Introduction

The little engine that could — did — and has ever since it was introduced in 1955: **THE SMALL-BLOCK CHEVROLET.** Who could have envisioned the world-beater it would become on the high-performance scene? Starting out at 265 cubic inches displacement, it's been bored, stroked and otherwise stretched all the way out to 400 cubic inches — in stock form. **This book tells you how to get the most out of your 265, 283, 302, 307, 327, 350 or 400 CID engine for street, strip — or all-out competition.**

We've attempted to reduce more than 15 years of small-block Chevy hardware to some printed pages. We've tried to nail down some facts, dispel some myths and put some half-truths in their proper places. Along the way we've added every fact or tip on high-performance Chevy engine building we could find — *and justify.* Above all, we've done our best to take the guesswork out of working on the small blocks. Advantages of stock and special parts are thoroughly discussed, together with the disadvantages. Where stock parts are best — we've said so. We have no ax to grind and we are not in the parts business.

Hopefully the photos and illustrations will help make your task an easier one, especially if you are new to engine work. This volume should not be considered a substitute for the Chevrolet Service Manuals or Overhaul Manuals which are available through Chevy dealers or from Helm Inc. We have tried to provide an encyclopedia of honest information which you can trust — written by some men who wanted this book to be right — just because the subject richly deserves creditable treatment. In several places we've pointed out the wrong way to do something; our purpose was not to discredit an engine builder or a product — but to lay bare those areas where mistakes are commonly made with a resultant loss of horsepower or component life. In some cases, the wrong way wastes a lot of time and money and we are committed to the idea that our books should help the racer or automotive enthusiast to enjoy his hobby — or profession — at minimum expense.

Any book of this kind has a certain degree of obsolescence because there is no way to capture more than a snapshot of development and availability of stock and special parts at that final moment when the printing presses are turned on. In this particular volume we've attempted to bridge a gap between current development and undying reference material — which is all too hard to come by in moments of heated bench racing. Remember that it's up to you to keep track of what's happening in small-block performance by following the availability of special parts from Chevrolet and by constantly reading automotive periodicals.

NOTICE: The information in this book is true and complete to the best of our knowledge. All of the recommendations on engine construction and modifications are made without any guarantees on the part of the authors or H. P. Books. Because design matters, engineering changes and methods of application are beyond our control, the authors and publisher disclaim any liability incurred in connection with the use of this data or specific details. Parts numbers will change and the availability of stock heavy-duty and special racing parts will change from day to day as improvements continue to be made in the small-block Chevrolet.

Smokey Yunick checks out an Edelbrock Tarantula manifold with Holley double-pumper carburetor as part of his seemingly never-ending test program to wring more HP out of the small-block Chevrolet engine.

ON THE COVER

    Smokey Yunick and the small-block Chevy have never really been separated — or if so — not for long. In January of 1970, Smokey got serious in pursuing a number of ideas aimed at wringing more horsepower out of the little engine. By mid-1971, he had 465 HP at 7600 RPM from 305 inches fed from a single four-barrel carburetor. This is the Yunick powerplant shown on the cover. Ed Sperko of General Motors Photographic applied his considerable talents to capture this mechanical beauty for posterity. It features angled-plug heads, Mark IV 1.7:1 ratio rocker arms, L-shaped head-land rings from Sealed Power, Weaver dry-sump pump, Holley double-pumper carburetor, National aluminum water pump, magnetic-impulse-triggered transistor ignition — and three highly visible "all-Smokey" items. That intake manifold started out as individually cast port runners mated to an old Rochester fuel injection bedplate. Months of changing, testing and refabricating made the Smoke Ram manifold the most effective single-four-barrel manifold known for the small-block Chevy. Those 4-into-1 exhaust headers are another mixture of art and science: equal-length, lightweight, equal temperature in each pipe — and an easy fit into most Chevrolet chassis. The finishing touch to the project is the cogged-belt accessory drive for the alternator and dry-sump pump. This troublefree, compact design is a racer's dream. With all this going for it, is there any wonder why we chose this engine for the cover?

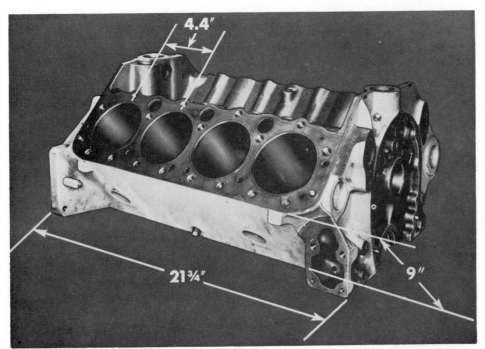

Keep it short, keep it light and keep the bore centers the same for more than a decade and a half and you've got the makings of the most popular V-8 engine ever.

The engine block measures only nine inches from the bottom machined surface to the lower edge of the head-seating surface. A 1/8-inch drop below the gasket-rail surface provides a register surface for the main-bearing caps.

When Chevrolet engineers initially planned the "small-block" V-8, their thinking ran along the lines of an engine of 231 cubic inches. Subsequent discussions — which included a closer look at the requirements of power steering, air conditioning, increasing frontal area and vehicle weights raised the size of the "paper" engine to 245 cubic inches displacement (CID). After basic dimensions were established, it was discovered that an engine of 260 or even 265 CID could be built with no penalty of extra weight. One engineer who was in on this early planning of the engine recalls some heated discussions about whether the engine really needed to be as large as 265 CID. But the engineers were well aware that adequate displacement is fundamentally the most economical method of ensuring high torque, sharp performance and reasonable economy.

Bore size was discussed and 3.750 inches was laid down. At this point the thoughts were still along the lines of a 260 CID engine and to produce this, the stroke needed to be 2.93 inches. For any number of production reasons, it was desirable to round off the stroke to 3 inches — which then produced the 265 CID engine that went into production. The compression ratio of the 265 CID engine was 8-to-1.

With the vital dimensions locked into place, the engineers went to work on compacting the engine. An SAE paper by R. F. Sanders, then the chief experimental engineer for Chevrolet, describes how the engineers spent hours slicing anything they could off the top, bottom or sides of the engine to lighten the engine and yield an overall compact design.

The length of the engine was determined by the crankshaft length — in other words, the engineers worked from the inside of the engine to the outside to eliminate cast iron and the water needed to cool it.

This is all of the coring for a complete block. Two one-piece jacket cores are set over the Vee cores and held in position by end cores which form the timing-chain-case and clutch-housing contours.

THE CYLINDER BLOCK

Structurally speaking, a V-8 design is relatively short and inherently stiff. Because of the extremely short couples, extra ribbing is unnecessary. Unlike other engineers, those at Chevrolet felt there was no need to carry the block casting below the centerline of the crank. Thus there was a drop of only 1/8-inch below the center of the crank. This is necessary to locate the main bearing caps in a broached longitudinal slot. By spreading the bolt centers and providing a rather deep section at the rear of the block, stiffness was obtained to support the transmission — again, without the penalty of added weight in the block structure.

The cylinder block was designed for high precision in the foundry as well as the machining operations. With a large number of cores, there is a problem of variation on every core and the stack-up of variations during assembly of the cores. Fewer cores mean that section thickness can be controlled quite accurately. In the final design of the small-block Chevy there was less sand to handle and the end result is a precision casting which is light and low in cost.

The cylinder-barrel cores are formed in pairs. One left and one right barrel are integral with a crank chamber core in a Vee form. Four of these basic cylinder-barrel and crank-chamber cores are set on a slab. Two one-piece jacket cores are then slipped over the cylinder-barrel Vee cores. Only nine major and three minor cores are used in the casting of the block. By comparison, another manufacturer uses 22 cores in the casting of a V-8 block.

CYLINDER HEAD

The main objectives in the casting of cylinder heads were precision, low heat rejection to the coolant, and low weight. The heads were designed to be interchangeable, with water outlets on the inner face at each end to eliminate any machine operation or core changes on the front and rear faces of the head. The cylinder-head slab core includes the contours for the four combustion chambers. The lower water jacket core is then set on the slab followed by the gas passage (intake and exhaust), and then the upper water jacket core. This "upside down" method of casting resulted in harder iron at the bottom of the head in the valve-seat area — a very desirable condition.

The combustion chambers are of high-turbulence, wedge-type design for combustion control and smoothness because the wedge controls the pressure rise in the chamber. The wedge is effective in exposing a high volume of mixture early in the burn cycle. Numerous detail changes have been made in the design of the combustion chamber for better performance, lower emissions, etc.

The combustion chamber is cast to shape — not machined — allowing the volume to be placed where designed because production is not limited by a cutter diameter. The only machining necessary in the chamber is for the valves. This operation is greatly simplified because the valves are all in a line. A number of distinct advantages come with the compact, wedge-type combustion chamber. For instance, a flat-top piston, which is economical and prevents excessive head mass, can be used. The quench area (of the 265) covers 23 percent of the piston area. Nominal thickness of the quench area is 0.045-inch with the piston at top dead center. The compression ratio of 8-to-1 was selected for the 265 for acceptable operation in the presence of moderate combustion-chamber deposits on regular-grade fuels available at the time of development.

Cylinder-barrel cores are formed in pairs — with one left and one right barrel integral with a section of the crank chamber core. Hmmmmm . . . good starting point for a V2. Four of the barrel cores per engine are set on a slab to form the cylinder-block inner core.

Locating the exhaust manifolds near the top of the cylinder heads not only simplified the coring of the heads, but got the manifolds up out of the way of the steering gear. The short exhaust passages are designed so they point upwards and out. And, the entire length of the ports, both top and bottom, are water-jacketed. Thus the transfer of distortion loads back to the valve seats is minimized along with valve burning due to uniform heat dissipation. Because these exhaust passages are short, the exhaust-port wall area in contact with the water jacket is very small, which accounts for one of the major gains in the feature of low heat rejection to the coolant.

Each cylinder head is secured to the block with 17 bolts arranged in a pentagon pattern of five bolts around each cylinder. Aside from the advantage of a weight saving through the use of smaller bolts which do not require externally ribbed bosses of any consequence, the use of five bolts instead of four around each cylinder bore results in less local distortion because less torque is required. With four bolts of larger diameter, higher tension or torque required on each bolt

would impose local stresses.

Complete jacketing provides cooling for the full length and circumference of the short cylinder barrels. A large drilled-in bypass was provided in the cylinder head, cylinder block and into the water pump for coolant circulation on cold starts before the thermostat opens. These drilled-in passages eliminate the use of outside piping or hoses.

A single water pump is used, and the first experimental model had a discharge scroll on the pump to divide the flow of coolant equally to the right and left sides of the block. But tests indicated that the contour and position of the water-pump inlet had more effect on water distribution to each bank than did the discharge scroll. The water-pump body was then simplified by use of a symmetrical-plenum-chamber design which shaped the inlet of the pump to provide an equal flow of coolant to the left and right bank. The water-circulation rate with the established pump design in the installed condition (including radiator) is 48 gallons per minute at 4400 engine RPM.

CRANKSHAFT

Forged steel was selected for crankshaft material because it has the advantage of a high modulus of elasticity coupled with a high specific gravity, and also because of the vast available forging capacity. The crank was designed with counterweights having the small outside radius of three inches positioned to minimize shaft bending. This was possible because of the short stroke and the use of the high modulus material and adequate cheek thickness which yields a stiff shaft.

Cheeking the sides of the crank arms and counterweights permitted designing for shorter overall length. This cheeking can be held to plus or minus 0.010-inch, while cast uncheeked counterweights require a minimum of 0.040-inch, which necessitates additional length at each crank arm to allow for grinding-wheel clearance. The crank design made it possible to produce one of the smallest and lightest commercial V-8's for its displacement — ever.

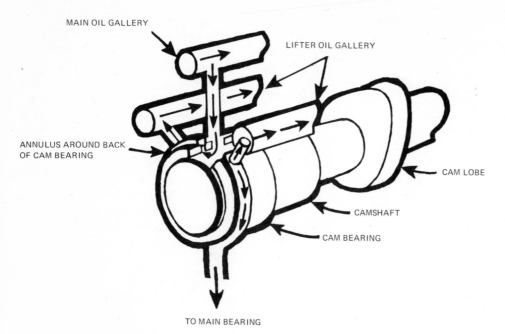

All 283 CID and later engines supply oil to the lifter galleries from an annulus around the backside of the rear cam bearing. The same annulus delivers oil from the main oil gallery to the main bearing. The other main bearings are similarly oiled, but only the rear cam bearing feeds the lifter galleries. 265 CID engines oiled the lifter galleries by a complex combination of extra holes in the cam bearing and a milled slot in the rear cam journal, as described on page 10. You'll have to add the milled slot in the rear cam journal on a later cam being installed in a 265 CID engine.

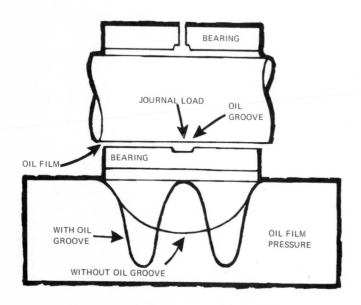

It just stands to reason that a groove in either the crank journal or the bearings will reduce the effective load-carrying area and this is reason enough not to run grooved bearings or journals.

Crankshaft torsional vibration is so slight that from the test made without a balancer, it was concluded it would not be important to crankshaft durability if a balancer was left off the crank, but when the engine was driven in a car, a harmonic could be heard and felt at approximately 2700 RPM. With the installation of a harmonic balancer of the rubber-and-torsional-shear type, the vibration could no longer be heard or felt in the car. The engines are balanced with the damper in place — so leave it there.

A relatively new balancing technique was used in small-block Chevy engine quality control from inception. Not only are all of the engine rotating and reciprocating parts precision balanced as individual pieces for use in either production or in service, but when they are brought together as an engine assembly in the plant, the complete assembly is balanced. Before the oil pan and heads were installed, the engine was placed on a newly developed machine which motors the engine, indicates out of balance of the engine assembly, stops the rotation at the indicated point and drills the crankshaft front and rear counterweights the required amount. This reduces any stackup of limits that might normally accumulate in the assembly of an engine, so that the overall result was a completely precision balanced engine. Through this new equipment every engine is balanced within a half inch ounce.

Naturally, in the period which has passed since the introduction of the small block this process has been refined and balancing is even more precise than it was in 1955.

MAIN BEARINGS

The five main bearings are of the same diameter, with the crank thrust taken at the rear bearing. In short-stroke, high-compression V-8 engines, the maximum main bearing loads are carried in the lower half under most operating conditions. By reducing the maximum oil film loads through the omission of the oil groove in the lower half, the capacity of the main bearings is increased approximately 100 percent, with the additional benefits of increased durability and greatly reduced wear. Keep this in mind before grooving a crank or running fully grooved bearings! With the grooved bearing, maximum pressure on the front bearing is 2929 pounds per square inch, and 2414 pounds per square inch for the grooveless bearing. On the rear intermediate bearing the loading is 3820 pounds per square inch for the grooved bearing, and 3141 for the grooveless type. Note how a groove increases the loads which the bearing has to support!

The accompanying drawing shows the oil-film distribution for both types of bearings. With the grooveless-type lower bearing, the pounds per square inch loading goes down as compared to the grooved bearing. Because the oil-film thickness is inversely proportional to the load applied, the film of the grooved bearing would be one-half the minimum thickness of the grooveless bearing. Conversely, with the same minimum film thickness, the bearing without the groove will carry twice the load. The primary reason for this is that the grooved bearing has twice as much side leakage as the bearing without a groove. In tests comparing the grooved lower bearing with the grooveless, it was found that the rate of wear was greatly reduced and the bearing life multiplied with the grooveless bearings.

CONNECTING ROD

In spite of the relatively large piston, the column section and weight of the rod was held to a minimum, still maintaining high structural rigidity because of the short length. The center-to-center distance was 5.70 inches, and the length-to-stroke ratio was 1.9. Standard Chevrolet testing procedure requires a connecting rod to withstand 10-million cycles on a hydraulically driven fatigue-testing machine. Connecting rods for the 265 were run up to 18-million cycles under 2400 pounds load tension, and 7000 pounds compression. This is the equivalent to a 10% overload at 4500 RPM in tension, and 10% overload at an 8-to-1 compression ratio. By way of further explanation:

One test cycle is equivalent to one engine revolution at 6800 RPM. If an engine ran for six hours at 6800 RPM, this would be equivalent of 2,448,000 test cycles. 10,000,000 test cycles is considered infinite life.

Stacked like cordwood, two dozen Chevy cranks begin inching their way down the line toward the first machining process.

Small-block crank is "attacked" by huge multiple head drill as part of the fast, but extremely accurate machining operation on the crank.

More than just a little thinking went into this — lubrication to the connecting rods from the drilled crank journal is plenty adequate for the task, thanks to the fact that the oil hole leads the position of peak load by 60 degrees. This assures a solid film between bearing and journal when most needed.

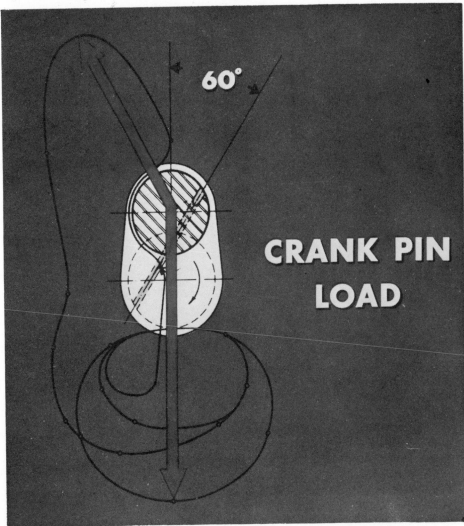

60°

CRANK PIN LOAD

No failures of any type were experienced. A pressed-in piston pin is used and proof tested to withstand a load of 2000 to 3000 pounds.

But no one at Chevrolet dreamed what the high-performance crowd would get or demand from the little engine. Rod failure became an almost chronic problem at one time and the rod has now been upgraded several times. Chevrolet has hardly dropped the ball in this area as their present standards are:

    compressive load - 15,000 lbs.
    inertial load   - 11,500 lbs.
An inertial load of 11,500 lbs. simulates a 302 cubic inch Z-28 running at 8685 RPM.

Z-28 rods on their way to be Magna-fluxed at the Flint engine plant. This bin was about four-feet by three-feet by four-feet deep. How'd you like to find that under your Christmas tree?

PISTON

A flat-top, steel-insert, slipper-type aluminum piston of autothermic design was used in the 265 CID engine introduced in 1955. The pressed-in wrist pin allowed bringing the pin bosses close together for efficient use of material. A 5/64-inch offset toward the major thrust face helped eliminate piston slap and allowed ample tolerances on piston fits for good manufacturing economy. The skirt was reinforced and the "tails" were fairly long to reduce deflections and cushion load transfer during the crossover from minor to major thrust sides.

PISTON RINGS

Three piston rings per piston were used. The two compression rings were thick wall alloy iron, 5/64-inch wide, taper-faced, with an inside bevel. The top ring was flash-chrome plated and lapped for scuff prevention during break-in.

One of the problems encountered was the difficulty common to many of the large-bore, short-stroke V-8's — that of getting good oil control under high vacuum conditions, such as decelerating down long grades, or in traffic where the engine tends to pull oil past the oil-control rings. Indications of that were frequently observed in visible smoking from the exhaust.

This smoking becomes more critical as engines go up in compression ratio and bore size. Tests showed that at 18 inches of mercury manifold vacuum, oil consumption is one quart per 1600 miles, while at 25 inches of vacuum, oil consumption is one quart for a little over 200 miles. Working with several ring manufacturers, a new type of expander for the oil rings was developed. The 3/16-inch-wide ring design finally adopted incorporates a circumferential expander which provides not only the desired axial load, but also a uniform radial load of relatively low unit pressure.

INTAKE MANIFOLD

The intake manifold area was greatly simplified and the end result was a casting which not only acts as the fuel intake manifold but also includes a provision for hot-water-heater take-off, cross-over for exhaust heat to the carburetor, distributor mounting, oil filler, thermostat housing, water outlet to the radiator and water-temperature-gauge hole.

In addition, the casting forms the top enclosure of the engine, eliminating any need for a separate tappet-chamber cover. Because of its construction, it is very effective in noise suppression; it adds considerable rigidity to the entire engine assembly; and it reduces assembly time. Molded oil-resistant rubber gaskets seal the ends to the block.

Small-block Chevy heads await another machining operation at the Flint plant. Literally thousands of heads can be seen from this vantage point.

Block begins going together on the assembly line with the installation of the crank. Workman uses a copper-clad hook on a rod journal to move crank from pallet to block. Note that main-bearing caps are already fitted with bolts and are ready for installation with an air wrench.

Rod and piston assemblies selected on a "go or no-go" weight basis, as well as bore sizing travel with the block during crank and cam installation.

The exhaust cross-over for supplying heat to the carburetor riser is brought from one port only in each cylinder head. Using one port instead of two minimizes valve-seat distortion because of the reduced flame-heated surface in the cylinder head as compared to a siamesed heat take-off. Also, it gives a more pulsating flow of hot exhaust gas in the cross-over. Two holes are in the carburetor throttle body which passes under the idle jets. The exhaust gases which travel through this circuit prevent carburetor icing during warmup. About 1964, this passage was moved to the intake manifold flange with a tin heat shield to allow using aluminum carburetor bodies.

EXHAUST SYSTEM

The exhaust system consists of three basic units — the left exhaust manifold, a cross-under pipe, and the right exhaust manifold. The external exhaust pipe crosses below the front of the engine. This is important because this location exposes it to the air stream from the fan and the air movement under the vehicle, and this piping reduces the build-up of high temperature under the hood. An automatic choke has always been standard equipment, its hot air supply being piped from a cast-in heat chamber located in the exhaust manifold.

Two men using over-center devices to push the piston and rod assemblies into place fit all eight bores in less than 30 seconds! Notice the clean gloves. Rod-bolt guides prevent bolts from nicking crank journal.

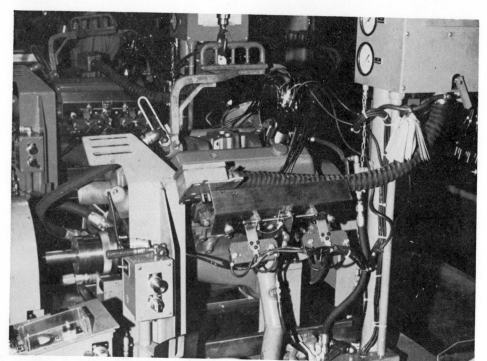

There's a small-block Chevy in there someplace — all engines are fired on natural gas; final timing set and finally balanced by drilling or weighting flexplate or flywheel. For a small-block-Chevy lover, this step is akin to hearing a baby cry for the first time.

Engines destined for California get the timing pointer welded directly to the front of the timing-chain cover.

Engines which are not destined for California retain the conventional pointer which wraps around the edge of the timing cover. Timing specs and methods of achieving them are different on the engines. Just thought you'd like to know about this if you're examining engines in a boneyard someday.

LUBRICATION SYSTEM

In the small-block lubrication system, all of the oil passages are drilled in the block. There are no drilled holes in the cylinder head for high-pressure lubrication. The drilled holes in the block are short with no sharp angular intersections. This minimizes the chipping of drills and the breaking off of particles of metal at the intersections — which helps keep the engine clean during construction. Three oil holes are drilled horizontally in the block, the main oil gallery and two tappet oil galleries.

Except for the rear bulkhead, vertical drilled holes from the main oil gallery pass through the bulkheads, through the centerline of the camshaft opening, and then through the bottom section of the bulkheads to the crankshaft bearings. Each of the bosses provided in the cylinder block for a camshaft bearing has a machined annulus which is covered when the bearing is installed. Oil under pressure in the main gallery moves downward through the drilled hole in the bulkhead and into the annulus under the camshaft bearing shells. Some of the oil is forced through a small hole near the bottom of these bearings. The remainder of the oil continues downward through the bottom section of

the bulkhead and into a hole in the upper half of each crankshaft main bearing, filling the groove in the upper half of the bearing.

A drilled hole from the high-pressure main oil gallery lines up with a small hole in the camshaft rear bearing shell, keeping high pressure oil on this bearing at all times. This bearing shell has a similar hole directly to the rear of the first hole and located in line with an annulus machined in the cylinder block. A hole from this annulus is drilled to each of the tappet galleries — thus there is balanced pressure to the two tappet galleries at all times.

A metering slot was milled in part of the outside diameter of the camshaft rear journal (265 CID only), just wide enough to cover the distance between the two holes in the bearing shell. Because the front hole is always exposed to high pressure oil, it keeps the bearing lubricated, and at every revolution of the camshaft, oil from the front hole filled the metering slot with oil under pressure. The oil crosses to the rear hole and down into the annulus, and then, at reduced and equal pressure, through the two drilled holes leading to the tappet galleries. The pressure of the oil in the tappet galleries was controlled through the length of

the metering slot milled in the camshaft journal. Oil flows out the top of the tappets, through the hollow push rods, and lubricates the rocker arms and valve stems.

The crankshaft oil hole to each connecting rod bearing leads the top dead center (TDC) position of the crankpin by approximately 60 degrees, which provides ample lubrication at the right time and position of the stroke, and furthermore, *the oil hole is never in a highly loaded area.* As a matter of fact, considering an engine lugging condition, the load is almost entirely removed at the oil-hole position, resulting in a maximum cooling flow of oil from the hole, and providing the bearing with an unbroken surface at the point of load application. This not only increases the relative effective connecting-rod-bearing capacity, but because the drilling is offset from the main journal, oil pressure required to overcome centrifugal force at the main bearing was reduced approximately three pounds.

The problem of supplying oil to the pistons under cold operation conditions was analyzed. During the early planning stages of the engine, an engine was set up in a laboratory for a stroboscopic analysis of oil flow and cold scuff tests were conducted. Oil holes in the connecting-rod-bearing caps at the split line were oriented so that the right hand bank of rods lubricated the left bank of cylinder walls and the left hand rods lubricated the right hand bank of cylinders.

This picture is a few years old, but in low-buck, down-South-style circle tracking, the small-block Chevy still brings home the grocery money on track after track.

VALVE TRAIN

The major development of the valve-operating mechanism was carried out by individuals and departments at General Motors. First seen on the small-block Chevy, the system is now in such widespread use that many enthusiasts have forgotten "who had it first." The effect one rocker arm may have on another through rocker-shaft deflection is eliminated because no rocker shaft is used. Each rocker arm is entirely independent of its brothers.

The valve rocker arms were 1010 steel stampings, carbo-nitrided and hardened to a case depth of 0.010-inch to 0.020-inch, and then surface treated. The rockers have been updated and are now constructed of A.I.S.I. C-1008 cold-rolled steel, P/N 3974290 (includes ball and nut).

This is a precision stamping of high physical characteristics, somewhat resembling an elongated cup with an oval-shaped hole pierced in the bottom. Studs, threaded at the upper end, are pressed into the cylinder heads under a minimum load of 2600 pounds. Each rocker arm is assembled over a valve stem and pushrod and retained by a fulcrum ball and lock nut. The rocker-arm development included Stress-coat analysis which, incidentally, also was used in the development of the crank, rods, and other parts.

The push rods are made from 5/16-inch welded steel tubing which has been formed and coined on the ends to produce a hemispherical surface, then surface hardened. A small opening at each end is provided for the passage of oil from the tappets to the rocker arms.

Valves are lashed by simply turning the nut, whether mechanical or hydraulic lifters are used. The lash change through the operating range is relatively low for both inlet and exhaust, and exceptional uniformity is obtained because oil of the same temperature is flowing through all of the push rods.

CLUTCH HOUSING

The clutch housing is bolted directly to the cylinder block, and extends over the flywheel ring gear. The starting motor is located on the clutch housing (early engines) and a rigid three-bolt type of mounting has been developed to eliminate all excess weight from mounting surfaces and pads. The housing was designed to be cast entirely in green sand and weighs nine pounds less than the bell-housing used on the Chevy six-cylinder engine.

The development of the small-block Chevy is the result of the combined efforts of all the resources of GM, GM Product Study, GM Research and the Chevrolet Engineering Staff. As you must have suspected by now, much of the information contained in this section is quite old — since some of the information does not now apply to the current version of the small block. This is correct — the bulk of the information came from a paper — The New Chevrolet V-8 Engine by R. F. Sanders. The paper was presented to the Golden Anniversary Annual Meeting of the Society of Automotive Engineers . . . in January of 1955. Careful rereading of the section will show a study of the concept, design justification and eventual hardware that came to be known the world over as the "small-block Chevy."

Acknowledgments

No one person wrote this book. We found it far more difficult to write the book than build a small-block Chevy engine which met our specifications. When the word went out that we were trying to put a "righteous" book together on the small block, guys all over the country began to help. Without their help, the effort would have died aborning.

We are deeply in debt to a number of men at Chevrolet. Chevrolet Public Relations' Jim Williams helped with specifications, photos and details that simply could not have been obtained elsewhere. Vince Piggens' Product Promotion group answered all of our inane questions with patience and "straight-skinny" information. Engineer Herb Fishel, resident small-block specialist in the group, served far beyond the call of duty. Herb lent criticism, integrity, and ideas to the project from start to finish and there is no adequate reward for effort of that depth.

Bill Howell and Paul Prior of the same engineering group made suggestions which made this book what it is. Bob Joehnck of Santa Barbara kept houndoggin' the project . . . "If you're gonna tell 'em this, you gotta tell 'em . . ." And so it went with guys like Bill King answering our questions at one in the morning. Dave Diamond, Mike Riley of the Carburetor Shop, Norm Brown of ChevTec, Bill Hielscher, and Neal Gates of Hooker who came up with parts, facts and experience in between making a living and racing.

Our favorite "old grouch," Racer Brown came up with much of the camshaft and valve-train information. Former GM engineer Doug Roe, plus Don Gonyou, Andy Guria and Mike Urich of Holley Carburetors helped separate the wheat from the chaff in the carburetor chapter. Ken and Ron Sperry kept saying, "what a guy needs to know is . . .", and it was that sort of spirit which built the book.

Dino Fry and Don Zandstra are two unsung heros who sorted through all of those part numbers and bins to tell us what you get when you order ". . . . ."; and if they didn't know the answer they ordered the part and found out first hand — and then passed the info on to us.

Jim Kinsler helped and so did Jere Stahl. Jim McFarland of Edelbrock was another of the willing helpers. Wayne Thoms came to our rescue time and again with needed photos, as did several magazine editors, notably Lee Kelley at Popular Hotrodding.

Ed Pink, Joe Reath and Hank the Crank (Bechtloff) made their shops available for photos time and again. Smokey Yunick's brain turns about nine grand all of the time — which was a problem for us since we don't turn but about half of that — and not for very long. But Smokey was patient and his contribution to the book is great.

Everyone involved was enthusiastic and helpful when they learned we really did want to "tell it like it is" about a formidable and highly respected piece of equipment — the small-block Chevy.

As you peruse these pages, you'll notice an unusual absence of speed equipment. This is intentional. Our feeling is that with so much very good Chevrolet equipment available — why bother with unknown and unproved qualities and quantities and end up with countless combinations which won't run as strong as a stock-out-of-the-crate engine? Don't misunderstand, please! We are not saying that all speed equipment is "BAD" — just that quite a bit of it is completely useless on street-driven cars. Our intention in writing this book was to provide a strong, reliable powerplant — not a base from which to spend money needlessly. We started with this premise and the more knowledgeable engine builders we talked with, the more we knew we were on the right track.

Penske/Traco 1968 Camaro with 2 x 4 bbl. carburetion draws air from fabricated cowl vent. A close look at the photo reveals a lot. Safety wire on headers, nylon-strapped plug cables, liberal use of steel-braid-covered lines, senders for oil pressure and water temperature. This is the type of engine that was used in SCCA Trans Am competition.

This is the highest HP small-block Chevrolet available as of 1972. It is the LT-1 370 HP 350 CID engine which was used in a few Corvettes and supplied as a service package complete or partial engine for small-block lovers. A similar engine is used in Z-28 Camaros with the 350 CID engine. Stainless-steel "doghouse" around tach-drive distributor shields ignition so no radio interference occurs.

SOLID HORSEPOWER ON THE CHEAP

One of the foundations of this publication is that you'll be dollars and horsepower ahead by buying the latest high-performance parts at the Chevy parts counter — doing what little (or nothing) needs to be done to the item and going racing. This chapter is a departure from that. We realize that there are a lot of used Chevy engines and parts around in enthusiasts' garages that are just waiting to be run one more time. Some of the parts can be turned into usable horsepower at zero cost — because you already have them. Again, we can't advocate buying some old blocks, cranks and heads when, for just a few more coins, you could get the very best that money can buy — but if they're out there gathering dust, why not use 'em?

As might be expected with any piece of hardware which is as potent, popular and long lived as the small-block Chevy, numerous design changes have been ef-
fected over the years. Some of the changes are very important to the performance enthusiasts and some are of no real importance at all. To the many students of the small-block Chevy, the engine of today which is called the "small block" or "little Chevy" is the same engine as the '55 version *in outward appearance only*. Just about every single piece in the engine has most likely undergone at least one design change.

Facing more than 15 years of small-block Chevy hardware, it is possible to put together some low-budget combinations of horsepower for the street or for amateur racing. There is no end to the way the parts can be stacked — some good and others terrible; but if you have a substantial supply of small-block Chevy parts then you probably just want to know how it all goes together without tying up a fortune in trick parts or special machine work.

Displacement — You'll find small-block Chevy engines around in displacements of 265, 283, 302, 307, 327, and 350 — engines out of one basic block. Then there is the new 400-incher which comes from a different block casting, but some of its parts will interchange with the smaller engines. The factory came up with all the above displacements simply by juggling the bore and stroke and even when they lengthened the stroke, they never varied the block deck height — which means there are interchange possibilities galore.

Filter & Cam Oiling Differences — When the "revolution" was introduced to the public in 1955, the 265 CID engine had no oil filter and no provision for one. When the 1956 models rolled out of Detroit, a filter boss had been cast in the block and all vehicles produced in that year (and since) were equipped with a full-flow oil-filter system.

The three motor-mount holes surrounding the forward freeze-plug location is the tip-off that this is a '58 or newer block — but could be one of most any displacement.

Those early 265 blocks without oil filters should be considered junk. No one anticipating rebuilding a small-block Chevy should start with this block . . . with one exception. If you are restoring a '55 Chevy to the Nth degree, this is the only block to have. Other than that — forget it.

All '55, '56 and '57 engines had a rear camshaft plug of 2-1/64-inch diameter while all '58 and newer blocks used a soft plug of 2-7/32-inch diameter. The desired (because of slightly thicker cylinder walls) '57 265 blocks are identified by the "C" at the end of the serial number located atop the front of the block.

The introduction of the 283 came in 1957. This block contained a subtle change in the rear cam journal under the bearing. On all small blocks three oil holes are located in this area. On all 283 and later blocks these holes are connected by an annulus behind the cam bearing. On all 265 blocks the holes are completely separate. This is in keeping with the change made in the camshafts. This is most important to anyone building an engine using one of the 265 blocks. All 265 engine rear cam journals were notched to provide lifter oiling. Later engines did not have a notched camshaft. Thus, any camshaft used in a 265 block must be notched as was the original cam or the lifters will not get any lubrication.

Bore Sizes & Boring to Oversizes — Most any of the 265-inch blocks can be safely bored 1/8-inch over the stock 3-3/4-inch bore to bring the displacement out to 283 inches. A stock 283 bore measures 3-7/8 inches. We'll probably get some argument here, but we won't advise boring a '57 283 past 0.060-inch oversize. Some blocks can be bored 1/8-inch — and some can't. A 265 bored 0.060-inch with a stock stroke yields 272 inches, a 283 bored 0.060-inch with a stock stroke gets you 292 inches, and a 283 ('58 and newer) bored 0.120-inch and with a stock stroke measures out at 301 inches.

The 283 introduced in 1957 came from the same basic block casting as the 265. In 1958, Chevrolet changed the block patterns around slightly and the result was a 283 with engine-mount bosses cast in the block sides. These blocks also had thicker cylinder walls that could be bored from the stock 3-7/8 inches to 4 inches. So if you're looking at a stack of wrecking-yard blocks, keep in mind that no 265 or any of the '57 283-inch engines had bosses for side engine mounts. These offer a shaky foundation from which to build a reliable horsepower-producing engine.

In 1959, the rear-main seal was changed from a graphite-impregnated rope to a Neoprene seal which is a far superior sealing method. All blocks from '59 to '62 are basically the same. All can be bored safely to 4 inches.

The 327 block introduced in 1962 was a different casting from previous efforts. Bore spacing remained the same, but the cylinder bore was brought out to an even 4 inches. They are relieved under the bores to clear the larger crank counterweights. A 327 block can safely be bored 0.030-inch. There are quite a few 327 blocks running which have been bored 0.060 — but this is a shaky deal.

Beginning in 1962, 283 blocks were produced with thicker cylinder walls which can be bored 1/8-inch over stock without problems. These blocks are relieved at the lower end to simulate the 327 block configuration so that the 327 crank may then be used. To identify these "goody" 283 blocks, look at the bottom of the cylinders. If the area around the cylinders is flat, you've got the "no goody" because the 327 crank counterweights will hit on the bottom of the cylinder walls. If the bottom of the walls are dished, the 327 crank will drop right in.

The 302, 327, 350 and 400 can all safely be bored 0.030-inch; however, there are a lot of these engines running around that have been bored up to 0.060-inch. We'd recommend sticking with the more conservative figure to keep the cylinder wall thickness closer to stock. Drastic overbores never seem to live very long.

A number of evolutionary changes made on the block defy specific dating, but are of some importance nevertheless. Blocks for truck use have two threaded holes above the oil filter boss for mounting the clutch hydraulic slave cylinder. But, just because these blocks were intended for truck usage doesn't mean all of them were installed in trucks. More than just a few were installed in passenger cars.

Many blocks contain one threaded hole above and in front of the rear freeze plug on the left side of the block to mount a clutch-linkage pivot ball. This could be very important if an attempt is made to install an early block without provision for the pivot ball into a later chassis which requires this type of linkage.

Starter Mounting — Early blocks fitted with cast-iron Powerglide and stick-shift transmissions mounted starters on the bell-housing. At some time during a production run, blocks were drilled and tapped to mount the starter on the block. This is another important consideration if you are contemplating connecting an early block with an aluminum-case Powerglide or a Turbohydro. Fortunately, the solution here is relatively simple. A 1/2-inch hand-held drill can be used (if you are careful) to drill the bottom of the block. A drill press is a better tool for this type of work. The two holes may then be tapped and a late starter mounted to an early block.

Connecting Rods — Chevy small-block rods have been updated several times, but center-to-center length has remained constant at 5.7 inches, except in the 400-inch engine, which has a special short rod with short rod bolts. When the 302 and 350-inch engines were introduced in 1967 (with the new large-diameter crank) the rod bolts remained at 11/32-inch diameter. Everything from '68 on up has the 3/8-inch bolt rod and the larger diameter journals. It must be remembered that stock rods with 3/8-inch bolts can't be had for the small-diameter crank. This means you can't build an engine with a pre-'67 crank and use a stock rod with the 3/8-inch bolts.

Over the years attempts have been made to install the larger bolts in the early rods to produce a small-displacement, high-RPM engine based on the early crank. Due to the availability of later hardware and many problems — and poor results — of installing the big rod bolts, this combination is not recommended.

Crankshaft Strokes & Stroker Combinations — Stock strokes offered by Chevrolet go like this. The 265 and 283 carry 3-inch strokes, both with the smaller diameter journals. The 327 has a stroke of 3.25 inches and is available in both small- and large-journal versions. The 302 crank goes back to the 3-inch stroke, but unlike the 265 and 283 crank, the 302 spins on large-diameter journals. The exception to this is the 1967 302 which had the small-diameter journals. The 350 crank has a stroke of 3.484 inches — also with large-diameter main and rod journals. The 3.750-inch stroke 400-inch crank is unlike any of the other cranks listed for the small block; it's cast, while most other cranks

are forged. Rod journals are common with those of the late 327, 350 and 302, but 400's main journals are a one-off size for the small block at 2.65 inches. The bore of the 400-incher is 4.125 inches.

One of the most popular of all combinations is the 327-crank-in-the-283-block trick. This can be done without machine work, but you'll need the early (small diameter) crank. There is a fly in the ointment though, and you should be aware of it before laying out cash for parts. Not all 283 blocks will accept an early 327 crank due to the counterweights on the crank contacting parts of the block. Two things you should not do is turn the counterweights off the crank or grind on the block until clearance is gained. The amount of material needed to be removed from the block is a bunch in at least one area and you are sure to hit water. Turning down the 327 counterweights will create a very bad imbalance situation so just keep trading or shopping until you come up with the right 283 block as described earlier in this chapter. This 3.25-inch stroke by 3.875-inch bore engine yields 307 CID when used with stock rods — which have to be the small-bolt, early rods. Don't confuse this home-grown mutation with the Chevy-built 307 which has a large-diameter cast crank and rods with the 3/8-inch bolts. The drawback to the Chevy-built 307 is its very-low-compression cast pistons. In the piston department (for the home-built 307) you have a choice of high-performance slugs, the 307 stock pistons or some of the TRW forged pistons which are the budget racer's dream come true. You can't use 283 pistons — they're the right bore but the wrong compression height.

Because the late 327 block is also used for the 350 CID engine, a 350 crank can be laid in the 327 block. The stock parts combination gets out of hand in a hurry and so does the endless variety of stroke combinations which can be obtained by turning the project over to a crank grinder. On engines to be built on the basis of a 265, 283 or early 327 block, a large-diameter crank can have its rod journals reground on an offset to produce a non-welded stroker. The maximum stroke to be achieved by this method is 3-9/16 inch on a 350 crank. By welding up the journals and then turning them down, most any stroke you can dream up

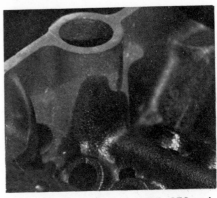

Front breather hole in the 302, 350 and late 327 blocks has been eliminated. These are popularly called "smog-control blocks." Therefore the block shown is a pre-smog-control product.

Beginning in 1970, Chevrolet began production of a 400 CID small block — a mighty long haul from the days of the 265-incher. Bore center remains the same as on the earlier engines.

Use the following computations of stock displacements as a starting point for figuring the displacement of any bored or stroked small-block Chevy.

CID = bore x bore x 0.7854 x stroke x 8 cylinders

302 Engine 4.001 bore x 3.00 stroke
37.71793 CID/cyl. x 8 = 301.743 in.[3]

307 Engine 3.876 bore x 3.25 stroke
38.34780 CID/cyl. x 8 = 306.782 in.[3]

327 Engine 4.001 bore x 3.25 stroke
40.86110 CID/cyl. x 8 = 326.889 in.[3]

350 Engine 4.001 bore x 3.48 stroke
43.75280 CID/cyl. x 8 = 350.022 in.[3]

400 Engine 4.126 bore x 3.75 stroke
50.13941 CID/cyl. x 8 = 401.1152 in.[3]

NOTE: Convert cubic inches to cubic centimeters by multiplying CID x 16.38716

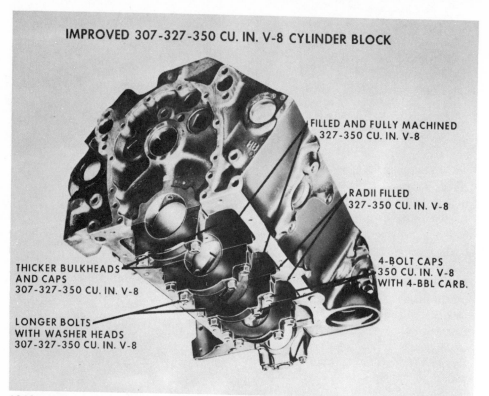

IMPROVED 307-327-350 CU. IN. V-8 CYLINDER BLOCK

FILLED AND FULLY MACHINED
327-350 CU. IN. V-8

RADII FILLED
327-350 CU. IN. V-8

4-BOLT CAPS
350 CU. IN. V-8
WITH 4-BBL CARB.

THICKER BULKHEADS
AND CAPS
307-327-350 CU. IN. V-8

LONGER BOLTS
WITH WASHER HEADS
307-327-350 CU. IN. V-8

1969 saw the introduction of a vastly improved block which is now used for all 302, 307, 327 and 350 CID engines. Use this as a reminder that in the long run you are far better off with the latest factory items than tricked-up earlier iron.

can be ground in. A 4-inch stroke may not be practical, but it is possible. The 3-5/8-inch stroker is one of the most popular, while the 3-3/4-inch stroke is around, but not plentiful. If you decide to go the stroker route, bear in mind that a stroked crank is more difficult to balance than an unmodified crank and for this reason you might opt to have the crank fully counterweighted. Also keep in mind that trick strokes require trick pistons — which cost money.

Only a cast crank is offered for the 400-inch block; the performance route lies along the lines of welding up the mains of the 350 (forged) crank and turning them down to the 400-inch crank diameter. The difference between the two is 0.200 inch. With a prudent stroke of 3.480 inches this produces a displacement of 370 inches — not bad for a small-block Chevy with all of the good stuff like a forged crank and the large-bolt rods. There are super-big combinations (how about 480 CID?) but they cost super-big and offer super-big problems to even experienced engine builders. If you're still interested, check with Moldex or Hank the Crank on one of their super-long-stroke small-block cranks which has been Tufftrided, balanced, straightened, chamfered and priced at about $500.

Cylinder Heads — Chevy has made several different cylinder heads for the little engine. Each differs in port and/or valve size and combustion-chamber volume. Chevy made both low- and high-compression heads for the 265 — but they are of little or no interest more than 15 years later. The 283 high-compression head was introduced in 1957. Combustion-chamber design was changed slightly and spark-plug cooling was increased. Valves are a rather small 1.72 inch on the intakes and 1.50 inch on the exhausts. Late part number on these heads is 3928454; an early part number was 3817682.

In 1960, some Corvette heads were cast in aluminum. Besides being lighter, these heads had larger ports and valves. Intake valve size was 1.94 inches. The heads were discontinued and called back because of casting problems. They're quite rare now — but there is no demand for them. There is no part number for the aluminum heads. Keep your money in your pocket if someone offers you a set because we'll tell you about newer and better heads.

The second-best heads for the little Chevy are the 1964 and newer high-performance units found on the old 327 fuel-injection engines, the 327/350

HP, the Z-28 302's and the 350/370 HP LT-1's. These heads have larger ports and big 2.02-inch intake valves with 1.60-inch exhausts. The present part number is 3928445; an earlier P/N was 3853608. In early 1971, Chevrolet introduced a variation of the "202" head popularly known as the slant-plug head. In all respects it is the well-known "202" head except for the angle of the spark plug — which is directed at the exhaust valve. Part number of the slant-plug head is 3965742.

All Chevy heads have a casting mark at both ends. If the mark is distinct, you can sometimes tell something about the head you're looking at — even if it's bolted to the block. Check the accompanying chart for the various casting marks. You'll note that all of the latest heads share the same mark, which means that you'll have to pull the head to see what you are buying — or own. One further tip on head evolution and identification involves placement of the rocker cover hold-down screws. 1959 and later heads have these screws directly opposite each other; earlier heads don't.

16

CYLINDER-HEAD CHART

Part No.	Year & Engines	Casting Mark
3773010	'55 '56—with 2-bbl.	(rectangle)
3729785	'56—with 4-bbl. (small ports)	Same as above
3734029	'56—with dual 4-bbl. (large ports)	(peaked mark)
3817682 3928454	'57-'62—with 2-bbl. '57-'65—283 '62-'64—327/250 '66-'69—307 '69—327/235, 350/255	(T mark)
3817681 3928494	'61—with 283 FI '62-'63—327/340, 327/360 '64-'68—327/300 '65—327/250 '66-'68—327/275 '69—350/300	(U/double mark)
3853608 3928445	'64—327/365, 327/375 '65-'66—327/350, 327/365, 365/375 '67-'68—327/325, 327/350, 302/390 '69—302/290, 350/350, 359/370	(curved mark)
3965742	'70-'71—service package (slant plug)	Same as above

Bill Jenkins' small-block-powered Chevrolet Vega uses two Holley center-shooters on an Edelbrock manifold. Pressure regulator for Holley electric fuel pump is mounted at the center of fuel-distribution log. Why the cut-off airhorns? For scoop clearance! This car brought the Chevy small-block to the forefront of drag performance by winning the 1972 Winternationals Pro-Stock class at Pomona, California. Car Craft photo (from May, 1972 article on the engine) courtesy Image International.

1970 250 HP and 300 HP engines are good foundations for high-performance street machines. Nodular-iron crank and cast-aluminum pistons are adequate for this type of use. It's no trick at all to swap the cam for a hotter Chevrolet or aftermarket bumpstick. Slant-plug heads can be added for another 10 to 15 HP boost. Restrictive single-snorkle air cleaner should be replaced with an open-element hi-performance type atop a spread bore or other double-pumper Holley carb.

Carbureted 327 CID small blocks can range from 250 to 365 HP, depending on the equipment: heads, carburetor, camshaft, pistons. This one with a four-barrel carburetor and clutch-type fan could be identified precisely if we just knew the last letters (suffix) in the engine serial number so we could look in the book at the Chevrolet parts counter. It contains this information for all engines. It would be a 1962 or earlier because it uses a generator instead of an alternator.

Rochester fuel-injection units: plain top on upper photo identifies 1960-62 unit. 1957-59 had same narrow plenums with ribbed tops. Bottom picture is 1963-65 design with removable ribbed top. Neither is competitive with current single four barrel installations on a HP basis. Small parts for any of these must be specially ordered through your Chevy store — and may take seemingly forever to arrive.

Plenum-ram forerunners — It should be obvious to anyone working with the Rochester FI units that these were the forerunners of the current-day plenum-ram manifolds such as the Edelbrock Tunnel-Ram and Smoke-Ram or the Weiand High-Ram. Although the FI units are limited from an air-flow capacity standpoint, they can provide exact F/A metering through the engine speed range without being affected by G forces or attitude of the car. For this reason, many autocross/slalom competitors prefer to use the units. Very few firms are left which will work on the units. Gail Parsons offers rebuilding and blueprinting of them on an exchange basis.

283 CID Corvettes had optional fuel injection from 1957 through this 1961 275 or 315 HP (depending on camshaft) model. FI option was also offered on 327 CID engines from 1962-65. Rochester FI is a curiosity item today — not a hot performance tip. Purchasers of the last FI units actually paid almost $300 more for 10 less HP than could have been available with a single Holley four-barrel.

Intake Manifolds & Fuel Injection — Chevy offers all kinds of ways to get the air/fuel mixture into the cylinders. We'll eliminate the Rochester fuel injection. This unit has not been offered from the factory since 1965. Most mechanics never learned how it operated and thus couldn't tune it. Parts are extremely hard to locate unless your Chevy parts man is willing to cooperate in ordering them for you. With all of the carburetion available there is little need for the Rochester unit.

In the Chevy parts book you have a choice of low-rise, cast-iron single four-barrel (one for Holley or Carter AFB and one for the Rochester Quadrajet), high-rise aluminum single four-barrel, low-rise cast-iron dual quads and high-rise aluminum dual ram quads, and the low-performance two-barrel manifolds.

One of the most desirable units for the street is the high-rise aluminum. It'll mount up to an 850 CFM Holley. This manifold is used on the 302 Z-28 engines as well as the high-performance 350 Corvette engines. The part number is 3958627. If you are short on cash and long on a shelf full of old carbs you might like to know that the big 750 CFM Carter AFB will bolt to the aluminum high-rise. Do not confuse this

manifold with the early high-rise P/N 3917610 manifold used on the '62-'66 'Vettes. The 3958627 manifold is the better of the two designs.

If you can't afford the high-rise aluminum job and you're running a two-barrel setup, you can still get quite a boost in performance with the regular cast-iron single four-barrel intake manifold. There are actually two cast-iron four-barrel setups. One is the older design for use with the small Holley or Carter four-barrels, part number 3813839. This manifold cannot accept large carbs because the throttle bores in the manifold are quite small. If you want to run a large four-barrel, you have to use the aluminum manifold already described or the Rochester Quadrajet intake manifold. From '67 on, Chevy has been using the Rochester Quadrajet on the low-performance small-block engines. The cast-iron intake manifold for the Quadrajet is P/N 3958624.

At this point we should again point out that this chapter is mainly intended to outline what is available (or has been) in the way of Chevy parts. The best current combinations are listed elsewhere in this book under the separate headings for the major components.

If you're a multiple-carb fan . . . take heart. Chevy's got two dual four-barrel setups. Neither is recommended for street use because a single large four-barrel gives all the performance necessary on the street — *minus the tuning headaches.* The first dual-quad setup from the old high-performance 283 Corvette engine mounts two Carter WCFB four-barrels. These carbs are obsolete and the manifold will not take large, late-model Holleys or Carter AFB's. The Carters sit inline on the manifold and look plenty hairy. Street roadster buffs go bananas over this arrangement. The part number is 3741029 for this aluminum manifold.

For even wilder looks and more mixture than you can use until the engine hits six grand, you can use the staggered-ram dual-quad manifold that is optional over-the-counter for 302's, part number 3940077. The usual carburetion for this manifold is two 600 CFM Holley double pumpers. Check the section in this book on carbs and manifolds *before* spending money.

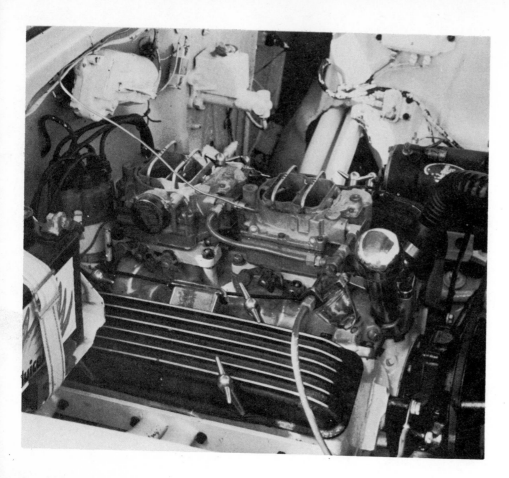

One of the long-standing favorites; a couple of Carter WCFB's on a '57 'Vette engine. Strong in its heyday, this setup now only makes sense for stock-class drag racing.

Camshafts — Several cams in the Chevy parts book can be considered high performance. Two are hydraulic and the rest use solid lifters. It is important to remember that Chevrolet always includes clearance ramps in their valve-timing specifications. Clearance ramps take up valve lash slowly before the valve begins to open or close. Because this distance can vary greatly, depending on the ramp and the method of measurement used by Chevy for that particular camshaft, the actual valve timing turns out to be a lot milder than the paper or theoretical timing specs.

The first "performance" hydraulic cam is used on all medium-performance engines like the old 327/275, 327/300 and the 350/300. Intake duration is 310 degrees. Exhaust duration is 320 degrees. Overlap is 90 degrees. Valve lift is 0.390-inch intake and 0.410-inch exhaust. The P/N is 3896929. On paper, this looks like a hot cam packing a lot of duration. In reality, it's a smooth-idling stick with good low-end torque and very little top end. Just keep in mind that those numbers are "paper timing."

The other hydraulic cam is pretty warm. This stick was installed on the old 327/350 Corvette engines. The stick is also used in the 327/325 Chevy II engines. Intake and exhaust duration is 342 degrees with 114 degrees overlap and a lift of 0.447-inch on both intake and exhaust. The P/N is 3863151. The 350 horse, 350 CID Corvette hydraulic cam has an intake lift of 0.450-inch and exhaust lift of 0.460-inch. The part number is 3896964.

There is quite a variety of solid-lifter cams to choose from. The first hot solid-lifter cam was used in '56 'Vettes. Timing was 287 degrees duration for both intake and exhaust. Lift was 0.404-inch, intake; 0.413-inch exhaust. This stick, P/N 3734077, has a lot of mid-range punch — with some sacrifice at the top end. In 1957, lift was brought down to 0.393-inch for the intake and 0.399-inch on the exhaust. Valve timing remained the same. This stick became famous as the Duntov Cam and remained unchanged from 1957 to 1963. It is still used by oval-track racers and some road racers today. The Duntov Cam carries 3736097 as its identification number.

In 1964, Chevy engineers went after top-end power and were willing to sacrifice a good deal of low- and mid-range performance to get it. The paper timing of the cam is 345 degrees on intake and exhaust with 0.488-inch lift on both valves. The cam was used on the 327/365 and the 327/375 engines. This same cam is used in the Z-28 302 engines. The cam is popularly referred to as the "30-across" cam. That (0.030-inch) is the valve lash for both intake and exhaust. P/N is 3849346.

A wilder cam is the optional service cam for the Z-28. The duration is slightly shorter — intake 333 degrees, exhaust 346, overlap is 118 degrees. The exhaust lift is quite high at 0.492 inches. Checking valve-to-piston clearance with this stick is a MUST! The part number is 3927140.

The current hot tip for a Chevrolet mechanical cam is P/N 3965754 as discussed in the chapter on camshafts.

Exhaust Manifolds — Chevy has never gone in much for cast-iron factory headers. They figured that most guys seeking performance would be investing in a set of steel-tube headers for maximum performance. As we've devoted an entire chapter to this subject, look there for the size and shape header to fit the various applications you might be considering.

Z-28's are the ultimate HP producers of the small-block line. Larger engines do not come close to the 1.53 HP per CID which has been obtained from this engine size with a single four-barrel carburetor — 460 to 470 HP on Trans-Am engines! Engines of about this size probably use the full air-flow capacity which is available from the cylinder-head design. Keep this in mind when building engines for class racing related to vehicle weight — if you can keep the car light enough.

Parts line-up for the 1967 Z-28 shows impressive array of high-performance goodies: four-bolt-main block, forged crank, forged rods, forged pistons, big-valve heads with 2.02-inch intakes and 1.60-inch exhausts, windage tray and mechanical-lifter camshaft. 290 HP factory rating for this engine is unusually conservative, as shown by vehicle performance data. Engine numbers end in "MO" for 1967-68 models, DZ for 1969's. 1970-72 models have 350 CID.

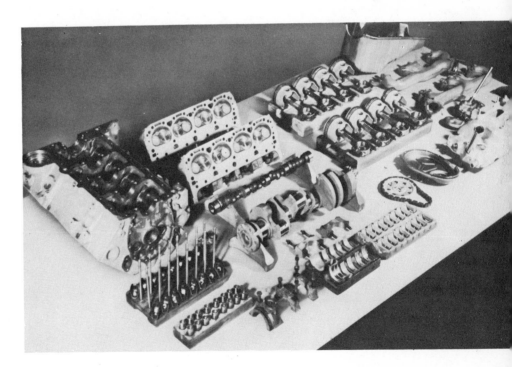

Two identifying features of the 4-1/8-inch bore small blocks (400 CID) are (1) siamesed bore with steam holes (arrows) which prevent steam pockets and enhance circulation and cooling; and (2) three freeze plugs on each side of the block. This block has been equipped with high-compression forged pistons.

Back in 1958, Chevrolet introduced the "W" engine. Performance enthusiasts remember it as the "348" and later the "409." When it came to racing applications, neither was really up to the competition and because of some other problems, the engines were subsequently dropped from production. The reason that the engine was introduced in the first place was because it was "obvious" that the "283" was as large as the small block could go on a production basis. The need for larger displacements continued and the engineers associated with the small block took it next to 327 CID, and then managed to stretch it again to a 350. Suddenly, in 1970, a 400-inch small block was announced. To those who affectionately call the small block a "Mouse Motor," this was "Super Mouse."

Surely this was advertising propaganda. Someone back in Detroit was getting the small block confused with the big block ("Rat Motor"). No indeed, despite all those inches, the new displacement was indeed contained within the dimensions of a small block. Design work on the 400-inch engine had started back in January of 1968. Engineers were looking for a high-displacement, light-weight engine that would be economical to produce and economical to operate. Higher (than 350 CID) displacement was needed because cars were getting heavier by the year, fuel octanes were going down — and the number of power-absorbing accessories installed on new cars was going up. Why not turn to the Mark IV — the 396, 402, 427, 454 big-block engine to solve the problem? Weight was one consideration. An "as-shipped" 400-inch small block scales 494 pounds; a comparably equipped large block weighs in at 609. The heftier

large-block engine costs more to produce and is a somewhat "dirtier" engine when the showdown came with emission-control standards.

Initial design considerations were in several areas — should the deck height be raised, should the bottom of the block be widened at the oil pan rail, and should the camshaft center line be moved up to accommodate a much longer stroke? Should the main and rod journal diameters be increased? Should the front accessory drive be redesigned? These were just a few of the questions which had to be hammered out. Along the line, two basic configurations were studied. A 4.000-inch bore by 4.000-inch stroke was one configuration. In the end, it lost out to the 4.126-inch bore by 3.75-inch stroke. This was chosen basically because of a more favorable bore/stroke ratio and the utilization of more existing manufacturing equipment which served to lower unit cost. Further savings are realized by the use of existing parts which (for the most part) fit small blocks all the way back to 265.

THE BASIC ENGINE

As this is being written, the 400-inch engine is designated LF-6, as it has been since its introduction in the 1970 models. It is available only with a two-barrel carburetor, low-compression heads with 1.9-inch-diameter intake valves and 1.6-inch exhausts, cast-aluminum pistons and a cast nodular-iron crankshaft. With this lineup of non-performance specifications, you should get the message in a hurry that racing was the last thing anyone ever thought about doing with the engine while it was in the design stage and the bookkeepers were having their crack at it. The engine has performed admirably in heavy sedans and station wagons. The large displacement delivers the torque necessary to move the weight and all of the accessories and still meet the requirements imposed by tightening emission controls.

You should note that there has been a steady decline in the HP ratings for this engine, just as for the other engines in

Low-compression heads, low-riser two-barrel intake manifold, tiny carburetor, nodular-iron crank, short connecting rods, cast-aluminum pistons and lots of low-speed torque are identifiers for the 400 CID small block. Unbalanced harmonic damper and flywheel are not evident from this photo. Cutaway photo courtesy Chevrolet Public Relations.

Chevy's line, over the past several years. Born a 265 HP model, the rating shrunk to 255 HP in 1971 and to 170 HP in 1972. The dramatic fall off in 1972 is due to the use of "as-installed" HP ratings by Chevrolet, primarily on the basis of compression reductions. For instance, the heads used on the 1970's had a combustion volume of 6.34 cubic inches in an assembled engine with the piston at TDC, while the 1972's had 6.98 cubic inches . . . a 0.64 cubic inch *increase* in chamber volume dramatically reduces compression ratio — from 8.9:1 to 8.1:1 — and performance.

SIAMESED BORES

The most striking feature of the 400-inch small block is the increased bore (4.126-inches, up from 4.001-inches) which necessitated joining or "siamesing" the bores. The area between the cylinders is a 0.274-inch-thick solid-iron web which prevents any water circulation between the cylinders where they meet. This web provides considerable strengthening for the cylinders. Like most modern-day blocks, this thin-wall casting does not take kindly to massive cuts with the boring bar. As detailed elsewhere in the chapter, consider +0.030 inch as the safe overbore limit.

"Super-Mouse" in street clothes masquerades as a 265 HP weakling. But, give him a forged crank and pistons, a healthy bumpstick and decent carburetion and then this "small block" will produce power like the original designers never dreamed of at introduction time 'way back in 1955.

Six steam holes per cylinder bank bleed steam and water from the block to the head through corresponding holes in the gaskets and heads. These holes are one of the few concessions which had to be made to allow manufacturing this engine with an extra 50 inches of displacement on the same production-line equipment as the smaller displacement engines.

The 400-inch block can safely be bored to 4.156 inch (+0.030 inch) and a number of aftermarket performance manufacturers are already making forged-aluminum high-compression pistons for the big bore. If you are concerned about the stock Victorcore gasket which may hang slightly into an overbored cylinder, don't be, because the rounded beaded edge of the gasket does not seem to cause problems. Chevrolet Engineer Bill Howell says that some people have been running the stock gaskets (even with the non-recommended +0.060-inch overbores) for two years without any problems being caused by the gasket.

PISTONS & RODS

Cast-aluminum pistons in the 400-inch engine use pressed-in piston pins. Because of this, and the cast-iron crank, the engine was obviously not intended for high-performance use. The connecting rod is identical to other small-block rods — except that it's 0.135-inch shorter. The standard center-to-center rod length is 5.700 inches while the 400-inch engine rod is 5.565 inches center-to-center. Also, the rod bolts are shorter to allow clearance at the camshaft. Unfortunately, the bolt-head seating area had to be reduced in these rods, so that they do not have the inherent strength of the longer rods. The shorter rod allowed maintaining the same compression height in the 400 CID pistons as for the 350 CID units, which gives additional commonality of parts — a Chevrolet tradition. Shorter rods create severe rod angles which increase the piston side thrust against the cylinder wall — and they also *increase torque*. They are not recommended for high performance.

However, longer rods can be used when hotrodding the 400-incher. If the 350 CID 3.48-inch

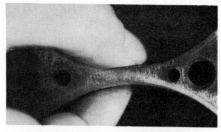

The bores of the 400-inch small blocks are siamesed. The stock bore is 4-1/8-inch. As you can see, there's little room to grow.

crank (with welded-up mains) is used, stock 350 rods work with the standard 350/400 compression height pistons so that there is no real problem getting the deck height established and no need for trick pistons with pins inserted through the ring grooves. If a forged crank is used, other rods may be required, depending on the total specifications to which the engine is being built. It's the piston and compression height problem which is most perplexing when trying to build a giant engine from one of these 400 CID blocks. That's why most of the builders have tended to use shorter-than-stock strokes in them.

BOTTOM END & CRANKSHAFT

To retain the famous Chevy reliability with the increased inches, the lower end of the 400-incher underwent some changes. Main-bearing diameter went from 2.45 inches to 2.65 inches. This required bigger main-bearing saddles, spreading the main-bearing bolts out to accommodate the larger diameter mains, and a wider bearing-cap channel. With the longer stroke, notches were needed at the bottom of each bore and also along the inside of the oil-pan rail to provide adequate connecting-rod clearance.

The front and rear main-bearing caps are of the two-bolt design with a bolt spread shared by none of the other small blocks. All of the intermediate main caps are of the four-bolt design.

All cranks for the 400-inch engine (at this writing) are cast nodular iron. Main-bearing diameter is 2.65-inches and the rod-journal diameter is 2.10-inches. Shoving this much bore and stroke in the small block doesn't leave a lot of room in the crankcase to start tacking on additional counterweights to balance all of that reciprocating mass, so the 400-incher gets a special harmonic balancer at the front of the engine and a special flywheel or converter flex plate to balance the engine externally. Thus, the flywheel and harmonic balancer on a 400-incher are inherently unbalanced and must not be used when building any of the other small blocks.

The cast-crank problem can be side-stepped by welding up the main journals on a forged 350 crank and turning them down to 2.65-inches to fit into the 400-inch bearing shells, then re-Tufftriding the journals. Joe Reath says you should expect to pay about $125 exchange for one of these cranks, which includes internally balancing the crank so that the 400 CID "unbalanced" balancer and flywheel will not be needed. Or, you can buy a forged crank specifically for the 400 from Hank the Crank or Moldex. Here, you are looking at about $450 for a crank ground on what is essentially a Chevy 350 forging. The stock forging is typically supplied with a stroke near the 3.50-inch-stroke dimension.

Or, Moldex will sell you one of their custom forgings with any stroke you like up to 4.25 — and that works out to 462 cubic inches with a +0.030-inch bore — for $650. This big-stroke unit requires Carillo rods — and there goes another $500. Building one of these super-big engines on a small-block foundation takes a wheelbarrow-full of $$$$ and a lot of patience for assembly. If you're really after inches, you can probably build or buy an iron or aluminum big-block Chevy for less money.

In the case of the modified-Chevrolet-type forging, Moldex suggests using the 454 CID big-block rods, P/N 3969804 or 3964552 (with ground-shank bolts 3969864) by taking 0.025-inch off each side of the rod and grinding a tiny bit off the corner of the rod bolt closest to the cam for clearance. Moldex widens the crank journal to allow using stock big-block rod bearings. Special pistons are required to get the correct compression height and pin-hole diameter.

If you are ordering one of the special crankshafts, be sure that you have made up your mind as to the kind of pistons and rods that you will be using — and make sure that they are available —

400-inch engine rod is shorter than those used in the other small-block configurations and the pistons are all dished and notched. Even with all the inches, the engine is still rated at only 265 horsepower, due to very mild valve timing and very low compression. As smog laws get tighter, you'll see a lot more of this.

Underside of a 400-inch block reveals four-bolt main-bearing caps and cutouts at the bottom of the block for connecting-rod clearance.

then you can tell the crank manufacturer what you'll be using so that he can build the crank with the correct balance.

CAMSHAFT, HEADS & MANIFOLD

The cam which comes in the 400 is the same as that used in the 350. Naturally, the Chevrolet four-barrel intake manifolds which are available for the smaller displacement engines may be used on the 400, including that fine high-riser model. The new service-package slant-plug heads (or other 2.02-inch-intake) may also be used *if* a 400-inch head gasket is used as a template and the heads are drilled for the previously mentioned steam holes.

HOTROD POSSIBILITIES

There are lots of possibilities in this block — even in the basic engine itself — for high-performance activities. Just remember that the short rods mitigate against using the engine for high-winding. But don't let that stop you from adding a larger carburetor, such as the Holley 500 CFM or 600 CFM two-barrel on the existing manifold. Incidentally, the 1970 400's had carburetors with 1.4-inch venturis, while the 1972's have 1.1-inch venturis to get better emission performance. Or, you could use a four-barrel carburetor on another manifold, a different camshaft or higher compression heads. The pistons will probably last a long while in moderate street-performance use, provided you keep the RPM's at some sensible limit. If you rework the engine, a rev limiter should be part of the package to help avoid over-enthusiastic use.

400 CID BASIC DIMENSIONS

Bore	4.126
Stroke	3.75
Deck height	9.025
Deck clearance	.025
Connecting rod length	5.565
Compression height	1.56

Examples using dimensions:

With 3.75-in. stroke 400 crank:

Deck clearance	.025
1/2 stroke	1.875
Rod length	5.565
Compression height	1.56
Deck height	9.025

With 3.48-in. stroke 350 crank (welded mains or special forging) and 350 rods:

Deck clearance	.025
1/2 stroke	1.740
Rod length	5.700
Compression height	1.56
Deck height	9.025

400 CID BLOCK BORE/STROKE COMBINATIONS

4.126 x 3.000 (283 stroke)	321 CID
4.126 x 3.250 (327 stroke)	348 CID
4.126 x 3.400 (special)	365 CID
4.126 x 3.480 (350 stroke)	373 CID
4.156 x 3.480 (350 stroke)	378 CID
4.126 x 3.750 (400 stroke)	400 CID
4.126 x 4.000 (Hank or Moldex)	427 CID
4.126 x 4.250 (Hank or Moldex)	454 CID
4.156 x 4.250 (Hank or Moldex)	462 CID

Arrows indicate unbalanced portions of the 400 CID flywheel converter flex plate and harmonic balancer. These must be used with the stock crank. Part numbers for specific years and applications are in the parts book.

These small-block 'Vette headers can be had at the Chevy parts counter. A muffler can be fitted in the long collector — so the arrangement is streetable and legal because the AIR fittings are in place on the primary pipes next to the flange. Looks like a cop-caller to us, though.

THE STOCK SYSTEM

Small-block cylinders exhaust through short exhaust ports into a cast-iron exhaust manifold which is connected to the exhaust system. A thermostatically operated exhaust heat-riser valve causes exhaust gases to be directed through the intake manifold until the engine warms up. If you block off the heat with blocker-type intake-manifold gaskets — or if you have blocked off the heat by installing steel shims between the head and gasket at the heat-riser port — you may want to block the heat-riser valve open or replace it with a Chevy spacer block. There are two sizes — P/N 3796797 fits the 2-1/2-inch exhaust flange hole and P/N 3750067 fits the 2-inch hole. Either one costs about $2.50.

If you want to keep your car *very quiet,* then the power-robbing stock exhaust manifolds are the answer. Their cast-iron construction effectively dampens exhaust noise, whereas tubular headers are almost "bell-like." If you are committed to the use of iron manifolds and the HP loss which they inevitably cause, you are "stuck" with the manifolds that came on your car.

Now let's get our heads on straight and look at the real problem. We have to drive our cars on the street, right? And tube-type headers are so noisy that they'll give you a headache with their constant ringing. You didn't know that? Well, it's the gospel truth and you'd better believe it! Headers give 25 to 50 more HP *with open exhaust.* If you have to use mufflers and a cam no stouter than the street mechanical, skip to page 36 where we tell you how to get what you really want: high performance for low bucks. All of the *absolute musts* that we talk about for headers relate to *competition with open exhaust.* End of lecture.

TUBULAR HEADERS

A good set of headers is HP that is the very cheapest that you can buy — lots of horses for few bucks.

As an average, you can figure that headers will add 10 to 30 HP to your small block — more if the engine is really a hot one. Your small-block Chevy can never reach its full potential if you insist on running its exhaust through the stock cast-iron manifolds.

Tubular headers are an absolute must for the performance-oriented small-block Chevy. They scavenge the cylinders of most of the burnt gases which are being expelled from the engine so that the engine draws in a completely fresh charge of fuel and air that can be ignited to make maximum power. With the restrictive stock exhaust manifolds, the burnt gases are not only not completely drawn out of the cylinder — part of the gases may be bounced right back into the cylinder before the exhaust valve closes, thereby diluting the incoming charge and reducing the amount of power which can be produced. Part of this problem is created by the fact that the exhaust manifold is a "log" with all of the ports on a head dumping into it. The log size and shape prevent isolating the ports from one another, so there is every good chance that the manifold will be running under pressure which is sufficient to drive part of the exhaust back into the cylinders when pressure in the still-open cylinder is less than that in the exhaust manifold.

You should note that headers usually cause the engine to run cooler. The stock exhaust manifolds are large heat sinks which store enormous amounts of heat right alongside of the cylinder head. This places an extra burden on the cooling system and also raises the temperature of the underhood air — detracting from performance unless the carburetor is being fed cool air from the cowl or front air scoops. The engine also runs cooler because the carburetor is jetted richer to take full advantage of the extra HP produced with the headers. A portion of the mixture is often carried through the combustion chamber and out with the exhaust on the overlap, cooling the exhaust valve, guide and port in the process.

Before outlining some basics on choosing headers for given applications, a few words about buying headers. Header sets can be store-bought or custom-built on the car. Custom-built headers are the order of the day when an engine swap has been performed and neither the stock exhaust system nor an existing header system will fit. Custom headers are also common on all-out race cars to fit around reworked suspension, engine relocation, or to achieve a given dimension or power output not possible with a production header. Custom headers are plenty expensive, and a set of custom-built headers is no guarantee that they are the ultimate in horsepower, or will even fit — unless they've been built on the car or boat.

Production headers are available in speed shops, department stores, discount houses, through the mail — and we wouldn't be a bit surprised to find a drugstore which sold headers for small-block Chevys. Needless to say, 99% of the non-stock exhaust systems running on small blocks are production headers manufactured by any number of companies. If you don't want to install the headers yourself, you'd best start shopping in a speed shop because many outlets for headers and other performance equipment will have nothing to do with installation.

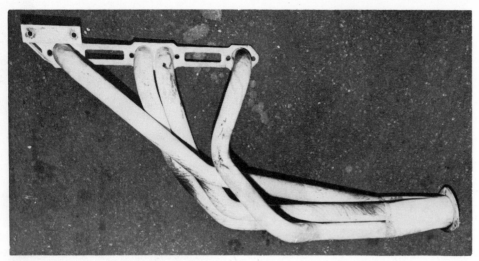

This is a "convenience" header designed to fit with maximum clearance for easy installation. The tube lengths are kept within about two inches — definitely not equal.

Because there are headers and there are headers, spend some time shopping. After eliminating some units due to tube diameter and length (we'll get to that) take a close look at the welding quality and the area where the tubing meets the flange. Does the tubing appear to be hammered roughly to meet the flange — or swaged on a mandrel to meet the flange smoothly? Just before you plunk down the bucks, place a straight edge along the flange head-mating surface and see whether the flange is true. If it's off more than 1/8-inch, pass up the header set or be prepared for chronic leakage — which is dangerous business. This could have been prevented at the time of installation if the flange had been Blanchard ground to a true flat surface or if the flange had been cut on either side of the two center primary pipes. This last step allows the flange sections to be pulled up snugly to the head with a minimum of leakage problems. Some of the newer Hooker headers are even being made that way.

The headers are the right size, shape, color, price and the flange is straight; give the man the money and leave? Not so fast. Do you get the headers in an unopened box from the manufacturer or does he take them off the wall or a display shelf? If they are out of the box when purchased, you'd better get a solid agreement — like in writing on the bill of sale — that you get your money back if the headers don't fit the car. Here's why. A set of headers built for a '67-'69 Camaro with power steering simply will not fit a '70-'72 Camaro — with

or without power steering. Just because both cars are powered by a small block and the dealer says they will fit does not mean the headers will fit. If the salesman takes them off the wall, you have only his word that the headers really were designed for the chassis you're buying for. Some manufacturers now stamp the flange with the header part number and this can be cross-checked in the manufacturer's catalog. Take the time to do so. Don't think that you are being obnoxious by demanding to see proof that you are getting the correct headers. You could waste days of time and dozens of Band-Aids trying to make the wrong headers fit on your car. That's Frustrationville!

READ THE INSTRUCTIONS!!!

Any dummy can install a set of headers. All you do is just unbolt the stock exhaust and bolt on the headers, right? Anyone who feeds you that line or believes it has never installed his first set of headers . . . yet!

READ THE INSTRUCTIONS!!!

On some cars, an engine mount may have to be unbolted and the engine jacked three inches up in the chassis so the header can be slipped in. Fine. Do you slip it in from the bottom or the top? Does a steering arm have to be removed? Does a tie rod have to be dropped? Installing headers can be a nightmare. If you immediately discover that one set of pipes can't even get close to the head, READ THE INSTRUCTIONS again. Several header manufacturers on the West Coast told us that they get calls every day from customers who can't in-

stall the headers, either because they have the wrong set to start with or didn't read the instructions.

More than one header manufacturer told us that the old Tri-Y design introduced in the mid-sixties is still the hot setup for the street. Because of the way the pipes were laid out and entered the collector, the design offered excellent low-end torque which continued right on up through the mid-range — which is the plan for a street-driven car. Unfortunately, the Tri-Y design is no longer being made — by anyone. Manufacturers cited the fact that the Tri-Y is much harder to build than the common "four-into-one" and that because they didn't look as good, most "street runners" who are really more concerned with appearance than with performance won't buy them.

On an all-out competition car — as in drag racing — header selection gets complicated in a hurry because the car weight, engine size, and RPM range through which the engine is worked all have a bearing on what the optimum header should be. Generally speaking, a heavy car with a small engine requires smaller diameter or longer primary pipes than the same engine installed in a much lighter car. In this example, the primary pipes might vary in length from 26 inches in a light car to 40 inches in a heavy car.

Jere Stahl says, "Small-block Chevys respond to header changes more than any other engine we have worked with. However, the engine always runs better with headers smaller/longer than optimum as compared with headers larger/shorter than optimum. Basically, pipe size should be 1-1/2 to 1-7/8-inch O.D. depending on displacement and power output. For example, all 265's in pre-1972 NHRA stock classes require 1-1/2-inch O.D. primaries — some as short as 28 inches with 2-3/4-inch x 13-inch collectors — up to 37-inch primaries with a 2-1/2-inch x 23-inch collector. All stock 283 to 327 CID engines — including the Z-28 302 CID — require 1-5/8-inch O.D. primaries with 2-1/2 to 3-1/4-inch diameter collectors. Modified engines from 288 to 302 CID work well with 1-3/4-inch O.D. primaries ranging from 26 to 34 inches long. 302 to 310 CID engines 'making' over 1.55 HP per cubic inch work well with 1-7/8-inch O.D. primaries. Unless a car has an extensively modified engine and a trick street system, the 1-5/8-inch O.D. arrangement works better than any other for street use."

Late engines — like the 350-inch engine with a hydraulic stick and relatively low compression seem to respond best to 1-3/4-inch primary diameter and super-long primary length of about 36-38 inches which dump into a 2-3/4-inch diameter collector 13 to 18 inches long. Because gear ratios, car weight, cams and intake systems differ widely, the process of trying to find the ultimate header for a small-block Chevy gets to be very time-consuming and involves making scores of runs at a strip and changing nothing but headers. That's how the pros do it — and that's why they can often run 4/10 of a second better than the field, because there is that much difference in a competitive drag-race car between header set A and header set B.

Road racing (as in Trans Am Camaros) and circle tracking (super modified, sportsman, late stocks, etc.) are as difficult to select headers for as a "right on" drag-race car. A Trans Am Camaro (302-inch) won't be too far off in exhaust system design with 1-3/4-inch primary pipes, 29 inches long (or 1-7/8 x 35-inch) dumping into a 3-1/2 x 50-inch or 4 x 65-inch collector/tailpipe for each side.

There are some header manufacturers who realize they can't custom-build headers in a box for every engine and car running — so they offer a "do-it-yourself" kit containing various lengths of slip tubing which can be used to lengthen the primary tubing, different length and diameter reducers which neck the collector down to the muffler and various length collector extensions to bolt onto the flange. Stahl pioneered this concept and both Stahl and Hooker offer several kits which prevent a customer "on the back 40" from becoming trapped with one set of header — any brand — which may or may not be the most effective for his particular application.

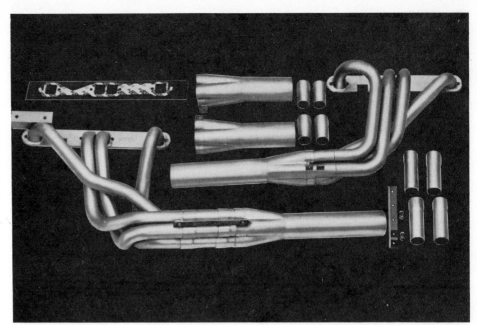

Race-car stuff. This particular set was used by Dave Strickler to win the Tulsa World Finals in 1968. Adjustable headers are available from Stahl to fit most popular Chevys. Primary-tube diameter is 1-5/8-inch, 1-3/4-inch and 1-7/8-inch. Primary length can vary from 26 to 34 inches long.

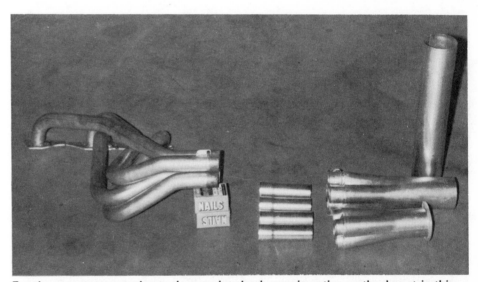

For the average racer trying to do some low-buck experimenting on the drag strip this adjustable-length header kit from Hooker is a godsend. Notice that the primary pipes can be lengthened as can the collector. Once you've settled on a combination, the tubing can be welded together in a solid, finished header. Stahl has similar kits.

This is a through-the-fender header built by Hooker for the '55-'57 Chevy. The header is installed on the car just as it sits here and requires a large hole be cut in the inner fender panel so the collector extends into the wheel well. This unit should be considered a drag-race header only, as plumbing this into mufflers gets complicated in a hurry.

29

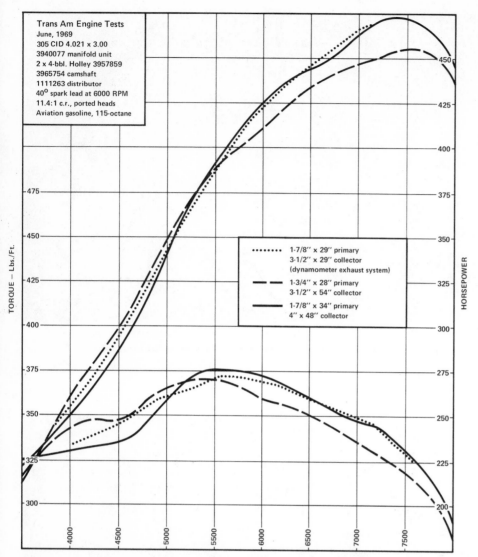

Trans Am Engine Tests
June, 1969
305 CID 4.021 x 3.00
3940077 manifold unit
2 x 4-bbl. Holley 3957859
3965754 camshaft
1111263 distributor
40° spark lead at 6000 RPM
11.4:1 c.r., ported heads
Aviation gasoline, 115-octane

TORQUE — Lbs./Ft.

HORSEPOWER

.... 1-7/8" x 29" primary
3-1/2" x 29" collector
(dynamometer exhaust system)

– – – 1-3/4" x 28" primary
3-1/2" x 54" collector

——— 1-7/8" x 34" primary
4" x 48" collector

Chevrolet engineer Herb Fishel points out that dynamometer headers can be built so that you can work around the engine easily and not get burned. However, the engine and header package requires changes to permit installation in a car. When these changes are made, the package should be requalified on the dynamometer to make sure that the power is still there. This chart shows such a comparison between dyno and vehicle headers, all of which are Stahl types. Note that 1-7/8-inch primary pipes worked better than 1-3/4-inch primary pipes on this dual-carburetored engine. A comparison for a single four-barrel engine is presented a few pages later in this chapter.

Look close. Road-racing headers built by Jere Stahl to fit small-block '67, '68 and '69 Camaros. They were used by Mark Donohue when he was Trans Am champion in '68 and '69 in a Chevy. They're also used by Don Yenko, Pete Hamilton, Tiny Lund and Joie Chitwood. They were not designed for street use.

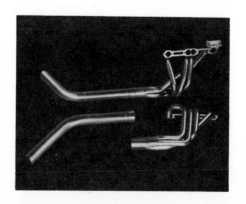

No one header manufacturer makes an ideal header for every chassis and engine combination — nor will he claim to do so. There are two types of headers which are usually offered: under the chassis and through the fender well. The fender-well types are in evidence at the drag strip because they apparently will make more HP. However, for a car to be run on the street, the tuck-under-the-chassis kind are preferred. If you live in a state which has roadside inspections, then you will probably have to get headers with the A.I.R. exhaust-air-injection provisions to match those which were on the original exhaust manifold. Californians take note!

Although the header manufacturer may offer some super-slick glass-packed straight-through mufflers which are guaranteed to sound like a 747 under full take-off power — avoid these like the plague. The kind of muffler that you can use on the street is fully described in the muffler section on page 36.

Decals should be considered as *meaningless indications* that hero racers are being paid big $$$$$ to stick them on their cars. This is especially true in the case of headers. Before you rush to buy the make of header claimed by your dragging hero's decal, check his car *very carefully* to see if his headers are the kind that *you* can buy. They could be made by another firm whose decal was soaked off for a bigger payoff. Don't be misled!

HEADER MAINTENANCE

Headers run on the street or race track need maintenance. At the head of the list comes bolt tightening. After installing the headers and running the car around the block a couple of times, retighten the bolts as soon as the engine cools down. Don't wait and don't try to run them for several days before doing this essential chore. You can't put it off or the exhaust will cook or burn the gaskets and you'll never get that set of gaskets to seal in a million years. Once a week for the next several weeks, tighten the bolts when the engine is cold. Then, after several weeks have passed, remove the bolts one at a time and apply Loctite as you reinstall and retighten the bolts. The idea here is to allow the header flange to "take a set" — or stabilize — before locking the bolts down. Due to the tremendous heat and vibrations, don't think that Loc-Tite is the cure-all — if you are going road racing, drill the bolt heads and safety wire them.

Headers will last longer if you'll keep them painted with some of the high-temperature paint made specifically for this purpose. This is especially true of headers run on the streets in the north and east where salt is used on the streets in the winter.

Never put the headers in a strain — or use them as a hanger for the rest of the exhaust system. If this is done, vibrations will crack the pipes. Make sure there is adequate clearance between the headers and any other part of the car. When the engine torques in the frame, does the header touch the steering box or frame? Clearance is a real problem on the later model cars, and all of this should be checked out when installing the headers — not after they have been installed on the car and have cracked — due to your neglect. The header manufacturer won't replace them or pay for your mistakes.

COSMETICS OR HORSEPOWER?

In attempting to wrap up this section of the book we contacted some of the major header manufacturers and asked them what their major problems were in dealing with the people who buy their products. Several of them pointed out that a lot of guys go to the drag races, lean over the hoods of the pro-stockers and see 2-inch tubing on a hemi or rat motor — then call the header manufacturer Monday morning and want 2-inch tubes for their small-block Chevy. There is still a lot of "monkey see, monkey do" in this business and this is part of it. The fact is that a small block — and some large blocks — falls on its face with 2-inch tubing. Follow the manufacturer's recommendation for your particular application unless you have money and time to burn in experimenting with unproved and untried combinations.

The 2 x 4-bbl. carburetion used on 305 CID Trans-Am engines in 1969 definitely made good use of 1-7/8-inch primary pipes as shown in the HP chart on the opposite page.

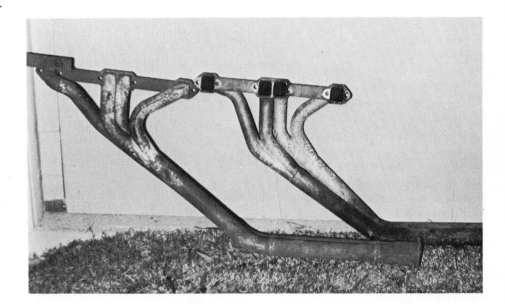

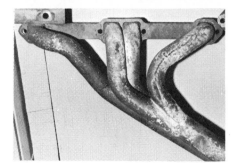 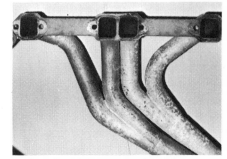

Once in vogue, Tri-Y headers phased out of the performance picture when street-machine owners started copying all-out racers, never noticing what the 4-into-1 systems did to low and mid-range torque. A small-block Chevy Tri-Y pairs cylinders 1 & 5, 3 & 7, 2 & 4 and 6 & 8. Perhaps users will wake up someday and demand the correct headers, even though they will cost more.

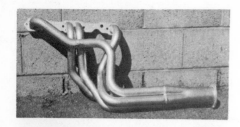

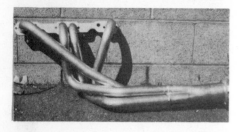

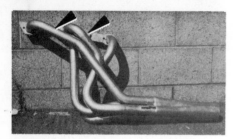

Hookers for Camaro's: one for '70-'72 and the other for '67-'69. Buy the wrong set and you've got a problem — because the headers won't interchange as the photos plainly show. Make sure you get the correct headers to start with and then READ THE INSTRUCTIONS. Lower Hooker is a "take-apart" header which is assembled in place on the car and then welded together at the collector to provide a rattle-free unit. Sometimes this can be a saving grace in an engine swap. Notice that flange is cut twice — at points shown by arrows.

NOTE: Perhaps the most important construction feature that you should check before signing that check for your new headers is this: can you get the plugs in and out after the headers are installed? And, do the plug wires and boots clear the headers? Don't take either of these points for granted. Check it for yourself, even if you have to carry a head into the store and bolt on first one header — then the other — to be absolutely sure.

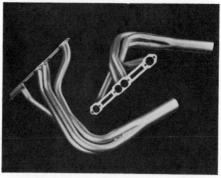

These Stahl headers for '55-'57 Chevys have been on more record-breaking NHRA class cars than all other headers put together. They're available in four pipe sizes: 1-1/2, 1-5/8, 1-3/4 and 1-7/8-inch. Primary length ranges from 28 to 37 inches. Five collector diameters and seven flange designs are offered. Complicated, ain't it? All Stahl sets are serial-numbered and a permanent record made of the original purchaser, type of header and application.

Realizing that he can't build production headers for everything, Stahl offers these equal length kits for small-block Chevys used in sprint cars. This could be the answer to a lot of engine-swap problems.

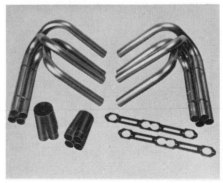

There were some steering-box clearance problems when this small block was slipped into an early frame. Exhaust pipe was hammered severely — an indication of poor engine swapping and a resulting loss of horsepower from the crimped pipe.

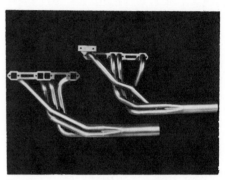

Don't confuse these with Stahl road-racing headers. These 1-5/8-inch primary-ed units are for 302 CID stock-class Z-28 Camaros used in drag racing. Tony Pizzi, Jim Hayter and a few other Z-28 shoes spread the Chevy gospel with these headers.

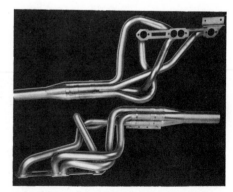

One of the "workinist" sets of headers ever built for the small-block Chevy: Stahl headers built for the racing '64 through '72 Chevelles. Note adjustable 1-3/4-inch primaries.

4-Into-1 HEADER COMPARISON

350 CID Chevrolet
2 x 4-bbl. Holley List No. 4224 carburetors
Edelbrock TR-1X Tunnel-Ram manifold
Diamond-Elkins Ported Heads
Racing camshaft
Vertex magneto 36° BTDC at 4000 RPM

HORSEPOWER

— 400 —
— 350 —
— 300 —
— 250 —

RPM

4500 5000 5500 6000 6500 7000

- - - 1-5/8'' x 35'' primary
3'' collector
Super-Scavenger
(Mickey Thompson)

——— 1-7/8'' x 28'' primary
3-1/2'' collector

······· 1-7/8'' x 28'' primary
3'' collector

– – – 1-3/4'' x 32'' primary
3'' collector

Holley Dyno Tests
December 8, 1971

Header tests run by Don Gonyou of Holley's Mickey Thompson Division show clearly that small tube headers ain't all bad for the street machine. Only at 5600 RPM does one of the three larger headers begin to produce more HP. The other two were better at over 6000 RPM. How often are you going to turn those speeds with your street machine? Maybe those 1-5/8 headers that have been hard to get rid of on the market are one of the smartest buys for the street runner. Pictured below is the 350 CID small-block that Holley uses for header and carburetor research. Large tubes connect into fans to carry exhaust away from the test cell. Instrumentation and controls are outside of the cell so that the engine can be operated remotely. This is a Froude high-speed dynamometer.

JETTING AND HEADERS

When installing a new set of headers, always install a new set of spark plugs of the same heat range you've been running and keep close tabs on how they look after several runs or after several days on the street. A header which is really "working" will lean the engine out. If you've been jetted too rich, the jetting could now be right, but if you were jetted correctly to begin with, you may now be too lean. Check this carefully with new plugs and be prepared to go 1 to 3 jet sizes richer — depending on the application.

READ THE INSTRUCTIONS

Read the instructions!

EXHAUST CHANGES REQUIRE TUNING

Any time that you change the engine so that it can breathe more freely, carburetion and ignition-timing changes will be needed to obtain the best possible performance. Typically, a slightly richer mixture will be required because the headers will scavenge the combustion chambers better than the stock exhaust manifolds. Slight retarding of the ignition may also be required under some circumstances.

EXHAUST SYSTEM APPEARANCE

Keeping your exhaust system "looking young" is no difficult chore if you will clean off the paint that the header maker puts on — usually by sandblasting — and apply Sperex VHT enamel to the pipes, flanges and collectors. The parts will look even better if you grind off any ugly welds before painting. VHT is the paint used on all sorts of race cars and boats. It is available in black, white and a wide array of colors.

TUNED EXHAUST SYSTEMS

We won't go into the construction of tuned exhaust systems because that's the subject of another book. You might want to read it someday. Get a copy of Philip H. Smith's "THE SCIENTIFIC DESIGN OF EXHAUST AND INTAKE SYSTEMS." In passing, we'll note that the four-into-one collector systems being made for the small block by most header makers are pretty close to what would be optimum.

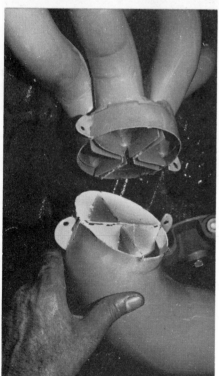

Smokey Yunick came up with these experimental headers. Check the number of pieces in each primary pipe. Holes near the flange in each 1-3/4-inch primary pipe are used for thermocouples during testing, can subsequently be used for observation of flame color after thermocouples are removed. Another set of the same type headers is on the engine shown on the cover. Interior shot of the collector shows how Smokey carried the primary tubes to much greater lengths than is immediately apparent from a first look. Primary pipes are kept separated through the entire four-inch-diameter collector. Individual flanges like these give the engine a cleaner appearance and make installation easier and gasket sealing more positive. Such construction is not used on production-made headers because it costs too much.

Tuned-length pipes to the collector and various collector lengths and diameters can be used to fine-tune an exhaust system. If you are drag racing, then such adjustable systems could be worth the effort. We've noted that Grand Prix racing teams — such as Ferrari — don't hesitate to use such tactics in fine-tuning their cars for particular courses. Stahl Engineering pioneered the use of adjustable headers for production cars here in the U.S.

Straight, open stacks were once regarded as the ultimate exhaust system. There's no denying that they made lots of noise and looked racy. But, their usefulness ended there because the dyno and the race track have both proved beyond any doubt that straight stacks do not allow the engine to produce as much HP as it can when a collectored system with the correct length primary pipes and collectors is installed. Unless you have HP to give away, there is no reason to even think about using straight stacks.

Tuned-length straight stacks are very "peaky," providing a large increase in power at a particular RPM — and detracting from power output throughout the rest of the engine range. In fact, tuned stacks never quite equal the collector-type system anywhere in the RPM range if the collector is correctly designed.

The trend is definitely away from straight stacks for any kind of racing car. You certainly won't see any on Formula A cars or on the top drag machines.

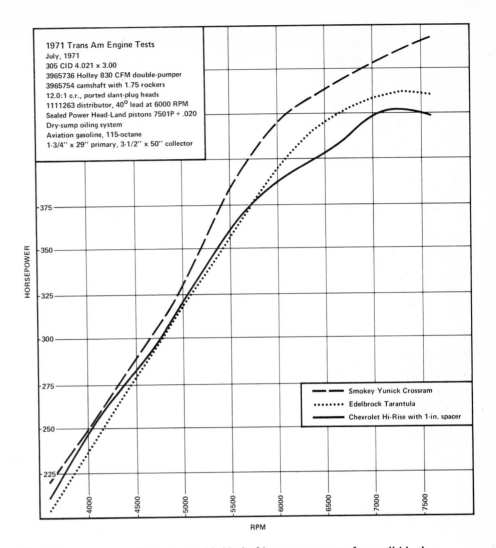

1971 Trans Am Engine Tests
July, 1971
305 CID 4.021 x 3.00
3965736 Holley 830 CFM double-pumper
3965754 camshaft with 1.75 rockers
12.0:1 c.r., ported slant-plug heads
1111263 distributor, 40° lead at 6000 RPM
Sealed Power Head-Land pistons 7501P + .020
Dry-sump oiling system
Aviation gasoline, 115-octane
1-3/4'' x 29'' primary, 3-1/2'' x 50'' collector

- - - Smokey Yunick Crossram
····· Edelbrock Tarantula
——— Chevrolet Hi-Rise with 1-in. spacer

All of the parts are available to get this kind of horsepower out of a small-block Chevy with a single four-barrel Holley carburetor. These are as-installed figures. Note that this combination with the one Holley carburetor works better with 1-3/4-inch primary pipes, while the graph shown a few pages back for the Trans Am engine with two Holleys showed that the best power was obtained with 1-7/8-inch primary pipes. This graph provides a good comparison of three manifolds: stock Z-28/LT-1 high-riser with a 1-inch spacer, Edelbrock Tarantula and the Smoke Ram which was designed by Smokey Yunick and is now made by Edelbrock.

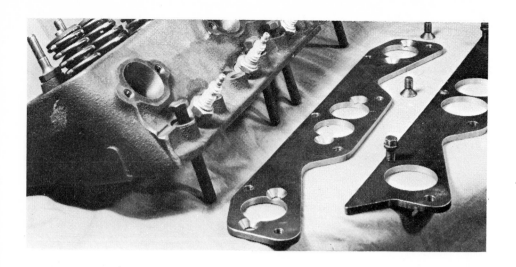

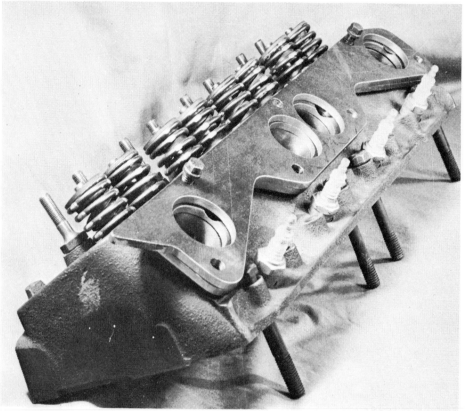

For years, guys have been trying to figure out how to run 1-7/8-inch and 2-inch primary pipes on the small block without dimpling the pipes for flange-bolt clearance. Stahl solved the problem early in 1970 and applied for a patent on the design. They are in production for those of you who have a fire-breathing small block with lots of cubic inches. Flange with 1-7/8- or 2-inch-diameter holes bolts to block with countersunk screws. Outer flange with attached pipes has holes which mate with and bolt onto the inner flange.

MUFFLERS

You'll want at least two — one for each side of the engine. Not for the extra noise that this makes — but to reduce the restriction in the exhaust system. It is absolutely essential that you replace the original skinny exhaust pipes. At least 2-1/2-inch exhaust pipes should be used from the header collector to the muffler. Get the muffler as far back under the car as you can and then make the tailpipe at least 2-1/4 and preferably 2-1/2-inch in diameter.

Ideally, four Cadillac reverse-flow mufflers should be used. Dyno tests have proved this to be the least restrictive system that can be installed. Add a 2-1/2-inch diameter "Y" immediately behind each collector and connect the "Y" into two Cadillac reverse flow mufflers *for each side* — four in all! Use 2-1/2-inch tailpipes out of the mufflers. This makes a heavy — but quiet and efficient — exhaust system. It is the one that the Detroit engineer street racers use and recommend.

If you don't have the room — or the $$$ for the four-Cadillac system — try a pair of the 2-1/2-inch Corvette mufflers or the ones from the Corvair Spyder. This will do a fairly effective job of silencing, especially if you add a balance tube ahead of the mufflers, as described on the following page. In the case of the Camaro optional mufflers which hang on the outside of the car, the only way to quiet these when used with headers is to add a balance pipe *plus* a resonator on each side, just ahead of the entry to the muffler/tailpipe combination. This modification will bring the noise down to a livable purr. You won't believe it's the same vehicle.

If you elect to use straight-through mufflers, good luck! Chances are that you won't be able to come close to the core diameter that you could use on a reverse-flow muffler (which are *more efficient* than the straight-through type, believe it or not!) and you'll probably have to drop down on core diameter to even drive the car on the street. As you go down on core diameter, you give away HP. Neal Gates of Hooker cited a test that they ran with a pickup on a chassis dyno in which 2-inch-core straight-throughs were changed for 1-3/4's and 16 HP was lost. This was done because the 2-inchers were just too loud to live with on the street.

So, which mufflers should you buy? Preferably *not* the straight-through "glass-packs" unless you have a bottomless wallet and can afford to put up with all the harassment that this brings from the men in blue. Keep it quiet! You'll have more fun with your car's performance as a result. Get the Cadillac, Corvette or Corvair mufflers that we've recommended, keep that exhaust and tailpipe diameter up — and add a balance pipe just behind the collectors.

Take a good look at the joints where the exhaust pipes attach to the exhaust manifolds (if you are using manifolds). Make sure that there are no restrictions at this point. Some late cars and trucks have necked down the entry to the exhaust (head) pipe. The net result is like stuffing a potato in the tailpipe. Make sure that this problem does not exist on your car.

The correct selection of a pair of mufflers can make a big difference in performance if they are connected through 2-1/2-inch head pipes as already described. Some performance difference can even be obtained when the free-flowing parts are tacked on behind the stock cast-iron manifolds.

Don't regard noise lightly if you want to use your engine's full performance potentialities. A quiet exhaust system attracts much less attention than a noisy one. The same is true of carburetor-intake noise because it can be louder than the muffled exhaust under certain circumstances. Don't neglect this point because the quieter the exhaust — the less traffic tickets — of all types. We have proved that time and again on street-driven cars.

Making it quieter

If you get the muffler system installed behind your headers and find that the whole affair is just too cotton-pickin' loud, run a balance tube ahead of the two mufflers between the two exhaust pipes. The larger you make the balance tube — the quieter the system will become. Use of a balance pipe to connect the two sides dampens the low-frequency pulses to a lesser sound-pressure level. The factory puts the single exhaust system on their bread-and-butter cars. It "speaks" at 16,000 pulses a minute when the engine is turning 4,000 RPM, or 266 pulses per second. This sounds smoother to our ears than the same exhaust split into two four-cylinder sets — each talking at a 133-pulse-per-second rate. Most dual arrangements are cop-calling stereo systems. But the balance pipe ahead of the mufflers allows each side to speak more softly — at the 266-pulse-per-second rate — and back pressure is reduced still further and the noise level approaches that of a stock single-muffler system.

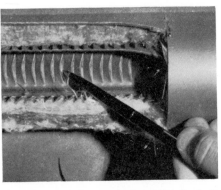

Worst offender of the straight-through muffler group is one in which a gang blade saw is used to create baffles. These rough edges slow down the flow and lose horsepower. You can spot this type easily — just look down the inlet and look for all of those burrs hanging in the wind.

Though they're painted and decaled when you see them in the store, this is basically what all of the straight-through muffler is about. They come in different diameters and lengths and most all of them turn out to be horsepower losers unless you go to the 2-inch diameter inlet — then you face a noise and gendarme problem.

A more expensive way of making the baffles in a straight-through muffler is by punching rows of louvers on the inner pipe. That's fiberglass packing between the inner pipe and the outer shell. This makes a louder muffler. More noise equals more HP — and more traffic tickets for anything the cops can dream up.

Blocking the heat riser for the intake manifold can never be recommended for the street. This modification creates numerous ills for the street-driven machine. It creates poor vaporization and this worsens mixture distribution to the cylinders. It also makes the exhaust system louder because the heat riser acts as a balancer between the two sides of the engine.

NOTE: Brake and fuel lines should be relocated so that they are not within two inches of an exhaust component. If the exhaust pipes come this close to brake or fuel lines, the lines must be equipped with aluminum heat shields and wrapped with asbestos.

Utter function for the drag strip. Dual Holleys on Edelbrock tunnel-ram manifold. This is Ed Nelson's small-block 'Vette which runs out of Bob Joehnck's Santa Barbara shop. Notice the Aeroquip fuel line. Aluminum "shelf" and foam rubber seal off engine heat from inlet air arriving via hood scoop.

Weiand Hi-Quad with two Holleys has a home in Dick Scritchfield's street roadster. It's the kind of carburetion that you'll find in super-light competition vehicles, or drag-race machines. You'll seldom find it on the street because the Hi-Quad runs best "upstairs."

Many Chevys are equipped with a Rochester Quadra-Jet (Q-Jet) or a Holley carburetor. Both of these four-barrel carburetors have two smaller primary "barrels." Some low-HP engines have two-barrel Rochester carburetors. We have assumed that you are not interested in these two-barrel carburetors and info in this book is devoted almost entirely to the four-barrel carburetors. Although photos of hot machinery with dual four-barrel carburetors for drag and boat racing — and injectors for Formula A cars — are included, emphasis is on streetable equipment. Our discussion is primarily limited to a single four-barrel installed on either a factory manifold or one of the aftermarket manifolds.

The carburetor is mounted in the center of the engine on an aluminum or cast-iron low-riser manifold, or on an aluminum high-riser manifold. Holley four barrels are always mounted on an aluminum manifold.

Because carburetion systems are inextricably tied into the emission controls, it is important to have a service manual for your particular car so that you can learn to understand the workings of the various emission-control devices. Some of these include transmission-controlled vacuum spark advance (TCS), specialized mechanical-advance curves in the distributor, carburetor-air heat, and on some models, a device which cuts in the air-conditioning compressor as you turn the ignition switch off to load the engine so it will shut off if dieseling (running-on) occurs.

NOTE: When checking for full-throttle, do not merely actuate the linkage at the carburetor by hand. Looseness and wear in the linkage or cable will not show up unless you include the entire system — which requires mashing on the foot pedal.

Lest you think that all of these items have been added to make your life harder, think seriously and unselfishly about the clean-air problem which must be solved if we want to continue living on Planet Earth. Make yourself part of the solution — instead of part of the problem — by getting acquainted with the systems and what each does.

We won't try to kid you — almost anything which makes an engine "cleaner" — so that it produces less emissions — makes the engine run poorer and produce less HP. Short-circuiting or de-activating these control devices can be helpful for winning at the drag races, but in California and certain other states, roadside inspections are made without warning to check that all systems are operable. The fines for deactivating the systems for *road use* are severe and getting more severe every year. Don't put yourself in a financial bind or destroy the engineers' efforts to clean up the air. Ecology is us and we are all part of the problem.

Carburetors supplied by Chevrolet have automatic chokes to provide easy starting and smooth warmups for the engine. These have fast-idle mechanisms to keep the engine running a little fast until the first time that you open the throttle after the engine has a bit of heat in it. Some Chevy engines have a device which pre-heats the carburetor air. This improves engine performance when the engine is cold, but after the engine warms up, the system, like all other smog devices, reduces performance. The system provides only heated air to the carburetor inlet until the air temperature reaches 85°F. When underhood temperatures exceed 128°F, the system provides underhood air which is not preheated by the exhaust-manifold stove. When it is time to race, you'll want *fresh cool air* directed to the carburetor.

BASICS OF CARBURETION

The carburetor is a mixing and metering device which automatically combines air and gasoline in the correct proportions for varying engine speeds and loads. Although it performs a complex job, the carburetor is a simple low-cost device.

A carburetor is a restriction (venturi) in the engine's air-inlet path to measure air and create a reduced-pressure area. Discharge nozzles in this reduced-pressure area connect to a float bowl which is vented to atmospheric pressure. Although the nozzle is higher than the gasoline level in the bowl, a predetermined decrease in pressure at the nozzle causes fuel to flow through it. As air is sucked through the carb by the piston strokes, fuel is added to the air stream in relation to air speed through the venturi.

At speeds above idle when fuel is flowing from the discharge nozzle, suddenly opening the throttle at low RPM instantaneously reduces the air velocity so that there is not enough signal to draw fuel from the nozzle. The mixture leans out. Fuel also deposits on the manifold walls, further leaning the mixture. The accelerator pump covers up this lean period by mechanically injecting fuel.

Good low-end punch with an excellent mid-range and a better-than-average top speed is provided by a carburetor system giving a minimum pressure drop not greater than 3.0 inches of mercury (Hg) at WOT (wide-open throttle). This is approximately what you get with the stock carburetion system. Racing systems are set up to give 1.0 inch — or even lower pressure drop in some cases — under full load at peak RPM and wide-open throttle (WOT). The pressure in the manifold is approaching atmospheric under these conditions.

This is not ideal for your street-driven car!

When you add carburetion capacity to get in this ball park you add more problems than performance. This is because adding carburetors or increasing venturi size decreases air velocity through the carburetors. When velocity falls below a "critical" value at which fuel and air cease to meter in the correct proportions, the engine is over-carbureted and produces little power at or near the RPM where the critical value is reached. Undesirable results include: poor low-speed torque, weak part-throttle mid-range, and a powerful top end once RPM is increased to the point where air velocity will cause fuel and air to meter correctly. The real loss for the street-runner is in flexibility of engine operation over a broad RPM range. Remember — the larger the venturi, the greater the top-end capability — but with a resultant

The sky — or your billfold — is the limit when it comes to small-block carburetion. This four-Weber setup graces the engine room of a roadster. Idles smoothly and runs like a champ. You can bet that no one makes an air cleaner for all of this. It's more show than go.

Never laugh at a two barrel. This small block is cooling off after a 13-second run through the quarter with a Holley 500 CFM two barrel providing the carbureting. A 600 CFM-er is now available. Note fender-well headers and cool can.

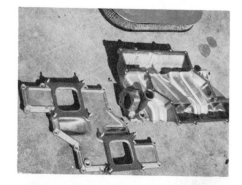

Chevy's own dual-quad (2 X 4) manifold that was an option for the 302. Part number is 3940077. Two 600 CFM double-pumper Holleys are used. Needless to say, this wakes up 'most any small block that's going to be run continuously at high RPM. Good for circle track and road racing.

loss in low-end response. Engines with a lot of venturi area . . . even large-displacement engines such as the 400-incher . . . can be said to have a "soggy" bottom end.

The problem is partially solved on your Chevy engine by the four-barrel carb which has both primary and secondary venturis. These provide additional carburetion in variable fashion so that the engine is neither over-carbureted at low speeds, nor undercarbureted to a great extent at high speeds. The primaries provide the air/fuel mixture for idling and mid-range — and two secondary venturis come in for top RPM. The secondaries, incidentally, are actuated by air flow through the carburetor in the case of the Q-Jet and "vacuum-operated" Holleys.

While the carburetor is off of your manifold, look at the area under the carb base. There is probably a divider under the base of the carb. So what is it, what's it for — and why do some manifolds have it and others don't? An explanation from Vic Edelbrock can help our understanding. "The divider separates the two planes of a 180°-style or two-plane manifold. The full divider isolates the two volumes of mixture in the manifold. These are alternately activated — first one plane and then the other — as the intake valves of the cylinders open. Each of these mixture volumes requires energy to be activated during intake-valve operation. Removing the plenum divider combines the two planes and increases the volume of mixture which must be activated each time that an intake valve opens. In terms of throttle response and mid-RPM torque, removal of the divider disrupts mixture velocity in this engine-speed range, leading to soggy response and poor off-the-line acceleration. It is simply a matter of more mixture volume requiring more energy to be activated. However, for engines normally operated above 4000 RPM, removing the divider lets the engine "see" a little more flow capacity at high RPM."

Edelbrock goes on to say, "In a sense, the divider can be used as a *fine trim tuning tool* by gradual removal of material from the divider until optimum performance is obtained for the desired RPM range. We suggest that the dividers be left undisturbed for all but long-cammed maximum-effort engines which require little — if any — low- and mid-range torque and throttle response." Incidentally, manifolds without the divider are termed "open-plenum" and manifolds with the divider are called "divided-plenum." Just remember that an open plenum "cushions" pulsations in the manifold so that they are not so harsh. The larger the plenum chamber volume, the more the softening effect. As the pulses are softened, the incoming air stream does not pull as much fuel from the discharge nozzles, so the mixture leans out in the mid-range. The cure is usually excessively rich jetting so that the mixture will be correct at WOT, which also richens the part-throttle mixture. You don't want these characteristics, so make such changes with the power valve channel restriction as described in H. P. Books' volume on Holley Carburetors.

Adding carburetion capacity (more carburetors or larger venturis) may cause flat spots at low speeds and reduces engine flexibility. You can't argue with the laws of physics — with the same engine speed and displacement, a large venturi area slows down the mixture and detracts from good mixing and metering. It may be almost impossible to get a smooth transition from idle to the mid-range. These problems won't bother a drag racer or road racer, but they can make a street machine extremely tough to live with for normal driving. A long-duration camshaft further complicates the situation by pumping back a part of the intake charge, further reducing the average air speed through the venturi.

Driving an engine with too much breathing capacity is work, not fun! It will stumble, cough and spit until 3000 RPM or so — then it'll really hustle to 7000 or so. You may not need *or even want* a 7000-RPM engine. You could be more interested in acceleration than top speed. The most important factor for acceleration is torque, not peak HP. If you need street performance concentrate on torque — which will take just one four-barrel carb for any small-block engine. A pair of Holleys — any size — on

a tunnel ram may look impressive to you and your friends, but they'll destroy torque at part-throttle for street operation. However, a pair of List No. 4224's on a high-quad or tunnel ram is the way to go for drag racing.

Don't buy the biggest carb that you can find. Chances are that your engine will run best with a 600, 650, 780, or 800 CFM Holley. Whatever you do, do not invest in the three-barrel 950 CFM Holley — or any larger carburetor — unless you are absolutely certain that this is what you really need to get your engine to run in the RPM range that your application demands. This is so much carburetion that we cannot recommend one for any street or street/strip application. The man who buys only one carburetor and figures that he has the ultimate "hot set-up" for his car is fooling himself. It is better to experiment with several carbs with different air-flow capabilities and let actual performance tell you which one is right for your job. A small carb often provides better drag ET's — and a lot more pleasure in driving — at the same time. Work with your friends who'll cooperate by trading carbs for a few test runs.

Quickly open the throttles of any carburetor arrangement with large venturi area and the engine will misfire momentarily — or even die! Why? Because manifold pressure rises almost to atmospheric, air velocity drops . . . and fuel deposits on the manifold floor and passage walls. The mixture, now mostly air, arrives at the cylinder too lean to support combustion. Many auto enthusiasts have the idea that quick throttle opening floods the engine with excess fuel, thereby causing the bog, stumble or roughness. 'Tain't so!

This is why experienced tuners direct their customers toward the use of a small carburetor . . . especially for exciting street performance. And, if you are buying a carburetor, consider one of the "double-pumper" Holleys which are set up to ensure that the engine gets a massive dose of fuel to help overcome the bog which normally occurs when you "jump on the throttle."

Holley engineer Don Gonyou says, "The wilder the cam and the bigger the carburetor — the more 'hole' or bog that must be covered up, hence the trend to larger accelerator

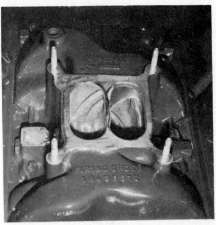

Divided-plenum cross-H high-rise manifold supplied on Z-28 and Corvette engines is hard to beat. Its mid-range HP is better than most replacement "performance" manifolds and its top-end HP is close to that provided by any two-plane or open-plenum manifold. Ribs in manifold runners are mixture-distribution devices. This is the best that Chevy has to offer in a single four-barrel intake manifold for the small block — and it's pretty good. The part number is 3917610. The aluminum high riser comes stock on the Z-28 and LT-1 engines.

An Edelbrock Tunnel Ram manifold mounting two mechanical-secondary Holley carburetors with "center shooters." This amount of plenum and carburetion is effective only at mid and higher RPM operation. Not recommended for the street under any circumstances.

Z-28/LT-1 high-rise aluminum intake manifold can be improved for high RPM by removing a section from the septum (plenum divider). Section removed should be 1-inch deep, 2-1/2-inches long. Notice that divider edge has been radiused and corners have been rounded off. This "no-buck" modification gives a slight horse-power increase in the upper RPM range only.

Considering that you saved some money and gained some high-RPM horsepower by cutting some material out of the plenum divider return the favor to your engine and fabricate a one-inch spacer from aluminum and bolt it directly to the carburetor pad of the manifold. Use a carb-base gasket as a pattern — leave any and all dividers out of the center. The spacer should be one-inch thick — not 3/4-inch or two inches — just one inch. Wondering what this is worth in terms of HP? About 8 to 10 HP above 5600 RPM.

pumps — such as the Reo type which we use — or dual-pumper carbs with two complete accelerator-pump systems."

IMPROVING STOCK CARBURETION

There are many reasons why you might want to improve stock carburetion, especially if you have a Q-Jet. You may want to contend in "stock" classes at either drags or autocross races — or both. Or, you could want every last ounce of performance which you paid for in the stock engine. Stock carburetion systems are fine for economy and all-around uninspiring performance. The small-venturi carburetor gives good low-speed torque, fine engine flexibility and restricted power output at high engine speeds. Simple changes to well-engineered stock-carb systems can provide enormous performance improvements, but you must keep in mind the fact that every "advantage" has an off-setting "disadvantage."

Careful tuning of the stock carb will usually add HP, but it's hard to find these missing horses unless you have a mixture analyzer or a dynamometer . . . or both.

The first thing you should do — even if you never plan to race — is to remove the air cleaner (temporarily!) so that you can peer into the carb's air-inlet horn. Have someone else mash the pedal to the floor as you check with a flashlight to make sure that the throttles fully open (not slightly angled). If they're not opening fully, figure out why and fix the problem. Any time you remove and replace the carburetor — check again to ensure that you have a fully opening throttle. It is the easiest thing to overlook and the cause of a lot of lost races or poor times. Any honest racing mechanic will admit that he's been tripped up by a part-opening throttle *at least once.*

Unless you are drag racing, put the air cleaner back in place. Don't leave it off. This is a temptation that you must overcome. The time-honored mark of the performance-oriented owner may be an engine with no air cleaner, but you can't afford to copy all of the things which have been proved not to work. You must proceed in a heads-up intelligent fashion to keep everything working for you — not against you. The engine needs all the help you can give.

The air cleaner directs the air into the carburetor in such a way that the vents work correctly so that the air gets into the air bleed jets in the correct fashion. A carburetor engineer can use almost any carburetor without the air cleaner or its base, but you may never acquire the specialized knowledge that is required. So, rather than work against yourself, use what has been proved to work successfully and you will be that much farther ahead of your competition. You have probably read a lot of articles which said to be sure to leave the air-cleaner base in place, even if you had to remove the air cleaner for some obscure reason. Lest you think that the writers have been kidding you, one dyno test series showed a 3 HP loss by removing the air-cleaner base. This little item causes air to flow into the carburetor with less turbulence. It is essential.

Air cleaners also protect against fires caused by starting "belch-backs" — reduce intake noise — and reduce engine wear. Intake noise can be horrendous — even worse than exhaust noise — on an engine that's turning up a lot of RPM.

Before leaving the subject of air cleaners, let us remind you to look at the way the stock cleaner is designed before you invest in some flat-topped short cleaner because it looks good. Note that the high-performance cleaner stands high above the carburetor air inlet. This design allows adequate space for the incoming air to enter the carb correctly and with minimum turbulence. With a flat filter sitting right on top of the air inlet you may get HP loss.

Naturally, the next thing to do is to bring the carburetor or carburetors up to the latest-year specifications as shown in the Service Manual. Of course, you'll want to make sure that the carburetor is clean and that the float level is correctly set.

In general, the main jet is correct for maximum performance at WOT. The latest models with low emissions are jetted so lean at part throttle that the engine runs hotter than would otherwise be necessary. Power valves are carefully selected to give best part-throttle performance with low emissions and best economy while maintaining best WOT mixture. If you make the mixture rich enough for best mid-range and part-throttle performance by changing the power valve restriction, mileage will suffer.

Changes which can affect carburetion include larger valve sizes, bigger displacement, ignition timing, special camshaft, changes in compression ratio, elimination of intake manifold exhaust heat, etc. An efficient exhaust system greatly affects the engine's overall breathing ability. Correctly exhausted cylinders have less residual burnt charge and can handle more intake charge. Slight changes in jetting may be required because the air flow through the carburetor may be caused to pulse more or less with such modifications.

You may be tempted to rip out the choke(s) until you look at the carb to see that there is so much area around the choke — as compared to the venturis being supplied — that there's no way to get more air through the carb by taking out the choke. Taking out the choke causes further wasted effort because then you still have to plug the choke-shaft holes so that all air entering the carb will come through the air filter.

Still further improvement is available by cooling the mixture, assuming that you are sweltering in summer's heat — because this is something that you don't want to do in wintertime or you'll get carburetor icing. Eliminating the exhaust flow through the heat-riser passage is accomplished by cutting a piece of tin or stainless steel to block the passage. A piece of tin can will work fine. Just loosen the manifold and slip the tin in on each side to block the exhaust which would otherwise flow into the underside of the manifold. Dyno tests show that this simple trick adds several horsepower with no other changes. It also increases the time required for the engine to warm up. It's not for the street!

To cool the mixture even further, use a "cool can." These standard items for the gung-ho drag racer use tubing coiled in a container of ice or dry ice to cool the fuel before it gets to the carburetor. The fuel line is merely cut apart so that the cool can be inserted as a section of the line. The HP improvement is minimal, but every little bit counts in drag racing.

If you live in "hot country" where summer temperatures go out of sight, consider installing a fuel radiator. You can run the fuel line through a Corvair oil cooler which you'll mount up in the airstream at the front of the car. Such a device will practically eliminate any vapor-lock problems. The radiator will not provide the cooling which can be had from a cool-can device, but is helpful for road-racing applications and ordinary highway driving.

RAM AIR AND COLD-AIR KITS

Some would-be speed tuners have the mistaken idea that they can add a mild form of supercharging at low cost by connecting rubber hoses to their carburetor(s) from scoops on the hood or under the front bumper. Any apparent improvement thereby obtained is due to the engine receiving cold air — *not from any supercharging or "ramming."* Ram air can provide minor HP improvement at very high speed: +1.2% at 100 MPH, +2.7% at 150 MPH, and 4.8% at 200 MPH. But, according to Colin Campbell, ramming to get this small power addition also creates problems. Unless the ram air is fed to all parts of the carburetors, including the float bowls and all vents — carburetion is disturbed, especially at low speeds. His book, *The Sports Car — Its Design & Performance,* states that a cold-air box arranged to feed the carburetors should be designed without ram effect by allowing free flow of the air out of the box feeding the carburetor filtered intakes.

Cold air will give you more improvement than ram air because 1% HP is gained for every 10°F temperature drop. This assumes that the mixture is adjusted to allow for the change in mixture density

Nothing mysterious about a fuel cooling can: fuel in the coiled metal line gets cooled because the can is packed full of ice or a combination of dry ice and alcohol which really gets the fuel temperature down there!

This is a homemade cowl-induction system for a Trans Am racer. The base of the windshield is a high-pressure area and therefore a good place to pick up carb air.

Constructing your own cold-air package is not as difficult as you might think. Many military surplus stores have the flexible ducting which can be mated to a reworked air-cleaner can. The kitchen utensil department of most any large store will yield a large funnel which can be fitted into an existing headlight housing.

You're looking at 465 horsepower from 302 inches. Bumped valve covers indicate Yunick is running the Mark IV rockers. Manifold is the Smoke Ram. Check the size of that fuel line.

Although this may look plenty backyard, it's the prototype of the Smoke Ram manifold being produced by Edelbrock. Milled slots in cover plate are for throttle and pump-linkage clearance. As this book goes to press, this is the best small-block single-carburetor manifold in existence.

An end view of the Smoke Ram reveals the long runner system which is employed to move the mixture from one side of the manifold to the opposite head. Arrows indicate openings which were used to house instrumentation during dyno testing. Notice how the manifold was welded up from many pieces — measured in cubic hours.

Inside the Smoke Ram. Carb sits directly over flat area which runs the length of the inner chamber. Mixture slams against the flat and then moves into the two "troughs." Smokey says the distance from the carb base to the "floor" is critical and has a stack of dyno sheets to prove it.

and that there is no detonation or other problems. Cold-air-box use is climate-limited because too-cold temperature will cause icing. Air scoops are o.k., provided that they are not connected to the carburetors — but to cold-air boxes or air cleaners which are vented correctly.

For complete details on ram tuning intake systems, refer to Philip H. Smith's book, *The Scientific Design of Exhaust & Intake Systems.* Perhaps one of the best single articles written on the subject was by Roger Huntington in the July 1960 HOTROD Magazine, "That Crazy Manifold." July and August 1964 HOTROD Magazines had two further articles which were written by Dr. Gordon H. Blair, Ph.D. All are worth reading, however, the use of a dyno to measure the real performance of a specially constructed "tuned" system — either intake or exhaust — is absolutely essential.

If you are running a cold-air kit which picks up cold air at the front of the car, be prepared to change the air-cleaner filter element at regular intervals, perhaps as often as once a week on the street in dustier areas. Front air inlets look "boss," but they are giant vacuum-cleaner entries to the carburetor. You'll be better off ducting cold air from the cowl just ahead of the windshield, using GM's standard parts for the task. That area still gets airborne dust, but it is several feet off of the ground — away from the grimy grit encountered at road level. If you like a car that looks "stock," the use of fresh air from the cowl is another way to get performance without making the car look like a racer.

SINGLE-CARB MANIFOLDS

Until 1971, the man wanting a four-barrel manifold for a Holley carb had few choices: stock Chevy manifolds — or one of the performance manifolds. All sold for about $100.

In January 1971, Edelbrock introduced a totally new concept in intake-manifold design. Their *Tarantula Series* is designed to work with a single four barrel. The manifold lists at $130, about $50 more than a stock aluminum high-rise or performance-type four-barrel manifold.

Although it is an open-plenum design, mixture velocity is kept high so that the low and mid-range performance are quite close to that provided by a divided-plenum manifold of the more usual 180° two-plane design. You can expect 15 to 20 HP more than the best previous single-carb manifolds produced — from 4500 RPM on up.

When you get one of these manifolds you will immediately think that some kind of a cruel joke has been played on you. The port runners don't even match with the ports in the head — by a long way! Don't you dare grab a grinder to match the manifold ports to the head openings — they're not supposed to match. That certainly goes against everything that we have ever been taught about building a high-performance engine, doesn't it?

Vic Edelbrock says, "We can only hope that most of the buyers will bolt the manifolds on and feel the difference in performance — or see it positively in their drag-strip time slips before making modifications which we guarantee will destroy all of the extra performance which we have built into these manifolds." Jim McFarland of Edelbrock Equipment says, "Flow characteristics of the port runners are so nearly equal that square jetting can be used with the 850 double-pumper Holley (78's all around). The 3310-1 works well with the stock 72 (primary) and 76 (secondary) jets and the Spread-Bore Holley works fine right out of the box.

"The manifold is unusual in that it makes the carb operate as if it were larger. Thus, a Q-Jet or spread-bore Holley can provide super punch off the line with good economy for around-town driving, yet gives good top end when the secondaries open. Using either of these on the Tarantula requires an adapter."

"Smoke Ram" is a name that you will be hearing a lot of over the next several years because it is a very efficient single four-barrel intake manifold for the small-block Chevrolet. Developed by Smokey Yunick for Trans Am racing, the manifold is now made by Edelbrock for the aftermarket. A HP comparison of the manifold vs the stock Z-28/LT-1 and the Tarantula appears in the exhaust chapter on page 35. Bear in mind when you look at the graphs

Holley Spread-Bore 650 CFM carb adapter-mounted on Tarantula manifold. Fuel bowls work with stock air cleaner. This combination with a high-performance hydraulic cam will wake up the most sluggish late-model small blocks, making them respectable street-runners—especially in the upper RPM range.

that this is for a fully tricked up engine with everything possible done to it to make a racing engine. Note especially the low-speed torque capabilities of the Smoke Ram as compared to the other manifolds.

Hilborn fuel-injection is commonly seen on circle-track and drag machinery. This is the current model as of 1972.

45

Holley's List No. 6210 of their Model 4165 Spread Bore is the most popular aftermarket carburetor for the small-block Chevy. Its bowl configuration, connections and linkage allow use with all stock equipment, including the air cleaner. Its large primaries give a good driving "feel" for around-town operation and a large accelerator pump on the secondary ensures that there will be no bog or hole when you "nail it" to go.

This is the Holley double-pumper made in several CFM ratings. It is readily identified by the accelerator pump on the secondary as well as the primary side of the carb. Although the carburetor is streetable, you'll probably soon tire of using one on the streets because of the time spent in conversing with John Law or getting filled up with gas. A 650 CFM Spread Bore is a better choice for a street-driven car.

HOLLEY CARBURETORS

Always use the smallest carb which gives best performance for the job. If your small block came equipped with a Holley, chances are you'll want to go right on using it. If you are in the market for a Holley you should have a pretty good idea of what you *really need* before buying first one and then another carb in quest of one which won't bog or stumble. One of the most common mistakes is simply bolting on too much carburetion. If you have to drive your car on the street, your best buy will probably be the 600 CFM carb for up to 350 inches and the 780 CFM carb for up to 400 inches. If you have a large engine and a performance cam, and want more "beans" on the strip then the 800 CFM double accelerator pump can be used to serve double duty.

A vacuum-operated secondary carb is better for high performance than most enthusiasts believe because it supplies the added air flow capacity only as the engine can use it. Thus, it is difficult to over-carburete when using the vacuum-secondary carburetor. Do not try to convert one of these to mechanical-secondary operation because the carb was not designed to work that way. You will create a bogging situation which cannot be alleviated easily — and the car becomes difficult to drive because of throttle sensitivity. If you have converted your vacuum-secondary carb to mechanical secondaries, change it back to regain that driveability, performance and mileage which you lost. If you need more performance, buy one of the double-pumper carbs with progressive-action mechanical secondaries.

Chevrolet recommends the use of 73 primary and secondary jets in the 780 to 800 CFM Holleys supplied as stock on some high-performance small blocks. Rather than change the jets, run it as it comes because the jets already in it may be perfect for your application — and you'll never know until you try it.

If you are going to use a double-pumper, buy an aftermarket version and run it as it comes out of the box. If you should fall heir to one of the 850 CFM 427 big-block Holleys, List No. 4296, change the stagger jetting to 73 or 74 primary and 76 secondary jets and remove the mixture-distribution tabs from the booster venturis. Aftermarket carbs are not stagger jetted and do not have mixture-distribution tabs.

If you are running two carbs, as on a plenum-type manifold, use the carbs recommended by the manifold maker. If you want to go racing with a single four-barrel, the choice is between the 830 CFM unit, List No. 4788 (with 1-11/16-inch throttle bores) — and the 850 CFM-er, List No. 4781 with 1-3/4-inch throttle bores.

Get the aftermarket models

When buying a Holley, get yours as an aftermarket equivalent. If you buy from a Chevy dealer, avoid carbs with a GM part number. GM is not trying to get rich by selling carbs at high prices. These are high-priced items and by the time that distributing costs are tacked on, the price for the factory-numbered part may go out of sight. Holley's lower priced aftermarket units are available to replace most of the original equipment carbs. Economy (in the form of gas mileage this time) is improved when the spread-bore type Holley (Quadra-Jet replacement) is used because these carbs have larger primary venturis and give better part-throttle response. There is less temptation to try for more performance by mashing harder on the throttle, as is required with the smaller Q-Jet. Keep in mind that fuel economy with any four barrel is achieved for the most part by keeping your big foot out of the throttle. If the secondaries are constantly being yanked open (especially with the double pumper) gas mileage will suffer greatly since the engine gets a double shot of fuel every time you "put 'er to the wood." The separate pumps are an advantage on a carb having progressive secondaries and being used for "serious driving" because the secondaries get an accelerator pump shot when they are being used.

If you are putting a new Holley on an engine, remove the float bowls and check the jet sizes and/or the number of the secondary metering plate. Write the sizes in a notebook or on the firewall for reference. Put it all back together and run the carb on the engine just as it came out of the box. Be sure to check that the accelerator-pump pivot arm can be moved an additional 0.015 inch with your fingers at wide-open throttle. For 90 percent of the engines, the jetting is plenty close. If the plugs start getting sooty (rich) or yellowish green (lean), motor over to the speed shop and pick up the next several jet sizes without having to pull the carb apart to see what the original jets were.

Just because you bore and/or stroke your engine, the jets do not necessarily need to be changed. If you have to use jets which are more than two or three jet sizes away from stock, the chances are very good that you have done something wrong.

Nearly every would-be racer starts out with the idea that the vacuum operating of the secondaries on any carb is wrong for performance. Thus, many of them spend countless hours playing with vacuum-diaphragm springs in an effort to get it "just right." Chances are it was right to begin with. In the main, vacuum-operated secondaries on a street/strip car don't hurt performance. The contrary may be true. Slow opening of the secondaries so no bog occurs when they come open may easily add speed and cut ET's. Opening the secondary throttle plates too quickly can easily make for slower times.

Vacuum diaphragm springs for the Holley vary from high tension, through medium to low. The lower the tension, the quicker the secondaries come in — and the more chance you have of creating a bog. Here again, most street cars run best with the springs supplied in the carburetor. The springs are fully detailed as to their operating characteristics — where opening begins, where full throttle is reached and load versus height — in the H. P. Book "Holley Carburetors."

There are a lot of things that can be done to tune a carburetor. Some of the "tricks" will work on one type of racer and not on another — hardly any of the racers' tricks do any good on the street. Here are a couple of areas which you might explore for a little better response, or in some cases, top end. If you make a change and the engine "falls on its face," go back to where you were with the carb before making another change, and then another until the car won't get out of its own way. Change just one thing at a time.

Some Holley carburetors have a secondary metering plate instead of removable jets. This can lead to wonderment about secondary jet size.

The secondary metering plate has the part number (34R-2007B) embossed upside down just below the top rectangular opening on the front side of the plate. An identifying number is stamped in the middle of the plate — also upside down, just below the part number.

When putting a single-inlet Holley together, don't shove the feed tube O-ring up to the lip on the tube. Put a drop of oil on the ring, just get it on the tube and let it roll back to the lip as you push the tube gently into the float bowl.

Amateurs rebuilding carburetors often cause themselves all sorts of problems. When you've stripped the threads out the fuel inlet, buy this little kit from the Carburetor Shop of Costa Mesa, California. It fits all Rochester and Holley's with a deep 3/4-inch inlet, the expanding plug does away with trying to repair stripped or corroded threads.

Smokey Yunick with a very smooth Camaro. Note the roll cage, Mini-Lite wheels, and front and rear spoilers. Carb on Smoke Ram manifold is fed cool air under pressure taken in ahead of the radiator by a very special hood. Note that the air cleaner is retained. It's a tall truck element which is not restrictive. Rocker covers are vented to catch-can breather behind firewall. Rocker covers have been bumped out to clear 1.7:1 ratio big-block rockers. Headers have 1-3/4-inch primaries, are the same as those on the cover photo.

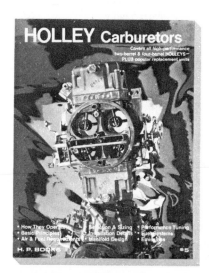

HOLLEY Carburetors is a complete book on these fine fuel/air metering devices. It covers all of the high-performance list numbers and details their selection, operation and tuning. It includes many charts, graphs, photos and cutaways which have never been previously published. It was written by Mike Urich, Engineering Manager for Aftermarket Products at Holley and by Bill Fisher of H. P. Books. The 160-page book sells for $5.

The secondary metering plate has two sets of holes in it. The bottom ones are secondary-metering restrictions. The other set of holes on the back side, near the top of the plate, are secondary idle-feed holes. Secondary plates with larger idle-feed holes may be helpful on big-displacement, hi-performance engines, especially with a racing cam. Richening the secondary idle provides better performance as the secondaries open.

The plates and their jet sizes (hole sizes, really) are described in the Holley High-Performance catalog and in the H. P. Book, "Holley Carburetors."

In a drag-race situation, richer jets are used because they *are* needed, although the reasons for this are not well defined. If 70's are needed on the dyno, then you may have to go to 72 or 74 on the strip for best acceleration. Double-pumper carbs help to reduce or eliminate this tendency and thus are quite popular for drag racing, even though they may murder economy on the street and highway. Having plenty of fuel available at the carburetor with large fuel lines and adequate pressure helps, of course. The pressure should be monitored with a gage connected just ahead of the carburetor. Pressure should not drop below four to six psi at wide-open throttle.

Holley's accelerator pumps are actuated by cams which can be changed to modify their action, or moved on the lever to provide a richer shot for cold weather operation. This is just one more of the areas for experimentation with these carburetors. Remember that whatever you do to the Holley, it is essential to check that there is an additional 0.015-inch of travel available for the pump pivot arm when the carburetor is wide open. You can check this by holding the throttle open and moving the lever with your fingers. If there is no clearance, adjust the screw which contacts the pump pivot arm. Failure to observe this causes overloading of the override spring which gives excessive throttle effort. Just the opposite is wanted at closed throttle or idle — no clearance can be allowed between the cam and the pump-actuating arm. You must have a pump shot issuing

from the discharge nozzles when the throttle lever is moved 1/16 to 1/8 inch.

Do not replace the power valve with a solid plug as many racers do. If the manifold vacuum is so low at idle and low RPM that the power valve is turning on and off and making it impossible to tune the car, replace the valve with one which operates at a lower manifold vacuum. When power valves are removed, the carburetor's fuel-handling characteristics are compromised. Richer jets have to be installed to make up for the lost jet area of the power-valve channel restriction and this makes the carburetor subject to flooding on stops.

Holleys have several fuel bowl types. The side-hung type is available with non-adjustable needle-and-seat assemblies and with externally adjustable needle-and-seat assemblies. The center-hung type has externally adjustable needle-and-seat assemblies. If you are buying a Holley, realize that the original stock air cleaner for a Q-Jet will not clear any of the fuel bowls except those on the 650 CFM Spread Bore which is designed as a bolt-on replacement. Center-hung bowls as found on the larger Spread Bores and on the double-pumper series require using an air cleaner such as the high-performance open-element type. Incidentally, the center-hung fuel bowls provide no real advantage, except for auto-crossing or road racing. A great number of drag-race cars use the side-hung floats. In fact, they are essential to allow jamming two carburetors close together — as on a high-rise dual-quad of the tunnel-ram variety.

Once you have installed the carburetor and have run the engine for several on-off cycles, so that the carburetor has been heated up and then cooled off, tighten the fuel-bowl screws *again*. They may appear to be tight because the fuel bowls are not leaking. But, remember that there is a second gasket between the metering block and the carburetor body. Any leaks here are not obvious but they play havoc with the way the carburetor functions. This gasket has to provide intact passages between the block and the body and it must also withstand vacuum applied to the back of the power valve. If a carburetor has been run and it is to be

I cannot tell a lie — it was I who swiped your two shower caps. They're being put to good use though.

disassembled, store the bowl and block gaskets in a handy coffee can full of solvent. Although the gaskets are reusable, they won't be if you let them shrink! A Holley which has been stored without gasoline or solvent in it and has dried out may require replacement of the bowl and block gaskets at each end.

One final point — the sintered-bronze filters just inside of the fuel inlet nuts at each fuel bowl should be removed for racing and a large paper-element fuel filter should be installed between the fuel pump and the carburetor. Keep the bronze filters installed for street use.

If you should happen to strip the threads in your fuel bowl, replacement needle-and-seat assemblies with longer-than-stock threads can be used for a low-cost fix. These are available from The Carb Shop in Costa Mesa, California.

Rochester Q-Jet is equipped with tiny primary venturis and huge secondaries. Secondary operation is controlled by an air valve to give good cruising gas mileage with adequate full-throttle power. It is one of the best performance/economy carbs in the industry and is used on millions of GM cars. Tuning details are provided later in the chapter.

Arrow indicates stock secondary lever which can be modified to open at 30° position of primary throttles instead of 50° as is stock.

QUADRA-JET

The Q-Jet carburetor comes stock on a vast number of small-block Chevys. It is a relatively sophisticated unit which is designed for smoothness, power, flexibility and long, troublefree operation. The carb contains four barrels: two primaries and two secondaries. The primaries are unusually small for excellent low-speed torque and good mileage. Secondary throttle bores are big. The centrally-located fuel bowl gives a compact design and more importantly helps to eliminate fuel starvation/slosh problems encountered in hi-perf cornering situations. The carburetor flows about 700 CFM at wide-open throttle.

The Q-Jet will usually be replaced by a Holley in time because the Q-Jet simply does not offer the response or HP of a correctly set up Holley. Thus, although the Q-Jet is a great carb for the street, it is seldom seen on the racing scene unless class rules require running the original carburetor.

To work on the Q-Jet with any degree of finesse requires following instructions in the Chassis Service or Overhaul Manuals for your particular model. Otherwise, trying to make it work — especially on the '70-72's with all that emission-control stuff — will be like trying to find your way out of a dismal swamp on a moonless night without getting eaten by alligators or bitten by snakes. Manuals are cheaper than new carburetors every time. It's amazing how many neophyte tuners will read a magazine article with all kinds of tricks and believe that this is really what the man did to his carburetor. So, they start drilling holes, filing things and tightening springs, etc. — getting the part into a condition so far from stock that a trained carb man may not be able to repair the damage without a lot of new parts. "A little knowledge is a dangerous thing."

Other than a good basic rebuild by carefully following the instructions in the kit *and* in the factory manual/s, a few modifications may be performed in pursuit of better response. First of all, if your carb has a bronze filter in the entryway, chuck it. Use an in-line filter with a replaceable element such as Holley's 62R-121A or 62R-123A. Don't take out the choke because there's no performance to be gained.

You may cause the carb to run worse because the choke is part of the air-horn configuration which makes the air bleeds work correctly.

Primary metering

Take the air horn off to get at the primary metering rods and jets. Pop out the power-piston assembly with the metering rods by bouncing the assembly lightly and rapidly with your finger.

There are 46 different primary jets, ranging from 0.050 to 0.099 inch. They can be ordered through your Chevy dealer or a United Motors dealer. However, you can't drill the jets so that they will flow accurately or even similarly, so buy pairs of jets in the sizes that you want to try. Then you don't have to do the job all over again when you think that you are finished tuning. Do not attempt to install Holley jets because they will destroy the different threads in the Q-Jet body.

The first mistake made by most people in working on any carburetor is to make everything *bigger*. Leaner jetting often provides sharper acceleration. With the Q-Jet you can install smaller primary main jets if you richen up the secondary system with different metering rods so that there will be plenty of fuel to avoid leaning out when the engine is putting out power.

If you install larger primary jets, the power system and wide-open throttle are also richened and the mid-range or part-throttle condition is also fattened up. Here is a relationship which you should note: for each 0.001-inch larger primary jet, install two sizes larger metering rod; for each 0.001-inch smaller primary jet, install two sizes smaller metering rod. Each 0.001-inch primary jet chance richens/leans WOT operation 0.5 A/F ratio. The rod number indicates the largest diameter of the rod portion which is fully inserted into the jet in the part-throttle position. The rods must be changed whenever you change the jets or the part-throttle operation will be excessively richened/leaned, depending on whether you installed larger/smaller primary jets.

Secondary metering

Each secondary barrel has a fixed jet. Fuel which flows through it is dependent on secondary metering rods (needles) attached to a yoke (hanger) which raises the rods out of the jets to flow more fuel as the air valve over the secondary throttles opens. The yokes are letter-coded. Each letter from "B" towards "V" drops the rod taper farther into the jet by 0.005-inch, leaning out the entire calibration by 0.2 A/F ratio.

Secondary metering rods are numbered with two letters (AT, AX, etc.). Your local United Motors dealer's charts describe the rods' small-end diameters which control fuel flow when the secondaries and air valve are fully open. Thus, a rod change alters A/F ratio where the air valve opens and/or at maximum flow. If you want to richen the mixture at the top end, reduce the small-end diameter of the rods about 0.003-inch at a time by using a file or emery cloth on the rod tips as they are spun in a lathe or drill press chuck or collet. Once you have found the correct diameter by experimentation, buy the right rods from the United Motors man.

Should your engine exhibit a mid-range stumble, you may be able to cure the malady by adjusting the secondary metering yoke so that the metering rods are caused to sit higher in the jets and so that they lift higher sooner. Bending the yoke is not recommended, but you can either change the yoke or epoxy a small piece of paperclip wire under the lift arm at the pivotal point as a starter for experimentation.

When installing the air horn on the carb body, don't jam the secondary metering rods into the jets because this can affect metering.

A pair of holes supply fuel to the standpipes which deliver fuel to the secondary barrels. Some tuners have added additional holes below the stock ones to add to the total fuel reserve available for the secondaries. Such holes can be plugged with lead shot to get the carb back to stock condition if the change does not help.

A few words about that air valve

Q-Jets have a giant pair of secondary throttles controlled by the accelerator. However, to avoid the bogging which is so common when a carb is quickly opened wide, both air flow and jetting of the secondaries are controlled by a unique air valve. As more air enters the carb, air gradually overcomes the spring pressure which normally holds the air valve closed. As previously mentioned, a cam attached to the air valve lifts a yoke with two tapered metering rods out of the secondary jets to increase fuel flow.

Air-valve opening point is controlled by a wind-up spring. The air valve is off-center on its shaft so that air acting on the larger area turns the spring-loaded shaft. As the air valve opens, it forms a crude V-shaped "venturi" with a sheet-metal baffle inside the secondary air horn. Fuel-discharge pipes here deliver fuel as air flows through the secondaries. The previous section described how the air valve operates the metering rods to affect the entire system.

When you open the throttle quickly, air flows immediately – but fuel lags – hence the use of an accelerator pump to add fuel to help make up for this lag. However, the secondaries do not have an accelerator pump of their own and you may want to increase the spring tension to slow secondary action. A very slight pause as you apply more throttle could indicate the need to slow the air valve by increasing spring wind-up, but not beyond one turn! Unfortunately, increased spring tension may cut down the carb's total air-flow capability because the air flow at peak RPM may not be able to open the air valve against the increased spring tension.

Adjusting the spring tension against which the air valve operates causes the air valve to open either sooner or later. To adjust the spring, loosen the socket set screw under the adjustment screw and back off the screw CCW 1/4 turn at a time until you reach the zero-tension point where the air valve barely closes when you tap on the carburetor. Then, preset spring tension by turning the adjusting screw 7/8 turn CW from the zero point. Hold the adjusting screw position as you retighten the set screw. Any experimentation from this

Pen point indicates pivot-point pin which can be extended to stop air valve in a slightly open position as described in text. Arrow points to yoke which can be raised by installing a piece of wire between yoke and its mount. Outline arrow indicates air-valve cam which lifts yoke as valve opens.

Pen point indicates air-valve adjustment screw. Arrow points to socket set screw which secures adjustment.

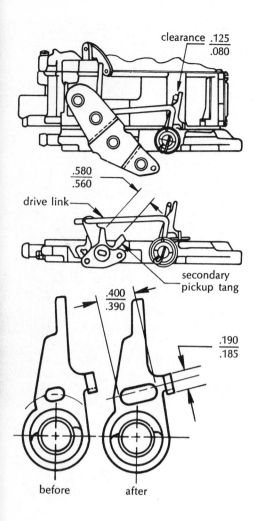

clearance $\frac{.125}{.080}$

$\frac{.580}{.560}$

drive link

secondary pickup tang

$\frac{.400}{.390}$

$\frac{.190}{.185}$

before   after

point should be 1/8 turn at a time, but the screw must not be tightened more than one turn from zero-tension or you'll distort the spring into uselessness.

A lot of owners try to quicken the air-valve opening, thereby interrupting the continuous smooth air flow that would be best for acceleration with this carburetor. Quick air-valve opening sends the car straight to Bogsville, which is located on the map a few feet down the road from where you buried your foot in the throttle. If you must experiment in this area, unwind the spring until the engine begins to "stumble" just as the car leaves the starting line, then tighten the spring a little at a time until it's eliminated — but not more than one turn.

Jim Baker, who campaigned a '68 Camaro (120.95 MPH at 11.67 seconds ET) used an elongated pin through the yoke pivot point to hold the air valves slightly open in their at-rest or "closed" position. This eliminates hesitation caused by sudden opening of the air valve and may allow running closer to the stock wind-up setting. However, this kind of mod requires tailoring for the individual situation. It may not work for everyone!

Accelerator pump talk

After setting the air valve, more pump action may be required. This is especially true if the air-valve setting ends up 1/4 to 1/2 turn weaker than stock. Remove about 1/8 inch from the end of the pump-rod assembly to increase the pump stroke. This increases the volume of gasoline delivered to cover up holes caused by too quick an air-valve opening, a lopey cam, or whatever. But, do this kind of mod on an extra pump assembly so you can switch back and forth to see whether you are helping or hindering performance. There must be a little travel left in the accelerator pump at WOT or the primary will not open all the way—and neither will the secondary.

Secondary opening change

Modifying the secondary lever as shown in the accompanying drawing starts secondary opening at 30° instead of 50°. If the vehicle is light or geared for quick acceleration, this can be *extremely helpful*, especially in auto-

crossing. This technique just about doubles the CFM capabilities at a 3-inch Hg pressure drop across the carb. But, if the secondaries are in excessively during highway cruising, economy will be *murdered*, according to sportscar carburetion expert Doug Roe.

Leave the float level alone

Changing the float level to cure ills is a poor way to go. This changes all kinds of characteristics in the carburetor, including where the jets begin to work and so on. Use the stock float level. If the carb needs more fuel, consider raising the fuel pressure to as much as 8 psi and install a larger needle and seat from a Buick, P/N 7023896. It has 0.136-inch diameter as compared to the stocker's 0.125 or so. The combination of a larger needle and seat and more fuel pressure may be the only way to cure a lean condition at high RPM.

If you get careless when installing or removing the needle seat of a Quadrajet you can strip the threads out of the carb body. The body is cast pot metal and the seat is a harder brass. When that happens you can either buy a new carb body or contact the Carb Shop for a special needle seat with another couple of threads to reach down in the threaded hole to grab the remaining good threads.

Q-JET METERING JETS & RODS

Primary metering rods[1]

7034832	0.032	7034843	0.043
833	0.033	844	0.044
834	0.034	845	0.045
835	0.035	846	0.046
836	0.036	847	0.047
837	0.037	848	0.048
838	0.038	849	0.049
839	0.039	850	0.050
840	0.040	851	0.051
841	0.041	852	0.052
842	0.042		

Primary metering jets[2]

7031950	0.050	7031973	0.073
951	0.051	974	0.075
952	0.052	975	0.076
953	0.053	976	0.078
954	0.054	977	0.079
955	0.055	978	0.080
956	0.056	979	0.082
957	0.057	980	0.083
958	0.058	981	0.085
959	0.059	982	0.086
960	0.060	983	0.087
961	0.061	984	0.088
962	0.062	985	0.089
963	0.063	986	0.090
964	0.064	987	0.091
965	0.065	988	0.092
966	0.066	989	0.093
967	0.067	990	0.094
968	0.068	991	0.095
969	0.069	992	0.096
970	0.070	993	0.097
971	0.071	994	0.098
972	0.072	995	0.099

1. Diameter is largest part of rod which is in primary jet at part-throttle.

2. Diameter is jet orifice with 90° included angle at entry and 60° included angle at exit.

On page 40 we show the stock 2 X 4 manifold off of the engine. Here it is installed on a Camaro with a stock fiberglas hood Chevrolet engineer Gerry Thompson is holding the air-cleaner-base assembly. All of the parts are in the HD Parts List.

Hoods that take advantage of the high-pressure area ahead of the windshield are real performance aids because they help to ensure that the carburetor gets cooler air than is available under the hood. Top is a Corvette optional hood, lower photo is an optional Camaro hood.

Some hi-rise-type manifolds require additions be made to the hood for clearance. This box is open at the back because there is a high-pressure area at the base of the windshield.

Two Chevrolet transistor ignition systems, distributors and amplifiers. Magnetic-pulse "sender" is below rotor of distributor at right. "Contact Controlled" means ordinary points . . . in distributor at left.

Don't be quick to do away with those stock ignition wire clamps. Plug wires must be kept separated.

Magnetic-impulse ball-bearing distributor for the big-block Chevy is acknowledged to be the finest Delco unit available. It can be fitted to the small block by changing the drive gear (to 1958599) and completing the groove around the area just above the gear (arrow). The reason you have to change the gear is that the distributor was originally designed for use with a gear-drive cam which turns opposite to a chain-driven camshaft or to a gear-driven camshaft which rotates the same as a stock small-block cam. The distributor is released with weak spring and a curve too long for racing use. It is necessary to shorten the mechanical-advance-limiting slot and to use stiffer springs. The recommended spring, P/N 1887302, measures 90 oz. tension at 0.725-inch length.

If you follow our recommendations in this chapter, you will save the cost of this book several times over. You can save lots of money by using stock Chevy ignition parts because no horsepower can be gained by changing to a special ignition system if your stock system is the correct one and is in good condition. Your Chevy ignition system will provide maximum power in the most strenuous racing applications. Although there have been many different Chevy distributors, the chapter tells you which ones to consider for use in your engine . . . and why.

Spark-plug selection is also important for performance and types for high-performance, high-compression engines are discussed. The two bugaboos of high performance, detonation and pre-ignition, are covered in detail.

STOCK IGNITION SYSTEM

The stock ignition system consists of the battery, a distributor, a coil, an amplifier for transistor-switched or magnetic-impulse ignitions, spark-plug cables terminating in boots over the plug connectors, and spark plugs. All of the stock distributors have one point set for the ignition system—or a toothed wheel which is surrounded by a magnetic-impulse pickup.

No point-type distributors are listed in the Chevrolet heavy-duty parts list as of 1970. We surmise that eliminating any need for checking point gap and ignition dwell has caused the complete changeover to the magnetic-impulse systems for high-performance engines. With one of these systems, you can be assured that ignition timing will not change as the distributor is used. Points, on the other hand, wear at the rubbing block so that the gap closes and dwell angle—

which determines coil saturation time—changes. Just as frustrating is the fact that this retards the ignition timing. But, there's some doubt as to how many builders will see their way clear to spend $200 to $300 for an ignition system when they can "get by" for a lesser investment.

Chevy refers to their magnetic-impulse system as a "transistor ignition system." It features a specially-designed distributor, ignition pulse amplifier, and a special coil. Two resistance wires are used in the circuit: one as a ballast between the coil negative terminal and ground, and the other as a voltage drop for the engine run circuit. This second resistance wire is bypassed during starting. Two magnetic-impulse distributors are offered. Both have a mechanical tachometer drive. The top-of-the-line $203 (list price) unit, 1111263, is an all-ball-bearing distributor. Because it is *strictly for racing*, it does not have a vacuum-advance mechanism. Its advance mechanism is controlled by weights which advance the toothed wheel as engine RPM increases. This is a truly maintenance-free distributor.

Next in line is the plain-bearing distributor with vacuum advance, P/N 1111267. At $83 (list price), this distributor has become a favorite with street/strip engine builders. The only maintenance recommended for this distributor's upper bushing is "at overhaul" when the plastic seal should be removed and SAE 20 oil added to the packing in the cavity. A new oil seal is required because the old one is destroyed by taking it out.

Each of the magnetic-impulse distributors is used with a $111 kit, P/N 3997782 to make a complete transistor ignition system. It is a "brute-force" transistor system which incorporates a certain degree of dwell "stretching" so that the coil will produce adequate sparks at very high RPM. But, contrary to what you may have read, the Chevrolet systems supplied for the big-block and small-block engines are not capacitive-discharge systems.

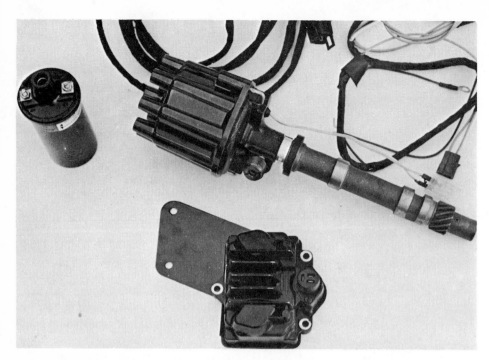

This is the good-guy distributor that Chevy sells for the real racers. It's a ball-bearing-equipped distributor with magnetic-pulse-triggered transistor ignition. All cables, amplifier and coil are parts contained in a transistor-ignition unit listed in the HD Parts List.

Delco dual-point distributor for the small block is equipped with a mechanical tachometer drive — which usually indicates that the distributor was originally designed for use with the Corvette engine. Points must be replaced with heavy-duty ones to allow high RPM operation as the stock points "sign-off" at about 6,000 RPM. This unit has a fixed point plate, hence only mechanical (centrifugal) advance. No vacuum advance can be fitted to this distributor, so consider it useful for racing only. Vacuum advance is a necessary requirement for the street machine.

If you want an all-Delco capacitive-discharge ignition system, buy P/N 1115015 with matching coil 1115248 at $115 and $12, respectively. These components have been offered since 1967 as parts of a mag-pulse-triggered C-D system on high-performance Oldsmobiles.

A point-type distributor can be converted to the breakerless triggering system by buying two parts: 1960779 and 1964272 — the rotating pole piece and the stationary pole piece with magnetic-pickup assembly. A distributor converted thusly will operate with the magnetic-pulse-triggered amplifier included in the kit mentioned in the previous paragraph.

A word of warning should be tacked onto any enthusiasm you might have about the magnetic-pulse-triggered-transistor ignition. When it works it works; and when it doesn't work, it doesn't work. In other words there is no gradual tapering off in efficiency. Efficiency is either close to 100 percent or dead zero. This is good and this is bad. First, the good news. When the unit is working, it is one less item to tune, to tinker with and to get out of adjustment through wear. In other words, you have eliminated a problem—until it quits. Now the bad news. Because the distributor cannot be checked out on a regular distributor machine you could find yourself in a severe bind in East Hogwash, Illinois.

Obviously, there is a trade-off here between the transistor unit and the conventional point distributor in terms of price and serviceability. Read on before making your choice.

Chevrolet also makes a contact-triggered transistor ignition system which works with the usual point-equipped distributor. This "amplifier" unit is 1115006 which lists at $68, as opposed to the $91 retail price for the magnetic-impulse-triggered amplifier. As already mentioned, neither of these is a capacitive-discharge unit.

A point-type distributor with tach drive and vacuum-advance is P/N 1111496. Another point-type distributor which is often used has dual points and a solidly mounted point plate— hence no vacuum advance. It is P/N 1110985. Or, you can add dual points to any of the Chevy V-8 distributors by installing dual-point plate 1953752.

HOW TO IMPROVE STOCK IGNITION

A few of the stock Chevy ignition-system parts are nearly always exchanged for other stock or "high-performance" parts by owners who are literally "taken in" by ads for super spark plugs, extra-special spark-plug wires, deluxe condensers, long-life points, and high-voltage coils. Save your money! If the distributor is not worn out, there is little that you can do to make the ignition system work better. Even the resistive-type cables and wide-space late-model "smog-type" rotor and cap won't cost you any horsepower if they are in good condition. The only reason to change them is if they are old and worn out. The stock coil works fine for high-performance. If yours has quit, try a Delco 1115207 coil, but don't expect any added HP. You can buy higher voltage coils from specialty ignition manufacturers, but good parts are usually cheaper at the Chevy store. If your stock one makes sparks, save your money for parts that you really need.

Chevrolet spark plug and coil cables are the "TVR" resistive noise-suppressor kind which reduce radio interference. Cut one apart and you will find that there is no wire inside of the insulation—just a piece of graphited string. You must be careful when installing and removing this type of wire because any sharp bend or

yank will break the connector inside of the insulation. You won't be able to tell that this has happened unless you use an ohmmeter to measure the total resistance of the wire. As a good practice, you should replace the plug wires every two years or so—and more often in smog-ridden areas because smog really wrecks insulation.

With coil, plugs and wiring under control, the only other area of concern in the ignition system is the distributor. There is more hokus pocus and more misinformation about modifying this one component than any other part of the engine. A stock distributor will feed an engine up to 5500 RPM before exhibiting point bounce. That's an average figure— so you'll know what to expect from the stock unit. Delco's heavy-duty point set (D112PHD) will go more than 8000 RPM without bouncing. The new Chevy coils make the long saturation characteristics of dual points unnecessary. Heavy-duty points, such as those made by some manufacturers, allow very-high-RPM operation without point-caused problems. However, the extremely stiff springs used in these units promote rapid wear of the point rubbing block. Thus, the point setting and timing must be checked regularly or your performance will "go away" as the points close and the timing retards.

Greatly increased advance in the lower-RPM range can usually be used in cars which will be primarily engaged in acceleration contests (drags). This is because the engine passes through the low RPM range very quickly, or is seldom operated there at all. Also, long-overlap cams pump part of the fuel charge back into the manifolds at low speeds, even at full throttle, reducing charge density and allowing more advance to be used. Thus, mechanical advance-curve changes can provide startling full-throttle-acceleration improvement. A total centrifugal advance of 26 crankshaft degrees should be "all in" by 3000 RPM or even sooner for best performance. There are two basic curves for this engine that work. One is designed for street use; the other for racing. No stock-type distributor comes stock with the correct curve for either street performance or the race track, so you'll have to head for a distributor machine no matter which distributor you start with. To get the distributor to advance quicker, lighter springs can be installed. Inexpensive kits supplied by several manufacturers can be used to make this an easy task. However, to be sure that the distributor is not altered to provide more than the 12° to 13° distributor advance (24° to 26° crankshaft) which the unit had originally, check the distributor on an ignition machine—or use your timing light on your degreed harmonic balancer to check that the recommended maximum total 38 to 42° BTDC advance is not exceeded with the suggested 14° BTDC static setting. If it is, you'll have to reduce the amount of advance in the distributor or use a less advanced static setting. The vacuum line to the distributor should be blocked off when making such checks.

The same modified curves can be applied to magnetic-pulse-type distributors because the centrifugal-advance mechanisms are the same for both point and mag-pulse types.

The full-race curve should just begin at 500 RPM (distributor); it should be smooth and gentle up to 1500 RPM with a consistent 10° advance showing in the distributor (20 crankshaft degrees). The curve should end at 1500 RPM (distributor). Add another 18° static advance (crankshaft) into the system for a total of 38° (on some engines this can be advanced to 40°). With this curve there may be a

These two parts can be used to convert any Chevy distributor into a mag-pulse triggered type, provided that the correct amplifier is also added into the system. Text explains possible combinations.

Single-point distributor with rotor removed to expose centrifugal-advance weights and springs. Increasing RPM causes weights to overcome spring tension, moving outward to advance cam and thereby advancing timing.

This could be the ultimate ignition for the little Chevy, but it is only offered for the 1971-72 Pontiac 455 CID 4-bbl. engine. It has no points or condenser and requires only one wire to connect to the ignition, plus the usual eight to the plugs. The coil is built in. We're betting that it will adapt to the small block with a minimum amount of trouble.

tendency for the engine to "run on" after turning off the ignition because of high cylinder-head temperatures. This, and hard starting because of static advance setting, are two of the reasons the curve is not recommended for street use. Point dwell should be 30°.

The street curve runs the same 38° total advance with 20° initial lead at the crank. This must not vary to about 600 RPM (distributor) at which point it should kick up fast to full advance of 9° (distributor) by 1,500 RPM (distributor). It is essential that the distributor return to the initial setting at idle or it will be almost impossible to get a stable idle and the engine will tend to die. This is one of the problems of using very weak springs which cause the advance curve to start kicking in close to the idle speed. Use the heavy-duty points and 30° dwell setting.

Remember that neither of these curves "creates" more horsepower or torque when the engine is smoking the tires through the quarter of a mile. The curves do increase the power at the bottom end of the RPM scale. Both curves described here are effective when used with any cam which is streetable.

Distributor Installation

Take the distributor out of the engine to work on it, period. Don't try to install special weights and springs or new points without getting that rascal out in the open where you can check it thoroughly for end play, shaft wear, smooth operation—and for actual advance characteristics by putting the distributor onto a distributor machine. For some reason, pulling a distributor just doesn't seem to be important to some mechanics or enthusiasts. Various reasons are given, including, "It takes too long," "It's not hard to work on it in the car," or, "I don't have a distributor machine." The real reason could be a fear of not being able to reinstall the distributor correctly. This is no big deal and no really special knowledge is required. Anyone can do it, including you.

While it can take a little coaxing to get the distributor gear and oil-pump drive tang to mesh sometimes . . . and it is possible to get the gear off by one tooth so that the rotor is "out of register," these little obstacles do not offset the advantages of having the distri-

butor out of the car where you can get a good look at it without straining your eyes and your back.

Always aim the rotor in the same direction before pulling the distributor out of the engine. Either aim it at No. 1 cable in the cap, straight back or straight forward, but always do it the same and you won't have to remember what was happening. Before you do anything else, make a drawing of the distributor showing the rotor position that you selected.

The absolute easiest and surest method is to always aim the rotor at No. 1 and make sure that the timing mark on the harmonic balancer is correctly aligned for the specification static advance. With a clutch-equipped car you can push the car in high gear until you have achieved the correct conditions. It is somewhat more difficult—but not impossible— with an auto-trans-equipped car. In this instance, you can "bump" the starter to get close to the correct conditions, then use a wrench to turn the crank with the harmonic balancer attachment screw. When you have done this, reinstallation of the distributor becomes dirt-simple.

Before you take the clamp loose, scribe a line on the distributor housing and onto the block. Take the clamp off, then carefully pull the distributor out of the block, noting that the rotor turns counter-clockwise (backward) as you lift the distributor out. Note or mark the distributor edge so that you will know where the rotor turned to as the distributor finally came loose from the cam gear.

If you point the rotor in this direction and watch that scribe mark which you made, you can literally drop the distributor back into the engine—assuming that you took the car out of gear and that no one bumped the starter for you while you had the distributor out. If the distributor does not drop into place, check that the oil pump slot has not moved. A slight movement of this slot may be required so that the driving pin on the underside of the distributor gear will slip in o.k.

VACUUM ADVANCE

Don't rush to disconnect the vacuum advance which the factory included on your stock distributor. And, don't think that you should buy a replacement distributor without a vacuum advance because "real racers" use centrifugal-advance-only distributors. They don't drive their cars on the street, so the equipment which they use is not the hot tip for your street-driven car. Vacuum-advance mechanisms provide advance in relation to load and should really be called *load-compensation advance*.

Over-simplified explanations merely state that burning the fuel charge takes a certain amount of time and that burning time remains much the same regardless of RPM. Because the compression stroke requires less time as RPM increases, ignition must start earlier to allow burning to be completed at an ideal time in the stroke. T'aint *necessarily* so! Such simple explanations completely ignore combustion-chamber turbulence which hastens burning. Turbulence moves unburned mixture into the area where ignition is occurring—instead of relying on slow travel of the combustion flame front. Moving the unburned mixture into the combustion area speeds up burning so that there's usually no necessity for the advance mechanism to continue operating beyond 3000 RPM or so.

Charge density further complicates the picture. A light charge—as created by part-throttle operation—is a "slow" burner . . . needing earlier ignition. Up to 20° additional advance can be tolerated by the engine under certain part-throttle conditions. And, we may see this amount increase still further as the emission-reducing trend away from "quench-type" combustion chambers continues. However, the hotter versions are usually restricted to about 12° (crankshaft) vacuum advance to avoid the rattle which would occur when the throttle is opened quickly.

A normal appendage on most small block Chevy distributors is a vacuum-operated diaphragm. At light throttle, high manifold vacuum advances the spark a considerable amount. As the throttle is opened further for acceleration or to climb a hill, etc., the manifold vacuum drops off and the vacuum-advance diaphragm relaxes so that the distributor assumes a more-retarded position. The vacuum diaphragm

Solid or stranded metal wire is often touted as the only way to get full power to the spark plugs. However, such wire radiates energy in the radio/TV frequency spectrum, causing unwanted and illegal interference. Magnetic-suppression spark-plug wire meets FCC requirements for high-frequency suppression without causing any loss in engine performance. Monel metal wire wound around a magnetic core stops unwanted radiation; gives negligible DC resistance. This is the only type of interference-suppression wire which can be used with capacitive-discharge ignition systems. Enlarged view illustrates MSW construction.

mechanism supplements the centrifugal-advance mechanism—which provides RPM-compensated spark advance.

Take off the vacuum advance—or disable it by disconnecting the hose—and you can expect awful gas mileage and spark-plug fouling because the engine is forced to operate with the spark retarded under cruising conditions. This reduces thermal efficiency of the engine. The spark plugs foul because they cool off, allowing soot to form on the porcelains and misfiring immediately follows because the spark travels along the soot to ground ineffectively—instead of jumping the electrodes to fire the mixture.

If you have installed a long-duration cam which reduces the manifold vacuum at low speeds—or installed a larger carburetor which drops the manifold vacuum more quickly on quick throttle opening—you may want to alter the vacuum advance mechanism. According to Jere Stahl, the spring tension against which the vacuum must work to advance the spark—and the amount of vacuum-caused advance—can both be reduced to make the car more drivable for street use. He suggests limiting diaphragm travel to $8\text{-}10^\circ$ (crank) and changing the spring tension so that the diaphragm will back off more quickly. He claims that this greatly aids economy on hotrodded engines which are driven on the street. Using such "tricks" reduces the rattle or hard pinging that is such a familiar sound when the throttles of a high-performance engine are suddenly opened during street driving.

Magnetic Suppression Wire

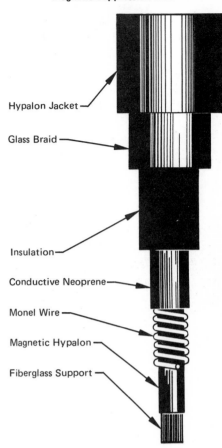

Hypalon Jacket

Glass Braid

Insulation

Conductive Neoprene

Monel Wire

Magnetic Hypalon

Fiberglass Support

SPECIAL IGNITIONS

Glamorous transistor or capacitive-discharge ignition systems are interesting technical achievements, *but they are expensive.* Their real advantages include long point life, easier starting in cold or damp weather and increased spark-plug life. This latter feature is the real "plus" of the capacitive-discharge systems because these will fire plugs which are too worn out for peak performance with a stock ignition system. But, special ignition systems do not increase acceleration or top speed and they do not give more gasoline mileage than the stock ignition system *in good condition.* Peak ignition requirements, according to Champion engineers, are for maximum voltage at the plugs when the engine is being accelerated at low speeds under full throttle. Transistor and capacitive-discharge systems are equal to—but not better than—stock systems under these conditions. Buy a capacitive-discharge unit if you are choosing between these two types.

And, if you can afford it, buy the magnetic-pulse-triggered type distributor with matching amplifier or converter. With a magnetically triggered system, there are no points and no dwell settings. This eliminates all future worries about points wearing out the rubbing block so that dwell, coil-saturation time and advance are reduced. These systems also eliminate the need for frequent inspection of points so that this time can be devoted to other maintenance. Actually, this is the most trouble-free type ignition system that you can install on your engine. That's why many racers figure that the advantages are worth the price. We'll probably see more and more stock cars equipped with these systems as the costs for automotive electronics continue to be reduced . . . and as the already-too-high costs for automotive maintenance continue to soar.

A magneto ignition system is the perfect answer for super lightweight dragsters or circle-track racers which will be push started and therefore do not need a battery. If you can really use a magneto to good advantage, then we'd recommend a Joe Hunt-adapted Scintilla Vertex magneto. But, if a battery must be carried to operate the starter—stick with the stock ignition and use the money you save to buy some helpful item of equipment which will add performance. The only time that a special ignition will produce more horsepower than the stock coil and distributor is when the plugs are worn out or there is some other problem with the stock system.

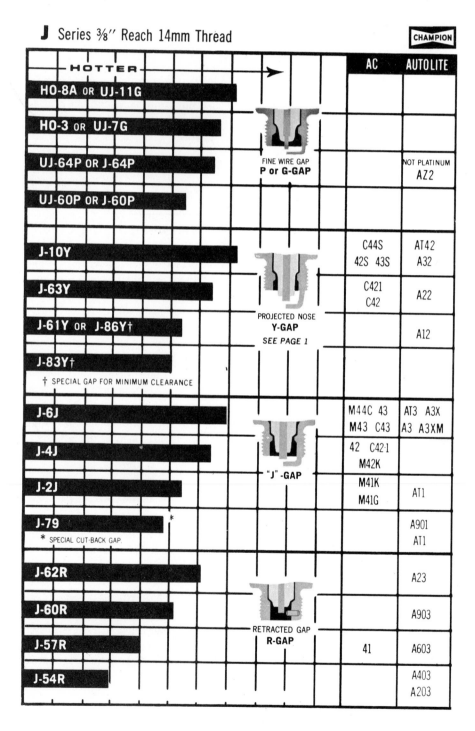

J Series ⅜" Reach 14mm Thread — CHAMPION

←HOTTER→		AC	AUTOLITE
HO-8A OR UJ-11G			
HO-3 OR UJ-7G			
UJ-64P OR J-64P	FINE WIRE GAP — P or G-GAP		NOT PLATINUM AZ2
UJ-60P OR J-60P			
J-10Y		C44S 42S 43S	AT42 A32
J-63Y	PROJECTED NOSE — Y-GAP — SEE PAGE 1	C421 C42	A22
J-61Y OR J-86Y†			A12
J-83Y†			
† SPECIAL GAP FOR MINIMUM CLEARANCE			
J-6J		M44C 43 M43 C43	AT3 A3X A3 A3XM
J-4J	"J"-GAP	42 C42-1 M42K	
J-2J		M41K M41G	AT1
J-79			A901 AT1
* SPECIAL CUT-BACK GAP.			
J-62R			A23
J-60R	RETRACTED GAP — R-GAP		A903
J-57R		41	A603
J-54R			A403 A203

SPARK PLUGS

Don't be surprised if the spark plugs "go away" in a hurry. The Chevy is noted for "eating" plugs. This is another way of saying that plug life in this engine is short!

Spark-plug life is a real problem in hotrodded engines. Even stockers can seldom get 10,000-mile plug life, even with a cleaning at 5,000 miles. The problem is complicated when you modify the engine for more horsepower and use the engine in varying ways—such as freeway driving, occasional drag races and the usual trips to work and the grocery store.

The reason for this is that combustion-chamber temperatures are considerably higher than those of many other engines. Any plugs used in the small Chevy usually fall off sharply in efficiency after only two or three thousand miles—or after 10 to 20 hard acceleration runs—especially if the stock too-lean-for-performance jetting is used in the carburetor. Some enthusiasts attempt to "cure" the problem by installing a much colder range plug for street application. This leads to premature loading up of the plugs—and thus still shorter plug life. In desperation, others have installed "guaranteed, life time, more horsepower, mileage and engine life" trick plugs. Don't bother. No one winning any races uses them—so why should you? Most of these plugs, easily identified by the full pages used to advertise them, appeal to the "something-for-nothing" owner who thinks that screwing in new plugs will give instant and enormous improvements in HP and mileage. We know that this is impossible and so do you. But, Barnum was right, there *is* a sucker born every minute.

The words "hot" or "cold," used in reference to spark plugs, often cause confusion because a "hot" plug is normally used in a "cold" low-horsepower engine and a "cold" plug in a "hot" high-performance engine. The terms refer to the heat rating or thermal characteristics of the plug— more specifically—the plug's ability to transfer heat from the firing end into the engine cylinder head and thence into the coolant.

Bartz-built Formula A small-block Chevy uses Joe Hunt Vertex magneto for positive ignition at high RPM. Magneto is set up to drive Lucas fuel-injection pump. One of the large braided-steel-covered lines is incoming fuel, the other is a bypass and the eight small lines feed the intake ports.

By definition, a cold-running plug transfers heat rapidly from the firing end. It is used to avoid overheating where combustion-chamber or cylinder-head temperatures are relatively high. A hot-running plug has a slower rate of heat transfer and is used to avoid fouling where combustion chamber temperature is relatively low.

The length of the core nose and electrode alloy material are the primary factors in establishing the heat range of a particular spark plug design. Hot plugs have relatively long insulator noses with long heat-transfer paths. Cold plugs have much shorter insulator-nose lengths and thus transfer heat more rapidly.

If the engine ignition timing, camshaft, compression ratio or carburetion is changed, heat-range substitution may be necessary. Stock-heat-range plugs recommended in the service manual may be replaced with *slightly colder* ones when you modify the engine. But cold plugs required for best all-out racing performance will not work for normal street/highway driving. They will make the engine spit back excessively, make gasoline mileage terrible, and the plugs will wear out or load up in a hurry, requiring frequent cleaning and/or replacement. On the other hand, a too-hot plug will last only a few miles and can cause destructive preignition. Extremely cold racing plugs do give better preignition protection *when fired by capacitor-discharge systems.* Keep in mind, though, that plugs thermally matched to combustion-chamber temperature are superior to too-cold plugs, regardless of the type of ignition system you are using.

"Hot" coils, special magnetos and transistorized or capacitor-discharge ignition systems do not require changes in spark-plug heat range. As previously mentioned, combustion-chamber temperature, not spark temperature, influences heat range. Spark erosion of the plug electrodes cannot be materially reduced by colder heat-range substitution, but erosion can be reduced with a C-D system.

A near-perfect plug is the projected core-nose which acts as a "warm" plug at low speeds and cools off to act as a "cold" plug as RPM's are increased. Some of these also have an auxiliary gap which increases plug life between replacement or regapping because it changes the spark-voltage characteristic. When the spark has jumped the auxiliary gap it has sufficient voltage so that the electrode path will be used, instead of leaking away ineffectually across fouling deposits which may have built up on the porcelain and shell.

Serious enthusiasts always run projected core-nose plugs around town and switch to colder plugs for dragging. There's just too wide a heat-range requirement for any one plug to do the entire job in a hotrodded engine, although the projected core-nose ones come close.

R. J. Gail, Champion Spark Plug's Racing Coordinator says, "The projected core-nose plug benefits from the cooling effect of the incoming charge at high engine speeds. This 'charge cooling' on the

projected firing end provides greater pre-ignition protection at high speed and makes it possible to increase the insulator length on a given design, thereby improving the spark-plug-temperature characteristics. In many racing applications, with critical spark-advance settings, the possibility of core-nose fracture from detonation would be more likely with projected core-nose plugs than with regular types."

The stock plug gap of 0.035-inch is fine for a modified engine. Setting extra-wide plug gaps because of exotic ignition systems presents risks. If ignition becomes marginal in a race, a closer gap might prevent the breakdown.

Plug life and consequently, replacement expense, can be enough of a problem to make buying a capacitive-discharge ignition system very worthwhile. Some Porsche 911's, for instance, are factory-equipped with capacitive-discharge ignition systems to overcome their short plug life.

According to an article in CAR LIFE Magazine, July 1968, a capacitive-discharge system increases usable spark plug life two to five times. Such systems greatly reduce the ills which may result from inadequate ignition when the conventional system nears tuneup time.

Capacitive-discharge ignition systems have the ability to fire fouled plugs and even worn-out plugs . . . as if they were new ones. Engines with C-D ignition systems can perform o.k. with plugs which are one to two heat ranges colder than stock, providing performance similar to that which you'd get with new projected core-nose plugs. If you are running a rev limiter with a C-D ignition, colder plugs are necessary to keep "glo-plugging" from cancelling out the speed-limiting effects.

Plug-seat type and thread length must be correct for the head type used. Small blocks prior to '69 used 3/8-inch-reach plugs with washers and a 13/16-inch hex. A taper-seat plug with 5/8-inch hex is used in 1969 and later slant-plug heads, in some 1970 heads and in all 1971-72 heads. It is important to check whether there are any exposed plug or head threads in the combustion chamber when you have the heads off. Exposed threads get red hot and can cause destructive detonation, plus bother-

some after-run when the engine is turned off. With tapered-seat plugs, any exposed threads must be ground off of the plugs themselves or out of the heads.

If you have to use a washer-seal plug with too long a reach — as might be necessary if plugs of the required heat range were not available in the correct thread length — a thicker washer can be used so that no threads will be exposed in the chamber. *Do not use multiple washers of the crimped-copper or crimped-aluminum type* because they will not conduct heat out of the plug. Champion has standard, 0.060, 0.080 and 0.100-inch-thick washers as stock items. Plugs with a shorter reach must never be used under any circumstances because these would leave sharp threads in the head exposed to the combustion process. Washer-seal and taper-seat plugs cannot be interchanged, ever.

Do not be quick to condemn a spark plug if it does not spark in a plug tester at an air pressure equal to or greater than the engine cranking pressure. This idea is entirely wrong because air pressure as read on a plug tester has no direct relationship to engine-cranking pressure for several reasons. In a plug tester, the plug stays cold. In the engine, the electrodes operate at high temperature and require less voltage to fire than when cold. Keep in mind that spark plugs normally do not fire at the point of maximum cylinder pressure, but well ahead of top dead center. For these and a number of other reasons, the efficiency of a spark plug

One of the small items which make life a little easier around the performance enthusiast's garage is a plug board. A two-foot length of 2" x 6" holds a lot of spark plugs—electrodes up for easy reading.

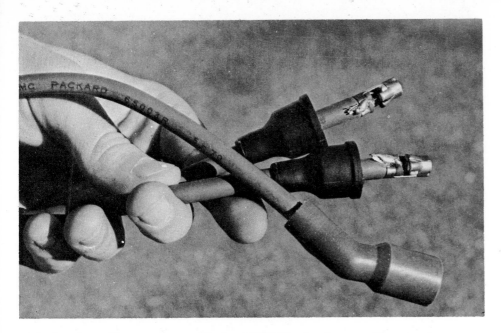

Chevy has these silicone-compound Packard 65003R wires for you. The complete soldered-terminal, steel-core set is listed in the HD Parts List. The insulation is heat resistant so that the cables will not be destroyed if you happen to lay one against a hot header someday while you are changing plugs.

cannot be measured in terms of "pounds per square inch"—which is what the plug tester attempts to establish.

Spark Plug Cables

Cross-firing or induction leakage between cables will occur when ignition cables are grouped closely together and run in parallel for some distance. This causes engine roughness and can result in damaging preignition and detonation.

Cross-fire is not caused by defective cable alone. It is traceable to the magnetic field which surrounds any high-tension conductor. Thus the lead which is carrying high voltage at any given instant tends to induce voltage into an adjacent lead. Troublesome cross fire is most likely to occur between consecutive firing cylinders when these cylinders are located closely together in the engine block. Never tape spark plug cables together and don't run spark plug wires through metal looms—no matter how neat they look!

Use the stock wire separators. Keep the cables in the correct slots and route the wires per factory recommendations so that cross firing cannot occur.

For racing, where plugs are often inspected and/or changed, install the silicone rubber-insula-

ted wire with stranded-steel wires soldered to connectors at each end. This set is in the HD parts list. Your dealer can get it to you for around $20. Holley, Auto Lite, Accel, Segal, Mr. Gasket—and a raft of others offer these wire sets. Silicone insulation is especially good where plug wires must be routed near exhaust headers . . . or where the wires might be laid against the exhaust headers as you change plugs.

Stock TVR cables do not work well with capacitive-discharge ignition systems. In fact, they can be expected to fail completely. Ted Trevor of Crown Manufacturing suggests using "MSW" (Magnetic-Suppression Wire) which is a coiled steel wire in spark-plug cable insulation. This type of wire will not fail when used with C-D systems and it suppresses ignition noise radiation so that you can listen to the radio. The use of the stranded-steel ignition cables typically used for high performance will destroy radio listenability for you and anyone who happens to be driving near you.

How to "read" plugs

Selection of the correct carburetor or injector jets can be aided by "reading" the appearance of the plug electrodes and porcelain insula-

tor shell. The accompanying plug color chart explains what to look for. Because the part of most interest is the base of the porcelain—which is "buried" in the plug shell, a magnifier-type illuminated viewer as made by AC or Champion should be an early purchase for your racing tool box.

Remember that new plugs will take time to "color." As many as three to four dragstrip runs may be required to "color" new plugs. If you are drag racing with plugs that have been run on the street—and we can't imagine why you'd want to—then keep in mind the fact that the plugs *may* clean out after several hard runs down the strip, but they will probably speckle the porcelain in the process.

Plug color is only meaningful when the engine is declutched and the engine "cut" clean at the end of a high-speed full-throttle, high-gear run. If you allow the car to slow with the engine still running, plug appearance will be meaningless. Plug readings can be made after full-throttle runs on a chassis dyno with the transmission in an intermediate gear so that the dyno is not overspeeded—but road tests require the use of high gear to load the engine correctly. Similarly, plug checks can be made where the engine has been running at full throttle against full load as applied by an engine dyno. It is easier to get good plug readings on the dyno because full power can be applied and the engine cut clean. Plugs can be read very quickly because you can get to them easier—as opposed to the usual car or boat installation. However, don't think that plug heat range and carburetion jetting established on an engine dyno will be absolutely right for the same engine installed in your racing chassis or boat. Conditions of air flow past the carburetor or injectors can easily change the requirements —and perhaps unevenly so that different cylinders need different changes.

It would be nice if every plug removed from a racing engine should look like the others from the same engine—in color and condition—but this is not easily achieved. Differences in color or condition indicate that combustion-chamber temperatures or fuel/air ratios are not the same in every cylinder, or that related engine components need attention.

If differences exist in the condition of the firing end of the plugs, the cause may be found in one or a combination of factors: unequal valve timing, weak compression, poor oil control (rings), weak ignition system, unequal cooling around the plugs or unequal distribution of the fuel/air mixture.

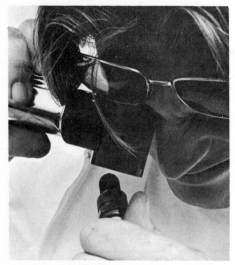

Color and appearance of plug porcelain can be checked with a Champion Sparkplug Viewer, No. CT 456. One of these should be in every tuner's tool kit.

If you correctly followed the procedures for blueprinting the engine then you should obtain equal cylinder pressure *at cranking speeds.* However, unequal cylinder pressures can lead to one or more plugs running "off." Check for incorrect valve lash, defective or unseated rings, a blown head gasket or severe differences in clearance on the cylinder walls. Problems within the ignition system which might lead to plugs not reading the same or misfiring include: a loose point plate, arcing within the distributor cap, a defective rotor or cap, cross-fire along with primary wiring, or a resistor which is opening intermittently. Pay special attention to cleanliness of the ignition system, including the inside and outside of the distributor cap and the outside of the coil "tower." Also clean the inside of the cable receptacles on the coil and in the cap. Any dirt or grease here can allow some or all of the spark energy to leak away.

You'll need two sets

Best performance in "strictly stock" drag racing or high-speed road work is not usually obtained by using the same plugs for street and race driving. Street plugs pick up deposits during low-speed running . . . deposits which tend to bleed away voltage (lessening the spark intensity) under high crankshaft speeds and heavy loadings. These deposits do not fluff off the plugs, but melt to form a conductive coating which causes misfiring. Thus, for a double-duty engine *at least* two sets of plugs are required: one set with heat range ideal for the street and another with the heat range required for the strip. Race plugs should be gapped closer—depending on the amount of compression and grade of fuel. Although a closer gap makes for an erratic idle, who worries about that when it's time to go racing?

A capacitive-discharge system creates a very "fat" spark which allows using plug gaps 0.002" to 0.005" wider than with the stock system.

BL Series .460" Taper Seat ⅝" hex — CHAMPION

HOTTER →		AC	AUTOLITE
BL-3	REGULAR GAP		AF901
BL-60			AF701
BL-57			AF501
BL-13Y or UBL-13Y		46T / 46TS	AF42
BL-11Y		43T / 43TS	AF32
BL-9Y	PROJECTED NOSE	42T / 42TS	AF22
BL-7Y		41T / 41TS	AF12
BL-54R	RETRACTED GAP		AF303

CAUTION! DO NOT EXCEED 12 FT/LBS TORQUE

If you are running a late engine (most 1970 and later) or slant-plug heads, the taper-seat plug is what you are using. If you have to borrow plugs at the strip, remember that Ford uses these plugs in Boss 302's, Cleveland 351 and the Cobra Jet 429 CID engines.

DETONATION AND PRE-IGNITION

Detonation or "ping" is a sharp knock which makes your engine ring or sing as if someone had hit it with a hammer. Skip Mason of Champion Plugs says, "It is like hitting the pistons, valves, spark plugs and other engine parts with a hammer." There is usually no problem in identifying detonation because you can hear it—unless you are running the engine with open exhaust. *Detonation is spontaneous combustion of fuel in the chamber instead of the desired controlled "slow" and even burning.* Perhaps the most common cause of detonation is over-advanced ignition timing, but there are other causes which should not be overlooked. It can also be caused by full-throttle acceleration with too-high a compression ratio; high operating temperatures, too-hot spark plugs, and lean mixtures can all be contributing factors to cause destructive detonation. Detonation results include hammered-out bearings, broken rods and crankshafts, sharp-edged holes in piston crowns, and broken ground electrodes on spark plugs. It also breaks ring lands and cracks piston skirts.

Pre-ignition is ignition of the fuel while the compression stroke is occurring, but much earlier than intended. It can be caused by glowing plug, sharp valve edges, overhanging gaskets. Pre-ignition can be temporarily reduced by retarding the spark, but this creates excessive heat and detonation sets in due to this heat —as a result the fuel fires as it enters the chamber. Complete chaos and a destroyed engine inevitably result from pre-ignition.

DO NOT DYNO-SET IGNITION TIMING

Dyno-set ignition timing will always be too far advanced unless the engine temperature has been allowed to stabilize at each timing setting. Spark plug temperature is greatly increased when the spark setting is advanced too far. Detonation and pre-ignition result in the worst cases. This all happens because the chassis-dyno operator sets the distributor for the best *flash* reading, and you drive off the rollers with the engine detonating merrily. Worse yet, you may not drive the car after setting the timing on the dyno. If you enter the car in competition the chances are very good that you will not hear the engine detonating because exhaust noise will mask the detonation. The dyno operator is not likely to pay you for a blown-up engine. It is essential that you understand what can happen to your engine.

While it is possible to cheat a little on the factory settings by advancing a few more degrees beyond the shop-manual recommendations, detonation must be listened for and the spark retarded if it occurs. If you hear detonation and the engine is not being run with close to 38° total advance (crankshaft degrees), try increasing the size of the main jet. Or, look for exposed plug threads or a sharp edge on a valve or somewhere else in the combustion chamber. Excessive carbon build-up can also be the culprit.

Barney Navarro, in a 1963 POPULAR HOTRODDING article, made the following observations. "Among the many things that affect the spark-advance requirements of an engine, we find engine temperature and air temperature. The hotter the fuel charge before ignition, the faster it burns, therefore requiring less spark advance. The speed of any chemical reaction is doubled by a temperature increase of 18° Fahrenheit, so it is easy to see that distributors should be fitted with temperature-compensating devices, especially those of air-cooled engines. The average modern overhead-valve engine can utilize from 5 to 8 degrees more advance when it is cold than when it reaches operating temperature."

Navarro's comments tell us why we can get away with cranking up the advance for quick blasts on the dyno or a fast trip down the quarter mile—but destroy the engine by trying to use the over-advanced distributor setting for everyday driving.

ARE's dwell-stretcher/RPM limiter allows presetting the desired engine-speed limit. When that speed is reached, the engine is automatically "held" at that limit. The dwell-stretch feature gives the equivalent of 45° dwell so that the stock coil can deliver 85% of its low-RPM voltage at small-block rev limits.

PLUG COLOR CHART

Rich - Sooty or wet plug bases, dark exhaust valves.

Correct - Light-brown color on porcelains, exhaust valves red-brown clay color. Plug base slightly sooty (leaves slight soot mark on hand when plug base turned against palm). New plugs start to color at the base of the porcelain and this is only visible with an illuminated plug magnifier.

Lean - Plug base ash grey. Glazed-brown appearance of porcelain may also indicate too-hot plugs. Exhaust valves whitish color.

NOTE: Piston top color, as observed with an inspection light, can be a quicker and sometimes more positive indicator of mixture than plug porcelain appearance. The careful tuner will look at all of the indicators to take advantage of every possible clue as to how the engine is working. Inspection lights are available from Charlie Hayes Racing Equipment and from Moon Equipment.

Falconer/Dunn Bosch timed fuel injection. Front cover encloses a gear drive which keeps pump in perfect time with the crank and cam. Nice, but expensive. Notice the Gilmer belts which drive the water pump and dry-sump apparatus.

Kinsler offers several fuel-injection systems for the small-block Chevy, including timed (shown here) and constant-flow. The constant flow units are more popular for drag applications due to the much lower cost. This Lucas-metered unit has the ignition and metering unit driven from a right-angle drive. Fuel control cam at the top of metering unit is linked to the throttles. A high-capacity fuel cooler is cast onto the backside of the runners to cool fuel returned to the supply tank via the bypass line.

Because the camshaft is seemingly easy to remove and reinstall in the Chevy, it is often one of the first items which the novice changes when chasing after additional power. But, it needs very careful installation to ensure that maximum benefit is obtained from its action and the knowledgeable tuner changes the cam only after he's "made" all the HP he could with the stock cam. And, then he may decide to use another stock Chevrolet cam.

The camshaft is only part of the valve train and the other items deserve equal attention if utmost performance is to be achieved. Lifters, pushrods, rocker arms, spring retainers, and valve springs interact in ways which are not completely understood by many mechanics. Installation techniques are also important because they affect camshaft life. The coverage devoted to these related parts and to careful installation will seem over-long to the casual reader, but the thoughtful engine builder will recognize that a short presentation does not give the complete picture.

Several camshafts have been offered in stock engines and each cam is well mated to its stock engine. Grinders of special cams can help with cams specifically designed to meet the requirements of non-stock applications. A detailed discussion of effective valve opening, as well as timing graphs relating stock cams to reground ones, will dispel some of the hocus-pocus surrounding the entire subject. Valve spring and retainer information is also included with specific directions for checking and changing camshaft timing at installation. Rocker-arm geometry and its effect on valve lift and guide wear is fully covered. The reader who follows all of this information with great care will discover that his engine has suddenly gained "free" horsepower—even with a stock cam—and that is the best kind!

HOW THE CAMSHAFT WORKS

It looks like a simple stick with bumps on it, but the cam is the major controlling element in determining your engine's ultimate behavior. The stock camshaft is carefully related to a

A dial indicator held by a magnetic base to a piece of angle iron can be very helpful when checking the valve train of a small-block Chevy—or any other engine. Valve lift and valve-stem height (part of getting rocker geometry correct) can be accurately checked. Needle-bearing rockers are strictly all-out-racer stuff—not for street machines under any circumstances! Adjustment of these rockers is quite touchy—move the feeler in from the side instead of straight into the roller.

fantastic number of factors, including carburetor area, compression, displacement, transmission and axle ratios, car weight, performance desires, driving habits of the buying public, and so on — ad infinitum. You cannot relate these factors to the same fine degree as the factory engineers with their experience and computers. We can consider what goes on during the intake and exhaust operations in a single cylinder.

Valve timing is related to degrees of crankshaft rotation, but avoid this oversimplification. Another relationship is more helpful in describing camshaft functioning. Where is the *piston,* in which direction is it going and what is its relationship to the valves — and in what direction are *they* going?

As high-school students

we were taught four-stroke internal-combustion-engine functioning in four unrelated 180-degree segments: Intake, Compression, Power, and Exhaust. If the valve mechanism could slam the valves open and shut precisely at the TDC (Top Dead Center) and BDC (Bottom Dead Center) points without delays, the engine would probably run — until some part broke! But, just as instantaneous valve action is impossible due to the severe forces such would impose on the valve mechanism, instantaneous movement of the intake and exhaust gases is impossible. So, the 180-degree-segmented description of valve opening versus crankshaft position does not work outside of the textbook covers. Now that another schoolboy belief has been destroyed, let's look at practical facts.

The intake valve is opened *before* TDC while the piston is still rising on the exhaust stroke. There is not much pressure left in the cylinder and the early opening is added to the textbook's 180°, even on "mild" engines. Valve acceleration rate can't exceed certain limits, so the cam designer may open the valve after the piston reaches its point of maximum velocity. By "lagging" the opening slightly, negative pressure in the cylinder helps to start *and sustain* cylinder filling until the intake valve closes. Opening the intake at almost TDC gives economy *and* low-speed torque beyond what you'd ordinarily get. Early opening is often touted as a cleaning device for pushing the exhaust out and helping to clean up the chamber of spent gases. According to Racer Brown, this may be true of a good hemispherical chamber with a tuned exhaust and intake system but it certainly does not apply to the small-block. Even at best, this so-called "scavenging action" is incomplete. Historically, there have been a great many more bad combustion-chamber designs, hemispherical or otherwise, than there have been good ones. Early opening should be approached with great care because the incoming gas has a decided tendency to do an "about-face escape act" through the convenient exhaust-valve opening. All you get for your efforts is increased fuel consumption, plus a few other disadvantages, and perhaps a bit of exhaust-valve cooling by the escaping fresh mixture.

Very early opening confuses the intake system at low speeds, causing the rough-idle trademark of a high-RPM engine. While early opening causes no particular problems at high speeds which provide an atmospheric-pressure operating condition, reduced speeds cause manifold vacuum to suck exhaust gases into the intake system. Results are diluted air/fuel mixtures, rough idling, spark-plug fouling in extreme cases, and fogging of the mixture out of the carburetor or injector throats. This dilution is one of the reasons why an accelerating racing engine tolerates full ignition advance at very low RPM.

There is good reason to leave the valve open *after* BDC to take advantage of the incoming-gas momentum. Although the piston starts its upward stroke after BDC, it is barely moving upward for quite a few degrees. The crank swings

through a considerable arc to swing the connecting rod big end sideways. The momentum of the inflowing gases gives additional filling during this period of piston "laziness." As piston-acceleration rate increases, the intake valve must be closed or severe reverse pumping and charge-density reduction will occur. It should be obvious that as engine RPM is increased, the closing point can be left until later than is desirable on an engine which has to produce good torque in the low and mid range. A tuned-intake system may increase charging-mixture momentum to improve cylinder filling in a limited RPM range. Reverse-pumping of the charge back into the manifold, as caused by late closing, is one factor allowing engines to be set up for drag-race competition with much higher compression than would ordinarily be possible with gasoline for fuel. The same cars would require lower compression if set up for continuous high-RPM operation, unless running at high altitude as at Bonneville.

If we consider four points only—intake opening and closing and exhaust opening and closing, *the one point that has the most dramatic effect on power output is the point at which the intake closes.* There is a fine balancing act going on here; trying to take advantage of the inertia of the air/fuel charge, plus any late arrivals in the form of positive sonic pulses and closing the intake valve *before* these forces are overcome by reverse-pumping action. This is particularly critical in a small-block Chevy with a short stroke and becomes even more critical as the connecting-rod center-to-center length is increased in relation to the crankshaft stroke.

Exhaust-valve operation can almost be deduced from what you have read about the intake, only in reverse. During the induction period, we do everything we can to fill a cylinder that is at or very near ambient atmospheric pressure. During the exhaust period, we try to unload the same cylinder of all gases, including residuals. The average pressure is six or more times that seen during the induction period. This is easier, therefore the exhaust opening and closing points are not so critical as those on the intake side. Because the exhaust valve needs its "head start" on the piston, part of the power stroke is "subtracted" by opening the

valve *before* BDC. This releases pressure from the cylinder so the piston works less to pump out the gases, and ensures that the valve is fully open by the time the piston is accelerating at its maximum upward rate. Pressure "blow-down" also starts the exhaust-gas flow out of the cylinder. Little power is lost by early exhaust-valve opening because the burning gases impart most of their available effort in the first 90° of the power stroke. Thus, some stock Chevy high-performance cams have dual patterns to give more exhaust than intake duration. When closing the exhaust valve *after* TDC—the intake action is overlapped—both valves are open at the same time. If this overlap is stretched too far, serious dilution occurs, especially past 70° overlap. When a tuned-exhaust system is used, late closing of the exhaust takes advantage of the momentum of the leaving gases to help discharge the cylinder. It is sometimes possible to reduce cylinder pressure on a momentary basis to below atmospheric (vacuum) so the incoming gases are started in by the draft of the exhaust gases, as well as by the increasing displacement afforded by the descending piston.

While the foregoing can be interesting in understanding the operation of your engine, it would not enable you to tell the cam grinder the precise number of degrees of overlap and duration which you would need for specific applications. Fortunately for most of us, the cam grinders use their superior knowledge of mechanical limitations and the physics of gas flow to protect us from ourselves. Cam patterns are available for every situation. You cannot go far wrong by relying on the recommendations of qualified cam grinders, especially if you are willing to follow through with careful installation procedures as will be described.

STOCK VALVE TRAIN

Chevy's valve train has been widely copied by the designers of other engines. A chain-driven camshaft of cast-iron alloy with 16 lobes has five bearing journals which operate in bearings pressed into the block. Lifters operate in holes bored in the block. Tubular-steel pushrods connect with stamped-steel rocker arms in the "tub"-shaped section atop each head. Each rocker arm pivots against a ball which locates the combination on a stud. A guide for each cylinder guides the pushrods close to their tops in Z-28 and LT-1 engines. Other small-block Chevys guide the pushrod with openings in the cylinder head. Camshaft motion is multiplied by 1.5 by the rocker arm which contacts the tip of an intake or an exhaust valve.

Valve stems are 11/32-inch diameter. Seating pressure for each valve is provided by one or more coil springs. Springs are retained by a stamped-steel retainer wedged to the valve stem by valve keys. Chevrolet's steel retainers are stout designs which are suitable for racing. They weigh slightly more than aluminum ones but their extra strength, fatigue resistance and low cost make these the parts to use in many applications. A stamped-steel cover or die-cast aluminum (Corvette, Z-28/LT-1) forms the outer half of the rocker-arm enclosure. Because these covers are always internally bathed in a thin film of oil, they can significantly aid in cooling the engine if you use non-chromed covers painted flat black.

STOCK CAMSHAFTS

The accompanying table indicates model, intake opening and closing, exhaust opening and closing, lift and duration for the stock small-block cams which were available as of 1972.

You will notice that these specifications do not agree with factory published specs. This is because factory cam-timing specs are "out to lunch." There's no way that you can make heads or tails out of them because each one must have been measured differently. Because there's no single standard, a user cannot actually compare camshafts to get a valid understanding of what's what. Perhaps this chart of stock timing and lift, plus the graph showing actual valve-lift patterns for stock small-block cams will help to sort out the hocus-pocus which surrounds the whole mysterious area of cam contours. Needless to say, the stock Chevrolet offerings can provide impressive performances when teamed correctly with carburetion, headers, compression, gear ratio, tires and clutch combinations that "get it all together."

STOCK CAMSHAFT COMPARISON

CAM & USE	TIMING[1] Intake/Exhaust	DURATION[1] Intake/Exhaust (Clearance)	LIFT Intake/Exhaust (Clearance)
3703906 3836862 1956-58 Hydraulic	23-88/58-37 14-55/49-4	291/275 249/233	0.334/0.334
3711355 3837137 1955-56 Corvette Mechanical	29-97/74-43 17-79/62-25	306/297 276/267	0.395/0.395
3732798 1958-66 Hydraulic	33-87/78-30 24-54/64-2	300/288 258/246	0.398/0.398
3736097 1957-64 Street Mechanical (Duntov)	50-87/78-30 38-69/66-12	317/288 287/258	0.382/0.386 (0.012/0.018)
3849346 1964-69 Street Mechanical	44-89/93-40 32-71/81-22	313/313 283/283	0.447/0.447 (0.030/0.030)
3863151 L-79 327 CID Hydraulic	40-86/88-38 31-73/79-25	306/306 284/284	0.447/0.447
3896929 1967-72 350-400 Hydraulic	38-92/88-52 29-59/79-19	310/320 268/278	0.390/0.410
3896962 L-46 350 CID Hydraulic	52-114/98-62 31-73/77-21	346/340 284/278	0.450/0.460
3927140 1969 Service Mechanical	40-82/90-46 28-65/78-28	302/316 273/286	0.463/0.482 (0.022/0.024) Open Exhaust
3965754 1971 Service Mechanical	49-96/96-55 40-72/91-31	325/331 292/302	0.495/0.512 (0.022/0.024) Open Exhaust
3972178 1970-71 Street Mechanical	42-94/112-54 25-75/95-33	317/346 280/308	0.438/0.455 (0.024/0.030)
6262944 1971-72 Calif. Hydraulic	44-96/88-60 14-50/58-14	320/328 244/252	0.400/0.410

NOTES:

1. Timing and degree indications are in crankshaft degrees. The upper set of figures for each camshaft is the factory specification. The lower set is the effective timing measured at the lifters. Hydraulic lifters at 0.008-inch lift; mechanical lifters at 0.015-inch lift. Cams above the line were estimated as to effective timing and duration. Cams below the line were actually measured.
2. Lifts are in inches.
3. The line drawn across the chart separates generally unavailable or outdated camshafts (above the line) from those which are current (below the line). You will be ahead in the horsepower game by installing one of the cams below the line.
4. Cams requiring open exhaust will not run well with mufflers. If open exhaust cannot be run, then install a cam with less timing. If you want less timing, but more lift, consider an aftermarket camshaft.
5. 3965754 requires springs with 130 lbs. seat pressure and 320 lbs. open pressure. Such springs were not available as Chevrolet parts when this book was printed. This cam and the 3927140 are not recommended for street use or with an automatic transmission.

As is the case with any production-made part, camshafts occasionally vary slightly due to the production tolerances which must be allowed to keep prices where ordinary folks like you and us'ns can afford to buy them. But you should become aware of the fact that automation has drastically improved production tolerances over the years so that factory parts are typically the most accurate that you can buy. You can disbelieve much of the scare propaganda passed out by hotrod parts makers who would have you believe that they are the original inventors of the wheel. The ones who scream loudest about quality hope that you will never measure one of their cams for timing or lift consistency or for consistency between the base circles.

Most magazine articles tell you to ashcan the stock camshaft: more baloney designed to please the cam grinders who spend big $$$ advertising their products. The writers of the articles have no choice. If they want to keep their jobs they have to push the products of the manufacturers who can afford to spend money for advertising. If stock cams are so bad, howcum so many million Chevy's manage to get their owners to where they are going every day? Chevy has a dozen stock cams and one of them may be just right if you select one that is correct for *your* application. And, the price is right!

When building up any modern high-performance engine it is difficult to avoid the temptation to "put a cam in it." In great part this is perhaps due to the penetration of advertising by those who sell camshafts for a living. Many cam grinders turn out excellent products — but they are for specific purposes. Despite advertising claims, the purpose is not usually street or highway driving. So, unless you are an old and experienced hand in the game of horsepower seeking, you would do well to consider the mechanical-lifter camshaft which was supplied as the street-mechanical cam for 1970-72, 3972178. It has 0.438-inch intake lift and 0.455-inch exhaust lift with about 274/282 degrees effective intake/exhaust duration. Or, you may want to consider keeping the hydraulic lifters in your engine to ensure quiet, troublefree valve-train operation. A high-lift, short duration hydraulic-lifter cam can often provide plenty of performance for the occasional stoplight Grand Prix or a trip to the drag strip on grudge night. Consider the L-46 cam, 3896962, or one of the aftermarket cams.

Although it is easy to buy a hotter cam from your dealer, the truth of the matter is that these cams do not work well if the engine has to exhaust through mufflers.

When you start cranking in extra duration, the engine begins to get "soggy bottom." You have to scream it up to get enough torque to move off the line or away from a stop sign—then the torque comes in "like gangbusters," usually when you don't really need or want it. That kind of engine behavior is strictly all wrong for the street, so think twice—maybe even three times—before stuffing a wild lumpstick into your go-to-work car or grocery-getter. Buy a decal instead. Decals are cheaper than cam kits anyway. If it makes you feel better, tell your friends about your "wild" camshaft and drive on by with your car in high gear and your engine going "pocketa-pocketa-pocketa." Happiness is often a stock cam.

If you are going racing or want exceptional performance for the street you may want to change the camshaft. But here again, don't be misled by the decals on your hero's car. Chances are that he's paid to run the decal, regardless of whose cam he selects. And, the decal is often changed at run-off time because *"money talks."*

Stock cams are priced *right*. The racer's "friendly price" for stock cams at most dealers will be about $25 for hydraulics, or for the street-mechanical. "Off-road" cams sell for about $40 net. Price alone could be a good reason to use the factory parts, but bear in mind that the street-mechanical cam is as far as you should go for a street-driven machine with mufflers. The off-road cams are for open exhausts and lots of RPM, so don't be confused. If you need more than the street-mechanical cam offers, consider one of the high-lift short-duration hydraulic camshafts that are available from some of the cam grinders.

NOTE: Although the camshaft is usually the last thing changed by a street rodder seeking after HP, this is fast changing with the advent of smog-type or emission-oriented cams. This is especially true for "base" or low-HP engines which have long timing but lazy action camshafts which kill the intake-manifold vacuum to about 10 to 13 inches Hg. If the stock engine refuses to idle at any vacuum higher than this, an amazing improvement in performance and mileage can be had by switching the cam for a pre-1970 stock camshaft, a high-lift high-performance hydraulic or a street-mechanical cam. Or, one of the aftermarket cams can be installed. Changing the cam to an earlier stock one will bring the vacuum back up — along with the mileage. Using one of the high-performance or aftermarket types may also help the mileage, although the manifold vacuum may be as low or lower than it was originally. Changing the camshaft in some of these emission-equipment-choked engines makes it feel as if there were two engines under the hood.

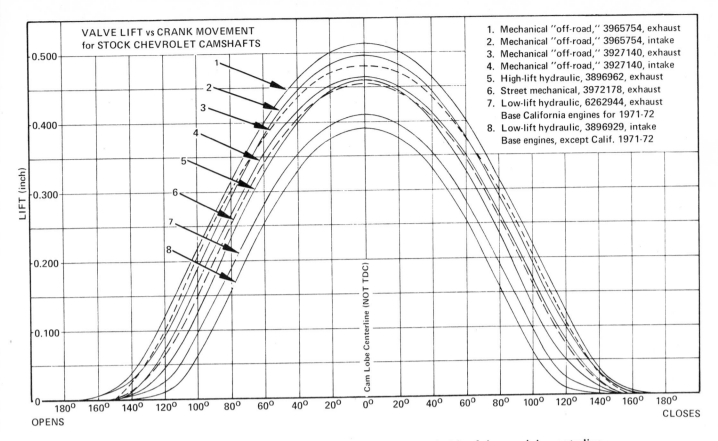

VALVE LIFT vs CRANK MOVEMENT
for STOCK CHEVROLET CAMSHAFTS

1. Mechanical "off-road," 3965754, exhaust
2. Mechanical "off-road," 3965754, intake
3. Mechanical "off-road," 3927140, exhaust
4. Mechanical "off-road," 3927140, intake
5. High-lift hydraulic, 3896962, exhaust
6. Street mechanical, 3972178, exhaust
7. Low-lift hydraulic, 6262944, exhaust
   Base California engines for 1971-72
8. Low-lift hydraulic, 3896929, intake
   Base engines, except Calif. 1971-72

These curves show actual intake-valve lift measured in crankshaft degrees on each side of the cam lobe centerline.

RACING CAMSHAFTS

Camshaft selection from amongst the thousands of "bump sticks" which are offered can be mind boggling — unless you know and understand what you are looking for. Although there are dozens — maybe even a hundred — cam manufacturers offering small-block cams, we called on W. G. "Racer" Brown to see what might be used to wake up the engine — beyond the factory's offerings.

In fact that's where we started our questioning, "If the factory offers a dozen cams ranging from streetable to wild — what more can cam makers offer to the small-block owner?" Racer rose to the bait like a hungry trout. "Factory offerings have to be more than somewhat reliable, so their designs have to incorporate a more decided degree of conservatism than those which we can make

and sell. Our dealers are not forced to service the entire automobile and hold still while a customer complains about a rough idle and so forth. Chevy cams are designed for either street use or far-out long-track competitive events such as Daytona for sports-car racing in Corvettes. As a result there's little middle ground. You can't put a road-race cam in a street machine and be happy and it won't work on a 1/4- or 1/2- mile track, either. So, that's where we come in — with duration, valve action and lift in enough different formats to allow tailoring the cam to give driveability with punch in the areas where it's needed. Because we can be bolder in our approach, we can nearly always add torque or HP in large amounts as compared to the factory cams."

Next we asked why there are not more hydraulic-lifter cams being used for fast street/strip machines. We were nearly overcome by the torrent of information

here because Racer seriously thinks that hydraulic cams are the most under-rated and overlooked components around the racing scene. "Lots of people distrust hydraulic lifters because the first ones were awful. And, most folks think that hydraulics pump up to cause problems. What actually happens is that the cam floats the valves and then the lifters automatically take up the clearance. But, lifter design has now reached such a state we can grind almost any kind of a cam in hydraulic form — and do. In fact, we recommend them for most street and street/strip applications and even for boats and some circle-track racers. With a hydraulic cam you can forget all that valve-adjustment nonsense and leave your tool box locked up. And, the hydraulic cams are easier on the lifters. The L-46 (350) hydraulic cam has been bench spun to 7200 RPM with stock springs. The GM-type lifters and our own private brand are self-purging because oil is always flowing through them to the upper valve train through the push-rod. Thus, there's no chance that air or dirt will be trapped in them to cause erratic action."

Racer continued, "Don't go wild on valve timing. Keep *effective* duration about 280 or 285 degrees as a reasonable maximum for wild street equipment with around 260 or so for sensible street applications, particularly on the inlet side. The exhaust can stand additional duration which will not detract from overall performance. Generally, valve lift should be in the range of 0.450-inch. Higher lifts show up somewhat better in an engine in which the heads have been correctly ported. Seems the "202" heads have a "knee" in the flow curve and real power gains with a higher lift cam are lessened unless the flow characteristics of the heads are improved.

"Longer duration can be used for competition, but even then the maximum should not exceed 300 to 310 degrees if the RPM drops to 3000 anywhere on the course.

"There is no *effective* timing until the valve is off its seat at least 0.015 inch to establish flow. It is easy to get added duration for advertising purposes by adding in the lengthy ramps which lift the cam gently off of its seat and return it the same way. When the *effective*-timing yardstick is applied, Chevy's street-mechanical and hydraulic cams show room for improvement. This is especially true of the hydraulic cams."

The "secret" of camshafts for additional performance is laid bare by lift vs. crankshaft-movement plots. Remember, too, that duration cannot be considered separately from overlap. We have included tables comparing the stock cams and another table comparing the offerings of one of the popular cam manufacturers. These are constructed on the basis of effective timing; that is, with the opening and closing measured with the valves approximately 0.015 inch off their seats.

Lift vs. crank-degree diagrams look similar for various cams because the designers must all work within the same limits for valve-train acceleration, spring pressure for returning the valve to the seat and compatibility of the tappets with the camshaft lobes under the spring loading, lubrication, and temperature conditions which exist. The rate of lift and descent, and therefore the curve shape, will turn out to be decidedly similar on various camshafts, provided the engineers know what they are doing. Be wary of vastly different curve shapes.

When comparing camshafts do not be impressed or swayed by a few degrees difference in timing or several thousandths lift. Such minor differences will not make two similar cams run that much differently.

If you plan to install a camshaft, order your cam and installation kit ahead of time, even if you are after a stock cam. Although Chevys are the most popular engines for reworking, there's always the chance that the particular cam you want was sold out yesterday.

Get the grinder's recommendations as to spring pressure so you will be able to install the appropriate springs.

CAMSHAFT COMPARISON TABLE
For Racer Brown! Camshafts

PROFILE DESIGNATION	DURATION	LIFT	APPLICATION	SEE NOTE
Hydraulic cams				
SS-H-23	270	0.470	Street-strip 302, 4-speed & Auto "stump-puller" in 327-350-400	1
SS-H-24	274	0.470	Street-strip 302, 4-speed. Very civilized in larger engines.	1
SS-H-25	286	0.485	Street-strip 327-350-400, 4-speed & Auto.	1
SS-H-44	292	0.510	Street-strip 327-350-400, 4-speed only.	2
Mechanical cams				
ST-21	286	0.520	Same as SS-H-25. Excellent short-track.	1
ST-12	294	0.485	Max street-strip 327-350-400, 4-speed only.	2
STX-19	296	0.530	Circle-track 3/8 to 1/2 mile 327-350-400.	3
STX-21	306	0.560	Comp. drag-race only 302. Circle-track 327-350-400. 1/2 mile & larger.	3
STX-39M	316	0.600	Comp. drag-race only 327-350.	3
Roller cams				
X-103	286	0.520	Short circle-track 302-327.	1
X-112	288	0.520	Short circle-track 327-350-400. Comp. drag-race heavy 302.	1
82-R	300	0.530	Similar to STX-19 above.	3
66-R	306	0.560	Similar to STX-21 above.	3
68-R	310	0.590	Comp. drag-race only 302.	3
70-R	314	0.590	Comp. drag-race only 302-327.	3
81-R	322	0.590	Comp. drag-race only 327-350.	3
84RM	320	0.620	Comp. drag-race only 350.	3

NOTES:

1. Normally, no piston modifications required for correct piston-to-valve clearance.
2. May require deeper valve reliefs in pistons for correct piston-to-valve clearance.
3. Will definitely require deeper valve reliefs in pistons for correct piston-to-valve clearance. No guesswork here!
4. Duration for hydraulic-lifter camshafts measured at 0.008 in. lift at lifter.
5. Duration for mechanical and roller lifter camshafts measured at 0.017 in. or 0.018 in. at lifter.
6. Valve-lift figures are for 1.5 to 1 rocker arms only.
7. Generally, camshafts specified for circle-track vehicles are also applicable for marine installations. Milder circle-track camshafts are usually acceptable for street-strip vehicles.
8. Maximum engine-speed limits when used with recommended installation package: hydraulic-lifter camshafts — 7000 rpm; mechanical-lifter street-strip camshafts — 7200-7500 rpm; competition mechanical or roller-lifter camshafts — 8500 to 9000 plus.
9. Racer's method of measuring duration is CONSERVATIVE so go easy! Too much camshaft is worse than not enough.

Fortunately there are several excellent factory camshafts which can be used to increase the performance of your small-block Chevrolet. Thus the burden of the performance enthusiast is reduced to the areas of correct cam selection, cam verification or checking, correct installation and maintenance. For the most part, cam selection can be taken off your shoulders by Chevrolet or any one of several reputable cam grinders who specialize in the high-performance field. First, decide exactly what the engine is to be used for — street and strip, street only, strip only, all-out road racing or whatever. The second step is to gather complete information about the engine in which the cam will be installed and the vehicle in which the engine will be installed. One of the better cam grinders in the country asks all orders for cams to contain the following information:

Engine make, year, original cubic inches, original bore, original stroke, bore now, stroke now, total cubic inches now; rocker arms: year, model, ratio, stock or high lift; valve size: diameter of both intake and exhaust; carbs or injectors: make, how many, total venturi area; supercharger type, drive ratio; cylinder heads, amount milled; brand of pistons, part number, manufacturer's claimed compression ratio, flat-top or deflector-head, cranking compression gage reading in pounds per square inch; chassis: weight, make, year; use of engine: drags only, circular track racing, size of track, exact drag class entered, street and drags, street only, marine, hull type, anticipated average speed and elapsed time, rear gear ratio, transmission type, tire diameter and size, make and grind number of cam used now, do you need more low-speed torque or more RPM?

Quite a list, isn't it? Chances are you might not be able to supply all of this information to a cam grinder, but the message here is clear. Most of them have years of experience and are willing to impart some of this knowledge in the form of a camshaft recommendation if you will only take the time to give them the correct information. The key here is correct information. All cam grinders and most speed shop operators have had experiences with a customer who said he wanted a cam for a racing engine, when in fact the engine would be used only for the street. In a case such as this the customer is the

These posed pictures show the difference between a head running stock (or nearly stock) valve gear and one (on the right) outfitted with one of the Jomar stud-stabilizing kits which space the valve cover away from the head. Jomar stud girdle clamps over rocker-stud extensions to prevent stud flexing during high-RPM operation. Roller rockers and extended rocker studs are all part of the racing game.

No matter what size, shape, color, grind or brand cam you stick in a small-block Chevy, it had better have these two holes drilled in the rear journal. If not, don't install it — you'll blow the rear cam plug out when oil pressure builds up. This is rare — but possible. Checking costs nothing.

All roller lifters have some type of device to prevent the lifters from rotating in their bores. Racer Brown-type shown simply anchors two lifters together with an arm to prevent either from rotating.

loser. A cam is installed which has almost no low-RPM torque which in turn makes the car all but impossible to drive on the street. Worse yet, the car has almost no performance at legal speed limits.

So at this point we would interject that in the end you are hurting only your engine and yourself if you are less than honest about specifications and intended use of the engine being built. This goes for all other performance equipment — not just camshafts. Lecture is over.

Two short items of note before getting into camshaft verification or checking, as it is most commonly called. Valve-lift figures are stated in a decimal fraction of an inch and are measured at either the lifter or the valve (usually at the valve). Overhead-valve engines such as the small-block Chevy usually rely on a rocker arm of some sort to actuate the valves. Normally these arms add to the lift caused by the camshaft. Thus a simple step of multiplication is necessary to determine the amount of lift at the valve. Simply multiply the lift at the valve lifter by the rocker-arm ratio.

In the case of the small-block Chevy, the stock rocker ratio is 1.5. In other words, the rocker multiplies the cam lobe lift by 1.5. Thus, 0.300-inch lift at the cam becomes 0.450-inch at the valve. In this chapter we also discuss installing the large-block Chevy rockers on the small-block heads. These rockers are 1.7 ratio which means that 0.300-inch lift at the cam becomes 0.510-inch at the valve.

Even if a camshaft is to be installed in an engine for checking purposes only, do not install the cam without lubricating the entire shaft. A medium-weight motor oil is o.k. when installing for checking, but specialized lubes sold just for the purpose of camshaft installation are highly recommended when the cam is being installed to be used. Modern valve-spring pressures are quite high, and without adequate lubrication on the lobes and journals, a camshaft can be ruined in the first few seconds of running.

ROLLER-TAPPET CAMS

If you are building a small-block Chevy for street use, forget you ever heard about roller-tappet cams because you can spend that $400 to $600 for other items which are far more necessary. There's even some disagreement as to whether the roller cams are required for an all-out racing small block, especially because the competitive machines — in most classes of racing — don't seem to be equipped with them.

When lifts soar into the 0.600-inch-plus region, such horrendous valve spring-pressure — typically approaching 500 pounds open pressure — load a cast-iron cam and flat-tappet lifters to the point where a lot of wear can occur very fast. Multiply this spring loading by the 1.5 rocker-arm ratio and you have an effective net load of 750 pounds against the cam. This unit loading approaches or exceeds 250,000 lbs/sq. in. where the lifter meets the cam lobe. For this reason, if no other, many drag racers and Bonneville machines are equipped with roller-tappet camshafts.

Owners of such machines are usually running the engines beyond the factory's rev-limit recommendation, often with nitro-methane-based fuel which reduces the oil's lubricating capabilities when the fuel dilutes the oil. For extreme engine speeds, the roller tappet allows using high spring loads, primarily because the roller tappet protects against destroying the cam lobe, assuming there is a reasonable shape. The tappets roll, helping the situation from a wear standpoint. The roller-tappet cam sometimes requires added spring pressure to hold the heavier tappets against the lobes. And the use of heavy spring loads and the extra mechanical complexity of the roller tappets with their guiding mechanisms increases opportunities for failures.

As a point of interest, we asked Racer Brown about differences in frictional loading in the camshaft and valve train — between the flat-tappet cam and a roller-tappet cam: He recollected that a small-block Chevy showed that the breakaway and sustaining torque required to rotate the camshaft was exactly half with the roller-tappet job.

GEAR-DRIVEN CAMS

Gear-driven camshafts are noisy, require a special high-cost ball-bearing distributor and are not necessary for street, drag-strip or most racing use. Save your money. You may see gear-drive cams being used in marathon race boats and in engines set up for long-duration racing, but there's no earthly reason to consider one for your street machine that gets rushed through the quarter mile a few times each month.

The stock nylon-toothed cam sprocket and matching chain works fine, assuming that you get a cam sprocket with concentric pitch line and hub.

The majority of small-block Chevys being used in Formula A, and all classes of drag racing are using stock or replacement chains. This may be another of those places where you can save your money to buy the parts that you really need. Didn't the factory continue in that direction? Think about that.

The argument is often offered that a chain will stretch during high-speed operation and thus effectively retard the camshaft and cause the engine to lose power. This may be true, but there are at least three reputable high-performance engine builders who have witnessed a gear drive lose horsepower as compared to driving the cam with a chain.

DEGREE WHEELS

Depending on the manufacturer, degree wheels are numbered or marked in different ways. Some are marked Zero, 90, 180 and 270 with appropriate gradations in between. On other wheels the Zero and 180-degree marks are shown as TDC and BDC and the marks halfway in between these two are represented as 90 degrees. Either is acceptable; you're still working with the same 360 degrees.

If a stock rocker is used, the tip for long life is an aftermarket grooved ball which has been treated with a dry penetrant lubricant. The tall adjusting nut with a lock screw is also an aftermarket piece which has found favor with many top engine builders. However, it must be used with a rocker stud which has been ground flat on the upper end.

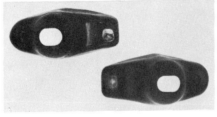

The lower rocker has been treated with a dry-penetrant lubricant, while the upper rocker is stock. Notice the difference in the amount of wear in the pallet area. Both rockers came from the same engine.

Chevy rocker ball at right has no grooves. Develco units are deeply grooved for oiling. The balls and mating surface of the rocker should be checked for galling anytime an engine is torn down.

Misalignment caused by high lift can sometimes cause an unnatural relationship between the end of the pushrod and the rocker. When this occurs the socket of the rocker will score, gall or blue. Check for this when disassembling a racing engine. The rocker should appear polished on the pallet, but examine the rockers for the end riding over the end of the valve stem. This should be checked when the engine goes together — before it is ever fired.

Three essential tools for camshaft installation in any high-performance engine are a degree wheel with pointer, a dial indicator with a magnetic base assembly, and some method for advancing or retarding the camshaft in relationship to the crankshaft indexing. In this photograph a series of offset bushings are shown. These are often used to advance or retard the cam.

Easy and accurate timing of the small-block Chevy requires a "degree wheel" to set timing. A machine shop can take care of this for you. Many speed shops sell a tape which wraps around the balancer to provide the same feature — at a fraction of the cost.

INSTALLING THE CAMSHAFT AND FINDING TDC

You will need a degree wheel or a degreed harmonic damper, a pointer, and a one-inch-travel dial indicator with clamps and brackets.

A slight modification must be made to two of your old valve lifters (tappet). The lifter needs a flat surface on which the stem of the dial indicator can ride for the following checks. A length of aluminum or steel rod can be fitted into the lifter body and a flat face turned on it. Don't use the radiused cup of the lifter as a contact point for the indicator stem, as it will cause inaccurate readings and possibly damage the indicator. Install the two modified tappets in the lifter bores for No. 1 cylinder.

Install the cam into its lubricated bearings in the block. Chevy suggests installing two capscrews in the cam nose to use as "handles" so that it becomes easier to install the cam without damaging the bearings with the lobes. Index cam sprocket onto the cam with the timing chain in place and install the cam-sprocket capscrews so valve-timing marks line up.

Install piston and connecting-rod assembly. Top and bottom rings should be used to hold the piston squarely in the bore, particularly if a dial indicator is used to find TDC. Attach the dial indicator so that its stem rests on top of the piston. Rotate the crankshaft slowly in its normal direction of rotation. When the dial indicator shows that the piston has reached its maximum travel, attach the degreed crankshaft pulley or attach a separate degree wheel to the stock pulley. Make an indicator tab from sheet metal or a piece of welding rod. Adjust the degree wheel and indicator to coincide with the TDC marking. Rotate the crank through an almost-complete revolution, stopping short of TDC when the dial indicator shows that the piston must still travel about 0.025-inch to reach TDC. Note the degree-wheel reading or make a mark on the crankshaft pulley. Continue rotating the crankshaft while the indicator passes through its maximum reading and backs down to 0.025-inch on the other side of TDC. Note reading. The ATDC reading should be the same as the BTDC one to show that you accurately located TDC. If not, start over again!

A large washer bolted to the deck surface of the block may be used to stop the piston to find TDC with the positive-stop method. This is a big-block, but the principle is the same, regardless of the engine.

Another method positively locates TDC without using a dial indicator. It is so simple that it amazes us how few engine builders are aware of it. Bolt a strap across No. 1 cylinder. The strap should have a cap-screw in its center, placed to extend into the cylinder. Set the degree wheel and indicator finger at TDC by guesstimate. Rotate the crank by hand until the piston stops against the screw. Note degree-wheel reading. Reverse rotation and turn the crank until piston again stops against the strap on the opposite side of BDC. Note the degree-wheel reading. Move the indicator to a point exactly between the two readings.

This same method can be used when the engine is assembled and in the car if care is used. In this instance, the stop is made from a spark plug. Braze a piece of steel rod into an old plug base from which the insulator has been removed. The steel should extend about 1 inch from the threads. Remove all of the spark plugs from the engine. Install your special "plug" into No. 1 cylinder. Rotate the engine by turning the crank-pulley nut with a box wrench in one direction; with the fan belt in the other. Use extreme care so you do not damage a piston!

NOTE: The factory's timing mark on the crank pulley, when used in conjunction with indicator on the timing cover, is not a positive or accurate TDC location. Do not use it! There are no really reliable shortcuts for finding TDC or checking camshaft timing, so do not look for any. However, you can compare your accurate TDC location with the stock markings and scribe a correct line or move the indicator to provide a true indication.

DEGREEING THE CAM

A modern camshaft is a precise piece of equipment, but never assume that as such they are always correct in all respects. A camshaft that is absolutely perfect is impossible to find.

All cam grinders have established their own quality standards to ensure that you will usually receive an accurately ground camshaft. However, errors can and do occur in manufacturing camshafts and they cannot control the other parts in your engine.

Cam check is up to the engine builder and checking must be done in the engine in which the camshaft will live because *individual engines are different* and their differences can and do drastically affect valve timing. If the camshaft is installed in another engine, or is reinstalled after being removed for an engine teardown, the degreeing operation must be repeated. Maximum performance is not obtained by short cuts. The cam grinder can only control the camshaft, not the rest of the running gear in your engine. The engine builder must ascertain if there are any errors present in the relationship between crank and cam and it is he who must also correct any errors for maximum performance.

You can obtain maximum performance by making sure that the cam installed in your engine opens and closes the valves as intended by the cam grinder. And there is a second valid reason which makes cam checking essential: consider the hours of wasted labor if subsequent removal of the cam is required to correct valve timing! It's no trouble to make an error when indexing the marks on the crank and cam sprockets.

There is no doubt that you can install a stock or special cam without checking. But, when you consider all of the tolerances working against you to cause less-than-perfect timing, why trust to luck? Some of the factors which affect timing include manufacturers' tolerances for the location of the keyways in the crank and cam sprocket dowels and their respective sprockets— plus the cam grinder's lobe-location tolerances. If, for instance, the location tolerance for the crankshaft keyway and dowel hole in the cam sprocket and cam nose is ±0.75°, you could get a tolerance "stack-up" of 4.5 crankshaft degrees total timing error with every item off by the maximum amount. It is assumed that you have carefully followed the instructions and have installed the degree wheel and accurately located TDC. With the lifter on the center of the heel of No. 1 intake lobe, adjust indicator stem parallel to lifter travel in all respects. Preload indicator about 0.010. Rotate crankshaft and observe the indicator, watching for the point of maximum lift. Mark "IN" in pencil on the degree wheel. Rotate the crankshaft exactly one turn in the same direction until the pointer again aligns with your "IN" notation. This places the lifter in the mid-point of the cam lobe's clearance section. The cam has turned exactly 180° (half-turn). Without changing the indicator pre-load, set the dial-indicator face to zero. Rotate the crankshaft in the direction of running rotation and observe the dial indicator. When it shows that the lifter has raised an amount equivalent to the checking clearance, record the degree-wheel reading. This will be a certain number of degrees BTDC. If no checking clearance is specified or the cam tag has been lost, use 0.020-inch (close for most camshafts). Stock cams can be checked with 0.015 clearance for mechanical cams and 0.008 for hydraulic cams if you use the data in our comparison table.

Continue to rotate the crankshaft in the same direction until the lifter has risen up in its bore and fallen back again as it followed the opening and closing flanks of the cam lobe. Watch again for the indicator to reach the checking clearance or the arbitrary figure of 0.020-inch just mentioned. Record the degree-wheel reading as the number of degrees between the pointer and BDC. Add 180° to your two readings to get duration of opening measured at the checking clearance.

When taking a reading with a dial indicator off the top of a lifter, the plunger of the indicator must run in the same axis as the lifter and preferably on a flat surface created by modifying a lifter with an aluminum button.

Repeat the process several times to eliminate the possibility of errors. Each repeat check must be started at the "IN" mark on the degree wheel and the indicator's needle and dial face must be at zero. Cam lobes and lifter bores must be scrupulously clean and lightly oiled so the lifter can move in and out of the bore without binding and of its own weight. With everything right, the indicator will reach zero and stay there before and after the mark on the degree wheel is reached.

Transfer lifter and dial indicator to No. 1 exhaust and repeat the entire process, beginning with finding full lift, then turning 360 crank degrees and marking the wheel "EX"— using this as your starting point. Exhaust-opening checking clearance will be reached at a point BBDC. As with the intake, the number of degrees from the BDC mark on the degree wheel must be counted to get the opening point. Record this figure.

Again, rotate the crank and observe the indicator as it indicates opening and then closing back down to the checking clearance. This will occur at a point ATDC, and the number of degrees from TDC must be recorded. Exhaust duration is calculated by adding 180° to the two readings recorded for exhaust timing. Again, repeat the process several times to eliminate the possibility of error.

Overlap is easily determined by adding the intake-opening degrees Before Top Dead Center to the exhaust-closing degrees After Top Dead Center. The entire cam-checking process presented herein has been taken with slight changes from Racer Brown's camshaft catalog which contains other data on correcting errors, etc.

Chrysler Corporation and some cam grinders use a different method of checking cam timing for high-performance engines. This is a quicker method but it is not consistently accurate unless checked at the lifter. It leaves the valve opening and closing points to fall where they may, but it is simpler because only one point is checked for each valve. Many builders check only the maximum intake-valve lift point when they are pressed for time. This is showing a lot of blind faith in the man who ground the cam, but suit yourself. This method consists of finding the points of maximum valve lift in relation to the piston position of top center.

Assume the valve timing is: Intake opens 34° before top center, closes 66° after bottom center, duration 280°; exhaust opens 70° before bottom center, closes 30° after top center, duration 280°. To find maximum lift of the intake valve, subtract the intake-opening point from half the duration. Using the figures above, half of 280° is 140° and the intake-opening point of 34° must be subtracted from 140°. The answer—106 degrees—is the point *after* top center that the intake valve should reach maximum lift.

On the exhaust side, the point of maximum lift of the exhaust valve is found by subtracting the exhaust-closing point from half the duration. Using the exhaust valve timing of 70-30 as above, the 30° exhaust-valve-closing point is subtracted from 140°. The answer of 110° is the point at which the exhaust valve should reach maximum lift *before* top center. This assumes cam lobes are symmetrical on both opening and closing sides, and that's not usual!

To establish these points correctly, the piston position of top center must be found accurately, as in the previous method.

Finding the points of maximum valve lift is really just a repetition of finding top center, except that the dial indicator is transferred from the piston to the lifters.

This check can also be performed by measuring for maximum lift at a valve re-

tainer in an assembled engine. The dial-indicator spindle must be parallel to the valve stem in both the longitudinal and lateral planes if the check is to be valid and one which will repeat.

This expensive dial indicator is graduated in inches on the linear scale and in thousandths on the dial—quite expensive, and certainly not necessary for occasional engine blueprinting. An indicator and base combination costing about $50 will do the job just as well.

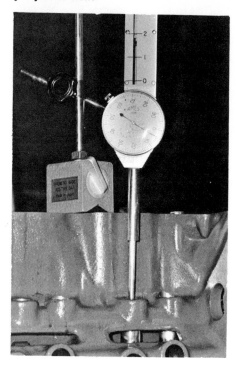

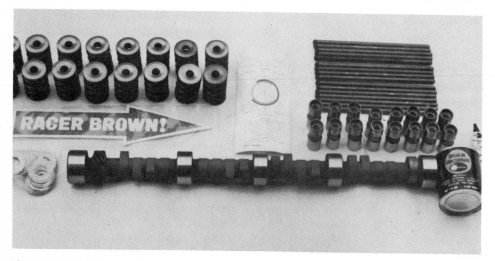

If you are seriously considering the purchase of an aftermarket camshaft, consider the kits that all of the cam grinders offer. The springs, retainers, and lifters are all designed to be compatible with the bump stick. If you didn't need the cam in the first place though, the kits are a double waste of money.

VALVE TIMING CORRECTIONS

The previously outlined procedure—under ideal conditions—will show that timing points coincide precisely with those shown on the cam tag. But, due to factors already stated, variations can occur. A difference of one or two crankshaft degrees between actual installed timing and the cam-tag specifications should be considered the maximum-allowable error. A closer tolerance of ±1° (crankshaft) is even better.

If the timing check shows that actual timing is 'way off —10° or more—then the timing sprockets are probably misindexed by one or more teeth. Correct such a situation and rerun the timing checks. Racer says that if an engine is run in this condition, or if the valve-timing check is made at the valves instead of at the lifters, it is a foregone conclusion that you will end up with an engineful of bent valves at the least. And, you'll also get bent pushrods, damaged rocker arms, and possibly even a bent or broken camshaft. These are a few additional reasons why the timing check should be made at the lifters, as opposed to checking it at the valves, or not checking at all. Checking valve overlap with feeler gages at the valves by the split-overlap method is not recommended under any circumstances because of the errors which are usually present in the rocker-arm geometry. *Feeler gages cannot be used for accurate checks!* Correcting a timing error requires rotating the camshaft in relation to the crankshaft, which can be confusing. It is important to take care to advance or retard the camshaft and *not one of the sprockets!* Remember that the sprockets retain their relative positions; it is the shafts which must be moved. This is true in all instances except where the cam and crank sprocket are misindexed, in which case the sprocket/shaft assembly is rotated. Assuming that the timing sprockets are held stationary, the drawing illustrates the direction that the crankshaft or camshaft must be moved to advance or retard cam action.

Three valve-event drawings compare specification timing with advanced timing (all events early) and with retarded timing (all events late).

Advancing or retarding the camshaft from the settings given by the cam grinder is idiotic unless you have access to a dyno and will actually run tests in the various advance/normal/retard settings that you are advocating. While this sort of jockeying has been known to cause an engine to run stronger at one end of the RPM range—or the other—most experts run their cams on the stock marks. In general, advancing the cam increases torque and HP through low- and mid-range RPM. Retarding the cam kills excessive low-end torque and increases HP at the top end. When an offset key or bushing is used, repeat the entire degree check to ensure that the correction has been made properly, that is, corrected *the right amount*—in *the right direction*. A movement of 0.0109-inch at the crankshaft nose (inside bore of crank sprocket) adjusts timing one crank degree (1/2 camshaft degree). Correcting a 5° timing error would require an offset key to offset the crankshaft sprocket 5° x 0.0109-inch = 0.0545-inch. Inexpensive offset keys or bushings can be used for making corrections. But, except for Racer Brown's, all are labelled in *camshaft degrees.* Keys or bushings can be made by any machine shop, but the readymade parts will be much cheaper. Rechecking timing after installing an offset key or bushing is essential!

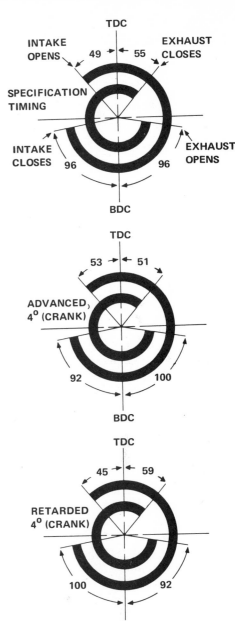

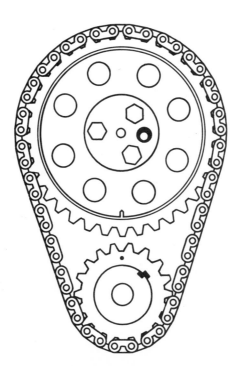

Comparison of normal specification timing with a cam which is advanced 4° (crank) and one which is retarded 4° (crank). 1° cam movement is equivalent to 2° crankshaft movement. Chevrolet's service mechanical cam 3965754 used for this example.

Drawing at left shows using bushing in the cam sprocket to advance cam. Offset key in crank sprocket advances cam when placed as shown. Reversing either retards the cam. Only one method needs to be used as various bushings and keys are sold.

In making valve-to-piston clearance check, clay is smeared in a thin layer over piston top. In lower photo, piston has pushed clay into valves, as described in text. A machinist's scale is being used to measure the clearance as indicated by the depressed clay on the piston. This is a big-block, but the technique is the same for the small block.

VARIABLE TIMING DEVICES

Be wary of buying any device which alters cam timing *as the engine is running.* Make sure that you have personally witnessed a horsepower increase on a dynamometer before investing in such gadgetry. One of the authors observed a test wherein one of these adjustable wonders "adjusted" a 25 HP decrease from a strong-running big block. You didn't read about that in the ads, did you? Racer Brown tells of one of his customers who bought such a device. He gave up on trying to make it work as the ads stated and locked out the adjustable feature to allow making quick changes of the cam timing manually to compensate for different-length circle tracks.

Remember that advancing or retarding the cam can change the relationship of the valves to the pistons, perhaps reducing the clearance to less than that which is required.

VALVE-TO-PISTON CLEARANCE

When installing a high-performance camshaft from Chevrolet or *any* cam manufacturer for the first time, the clearance between the valves and pistons during the overlap period must be checked to determine whether adequate clearance exists between these components. This clearance should be checked if the cam has been running in the engine with success but other components are changed—such as rocker arms with a different ratio than original equipment, a stroker crank, a different piston type, or a larger-diameter valve head, or a longer connecting rod. A change in any of these components may cause the valve and piston to collide where the problem did not exist previously. Of utmost importance is the fact that just because a manufacturer says the cam won't push the valves into the pistons doesn't always make it true. He has no way of knowing what you have done to the engine to affect clearances . . . so don't expect him to buy new parts because of your haste or his assurance that piston notching would not be needed.

The checking of valve-to-piston clearance should be done only after the camshaft has been installed and degreed to the crankshaft as it will run. Clearances during the check will thus be the same as when the engine runs.

On a competition small-block Chevrolet with steel rods, the valve-to-piston clearance must be at least 0.090-inch for the intake valves and 0.100-inch for the exhaust valves. If the engine is to be run with aluminum connecting rods, increase the above clearances to 0.110 and 0.120 minimum, respectively, to compensate for expansion of the rods.

Something to watch for in an engine when the camshaft is advanced or retarded is the clearance between the valves and the pistons at their closest points. When a camshaft is advanced, intake-valve clearance at the piston decreases and exhaust-valve clearance increases; conversely, when a shaft is retarded, intake-valve clearance at the piston increases and exhaust-valve clearance decreases.

There are at least three methods for checking valve-to-piston clearance. The "feeler-gage approach" will be discussed first. With pistons, rods and crank installed in the block, lay on a compressed (used) head gasket and a cylinder head or just the cylinder head without a gasket. One cylinder of the head should contain an intake and an exhaust valve—held in place and in the closed position by Perfect-Circle or Raymond valve-stem seals. Install lifters, pushrods and rocker arms for this one cylinder. Adjust both valves for zero lash. Rotate the crankshaft one complete revolution to TDC. Lift each rocker arm up, push the valves against the piston head and measure the gap between the valve stem and the tip of the rocker arm. The measurement is the gap between valve and piston. If the measurement is made without a head gasket in place, add the thickness of a compressed head gasket to the measurement for an accurate indication of the valve-to-piston gap at TDC.

Check the valve-to-piston clearance for both valves in 5° steps to 30° or more on each side of TDC. Valves are sometimes closer to the piston when the piston is slightly away from TDC, so a single check at TDC is not a safe indication.

The "clay method" has been around for years, and offers a real advantage over the feeler-gage method because the valves are rarely closest to the piston at TDC. Lay two strips of modeling clay, each at least 1/4-inch thick, on the head of one of the pistons so that the strips are directly under the low side of the valve heads. Install the cylinder head which contains the valves for the cylinder to be checked. Place a used head gasket between the head and the block—making certain that the gasket is of the same type to be used in the final installation. A thin coating of oil on the valve heads will prevent clay sticking to the valves if they should touch. Secure the cylinder head to the block with capscrews tightened to the correct torque to duplicate final-installation conditions.

With the camshaft in the position that causes both valves for the cylinder to be closed, install the lifters, pushrods, and rocker arms for the cylinder and adjust the valve lash to .002 inch. Slowly and carefully rotate the crankshaft. Feel carefully for any tendency for components to bind or stop. If the shaft reaches a spot where binding is apparent, STOP! The valve may be hitting the piston, so don't use excessive force. Only a very light force should be required for the piston and valves to compress the clay, squeezing it out of the way. You should be able to feel what is occurring well enough not to damage anything.

Rotate the crankshaft at least two full revolutions, then remove the head carefully. Examine the clay. If either valve head touched the clay, slice the clay lengthwise with a sharp knife through the middle of the depression made by the valve. Peel one-half of the clay section off of the piston. The thinnest section of the clay can then be measured with a micrometer, vernier caliper or even a thin steel scale.

Although some "pros" might tend to look down their noses at the clay method of measuring piston-to-valve clearance, it is highly recommended for the beginning engine builder. First,

this method gives the piston-to-valve clearance *accurately*. Second, a visual representation of the corrective cut is available so that you can use it as a guide to notch a piston. While experienced engine builders might not need this, it can be of immense help to someone who has never had to notch a hundred-dollar set of pistons.

To check valve-to-piston clearance by the "light-spring method" you'll need two light springs installed in a conventional manner on the intake and exhaust valves of the No. 1 cylinder. You don't need any trick springs here . . . fuel pump springs are lovely. Install a gasket and the cylinder head with two or three bolts. Install tappets, pushrods, and rockers. Install the camshaft to be run in the engine. Adjust valve lash to 0.002 inch. Rotate the crankshaft and stop at TDC with the intake and exhaust partially open in the overlap position.

Mount a dial indicator to the top of the cylinder head with the indicator "probe" resting at the top of the valve spring retainer. Set the indicator dial to zero. Now exert thumb pressure on the rocker arm until you feel the valve head touch the piston. By reading the dial indicator the valve-to-piston clearance may be determined.

To be double dead-sure about this, check the valve-to-piston clearance for both valves in 5° steps to at least 30° on each side of TDC. In some cases, due to piston approaching TDC and valve position, the valves will be in closer proximity to the piston when it is slightly away from TDC.

If the clearance is less than specified, the pistons will have to be notched or fly-cut to be run with that camshaft and rocker-arm set-up. Such notching should be done prior to balancing the engine assembly. Always notch the pistons to gain clearance. Never sink the valves!

ROCKER ARM GEOMETRY

In addition to installing the camshaft in the correct relationship to the crankshaft, you must observe another important point of engine construction: the relation of the rocker-arm-tip radius to the valve-stem center. If this is correct—with the centerline of the rocker's radiused tip coinciding with the valve-stem centerline at 50% lift—good

things happen! Specification lift throughout the lift cycle of the cam is assured, side thrust of the valve stem against the guide bore is minimized to reduce wear and consequent oil consumption, friction is reduced, and higher RPM can be reached before valve float occurs. This is a point of construction which is often overlooked but it makes a vast difference in engine performance. Motorcycle race-engine constructors used and wrote about these things for decades; most auto-engine modifiers still refuse to realize that extra HP can be gained through careful attention to all details. Care produces more HP than a truckful of "black-magic" tricks. Bike builders often had only one cylinder so they had to make it produce maximum HP. Always watch current development in motorcycle engines and tuning procedures.

NOTE: The small-block Chevy piston should have a full-width notch across the dome to accommodate both intake and exhaust valves — as opposed to individual notches for each valve. This permits better breathing during the overlap period, particularly at high engine speeds. It gives better power, even though it involves a slight loss in compression ratio. It also eliminates a stress-raiser in the area of the dome with the highest load, thereby postponing cracking at this point.

When notching is required, it is sound practice to notch the pistons 0.040 to 0.050-inch deeper than actually required. This allows advancing or retarding the camshaft without disassembling the engine to perform the notching operation a second time.

Getting back to the tip/stem relationship, there are several things which can affect this relationship: head milling, cam base circle, valve-seat location, valve-stem length, lifter dimension, rocker-arm differences and pushrod lengths. Some of these things become immediately obvious as sources of problems when we are working on the engine—then we shrug our shoulders and forget about the problems and go right ahead with the engine assembly, never realizing that in so doing we have seriously shortchanged the engine's breathing ability. Adjustments are possible through varying the height of the valve stem and/or the pushrod length; do not "sink" the valves!

Before continuing, let's look at some of the other aspects of ball-pivot rocker arms. Although these have virtues of light weight, low manufacturing cost, and simple installation, they also present problems and must therefore be considered a mixed blessing. The rocker opens and closes the valve with a continuously changing pivot-to-tip radius, moving through arcs of varying radii. With this changing situation, the rocker-arm ratio is highest at maximum lift, let's call it 1.5:1. It lessens as the pushrod moves away from the pivot, say 1.4:1. These figures, incidentally, are merely examples chosen to illustrate the problem and do not represent actual ratios which may occur. The problem is complicated by variances in the distance from the ball seat to the rocker tip. Just measure the valve travel with the cam at half and full-lift, using all 16 rockers, one at a time, on the same valve and cam lobe. Some produce more than 50% expected travel at half-lift, while others will show the opposite to provide more than specified valve travel at full-lift with less than 50% at the half-lift point. Obviously, you want 100% valve travel with the cam at full-lift position.

Make all of the valve-stem heights (*not lengths*) identical within ±0.005 inch (the rocker-arm-cover-gasket surface can be used as a reference point from which to measure heights). If any of the valves have to be shortened by grinding on the tips, reharden the ends by heating them cherry red and quenching in oil. Use a fairly large torch so the tip quickly gets cherry red without heat extending to the keeper groove. Hardening is wanted only on the tip. It is assumed that you have already seated the valves per directions in the section on cylinder heads. Reseating changes the stem heights, so do any seating *prior to establishing the heights.*

"Rocker-arm geometry is particularly important with the Chevrolet-type rocker gear. Nearly everything you touch affects rocker-arm geometry, usually for the worse . . . and nobody every heard of it," says Racer Brown. "We do something with Chevy pushrods and don't tell anyone about it. We make them *all* 1/32-inch shorter than stock to compensate for block decking, head milling, etc. It compensates in the wrong direction for facing valves and seats, but if it is necessary to make a deliberate 'error,' it's better to go in the direction of a shorter pushrod by far than to go for a longer pushrod 'by a little.' All this points out that rocker arm geometry, although extremely important, is usually completely neglected when building a Chevy engine.

"You can make individually tailored pushrods so that each valve, rocker and pushrod work as an integrated set to line up the center of the rocker-arm tip with the center of the valve stem at half-lift. But, this unnecessarily complicated procedure makes no provisions for broken or damaged parts. A better plan is like so: Get friendly with the local Chev parts dispenser or speed shoppe, depending on the brand and type of rocker arm to be used. Fill a bushel basket with the rockers of your choice and check them out in the engine using the *same* lifter, the *same* pushrod with the *same* valve on the *same* cam lobe.

"Set up the valve in the head with a light fuel-pump spring and set a dial indicator on the spring retainer. Install the rocker arm and pushrod and related bits and tighten the adjusting nut until the valve is off the seat, say by 0.002". Record the point of maximum valve lift with a chalk stripe on the degree wheel that's on the end of your crank. Rotate crank exactly one turn to the same mark to put the lifter in the center of the cam-lobe heel.

"Now very carefully measure valve duration in crankshaft degrees at 1/4, 1/2, 3/4 of full valve lift. Repeat the procedure on all rockers in the basket until, ideally, you get 16 rockers that are all exactly alike at all points. That would be ideal—and ideal things just don't often happen—so be prepared to accept at least eight rockers, plus a couple of spares, for the intakes. These should be as close as possible at all points. Ditto for the exhaust rockers.

"At this point, rocker ratio and rocker geometry do not mean anything. You are just trying to dig up an acceptable set of rockers, plus spares. Next, make up one intake and one exhaust adjustable pushrod and adjust the length of each to optimize rocker geometry. I prefer to do this with zero lash or close to it to ensure that the rocker arm is not cocked at an angle in relation to the valve-stem tip. At 50% lift, the center of the rocker tips should be in the center of the valve-stem tip.

"Why not just use adjustable pushrods and save the bother of making special-length pushrods? Adjustables are made for the engine but they are somewhat heavier and could require higher valve-spring pressures. However, the idea of using adjustable pushrods in these engines is not all bad.

"Rather than buying two adjustable pushrods for making this check, make them from stock parts. Braze a piece of a machine screw into one part and leave enough of the screw protruding so that it will accept a nut and extend into the other part of the pushrod for holding the two parts in alignment. The nut can be used to adjust the length.

"With the pushrod length established, it is no problem to get pushrods made to the required length, plus a couple of spares. We do it all the time. This plan gives interchangeability of pieces not obtainable in any other way.

"If the rocker-geometry check is made as described, but with zero lash, the pushrods will be a very small amount too short, but again, this is better than having them too long because valve-stem side thrust and valve-guide-bore wear are minimized.

"Doing things this way more-or-less ignores actual measured rocker-arm ratio, but the end result is better functioning of the entire valve train and hardly justifies 'squeaking' about a few thousandths valve lift gained or lost from theoretical numbers."

Several cam grinders offer unassembled pushrods with the top end left out so the tube can be cut to length prior to installing the hardened end.

By now you are perhaps wondering why so many engines run as well as they do. You can begin to understand why the top tuners always run in front—but never brag about how quickly they can assemble a winning engine. Now that the need for careful assembly has been re-emphasized, let's proceed to the next item.

STOCK ROCKER ARMS

These stamped-steel parts were the pieces that weren't supposed to work back in 1955 — but they worked then and they're working even better today. The rockers are lighter than any of the trick replacements that can be had; they cost less and they almost never fail if they are installed properly and used with the aftermarket grooved rocker balls. The grooves hold oil in the high-load areas to provide long life under the high heat and marginal lubrication conditions to which the rockers are continuously subjected.

Chevrolet does not manufacture grooved rocker balls for the small block — but a number of manufacturers do, including Develco. Part number D 11 50 identifies Develco's grooved balls. The balls will fit all sizes of the small block but will not fit any of the large blocks (396-454). The Develco units are machined from a bar, heat-treated, and Tuftrided. About the only thing you could do to improve them would be to have them Micro-Sealed or treated with some other form of dry-penetrant lube. These aftermarket grooved balls are not necessary for the street but are a must for all forms of competition.

If an engine is being assembled try to get some used rocker balls from intake positions to use on the exhaust rockers. The reason for this is that used balls that are in good condition have already been burnished and are less apt to fail during the critical break-in period. Exhaust balls almost always fail first. When failure does occur, move a used intake ball over onto the exhaust rocker and install a new ball on the intake rocker. When assembling the balls and rockers (at any time) coat the parts with GM's Engine Oil Supplement (EOS) or Molykote.

Another Racer Brown tip: get the rockers and balls Parker-Lubrite treated and then paint each ball and ball socket with molybdenum-disulfide and you'll have zero problems with rocker wear. About $10 should treat all 32 pieces.

Chevrolet goes to great lengths to case-harden the rockers so they will have long life. This case-hardening is immediately removed if you attempt to reface the rockers. If the pallet is scored or pitted, resist the urge to "just touch it with crocus cloth." Discard the part and start with a new one. Use the locking-type adjusting nuts which have a large contact area between the nut and the ball. These require grinding a flat on the end of the rocker stud. Relash valves frequently during run-in of new parts.

There are a couple of little tricks which can be done with the stock Chevy rockers — none necessary for street engines, but if you are going serious racing — they bear investigation. Smokey Yunick made up a fixture (pictured here) to hold the rocker arm so that a grinder could be used to remove some of the edge all the way around the top of the rocker arm. Smokey takes off about 3/16-inch with a die grinder. This serves to lighten the rocker and he says there is no indication that the strength of the rocker is adversely affected.

There are two approaches to the second trick. Yunick's approach is to cut a small tab of metal from light-weight sheet metal and heliarc the tab over the top of the area where oil squirts through the pushrods. This acts as a deflector and keeps the rocker ball well saturated with oil.

The next way to do this is to get a set of Traco's clips for the rocker arms. These snap onto the rocker arm to direct the oil right onto the rocker ball to ensure improved oiling. As a side benefit, they keep oil off of you when you are adjusting the rockers with the engine running. One thing to remember when using them is that the cast-in drippers in the rocker covers have to be removed for clearance. If you send $9 to Traco, they'll mail you a set of the clips postpaid.

Another Yunick experiment — rocker is clamped in the aluminum fixture which serves as a grinding guide. About 3/16-inch of metal is ground off the upper lip of the rocker to lighten the unit.

To replace press-in studs with the screw-in variety, you'll need a facing tool to top off the stud boss. A machined surface is required for the seating surface of the screw-in stud. There's info on pulling the stock studs in the cylinder head chapter.

When Chevrolet's or any other screw-in rocker studs are used with needle-bearing rockers or any other rockers which have a setscrew locking device on the adjusting nut, it is necessary to grind a flat on the upper end of the stud as shown here.

ROCKER-TO-STUD CLEARANCE

If you're running stock rockers with a big-lift cam or even a mild stick with the heads or block milled, check to see if the rockers may be binding on the studs or coming dangerously close to doing so. Bend a small piece of wire and see if it will fit between the rocker and the stud when the valve is in the fully-open position. Use a wire of no less than 0.030-inch diameter because this is the minimum clearance you should have between stud and rocker. Grind the slot out to achieve the clearance or buy a set of long-slot rockers from Manley Performance Engineering which features a 1/8-inch longer slot.

In addition, the 0.625-inch radius tip on the Manley rocker is much broader than any roller tip currently available. The reason for the large area is that their tests show that because most roller-tip rockers possess less than one-half that radius they tend to ride incorrectly on the valve stem, especially with a high-lift cam. The further the valve is opened, the more the rocker arcs about its center pivot, thereby riding off the valve centerline. Naturally, this causes rocker, valve-stem and valve-guide wear.

Manley also offers two pushrods for the little Chevy. Whereas the stockers are 7.794-inches long, the Manley units are available either 0.050- or 0.100-inch shorter. If you mill the block 0.050 to correct any number of register defects, the heel of the rocker arm will remain in the same location (distance above the block) while the nose will be 0.075-inch lower due to the 1.5:1 ratio.

Things get more complicated in the area of valve-train geometry when a high-lift cam is installed. This could cause the rocker nose to ride right to the very edge of the valve stem, or even off it. This side-loads the valves and guides, places the springs in an unnatural bind and generally leads to a short life for a lot of components. Shorter pushrods can then be used to restore the angle of the rockers to stock.

Even though the Chevy "rocker-on-a-stud" valve-actuating mechanism is widely copied, low cost and practically idiot-proof, high-performance enthusiasts have long wondered just what could be done with the little Chevy if a really good rocker-shaft assembly were used. When the Chevy was first introduced, a couple of aftermarket attempts to produce such a rocker-shaft kit got started, but none got off the ground. Fifteen years after the introduction of the engine such a kit became a reality. With fifteen years of development on all of the high-performance valve gear surrounding the rocker/stud arrangement it will be interesting to see if the rocker shaft is the hot setup that everyone thought it would be.

The rocker shaft for the Chevy is manufactured by Webster Racing of Mill Valley, California and is the brainchild of Marvin Webster who reasoned that valve-train geometry could be much more accurately controlled with a shaft than a stud. It is known that the studs do flex under high RPM, high-load operation. There are even stud girdles (Jomar) which tie all of the studs together to negate the flex of the individual studs which changes valve lash and thus the effective cam timing.

As we said, the Webster shaft arrangement is relatively new and unproved on the race course — but it is mentioned here because it will be interesting to see if, with some experimentation, even more horsepower can be gained from the little Chevy.

On the LT-1 heads or slant-pluggers with the screw-in studs, the shaft kit may be installed without pulling the heads from the engine. All of the earlier heads must be pulled and the stud bosses milled slightly to provide a parallel seating surface for the rocker-shaft stands.

The kit contains the rocker shaft, stands, mounting hardware, rockers, valve covers and all of the necessary oil lines and fittings which are needed to provide lubrication for the rocker arrangement.

Oil is taken from the front of the block and routed through the valve covers and into the hollow shaft. As we said, only time and competition will prove the merit of the rocker-shaft arrangement. Theoretically, it should permit the use of a wilder cam, promote longer component life and higher RPM. The higher flank rate cams could then be coupled with even heavier springs without danger of moving the studs around.

Incidentally, Webster Racing is at 244 Shoreline Highway, Mill Valley, CA 94941. The kits range in price from $230 to $340, depending on the application.

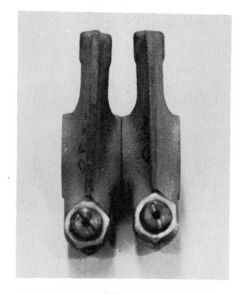

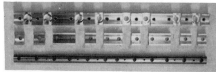

Appearing for all the world as if it grew there, the Webster rocker-shaft assembly bolts onto any small-block head. Oiling is through a fitting on the end of the hollow-steel rocker shaft which rests on the machined aluminum block and is held in place by the smaller aluminum pieces which bolt into place. Rockers are forged with slightly different configurations used for intake and exhaust. Lash adjustment is by conventional screw and jam nut method on the pushrod end of rocker. The competition kit, which includes dry pushrods and valve caps, allows blocking off the oil to the lifters and reduces the pushrod weight because there is no oil in the pushrods.

NEEDLE-BEARING ROCKER ARMS

Do you really need them? Probably not! A lot of $$$ are wasted every year by enthusiasts who whip out their checkbooks before putting their minds in gear. Spending money is apparently less painful than thinking . . . or perhaps more enjoyable. Somehow, the possibility that super-expensive trick parts *may not be required* never seems to sink in. Parts manufacturers and speed-shop owners love their customers for their inability or refusal to think about what is really necessary in their engines.

Your street-driven engine is not launched from every stop light with the RPM approaching 8000 as are the engines of drag racers. You are in a different ball game. And, we might mention in passing that a lot of the small-block drag racers still use the stock rocker arms, especially those that don't get the parts "laid on them" for free. Your street machine is not equipped with a dry-sump system that needs reduced circulation to the rockers so that the sump can be kept adequately pumped out in long-distance events.

Here are some facts which you may have overlooked. Needle-bearing rockers are often used because they reduce the side loading on the valve stems, thereby reducing friction and perhaps reducing heat. This is the single positive reason for using these rockers in anything. Needle rockers aggravate stud breakage to say nothing of the fact that the rockers themselves break. This makes it essential to use special rocker studs or to shotpeen the radius at the top of the stud base. And, the the top of the stud must be machined flat to allow using the setscrew inside of the adjustment nut used for these rockers. The stud-breakage problem could lead you to buy a stud-stabilizing device such as the Jomar Stud Girdle. Now you have doubled what you had planned to put into your engine when you started out to add the special rocker arms.

As with stock rockers, not all of the needle-bearing types provide full lift. The ratio can be less than 1.5:1 and you'll have to install a set in an engine to find out whether the type that you are thinking of buying gives full lift. Further, the longer rocker-adjusting nuts may interfere with the rocker covers so that you have to use double gaskets or shims for installation.

When using the needle-bearing rockers, the edge-orifice mechanical lifters should be used to reduce the flow of oil to the heads, see page 87.

If you have had problems with your stock rockers, check out that rocker-arm geometry before throwing brick bats at the stock parts. Getting the geometry correct — as described elsewhere in the chapter — could solve your problems for a lot less money than you had been planning to spend. Stock parts nearly always get the job done if you'll think about what's happening and remedy the problems which have been caused by deviating from stock combinations.

Most needle-bearing rockers are aluminum and therefore have no fatigue resistance. They have been known to fail. One builder claims six hours as a maximum "safe" life for an aluminum rocker. George Bolthoff and Bill King both suggested that a maximum of 2,000 racing miles could be run before replacing them. And, the roller tip on these arms is not particularly helpful, regardless of what the ads say. So, you might be better off with steel rockers.

A competitor, name of Ford, supplies needle-trunnion assemblies, DOZX 6A585-A ($6.25 each) for their Trans-Am Boss 302 rockers, C60Z 6564-B ($1.80 each). These fit the big-block studs as if they were designed for that specific application. So, for about $130 list price you can have 1.75:1 steel rocker arms and elsewhere in this chapter we tell you where the big-block stud can be located on the small-block head for just this purpose. However, you should have the rockers Tuftrided because Ford says that's the way to do it. As with the Chevy parts, Ford's vary, and it may be necessary to go through a whole bunch of them to get the rocker geometry sorted out as you'd like it.

Ron Sperry points out that while these rockers will give more lift than the Mark IV rockers, annealing and relocation of the oiling hole is required. The re-case-hardening and Tufftriding treatment is too complex to list here, but if you are making this modification, Bill King can handle these modifications along with the actual stud relocation, pushrod-guide-plate modification and the needed pushrods. In general, the high-lift rocker arm setup *is not a simple bolt-on.*

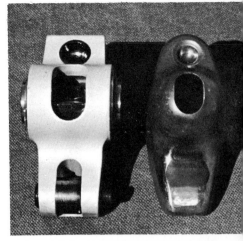

Roller-tip needle-bearing aluminum rocker arm compared with a stock Chevy part. Stock piece represents the simple, direct and extremely reliable approach used throughout all Chevrolet engines. Correctly installed stock rockers are adequate for almost all types of racing. Their use can help to reduce your engine-building costs drastically!

Boss 302 needle-bearing rocker is a steel stamping which should be Tufftrided before severe competition use. Needle bearings are held onto precision trunnion by rocker sides. Special nut supplied with the trunnion assembly requires machining flat on top of rocker stud to work with setscrew locking device in nut. This rocker could be used with the 1.7 big-block rocker conversion described on pages 92 and 93. It cannot be used to replace the stock 1.5 rockers.

Three Chevy timing chains. Left is split-bushing type used in some trucks. Center is Link-Belt type used in hi-perf engines since '67 and in all '65-'66 models. Right is narrow Morse chain typical of low-perf big-blocks since '67 model introduction. Cast nylon teeth are often non-concentric to sprocket hub creating weird cylinder-to-cylinder timing variations.

TIMING CHAINS & SPROCKETS

Small-block timing chains and sprockets are not all alike. Three styles have been supplied directly from Chevrolet. First was a 3/4-inch-wide Link-Belt chain used in all 1955-66 models. The Morse chain, introduced in '67, is 5/8-inch wide. The third chain is sometimes referred to as a roller chain, even though the split bushings do not roll. It is used in some truck applications. It is generally accepted that the truck item will stand more punishment than any of the other Chevy timing chain/sprocket combinations. P/N for the chain is 3735411, crank sprocket is 3735413, cam sprocket is 3735412. These parts will fit any year or size of the small-block Chevy.

It is generally accepted that the wider Link-Belt-style chain is the one to use for high-performance applications because it is less prone to stretching than the skinny chain. See caption, right.

If you are building an all-out racing engine, consider the Cloyes Tru-Roller chain 9-3100 which lists for about $60 for the chain and two sprockets. It is stronger than the stock chain and less prone to stretch than any of the stock chains. The chain is made for Cloyes by Reynolds, the famous English firm, and the solid-bushing rollers really *roll.* Cloyes guarantees that this chain eliminates chain-stretch problems and states what the timing error due to stretch or slop will be when the chain is installed. It has been measured to be only 3/4° at the cam, or 1.5° crankshaft, as compared to a typical 3° stretch error common with split-bushing-type "roller" chain sold as a truck replacement by Chevrolet and touted as roller chain by other timing-chain suppliers. Cloyes' cam sprocket is Tuftrided and Magnafluxed cast-iron, dynamically balanced to 1/8 inch ounce at 5,000 RPM. That's equivalent to 10,000 engine RPM! The pitch diameter of the sprockets is larger to accommodate the large rollers used in the Reynolds chain, so you can't buy just the chain alone to work with your stock sprockets.

You'll note in the accompanying photo that there are three keyways in the crank sprocket to allow installing the cam with the standard setting or 4° advanced or 4° retarded.

Three keyways in Cloyes Tru-Roller crank sprocket allow installing cam in stock position or advanced or retarded by 4°. Drill indentations in cam sprocket are made during dynamic balancing of this part — another plus that makes these sets worth their price. Below — Tru-Roller's wide teeth and bushings compared with Chevy truck set at right.

If you have had your block line bored and the cam-to-crank center distance has been reduced approximately 0.005-inch, Cloyes offers sets on special order with sprockets having larger pitch diameters to compensate for the closer positioning of the crank and cam.

Cloyes also offers a high-performance split-bushing timing-chain set which uses the same type of steel crank sprocket with three keyways, but without the no-stretch feature of the Tru-Roller set.

Two lifter types used with mechanical lifter cams. Inertia-flapper type (left) is called "piddle-valve." Edge-orifice (clearance-orificing) lifter should be used as is in engines with needle-bearing rockers, but 0.003 to 0.005-inch flat should be added between hole and groove (arrow) if engine has stock rockers. Edge-orifice lifters reduce total oil circulation by 10 to 20%—especially helpful for dry-sump oiling or restricted oil-pan capacity. These lifters usually eliminate any need for restricting the lifter galleries. Racer Brown offers pushrods with restricted oil flow if further help is needed to cut down oil circulation.

TAPPETS (valve lifters/cam followers)

Regardless of what you call these parts that convert the rotary motion of the cam lobes to a linear motion for the valve opening and closing, they are extremely important . . . and deserve more than a passing mention.

The camshaft and lifters must be "compatible" or extremely rapid wear results. Why? Because the force of the valve spring, multiplied by the rocker arm ratio, works to keep the tappet in contact with the cam lobe. This force squeezes out and wipes away or vaporizes the lubricant, thereby promoting wear. Unless the metal types of these rubbing parts are exactly compatible in metal composition, hardness and surface finish, very fast wear results.

Tappet faces are not flat incidentally. They are slightly convex with about a 30-inch radius. This is done to make the tappet turn as it works against the camshaft, thereby constantly exposing a new surface under the load so that the cam lobe and tappet will not wear out in a hurry. So, don't face tappets flat with a valve facer or you'll be rebuilding your engine. You can quickly check whether tappets have the desired curvature by holding the faces of two tappets together. They should "rock." If they have "gone flat"—get new ones.

If tappets have a few small pits in them—without any swirl marks, radial lines or other evidence of excessive wear—it's o.k. to use them again—if they are not flat. But, you'll have to install them "back home" against the same lobes of the old cam, right where they ran originally. If you are installing a new cam or a reground cam, spend the money for a new set of genuine Chevrolet lifters (or use the lifters recommended by the cam grinder). Lubricate the cam and lifters carefully as described in the engine assembly chapter. Hydraulic tappets are highly recommended, even for high-performance engines.

Two Chevy mechanical valve lifters are available for the small block. One, P/N 5232695, appears similar to a hydraulic lifter and controls oil going out the top of the lifter with an internal flapper valve actuated by inertia. This is the most common type of big-block Chevy lifter and it's also used in the Z-28 version of the small-block engine. Lifter 5231585 is found in the 327 engines manufactured from 1962 to 1965 and also some of the later 302 engines. The lifter controls oil moving out of the top on the basis of clearance available between the lifter and the bore. Using this lifter reduces the total oil-circulation rate into the head by as much as 20% — which

should be considered if you can't easily add to the capacity of the oil pan in your vehicle or plan to install a dry sump oil system on the engine.

Although it is a commonly used trick among the experienced engine builders, Gerry Thompson of Troy Promotions was the first to tell us about what to do to the lifter bases to get better longevity and to ensure that the cam has the best possible chance of living—especially during those first few critical minutes right after the engine is fired up. The factory finish on new tappets or lifters is "too aggressive" so Gerry and other engine builders recommend that you prepare the tappet faces by chucking each tappet in a lathe and running the lathe at high speed. Hold a piece of solvent-wetted No. 600 Wet-or-Dry abrasive paper against the tappet base very lightly so as to "dust it off." You can hand rub the tappets against abrasive paper supported on a flat surface (such as a piece of plate glass). Thompson also suggests that the best reliability combination is a used cam with used lifters treated as just mentioned. Next in order of reliability — or freedom from trouble — are new lifters, treated as recommended and installed onto a new cam. "Scariest of all and most failure prone," according to Thompson, "are new lifters installed onto a used cam — even if they have been correctly treated with abrasive paper and installed with correct lubricating techniques."

This arrangement is Cloyes' "Super Chain." Double-row roller chain runs on precision sprockets. Crank sprocket has three key ways to allow up to ±4 degrees adjustment.

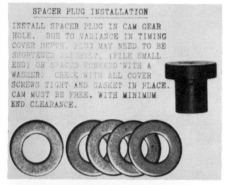

SPACER PLUG INSTALLATION

INSTALL SPACER PLUG IN CAM GEAR HOLE. DUE TO VARIANCE IN TIMING COVER DEPTH, PLUG MAY NEED TO BE SHORTENED PROPERLY. (FILE SMALL END) OR SPACED FORWARD WITH A WASHER. CHECK WITH ALL COVER SCREWS TIGHT AND GASKET IN PLACE. CAM MUST BE FREE, WITH MINIMUM END CLEARANCE.

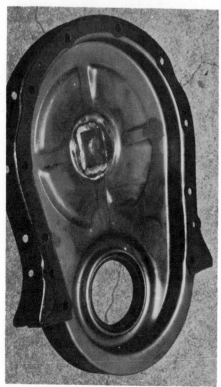

All of the cam grinders offer simple little spacer plugs which prevent the cam from working forward in their journals and altering timing. Plugs are generally made of Teflon for minimum friction between the plug and the timing chain cover. If you run a button in the nose of a cam to keep it from walking back and forth in the block, braze or weld a small piece of metal to the inside of the timing cover to strengthen cover area where button touches.

Cam thrust buttons are sometimes used on the cam nose. This needle-bearing type sells for about $5 and works against a 1/8-inch-thick steel pad brazed inside the cam cover. About 0.008-inch end clearance will end spark scatter problems because the end button will keep the cam from walking back-and-forth in the block. Roller cams without "straddle"-type tappets are the worst offenders in this regard and an end button should be considered absolutely essential for any engine so equipped.

HYDRAULIC TAPPETS

If you are building a street machine or a street/strip machine, give careful consideration to the use of hydraulic tappets. Because these almost never need adjustment, thay can take much of the work out of owning a high-performance car. As you can see from the cam comparison tables earlier in the chapter, hydraulic-lifter cams are available with a wide range of lift and timing characteristics to fit any street or street/strip—and many all-out-competition applications.

Stock Chevy hydraulic tappets, P/N 3799644, are recommended for your stock or reworked engine equipped with a hydraulic-lifter camshaft. These lifters, when preloaded by turning the adjustment 1/8 to 1/4 turn in from clatter, operate faultlessly beyond 7000 RPM if the cam lobe shape and valve-train combination is "right-on."

Chevy expert Larry Eave points out that hesitation and rough idling which often accompany turning in the adjustment from clatter can be avoided by backing off the nut until the clatter occurs, then just tightening the adjustment nut enough to eliminate the clatter. Do not establish the preload at that time, but continue to the next valve. Adjust it the same way and continue through the entire valve mechanism. When all of the valves have been set at the "just-not-clattering" point, shut off the engine. Now establish the 1/8 to 1/4 turn preload at each adjustment nut. It works!

Never run old tappets on a new cam or mix your tappets if you are reinstalling the old tappets on your old cam. Keep each tappet with the cam lobe on which it has been running or replace all of them. You can precondition the lifter bottoms with abrasive paper as described in the previous section.

Avoid the so-called fast-leak racing tappets as these are known to collapse at both idle and high RPM.

VALVE SPRINGS

If you are fairly new to the game of putting a little heat to a small-block Chevy, maybe we can save you some time here. If you're an old hand at this and have been fighting the battle of valve springs on small blocks we can't offer anything you haven't learned the hard way. If the engine is going on the street or moderate racing with a cam such as the Chevy 3927140, then the heavy-duty, optional Chevy spring 3927142 is the way to fly. The identifying paint code on these springs is reddish-brown. This spring combination is an outer spring with a damper. Specs are 110 pounds on the seat (1.7 inches) and 260 pounds open (1.25 inches). In all applications, CHECK FOR COIL BIND, regardless of cam. This spring coil-binds easily and it is suggested that lift be limited to 0.485-inch maximum. Use with 0.510-inch-lift cams shortens its life. The spring installs in the stock spring pockets.
spring pockets.

If you install the service mechanical cam 3965754 or any aftermarket cam with over 0.500-inch lift, a better spring is required. At the time this book went to press, Chevrolet did not have anything to fill the bill, but several springs are available. We found four, and there are probably others.

One of these fits the stock spring pockets. This Racer Brown's No. 962 with damper, which sells for $32 per set. It provides 115 lbs. seat load at 1.75-inch installed height and 330 lbs. at 0.520-inch lift. It is limited to 0.530 lift. The other three springs we found all require enlarging the spring pockets in the head. This is somewhat risky on late heads: the LT-1 and slant-plug style heads with guide plates—or with any of the heads with the three-bolt accessory-mounting pads on one end. These are very thin around the end spring pockets and it is easy to cut into the water jacket on those. King Engine Service offers their Part No. 439 which provides 135 lbs. seat pressure at 1.75-inch installed height; 304 lbs. at 0.550-inch lift. A set of these costs $44. Traco's T207 inner/outer spring set provides 125 lbs. seat and 300 lbs. open pressure at 0.500-inch lift. Price is $44 per set. Racer Brown has a set which includes a 957-A outer with a 957-C inner for $56 per set. This combination provides 110 lbs. seat load at 1.75-inch installed height;

365 lbs. at 0.560-inch lift—400 lbs. at 0.625-inch lift. When this combination is used with a roller-tappet camshaft, the installed height is reduced to 1.687-inch and the seat load then increases to 135 lbs. and the open load goes up to 395 lbs. at 0.560 or 440 lbs. at 0.625-inch. This spring combination is assembled with an interference fit. Opening the spring pockets is accomplished with a loaner cutter (used with the shim technique described below) which provides a slight interference fit in the head (about 0.003") to provide an opening for the 1.440-inch-diameter spring. Some street machines are equipped with just the outer set of 957-A springs (which includes the damper spring) at $38 per set. This provides 105 lbs. seat load at 1.687-inch installed height and 330 lbs. at 0.550-inch lift.

Chevrolet's own "bulletproof" big-block spring can be used when the 1.7 rocker arms are installed. This requires extreme care to open the spring pockets without opening up the water jacket. Use a 1.48-inch-diameter cutter with a radius on its outer edge. Place a 1/32-inch shim over the guide and cut the seat down until the cutter contacts the shim, leaving a center step-up in the pocket. This should be shaped by the cutter to locate the inner spring, too. Use of the springs, P/N 3989354 ($6 each) requires a special retainer to provide the correct installed height. This should be 1.9-inch for a seat load of 158 lbs. and an open load of 350 lbs. The inner spring requires a 1.8-inch installed height.

When such large springs are used, clearance between the bottom of the rocker and the top of the retainer must be checked throughout the operating cycle. Depending on the retainer, rocker and head machining, the stock rocker cannot always be used.

It is not unusual to hear of an engine builder installing heavier valve springs without making any other changes to the valve train. There is no sense in running more valve-spring pressure than is absolutely required because this just takes more HP to turn the cam over in its bearings. Don't buy the all-out triple valve springs for your high-lift

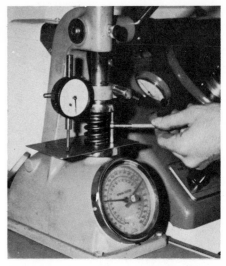

A given spring height and pressure are measured on a special scale built for the job. The hand-held snap gage simply makes the job go faster on a long run of springs to be checked.

Traco aluminum retainer (hard-anodized) and dual counter-wound valve spring combination is used as standard item in many high-revving small-block engines. It is the same diameter as the stock spring so the spring seats do not have to be opened up.

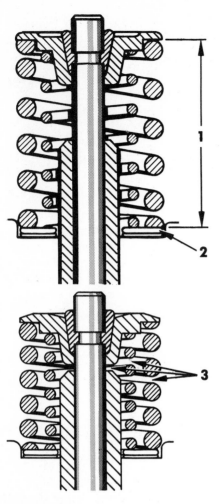

1. Installed height must be correct for each spring.
2. Valve springs seat on heavier shims, thinner shims go against head.
3. With valve at full lift, inner/outer spring coils should have 0.012-inch clearance between each coil; retainer and guide — at least 0.060 inch.

NOTE: Pushrods have hardened-steel inserted tips on one end. This end must be installed to contact the rocker arm. It may be difficult to spot which end this is on a used pushrod, but look carefully and you should be able to see a hairline where the tube joins the tip. New pushrods have the rocker-arm end marked with a blue stripe.

hydraulic or your street-mechanical camshaft. Use the factory recommendation for the camshaft—nothing more—nothing less!

Measuring valve springs

An accurate spring-testing fixture is necessary for these tests. Your local garage or parts house may have one. The tester is essential, so look 'til you find one. Installed-height specifications are the next thing that you'll need.

Note that the inner spring sits on a step in the retainer. Using the retainer when testing the springs simplifies the job. Remove the springs, place them in the spring tension tester, compress them to the installed height and note the reading. This is the seat-pressure measurement.

Now simulate valve opening by compressing the spring assembly to full lift and read the open pressure. The important thing here is to watch for coil bind, or solid stack, when the valve is fully opened. The springs should have at least 0.060-inch travel beyond the full valve lift for a margin of safety.

Tension on all valve springs should measure within 10 pounds for use in a high-performance engine. Every spring must be tested, even brand-new ones.

When you have established that the springs are within specification, cut a length of welding rod to the installed height for the outer spring. This will be 1.70-inch for the stock high-performance springs. It may be different for springs provided by a cam manufacturer. Install the valves in the guides and add the retainers and keepers without any springs.

Pull against the retainer to hold the valve against the seat. Insert the measuring rod between the valve-spring seat and the retainer. There will probably be a gap: the rod will be shorter than the space between the spring seat in the head and the retainer ledge. Insert valve-spring shims between the end of the rod and the retainer to take up the gap. Remove the retainer and *install those shims over that guide.* When stacking shims, always stack thin shims below thick ones to avoid crushing the thin shims. Mark that retainer so that it can be reinstalled on that

valve. Do this for each of the valves. Unless the springs are installed at the correct height, you will not have the correct seat/open pressures and valves may float 'way before the desired RPM has been reached.

In general, you can figure that springs which have run for more than six months in a passenger car will not be usable for an engine which is to be turned to specification RPM.

Spring-retainer-to-valve-guide clearance

Make this check before installing the springs, but after any seals have been installed. A machinist's scale can be held alongside of the retainer as you move the valve to its specification lift. There must be at least 1/16 to 1/8-inch clearance between the valve-guide end or installed valve-stem seal and the spring retainer when the valve is in the open position. Valve guides may stick out of the cylinder head far enough to interfere with the spring retainers if a high-lift camshaft is also being used. It may be necessary to machine valve-guide ends when a high-lift cam is installed. Most valve guides are installed with adequate clearance for the stock low-lift hydraulic cam.

RETAINERS

Valve-spring retainers are another of those romance items where the good stuff in the HD Parts List is often overlooked because the enthusiast engine builder is blinded by all of the trick multi-colored aluminum retainers offered by the cam grinders. General Kinetics' catalog tells it like it is, "High-strength steel retainers are recommended whenever the engine is to be driven at high RPM over an extended period of time such as in sports-racing or dual-purpose cars. If aluminum retainers are used they should be inspected and replaced periodically."

A major point of erosion is usually found where the flat damper coil contacts the aluminum retainer. If you see aluminum specks floating around or deposited on the head when you remove the rocker covers, this indicates that the retainers are being eroded by the springs. The oil may look "glittery."

While not all cam grinders will agree with us, we'll stick our necks out and say that you won't be wrong in using steel valve-spring retainers, preferably the best stock ones, P/N 3896934. This recommendation applies to any and all uses except perhaps pro-stock drag-racing engines where the need for higher revs could make it worthwhile to spend the $90 required for a set of Mr. Manley's *titanium* retainers.

Aluminum valve-spring retainers must be used with care with any valve spring giving near 300 pounds open-load pressure because the lower side of the retainer can be eroded away by the contact with the vibrating spring, especially in a valve-float situation. Hard-anodizing the retainers and closely fitting them to the valve springs helps to retard such wear. The factory supplies steel retainers on all small blocks.

LIMITING OIL TO THE LIFTERS

There is some disagreement as to whether the oil supply to the lifters should be restricted at the two entry holes at the rear cam bearing annulus. Chevy engineers we talked with insisted that the edge-orifice mechanical lifters are an adequate restriction in themselves and that no added means of reducing oil circulation be installed. But, several small-block engine builders, including Bob Joehnck and Bill King, were equally insistent in recommending that the oil supply to the lifters be choked down *in racing engines only*.

These men feel that the small block simply feeds too much oil to the lifters — which in turn places too much oil in the "upstairs" or rocker arm area of a racing engine. The danger, they point out, is not in overlubrication, but having both rocker covers full of oil and a minimum amount in the sump around the pickup. There are two slightly different ways to make such a modification to reduce the oil flow into the lifter galleries.

Turn the bare block upside down and look at the rear cam bearing area (with no cam bearing installed). Notice three holes in the deep groove (annulus) The center hole connects to the main oil gallery. Leave this hole alone — or open it to the same size as the hole between the cam bearing and the main bearing as described in the block prepping chapter. But, if you do this remember that you are working with a very long drill and it's easy to break the drill bit in the process. The two outer holes feed the lifter galleries and they can be tapped with a 5/16-18 tap. Two socket setscrews with this thread can be drilled to 0.080-in. and installed as restrictor jets. These get screwed in place just before installing the cam bearings in the clean block.

Bill King goes about it slightly differently. He taps the two rear holes as previously mentioned and installs setscrews without any holes in them. This shuts off the oil to the lifters as supplied by the rear feed holes. He then drills two 0.080-in. holes from the annulus behind the front cam bearing into the lifter galleries — one hole into each of the galleries. This makes the lifters the last thing that are in the lubrication chain.

Don't be surprised that the oil pressure becomes uncommonly high (80-90 psi) when the engine is cold. Remember that the distributor shaft drives the oil pump — which is heavily loaded when putting out this much pressure. So, don't jazz the throttle when the engine is cold and such pressures are showing.

Start "living" with the oil-pressure gage once the engine is installed in the car. In other words, you should become familiar with what the gage does with a dead-cold engine and where the pressure reads after a given warm-up period and then how the pressure is as the car is going through the lights (drag race) or along a certain straightaway in a road race. If reading the pressure gage becomes second nature, you will have a ready reference if trouble develops. A bearing problem would mean an instant change in the oil-pressure reading, for instance. This is just more along the line of what Bill Hielscher has to say. about living with the car in the tuning chapter.

For a racing engine with needle-bearing rockers only, some benefits can be had by restricting the oil going to the lifters. The two outer holes shown can be tapped and plugged with a drilled allen screw. Leave that center hole alone though.

Here's what you'll need to restrict oil to the lifters as described in the text — a tap, two socket setscrews and a drill to run through the centerline of the screws before they are installed. This is not recommended for street use.

PUSHRODS

There is only one diameter, one length pushrod from Chevy for the small block. Buy them at the Chevy parts counter—use them. When a competition engine is torn down for a rebuild, check them all for being straight and for signs of galling on the tips.

With all of the problems that aftermarket pushrods cause in small blocks, you should have a very good reason for using other than the stock Chevy.

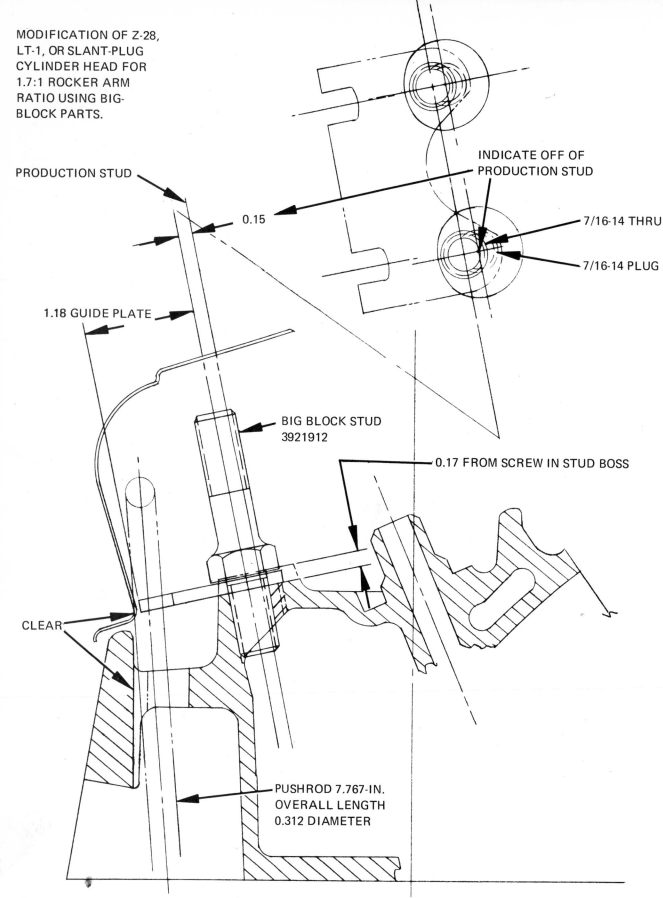

MODIFICATION OF Z-28, LT-1, OR SLANT-PLUG CYLINDER HEAD FOR 1.7:1 ROCKER ARM RATIO USING BIG-BLOCK PARTS.

PRODUCTION STUD

0.15

INDICATE OFF OF PRODUCTION STUD

7/16-14 THRU

7/16-14 PLUG

1.18 GUIDE PLATE

BIG BLOCK STUD 3921912

0.17 FROM SCREW IN STUD BOSS

CLEAR

PUSHROD 7.767-IN. OVERALL LENGTH 0.312 DIAMETER

Modifying the small-block head for the 1.7 large-block rocker arm assemblies is no easy task. It should not be attempted by other than an accomplished machinist. Drawing shows correct location of the big-block stud as related to the production stud. If you intend to farm out such work, Bill King says that this job should be worth about $160, including the new pushrods, but not including the other parts. His shop will do the work.

Head machined for 1.7 Mark IV rockers and the Mark IV (big-block) springs. Arrow indicates where casting is thin (both end pockets) on all late heads which have the three-hole accessory-mounting pads. Spring pockets must be machined by using a shim over the guide so that the pocket is not deepened. Use a radiused cutter so that minimum material is removed at the O.D. Never deepen a small-block spring pocket to get more installed spring height. Use different retainers to make such adjustments if needed.

BIG-BLOCK ROCKERS ON SMALL-BLOCK HEADS

Smokey Yunick stepped out on a limb more than a year before this book went to press and began experimenting with running the big-block rocker, stud and ball on the small-block head. Smokey didn't get into the project without some thought — and even though the real work of the project has now been taken care of with the accompanying drawing of what needs to be done, no one should just attempt to "tack on" the big-block rocker system. Smokey feels that up to 7600 RPM, the stock 1.5:1 ratio rockers work as well as any combination he's ever tried on the little engine. Other builders we talked with feel that lift helps all through the range — and far below the 7600 figure. In any event, the 1.7 ratio of the big-block rockers gets the valves off their seats in a hurry to improve air flow through the cylinder head. It increases the total lift available at any point in the operating cycle.

There is more than just a casual amount of machine work which must be effected in order to make the conversion. We can't do machine work in a book, but maybe we can point out some of the problems and pitfalls of the project.

In the first place, there is little point in going to the big-block rockers unless you intend to use the larger diameter big-block valve springs. As we've pointed out elsewhere in our discussion of the stock small-block valve springs, they simply will not give good service over long periods of time at extended RPM. So you should go to the Mark IV valve spring along with the Mark IV rocker. Smokey warns that on several occasions he has run into water when attempting to enlarge the valve-spring seating surface. The problem comes on the valve-spring seats serving the end-most cylinders. To attach the project prudently, this machine work should probably be done before any other steps are taken with a head; the thought being that if you must scrap a head, there's no sense in scrapping one which has a lot of time in it.

Secondly, you'll have to lay the accompanying drawing on a competent machinist along with a set of Z-28/LT-1 or slant-plug heads so he can figure out how much time it will take him to do the job — so he can do the job without losing his shirt or without driving you to the poorhouse in one easy pass. The small-block screw-in studs must be removed from the head. Then an iron plug must be tightened into the head with the threads coated with an epoxy. Then that area of the head must be milled.

The third step is to drill and tap all of the holes for the big-block rocker studs. Notice that the centerline of the big-block stud is moved to the outboard side of the head 0.150-inch from the centerline of the production (small block) rocker stud. This is a must! Do not try to screw the big-block studs in the small-block head and run the big-block rockers because this just will not work. Notice also that there is a pushrod-clearance problem with the outer valve-cover mating surface of the head and that things are also on the tight side where the pushrod goes through the head. This will have to be touched with a die grinder and checked carefully when everything goes together for a checking assembly of the engine.

The last fly in the ointment is relatively simple — the stock rocker covers won't fit on over all that high-lift rocker gear, although as pictures on these pages indicate, Smokey went to the trouble to modify stock covers to do the job. You might find accessory covers which will clear the rockers.

Yunick obviously chose this high-ratio rocker method of getting more lift so that a flat-tappet cam ground on a stock Chevrolet camshaft with the stock lifter diameter could be used to provide lift which would take advantage of good-flowing ports. It should be noted, however, that there are other methods to get similar lift figures. There are roller camshafts which will give lifts in the 0.640-inch range, with 1.5 rockers. And, there are needle-bearing roller tip rockers with 1.6:1 rocker ratios (Crane) which can be used with these cams to give net lifts in the neighborhood of 0.620-inch. This can be done without remachining the cylinder head and without any need for the extra-large-diameter big-block "bulletproof" springs.

We are completely sincere in suggesting that you should run the rocker arms and valve springs which the cam grinder recommends. And, high lifts— especially those over 1/2-inch, should be approached with great care by the experienced racing engine builder—and not at all by the novice. There are just too many little things that can rise to bite you when you start playing with lots of lift. Lots of valve-spring pressure does one thing in a hurry—especially to a street-driven machine—it keeps you busy changing cams. Anything more than 320 lbs. open pressure and 0.520-inch lift is *too much* for the street, according to Racer Brown.

Arrows indicate clearance bumps for the 1.7 rockers. Aluminum covers could not be used to provide this much clearance. Smokey Yunick Camaro engine.

ROCKER ARM COVERS

Rocker arm covers might not seem like a part of the valve mechanism, but they can interfere with valve action. When using a high-lift camshaft with needle-bearing rocker arms, bolting the valve covers on may open a valve or the adjusting nuts could hit the built-in oil drippers. Don't think for a minute that this kind of problem hasn't created its share of frustrated mechanics. Spread machinists' blue dye on the inside of the stock covers before installing them so you can check whether the rockers are hitting. Look for bright spots when you pull the covers off after turning the engine through several revolutions.

If there are places where the rockers contact the stock steel covers, place the cover over a socket and dimple it slightly with a ball-peen hammer. With solid aluminum covers such as Corvettes or those made by Edelbrock or Mickey Thompson, use a rotary file to make clearance. If the oil drippers have to be modified for clearance, leave the exhaust drippers intact if you are using stock rockers. If you cannot do this, get other covers or use your stock ones. If the interference is severe, double gaskets or spacers can be used to get the covers away from the adjusting nuts on needle-bearing rockers. Make sure that any covers you buy have adequate clearance. If your car is a 1969 or later model, be sure there is an oil-filler hole in one of the covers. "No-name" finned covers, as made by several manufacturers, look very nice. However, these do not include smog-equipment fittings or openings and some have no provisions for an oil-filler cap.

CAM BREAK-IN TECHNIQUE

Most camshaft wear occurs in the first 30 minutes of operation. Professional racers are known to set up their engines with lightweight single valve springs, douse the lifters and cam liberally with E.O.S. and then overfill the crankcase. The engine is then run for 30 minutes to an hour at not less than 2500 RPM with zero idle-speed time.

New valve-train parts go through quite a change in lash during run-in and the lash should be checked frequently until it is stabilized. Remember to check the lift at the valves to determine whether any of the cam lobes are experiencing undue wear.

Valve lash is rechecked after the fast-idle run-in and any excessive lash is carefully noted so that cam lobe can be measured for lift before running the engine again. If the cam lift is not up to specification, the lobe has worn and it is time for another camshaft. This can and does occur. If the cam has not worn, then the valve springs are changed for the correct ones and the crankcase is drained and refilled with racing oil.

Use a fitting which screws into a spark-plug hole in conjunction with compressed air to hold the valves against the seats while changing the springs without removing the heads. Valve spring compressors which work in conjunction with the rocker-arm studs are available.

The run-in procedure just described is especially recommended for flat-tappet camshafts which are to be run with very high spring pressures.

HOW TO SET VALVE LASH

1. Stabilize the oil and water temperature by idling the engine for at least 30 minutes for a cold engine and about 10 minutes for an already warm engine. While the engine is stabilizing, remove the rocker-cover bolts and whatever else is necessary so that the rocker covers can be removed rapidly.

2. Shut off engine. Remove the most difficult to remove rocker cover. Inspect for burned balls or broken valve springs. Run a magnet around the head and inside of the rocker cover to pick up any chips, etc.

Start engine and lash the valves to the specifications shown in the table. Lash should be adjusted for a snug fit on the feeler gage. The rocker arm must not be cocked to one side or a faulty lash will be the result. The feeler gage should be inserted and removed straight in toward the rocker-arm stud—NOT pulled from the side of the valve stem. The feeler gage should be free of burrs on the end, of course. If a feeler gage is used to check clearance while the engine is running, consider that gage as a throwaway item after lashing the valves one or two times. When correctly lashed, the valve train should have only a slight mechanical noise at idle and the engine should idle slightly roughly at 700 to 800 RPM (street cams) or 1000 to 1200 RPM for high-performance (off-road) cams.

3. If you want to lash the valves with the engine not running, follow Racer Brown's recommendations before you ever start the engine the first time. He suggests that the flywheel or crank pulley be marked to show the point of maximum lift for a valve, then rotate the crank exactly one turn right back to the same mark so that the tappet is in the center of the cam-lobe heel. Set the clearance on that valve, preferably with the P & G gapping tool. Proceed to the next valve and repeat the operation. Once the marks are permanently made on the flywheel or crank pulley and the order of setting the valves is established, this method is very quick and much more accurate than any other. If it takes more than 10 minutes to do the first side, warm the engine by idling it again for 10 minutes with the rocker covers in place. The inspection procedures recommended in **2** should always be carried out, regardless of which valve-lashing method you choose.

Cylinder heads 8

A small-block Chevy head before any machining — the Flint plant machines and installs 600 heads an hour. This is just one more indication that the Chevy is a production engine and not a racer as it comes from the factory. You've got to help it. Arrows point to locators used for a host of machining operations.

Just as it comes from the factory — the 1969-70 Z-28/LT-1 head with the 2.02-inch intake valves and 1.60-inch exhaust valves. As you buy it, the combustion chamber holds 63.99 cc — plus or minus a cc. This is the conventional straight-plug head — not the slant-plug version. Slant-plug heads are not supplied on any of the stock engines as they come from the factory, so this extra HP has to be purchased at the local Chevy store. Valves, screw-in studs and pushrod guide plates are the same for the head pictured here and for the slant-plug head. However, not all of the Z-28/LT-1 heads have the screw-in studs.

The basic design principles of the small-block Chevy head are unique. This is especially true, considering the time of its origin and the fact that only gradual improvements and modifications have achieved the head's present-day outstanding performance. In the small-block-hardware evolution chapter we've briefly outlined the basic changes made to the head. Let's pick up the story in 1964, when Chevrolet introduced the "fuel-injection heads," called that because they were first offered on fuel-injected engines. Later they were used on the 350-horse 327 and then the factory termed the head "special high performance" and the basic design found its way onto every small-block Chevy. The current head found on new high-performance cars rolling off the assembly line have 2.02-inch intake valves and 1.60-inch exhaust valves. As of 1972 models, 1.94-inch is the size of the intake on all four-barrel Quadrajet engines except the 350 HP, 350 CID 'Vette. At the Chevy store you'll find this head under part number 3928445.

Head A is a straight-plug, small-valve, very-low-compression head which is showing up on more and more engines due to emission-control requirements. Head B is a stock slant-plug head. Notice the great difference in shape and volume of the two chambers. Head A wouldn't produce enough horsepower to pull a fat girl off a tricycle.

Slant-plug heads not only have the plugs relocated, but use an entirely different plug. The J-83 Y is for the straight-plug head, while the BL-57 fits only the slant-plug head. Notice the no-gasket, tapered seat on the BL-57.

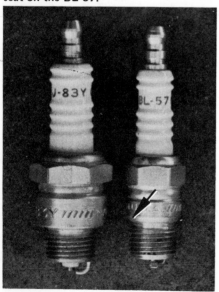

SLANT-PLUG HEADS

In late 1970, word spread like wildfire through the ranks of Chevy enthusiasts: Chevy had a new head — a slant-plug head that "made more HP." The rumor was correct — the heads appeared on a few drag-race cars (that ran better than most), the Jim Hall Trans Am Camaros, and Vic Hickey's off-road racing trucks.

The new slant-plug heads were good — plenty good. But how much different were they? Just enough to give the little Chevy a solid 10-horse increase (minimum) across the entire RPM band. Chevrolet started with RPO Z-28 heads obtained from the production line before the spark-plug machining had been done. A new plug location was added in a separate machine operation and the "slant-plug" head became available as a service part identified by P/N 3965742.

The new plug location does not restrict the head's usage as original service equipment. Small 14mm taper-seat plugs are angled toward the exhaust valve to ignite the hottest portion of the mixture initially. The new location places the plug closer to the charge center and also closer to the squish area. Maximum turbulence is directed toward the plug which improves the speed of combustion and pressure rise. By achieving optimum flame travel, maximum energy is extracted from the fuel/air mixture and transferred to the piston head with minimum piston travel because the amount of piston motion per degree of crank travel decreases approaching TDC.

Sounds good, doesn't it? There's more. Because of the increase in combustion efficiency, a higher compression ratio can be used with slant-plug heads. This is of little use on the street because very high octane fuels are no longer available, but the competitor who has access to racing gasoline can take advantage of this combustion efficiency by running as high as 12.25:1 compression.

The slant-plug heads have screw-in rocker-arm studs with pushrod-guide plates.

A set of slant-plug heads costs about $132 at the Chevy store, including screw-in studs and guide plates.

Chevrolet merely relocated the spark-plug hole in an existing casting by taking advantage of the small surface of the tapered-seat plug. This means that older heads can be reworked for the slant-plug configuration. Let's say that you've just completed a double-trick valve job and a lot of hard-earned cash on a flow-bench-porting job — only to read here that your efforts were applied to "outdated" heads. King Engine Service (address in the back of the book) takes 80 more of your dollars and your old heads. They fit the original spark-plug hole with a cast-iron plug, using high-temperature epoxy. And then they machine the new slant-plug location. In case you think that with a 1/2-inch drill motor and a big vise you can do the job yourself — don't bother, because there's no way! There is plenty of precise milling-machine work in this operation. It's absolutely no job for the run-of-the-mill machine shop because plug angle and location are quite critical.

The slant-plug head (new or reworked) is definitely the current launching pad for small-block Chevy horsepower. What we have to say about porting, CCing, and valve jobs for the little Chevy apply without favor to both slant-plug and straight-plug large-port 2.02-inch-intake-valve heads.

If you have one of the early sets of "202" heads, you should be aware that they have a cracking problem in the combustion chamber in the inlet area about 45 degrees from the spark plug. While this is not a disasterous condition, we couldn't recommend that you start with a set of these earlier heads for an expensive porting job — one more reason to spring for a set of the slant-plug heads.

Never assume that the block-mating surface of a head — even a new one — will be true. Heads warp and distort after they've been run hard and from time to time will need to be resurfaced; but a top engine builder will never assume that factory-fresh heads will be true because they rarely are straight enough for race-engine use. If you have CCed the heads, specify how much is to be taken off when grinding or milling the head surface. Otherwise, send the heads out to have a "clean-up-cut" taken. Don't specify how much is to be taken off the head; leave that to the machinist. Some heads may need as much as 0.008 inch removed before the surface is true — although this is the exception rather than the rule.

PORTING

If you pursue information on the small-block Chevy on a regular basis, you have undoubtedly encountered claims about ported, polished and reshaped heads that would produce 30% more horsepower than stock, 50 HP more than stock, were NHRA legal or were "cheater stock." In other words, to the guy building a small-block engine, confusion (not Confucius) is the name of the game when it comes time to select a set of heads.

Previous information in this chapter and that in the evolution and parts swapping chapter points to the new slant-plug head and then the Z-28/LT-1 heads as the only two "keepers" among the variety of heads available if you're serious about horsepower. But what about porting and polishing, will this increase horsepower? Maybe. If the heads are correctly reworked, they will produce more than stock heads. If they are not correctly reworked, they will produce the same or less horsepower than stock heads. Unless you are an expert, you cannot look at a set of reworked heads and tell if they are correctly done. The proof of a set of reworked heads is bolting them onto the engine and running the combination on the race track or the dyno.

One of (if not) the best small-block Chevy men in the world, Smokey Yunick was asked to comment on reworking small-block Chevy heads for more horsepower. Smokey drawled, "I just don't know where to start in describing how much work and time it takes to

So you want to do head work? This is just a small part of the flow bench facility at Smokey Yunick's. The fixture and dial indicator allow the flow to be measured at any valve lift — a very time-consuming (but rewarding) enterprise.

get one head correct — much less two heads." Yunick said that he found it impossible to duplicate four good exhaust ports on the same head without resorting to his flow bench and that he had spent as long as a full eight-hour day in attempting to get ONE exhaust PORT where he wanted it. Work of this quality is very rare and quite expensive. Smokey doesn't port or polish heads on a commercial basis — just for his own use. Good head work, regardless of where it's done, is plenty expensive. And, until the heads go on the engine you can't always be sure of whether you've gotten what you've paid for.

So where does this leave the guy with limited facilities who wants to build a small-block Chevy to the best of his abilities and resources — both of which get severely limited very quickly when dealing with head work?

Do not change the SHAPE of the ports in any way. Some horsepower can be gained by enlarging the intake port, but if you remove 0.040 inch in one place, you must be prepared to remove a like amount throughout the entire port. This means that the port must be measured sectionally throughout its length before anything is done. Then as the material is removed, the checking

must continue. Needless to say that when you are grinding on cast iron, none of this comes very easily or quickly. The job is simply more than most guys can handle.

Because the exhaust ports are shorter and smaller than the intake ports, they appear to be less work for the enthusiast and they are often opened up without regard to flow characteristics. As a consequence a lot of small-block Chevy heads are ruined for high-performance by well-meaning hot rodders who attack the exhaust port with more energy than restraint. Yunick recommends that the "backyard builder" match up the outer edge of the exhaust port with the grinder and leave any other work to a professional head grinder.

High-winding Chevys starve for air — there's no secret about that — but the problem is not solved by hogging out the intake port and then polishing it until it's "smoother than a kitten's belly." A radiused valve seat (described elsewhere in this chapter) is desirable — but not an absolute must. Don't get carried away with this. If you have the facilities and experience to do it, this step should definitely be considered for a competition engine; if not, don't lose sleep over it.

As this book goes to press, the current science regarding reshaping the combustion chamber goes something like this. Assuming that the block-mating surface of the head is true and clean, paint the areas around the combustion chambers with machinists' bluing (Dykem). Let it dry and then lay on the head gasket. Scribe the combustion chamber outline of the gasket onto the head. The combustion chamber should *not* be opened out to the edge of the head gasket as indicated by the scribed line. The most important area to rework is the shrouded side of the intake valve. Next in order of importance is the shrouded side of the exhaust. Do not grind and polish, grind and polish, ad nauseum, on a combustion chamber since every pass with a grinder or polisher lowers the compression ratio — which certainly is not the desired effect. The guide given here is intended for slant-plug and straight-plug (Z-28/LT-1) heads. If you are new to head reworking and are serious about doing a good job, you should know that most amateur attempts fail because the beginner spends three hours on the first chamber. At this point his eyes burn, his wrists hurt, his neck aches and the realization becomes all too clear: there are seven *more* combustion chambers to rework, and he really wasn't that interested in reworking heads after all. Thus, the other chambers get short-changed and the result is an engine which would have been much better off with stock heads bolted into place. If you're still with us at this point ahd have methodically opened all of the combustion chambers up in the intake valve area and all of the chambers "eyeball" the same, the job should be followed up by the CC-ing operation outlined in this chapter.

If you feel that you want to tackle the intake ports, keep several points in mind. For most high-performance applications, intake-port work is definitely needed. But, to be done correctly, the entire port should be brought up to scale and as pointed out earlier, this is easier said than done. Little, if anything, is gained by making the intake runners satin-smooth. If you have a chance to examine some of the head porting done by some of the real "names" in the business, you'll find that some deliberately leave the casting roughness on the long side of the runner. Their theory (which has some substance) is to slow down the

A prime example of Joehnck's porting — mainly a steady pass into the throat with a 70-degree stone and a bit of metal removing in the intake-valve area (lined area).

Using a high-speed die grinder for head work is fun on the first combustion chamber and torture on all the rest. This work takes a special touch and a mountain of patience. Always use goggles to keep those very small metal particles out of the eyes.

Bob Joehnck at work on a small-block head. If the engine put out 900 horsepower, he'd come to work the next morning looking for 901. Quite a guy.

mixture on that side of the runner and attempt to equalize the velocity with the mixture on the short side of the runner.

Sooner or later you'll look into an intake port and figure that the seemingly narrow area around the pushrod is choking the runner and that particular area of the runner needs to be "opened up." Yunick points out that if you'll measure the port sectionally, you'll find the smallest area of the port much closer to the valve. So you won't be gaining (and could be losing) by trying to open up the runner in the pushrod area. Again, the plan is to bring the entire runner up to scale if any work is done at all.

Until you have ported and polished a set of heads (correctly or incorrectly) you have no idea how much work is involved so don't figure you are being held up if you are quoted a price of three- to seven-hundred dollars for one pair of heads. The robbery of the situation comes through when you learn that the "double-throw-down, super-trick" heads don't work any better than a set out of a box. This is too often the case if you work with head modifiers who have not yet figured out what to do to the small-block heads, because it is *not* obvious.

Are we against ported and polished heads and are we trying to steer you away from them? No, we're just pointing out a few facts. Dollar-for-dollar, a set of expensive ported and polished heads will give you less horsepower than most any other piece of small-block high-performance equipment or modification. HOWEVER, if you want to be competitive, make no mistake about it, sooner or later you'll have to have a set of correctly modified heads. As this is being written, a number of firms scattered around the U.S. specialize in head porting. Kay Sissell Automotive and Joehnck Automotive in the Los Angeles area and King Engine Service in the Detroit area have built impressive reputations on consistent high-quality work. The addresses of these firms and others who do such work are listed on page 160.

What must be remembered is that head work is a function of the man behind the grinder and seating equipment — and the willingness of the proprietors to check each and every port on a flow bench to ensure that the ports are flowing up to their best quality. If the man who does the work correctly this week decides to quit, where does that leave you? There are no easy answers to this question. Believe us, we've tried to find them!

If you are going to have a set of heads ported and polished, start with the slant-plug heads for sure. However, if you already have four or five-hundred dollars invested in a set of ported and polished heads then have Bill King convert them to the angled-plug design for $80 and pick up another 10 horses.

Bob Joehnck, Smokey Yunick, Norm Brown and several other small-block Chevy builders report that because of a flame-propagation restriction in straight-plug heads, nothing is gained if the compression ratio is raised to more than 11:1. However, with the slant-plug heads you can get away with up to 12.25:1 and pick up a few more ponies from the compression increase.

Bob Joehnck rightfully points out that to gain real performance by porting, it's not how much material you remove, but where it is and that one flat spot or pocket ground into the port can undo the good you've ground in somewhere else along the line.

NOTE: Different head porters will approach the porting in ways which are not the same. Remember that it is the end combination that counts. Don't try to take what looks to be the best ideas of one and then attempt to incorporate all of these in one grand port. This will not work.

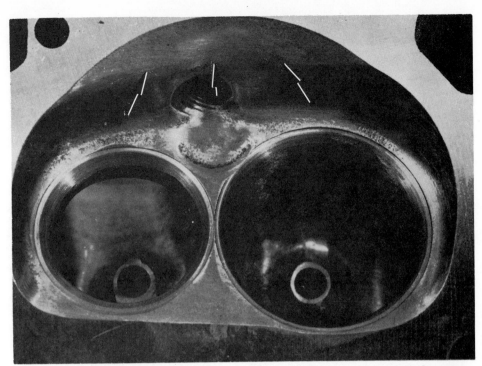

Slant-plug head reworked by King Engine Service for an all-out racing engine. Compare the added radiusing which has been done in the area indicated by the arrows. However, this smoothing does not take away much metal, so the chamber volume is not increased by very much. King says that he typically tries to keep the milling cut to 0.035-inch to get 64 cc chambers.

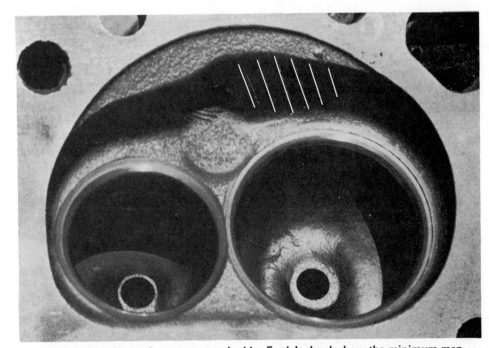

Combustion chamber and ports as reworked by Fred Joehnck show the minimum mandatory amount of metal to be removed when reworking a head. Notice that metal has been removed on the rear side of the spark-plug hole (toward the intake) in the lined area, but that most of the rest of the combustion chamber has just been touched and deburred to retain compression. Notice that the intake-valve-guide area has been left practically stock, while the same area in the exhaust port has been reworked and thinned.

A good example of "make-sense" port-entry shape and size. Notice that the manifold-mating area was blued and then scribed before porting was started so that realistic guide lines could be established and then followed during the reworking.

Stock slant-plug combustion chamber shown here can benefit somewhat from SLIGHT metal removal in the area indicated and by blending the lower portion of the valve seat into the port. For this last operation a small piece of crocus cloth held by hand can be used to break any edges.

Intake side of a stock LT-1 head. Notice that the rocker-stud bosses are machined flat for the stock screw-in studs. Notice also that the intake-port area has been blued and scribed to match the intake-manifold gasket.

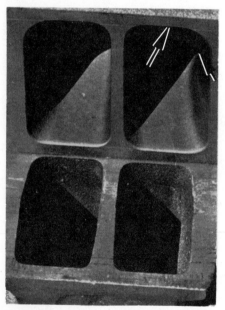

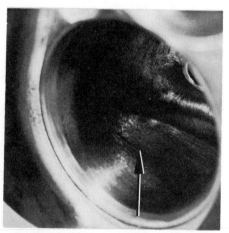

When you get into the ports just below the valve seat (1/2-inch or so) you'll find a casting lap which will give the appearance of a crack — which it is not.

Another example of some realistic porting by Fred Joehnck. Arrows indicate high-flow areas of the port. Notice how the walls have been straightened. This treatment is especially helpful when used with the high-velocity, small-cross-section Tarantula manifold. Gaskets and manifold will fit correctly and there has been no major metal removal through the cross section. The floor has been deburred, but no metal removed.

You name it and it's been tried on the small-block Chevy. Someone went to a lot of trouble to bring the intake ports out on the same side as the exhaust for a side-port effect. There are easier — and more positive — ways to find horsepower.

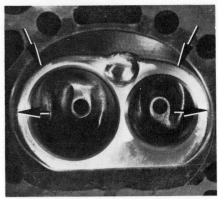

Obvious unshrouding of the valves has been attempted here. Doing this much work around the exhaust valve gets difficult in a hurry. This also takes away the compression in a hurry. Get some wrecking-yard heads to practice on if you plan to get serious about head work . . . and consider investing in a flow bench. If you're not REALLY serious about it, save your time and patience.

Here's an example of a lot of wasted work. The section between the ports (A) has been thinned to the point where the gasket will now hang into the port and disrupt the flow; so what has been gained? The high-flow area is (B) which has not been raised and should have been just to match the manifold after the head has been milled. The floor of the port (C) is beautiful — metal removed and a nice polish, but since there is very little flow here, what has been gained?

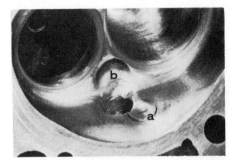

Early (straight-plug) head which King Engine Service of Detroit has plugged and then reworked to accept the angled spark plug. (a) indicates where King installed a cast-iron plug in the existing spark-plug hole. (b) indicates the "dimple" you find on all heads. Rumor and myth to the contrary, the reason for this depression is so that fixtures can clamp here in the factory during machining operations.

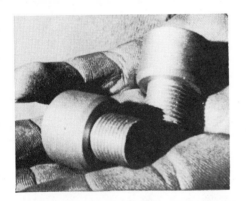

These machined plugs are epoxied and threaded into the existing spark-plug holes to begin the operation of converting the Z-28/LT-1 heads to the new "service-package" slant-plug design.

The '68 and later head is shown on the left while the much talked about all-aluminum head is on the right. The aluminum units were called back and discontinued in the same year of their release due to casting problems.

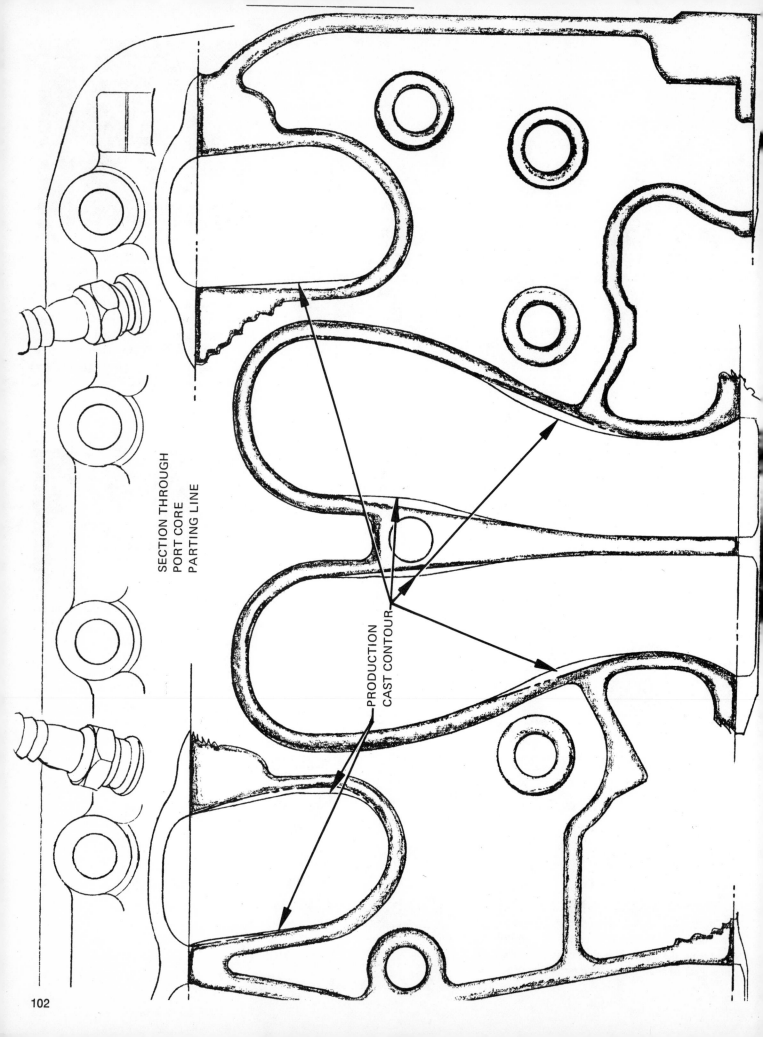

SECTION THROUGH
PORT CORE
PARTING LINE

PRODUCTION
CAST CONTOUR

102

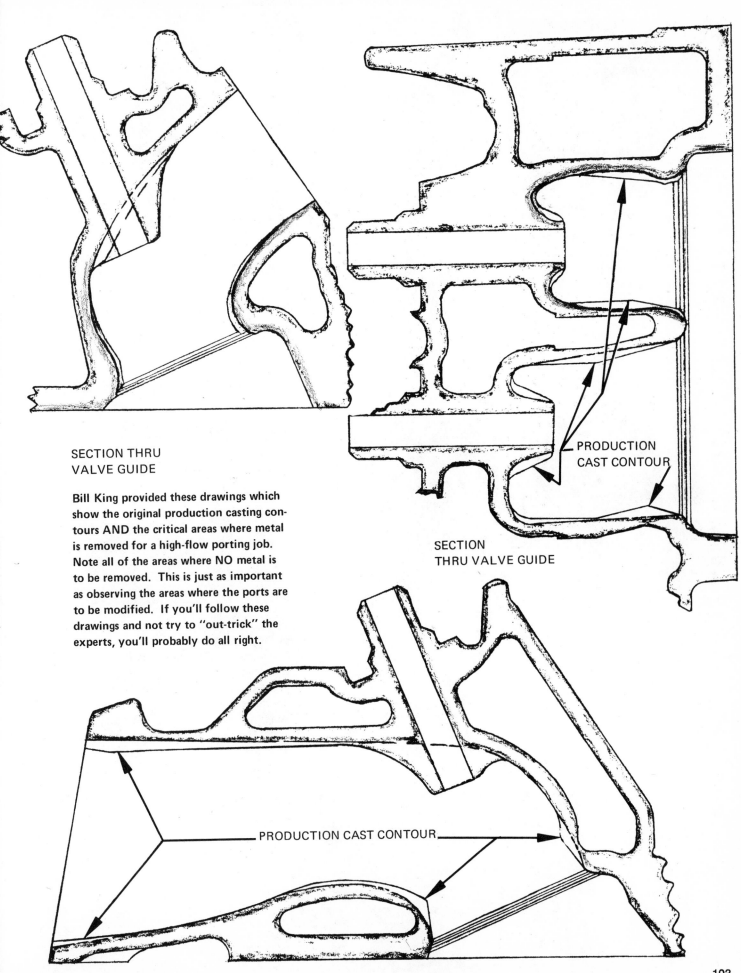

SECTION THRU
VALVE GUIDE

Bill King provided these drawings which
show the original production casting contours AND the critical areas where metal
is removed for a high-flow porting job.
Note all of the areas where NO metal is
to be removed. This is just as important
as observing the areas where the ports are
to be modified. If you'll follow these
drawings and not try to "out-trick" the
experts, you'll probably do all right.

PRODUCTION
CAST CONTOUR

SECTION
THRU VALVE GUIDE

PRODUCTION CAST CONTOUR

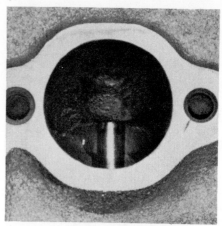

This is the shape of exhaust ports after they leave Bill King's shop in Detroit. His work is precise and he's regarded as one of the best head porters in the country.

For the guy without a flow bench and a lot of time to spend, this is just about the ticket for the exhaust port — clean up the port slightly around the valve seat, match the head to the gasket and leave it alone.

Good example of an exhaust port re-shaped to match up with a header system using 1-5/8-inch diameter pipes.

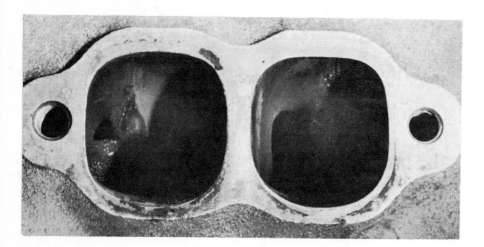

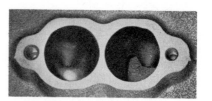

There are a number of approaches to shape of the exhaust-port exit. The biggest problem in this area is the head-work customer who feels he is being cheated if the shape at the exit is not altered. So shops alter the shape and the customer is happy. Shape at this point is relatively unimportant. The place to really change the flow of an exhaust port is just under the valve and where the port begins to turn.

VALVE GUIDES

Like many parts of the small-block Chevy, valve guides don't give any trouble. Leave the engine stock and run it a jillion miles. Trouble starts when the stock cam is replaced with a hot-rod item with radical lift and/or a drastically modified base circle. This usually leads to incorrect valve geometry — which produces guide wear in a hurry.

Once guides are worn, the tendency is to rush out to have them knurled. If the guides have been cut for seals, knurling tools can break the guides at this point. In general, a head for racing should not be "fixed" by knurling the guides. Two other ways can be used. The first requires access to an engine rebuilder equipped with a machine which locates the head according to the valve guide bores and valve seats. The stock guides are bored out and new cast-iron guides are installed. These should be reamed to 0.0014 for the intake and 0.0018-inch for the exhaust.

The second commonly used method is that known as the Winona Bronze-Wall Rebuilder. This method taps the guide with a coarse tap and then a bronze wire is wound into the threads so that the wire is captured in the guide. The bronze wire can be reamed for a perfect fit as described previously. This method is next-best to the replacement with new guides. It preserves the concentric relationship of the valve-guide bore with the seat — which can be worth a bunch of time right there. The price for the Winona work is usually about $4 per guide — or you can buy the tool with supplies for doing two sets of heads for about $130 from Manley dealers or automotive tool suppliers.

It should be noted that the Winona method suffers from the same problem as ordinary knurling — it will tend to break guides which have been cut for the installation of seals. So, if you are rebuilding guides with this method and plan to install seals, tap the guides and install the bronze wire *before* you cut the guides for the seals.

1968 and newer heads are commonly called "2 by 2" as a reference to the intake-valve size of 2.02 inches. Exhaust-valve size is 1-5/8-inch — as you can see, that's the limit for this head. They breathe quite well "as is."

LARGER VALVES

Can larger than stock valves be installed in a small-block Chevy head? Yes, and no. How's that for a straight answer? On the two latest heads, the Z-28/LT-1 and the slant-plug units, Chevy did the job for you. Larger valves can be installed in earlier heads, but why? With better heads available on the dealer's shelves, putting larger valves in the old heads is throwing good money after bad. Shrouding problems in the earlier heads are compounded with the larger valves, so instead of solving problems, you worsen them. In other words, putting larger valves in older heads costs time and money and compounds breathing problems, and does not always produce measureable increases in horsepower or torque. That slant-plug head gets more tempting every time you look at it!

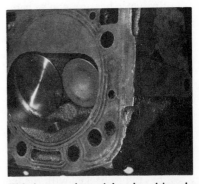

This is a stock straight-plug, big-valve head (2.02-inch intake). All of this combustion-chamber machining was done at the factory.

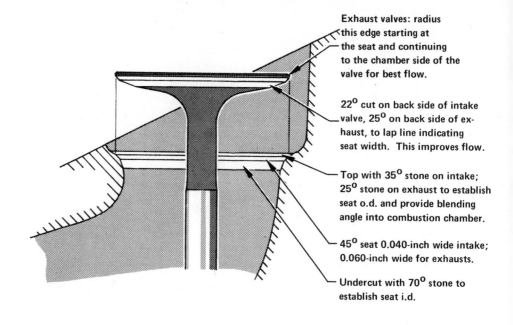

Exhaust valves: radius this edge starting at the seat and continuing to the chamber side of the valve for best flow.

22° cut on back side of intake valve, 25° on back side of exhaust, to lap line indicating seat width. This improves flow.

Top with 35° stone on intake; 25° stone on exhaust to establish seat o.d. and provide blending angle into combustion chamber.

45° seat 0.040-inch wide intake; 0.060-inch wide for exhausts.

Undercut with 70° stone to establish seat i.d.

VALVE SEATING

Close attention to the valve-seating task adds HP with such a minimal investment that you could almost call it "free." It's the factory's gift to you—just a little loving care and attention make it happen.

Stock valves overhang the seat opening by a large amount, reducing flow capability of the valve/port combination and stealing *at least 10 to 12 HP!* You need to trot out *all* of the horses from your engine's stable because your competitors will get them out—believe that! But, understand that there is a lot of metal to be removed to do the seat job recommended by Chevrolet. Paul Hogge of Racing Parts and Machine Co. in Baltimore, Maryland, says that the first competition valve job is worth about $50 and it is no money-maker as far as he's concerned. However, every small-block engine needs this type of valve job, even a brand-new one.

You'll note that it is so simple that any competent machinist should be able to do it—if he has the time and doesn't run out of patience because you've hammered him so far down on price that he can't make wages.

Make sure that the seats are checked with a seat indicator gage to ensure that seat runout does not exceed 0.001 inch. If the machinist does not have this kind of measuring equipment, don't take his word for it that he's measured his tools and they always produce this kind of accuracy. Baloney! Each and every seat has to be checked with the indicator to see whether that kind of accuracy has indeed been achieved *on that seat.* There's no way that this can be done unless the measuring tool is right there. What we are saying is that it is possible to have beautiful-looking seats which are 'way out

There's 12 to 15 HP just waiting for you if you'll just do a seat job according to the factory's recommendations — as presented in the drawing above. But, it's not a job for a vacuum-cupped stick and a can of valve-grinding compound. This requires four to five hours — or more — with professional valve seating and grinding tools.

and will not last. To get the best flow through your new seats, we have also added additional details of radiusing which can be carefully done with a hand grinder, fine stones, sanding sleeves and Cratex tools. The inside and outside of the seat can be radiused into the top and bottom angles.

Lapping the valve against the seat won't tell you anything except where the seat is in relation to the valve. Lapping does show you where you can take the back angle cut to, however.

The circumference of the valve seats should be increased to equal the valve o.d.'s. Then the inner diameter of the inlet seat can be ground with a 70-degree stone (we'll talk about fancy multi-angle valve jobs later on) to get a seat which is at least 0.040-inch wide. Use the same technique to get 0.060-inch-width for the exhaust seats. The valve seats themselves are all ground at 45 degrees. A further topping cut above the seat can be made with a 35-degree stone on the intake and a 25-degree stone for

the exhausts. The edges of these cuts should be blended into the combustion chamber with rotary files, mounted grinding stones and subsequently with sanding sleeves and Cratex tools. The edge of the topping cuts can be blended into the 45-degree seat with a slight radius *if you have a steady hand* and if you have an adequate supply of fine-grit sanding sleeves and Cratex at hand. The 70 degrees can be blended into the 45-degree seat similarly. And, the 70 degrees can be blended into the port throat with rotary files or mounted grinding stones.

Further aid to flow is given by making a cut on the underhead of the valve itself (22° for the inlet and 25° for the exhaust) so that the valve face is matched in width with the valve seat. The edge of this cut can be radiused into the 45-degree seating portion and the area at the other end of the 22-degree cut can be blended further into the backside of the valve head with additional blending cuts which you can "eyeball-in" with the valve grinder.

WIDER SEATS WILL LAST LONGER

Although narrow seats have long been considered optimum for racing, especially when the seat edges are radiused into the adjoining angles, the narrow seats won't last on the street. And, it is well known that narrow seats must be right on as regards run-out — within 0.001 inch, certainly — if the seats are to live for one or two races. When the narrow seat is used, especially with lots of valve-spring pressure, the valves erode the seats and the seat job gets in deep trouble before very many thousands of miles have passed under the tires. Our own flow-bench tests at Kay Sissell's Automotive in South El Monte, California have not shown any real hinderance to flow from using wider seats. In a few cases, wider seats improved the flow!

Bob Joehnck recommends that the intake-seat width be 0.070 to 0.080-inch. and the exhausts be at least 0.100-inch. The face on the valve itself should be 0.010-inch wider than the seat in the head. Narrowing the inside of the valve seat with an angle cut as shown in the accompanying drawing is o.k., so long as the valve face is not narrowed to less than the seat width. More research is undoubtedly needed to determine optimum seat widths, but wider seats will definitely last longer in a street-driven engine.

RADIUS & MULTI-ANGLE SEATS

Flow-bench work has shown that more air will flow through a valve/seat combination if there is a radius on the seat instead of a flat surface formed by a discrete angle. Similarly, the valve itself can be faced with an opposite radius so that the two radii are tangent to each other when the valve is on its seat. In this instance, the actual line of contact may only be 0.020 to 0.030 inch, as established by lapping to show the contact area. Seat runout must be tightly controlled with the radius-seat setup.

Radius seats can be machined into the heads with cutters or ground in with radiused stones. The valve can be made to approach a radius configuration by grinding a series of angles onto it and then blending these into a radius with a specially set up valve grinder.

An approximation of the radius setup can be accomplished on the cylinder head by using a series of angles. This has been done for many years by knowledgeable racing mechanics.

Several of the shops listed in the Suppliers List at the back of the book have the capability for installing radius seats. King Engine Service and Diamond-Elkins Porting are two which can do this type of work.

We should mention that such work is really only for the all-out racer and is not for the street-driven machine.

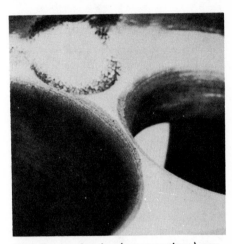

King Engine Service (among others) can machine these venturi valve seats. Done correctly it is worth a few horsepower — but consider it only for an all-out racing engine. Figure on spending $150 or so for the job.

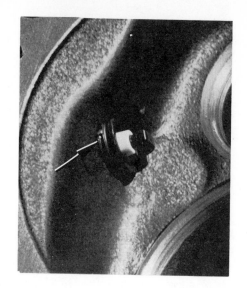

Small-block heads — stock or reworked — commonly crack in the area indicated. The head can continue to be used if a seat is maintained and if water does not seep out of the head when under pressure.

When a slant-plug head is reworked you might just find several plug threads sticking into the combustion chamber. Because these are taper-seat plugs you can't back the plug out of the hole with a washer, so if you are concerned about this, go lightly when removing metal from the chamber and consider removing a thread from the plug so that there will be no sharp edges in the chamber to grow red hot.

Box-stock, late Z-28/LT-1 head showing the shape of the valve-guide boss and how the stock head appears when cut for the stock spring. Those are also stock Chevy screw-in rocker studs and guide plates. Below: Same head after the valve-guide boss has been machined to accept the Hastings or PC teflon seal. Notice also that the head has been cut to accept a larger diameter valve spring. Most any automotive machine shop can handle this chore. Cutters which can be driven with a 1/2-inch drill motor are readily available.

CYLINDER HEAD CCing

Generally, the assumption is made that in a modern multi-cylinder engine all cylinders are doing an equal amount of work and contributing their fair share to the total horsepower and torque output of the engine. This is not the case. For the cylinders to produce equal amount of work, the total volume of each must be equal. As the engine comes from the factory, they are nearly equal — but in a high-performance engine where two or three HP are hard to get, it stands to reason that individual cylinder volumes must be equal.

Why should you spend the time and/or money to get your heads CCed to the minimum allowed for the class in which you will be competing? Well, this does produce the highest compression which is allowable. And, it does so for all of the cylinders. The less obvious, but just as important second reason is the need to know the compression ratio so that it can be adjusted if it is too high or too low for the intended use of the engine, fuel octane, etc.

The process of making all of the cylinders nearly equal in volume is called CCing. And, this provides the measurements which you need to calculate compression ratio. Getting the volumes equal not only requires making all of the combustion chambers equal, it also requires equal deck clearance at each combustion chamber.

If you are preparing a set of heads to be used in a competition engine which must "pass" as legal if torn down for technical inspection, be sure that you read and understand the rules. Know what is required for minimum head volume (hence the need for CCing as we are about to discuss), what chamber modifications are allowable—if any—and what type of valve-seating job is permissable for the class.

The job is not difficult, but is time-consuming and requires considerable patience on the part of a novice. A relatively small amount of equipment and money is involved, except for the final steps which require the services of a competent automotive machinist.

Begin with a cylinder head which is spotless. If the head has been run before, have it sandblasted, glassblasted, boiled out or scrubbed clean with a stiff wire brush attached to the end of an electric drill. It is most important to remove all deposits of carbon from the combustion chambers. Make certain that the machined surface of the head which mates to the block is straight. This may be checked in most cases with a steel straightedge such as a large machinist's rule. If there are any doubts in this area, have a

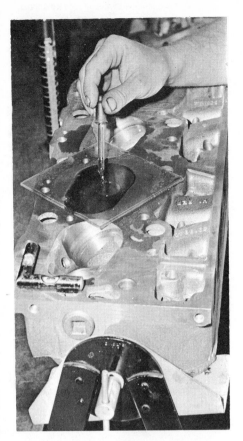

Head CCing can be done with an eye-dropper but to save your sanity—buy a burette. Here the dropper is used for the final filling.

machine shop mill or grind the head 0.003 inch to true the surface. Rough in a valve job and install the valves, springs and keepers and the type of spark plug to be run in the engine. Roughing in the valve job means having a valve job done on the head up to the point of making the final pass with the finishing stone. This will be done after CCing has been completed. As the valves are being installed in the head, coat the valve seat with a very thin coating of lightweight grease. You want a liquid-tight seal between the valve and the seat. Because the valve job is not yet finished, we cannot rely on the two metal surfaces to accomplish this seal—hence the light grease coating to retain liquid.

For the actual CCing, you'll need a chemist's burette and a small piece of plastic. This plastic should be a minimum of 1/2-inch thick and large enough to completely cover one combustion chamber with at least two inches of overlap all around. Drill a small hole near one edge of the plate. The hole should be about 1/4-inch in diameter and be countersunk on one side with a larger drill in order to ease filling the chamber.

The other tool needed for the job is the chemist's burette. This instrument is nothing more than a graduated glass tube with a petcock at one end to dispense accurately measured amounts of liquid.

For a measuring liquid you won't have to look far. Just use clean solvent. If you're wearing bifocals and starting to squint, add a few drops of food coloring to the solvent. You'll probably need about a quart for each head. The color and viscosity of this mixture contributes greatly to the ease of measuring.

Block the cylinder head up on a bench or table so that one side of the head is higher than the other by about an inch. This is done so the hole in the plastic plate may be positioned at the upper edge of the chamber and the combustion chamber can be completely filled with the measuring fluid. If the machined surface of the head is set level, then it becomes all but impossible to chase the bubbles out of the fluid when attempting to determine accurately how much fluid is contained in the enclosure. The head should be clamped or blocked so that it will not move during the operation. Fill the burette with the measuring liquid to the zero marking. Use the petcock to drain some of the liquid out to get the level exactly on the zero mark. This is critical! Note that there are two types of burette markings: zero at the full mark and the capacity of the device at the full mark, i.e., 100 cc's, etc. If you are buying a burette, get one that is marked with zero at the full mark because it reads directly as the fluid is metered out into the head.

Before pressing the plastic block into position over the chamber to be checked, coat the outside edges of the chamber with a very light coat of grease. Spread the grease evenly; then press the plastic block into position, leaving the small hole near the upper edge of the combustion chamber. With the burette over the hole in the plastic plate, slowly open the petcock and begin filling the chamber. As the fluid reaches the seal between the plastic and metal watch for leaks. If there's any seepage between the head and the plate, you'll have to go back to the start. Remove the plastic plate, pour the fluid out of the chamber, reseat the plate and remeasure the liquid. Don't attempt any shortcuts, 'cause there ain't any.

Paul Hogge of Racing Parts and Machine equips his plastic plates with head-bolt holes so that bolts can be used to clamp the plate to the head without any grease for sealing the plate so that no error will be introduced by a heavy coating of grease.

Barring complications with the seal, fill the chamber until the liquid just touches the bottom of the hole in the plastic plate. Although it may seem nit-picking, check the chamber for bubbles because they displace volume and will affect the measurement of the chamber. Carefully record the amount of liquid in the chamber; move on to the next chamber and repeat the measuring process.

We'll now assume that all chambers of one head have been measured and we have readings of 63, 64, 64.9 and 65.2 cc's (cubic centimeters). This may seem close enough — and it is for the run-of-the-mill engine. For our purposes we're going to make all the chambers measure the same. To aid our explanation process here, we shall assume that the head is going to be used on an engine in some stock class of competition which will not allow any removal of metal or polishing inside the combustion chamber. Let us also assume that rules from the same racing association will not allow the addition to or removal of metal from the face of any valve. As a further stumbling block, let us assume that for this particular engine the minimum head volume per cylinder is set at 64.5 cc's.

The next step is to bring all chambers up to the volume of the largest of the group — in this case, 65.2 cc's. This is accomplished by "sinking" valves. This nomenclature describes moving the valve seat further down into the head to increase the volume of the chamber. Careful thought should be given before any metal is moved around. It is most important to remember that any valve which is sunk cannot be raised. Keep planted firmly in mind that overly enthusiastic activity in the area of valve sinking will soon put you in the market for a new cylinder head.

Any valve which is sunk changes the flow characteristics in the cylinder and port area. An intake valve should not be sunk unless it is absolutely necessary, and then not more than 0.040 inch. This should be considered the absolute outside limit. Sinking an exhaust valve is not nearly so critical, so if you must sink a valve, make it an exhaust.

The process of sinking a valve runs something like this: Top an intake valve seat with a 35-degree stone; an exhaust with a 25-degree stone. This unshrouds the circumference of the seat. Next, re-establish the valve seat with several light passes with a 45-degree stone. Now carefully clean the chamber, install the valves, springs, retainers and spark plug and follow the previous steps until the chamber will hold the exact amount as the largest chamber in the head (in this case – 65.2 cc's).

Although it might appear that there is no simple method to determine how deep the valve should be sunk to gain the needed volume, it just takes a simple formula. The valve area times the amount sunk equals the volume which will be gained. However, the whole deal is painstakingly slow going. The first set of heads will be the hardest—on this set you'll want to take off only the slightest amount of metal on each pass. After running through this process on a couple of cylinders, you'll most likely determine that one is close enough.

Remember that this should be only when all chambers measure *exactly* alike. What do you have to lose if one cylinder runs a cc off? You tell us when the other guy wins the race.

With all chambers now measuring the same, the valve job may be finished off. With repeated passes of the stone to sink the valves, some of the seats might be quite wide. The remedy is to narrow the seat with a 55-degree stone and then move into the throat of the port for a pass with a 70-degree stone (if four angles are allowed by the class rules).

To round out the process of head CCing we need to reduce all the chambers to 64.5 cc's. As you recall, all of them now measure 65.2 cc's which is too large to provide the allowable compression ratio for the class.

With valves and spark plug installed in any of the chambers, block up the cylinder head until the machined block mating surface is exactly level. Be sure that you are using the type of spark plug which you plan to use in the engine. *The head must be level.* Fill the burette and then carefully drain exactly 64.5 cc's into the chamber. Rig a depth micrometer over the chamber to indicate the difference between the machined, level surface of the head and the surface of the fluid. Read this micrometer just as the fluid in the chamber begins to "jump" from the chamber to the micrometer shank as it is lowered toward the fluid. The reading at this point is the amount of metal to be ground or milled from the head to produce the desired chamber volume in all chambers in that head.

The prudent plan at this point is to remove slightly less metal than the amount indicated by the micrometer. By slight, we mean 0.002 to 0.004-inch. If too much metal is removed from the head and an overall lower chamber volume is produced, the head may be illegal when running in certain classes of competition. The head may now be taken to a competent automotive machinist. Tell him how much should be removed from the head surface. If at all possible, stand and watch—making certain that the head is jigged absolutely dead level on the mill table.

If all steps have been followed correctly up to this point, the chambers will now hold equal amounts of fluid; thus one less variable to high, consistent performance exists.

On the stem side of the cylinder head some of the valves are now "longer" than the others since they've been sunk deeper into the chamber. Changing the effective length of the valve stem alters valve timing and lift. This is a sure horsepower loser, and can negate all of your previous labors with the cylinder head.

Bolt a machined plate to the stem side of the head to serve as a resting place for a dial indicator. By moving an indicator along this plate and stopping at each valve stem, the relative height differential may be found. Measure them all—determine which is "shortest," mark valves as to location, and bring all of the rest of the valve stems down to that level. Do this on both heads. Most all valve grinders have an attachment for refacing the end of a valve stem—which makes the job of shortening a stem relatively easy.

The chamber-volume measurements used in this explanation are actual measurements from a small-block head. Naturally, for a variety of reasons, all heads will not measure the same — the figures used here should be considered only as an example.

When CCing piston-dome volume, locate piston 1.000 inch from deck if deck clearance is zero. Lightly grease rings and piston edge for a seal. Coat deck with grease before installing plate with filler hole to one side of cylinder bore.

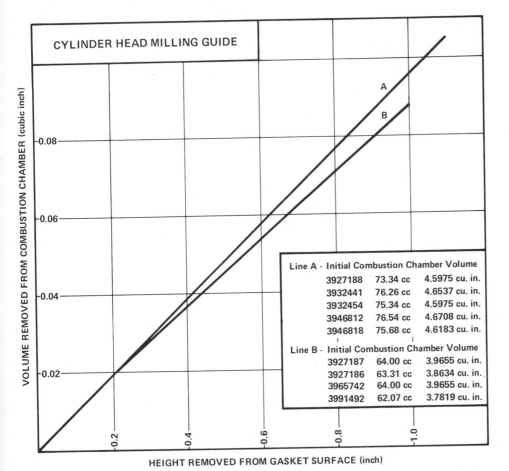

CYLINDER HEAD MILLING GUIDE

Y-axis: VOLUME REMOVED FROM COMBUSTION CHAMBER (cubic inch) — 0.02, 0.04, 0.06, 0.08

X-axis: HEIGHT REMOVED FROM GASKET SURFACE (inch) — 0.2, 0.4, 0.6, 0.8, 1.0

Line A - Initial Combustion Chamber Volume

3927188	73.34 cc	4.5975 cu. in.
3932441	76.26 cc	4.6537 cu. in.
3932454	75.34 cc	4.5975 cu. in.
3946812	76.54 cc	4.6708 cu. in.
3946818	75.68 cc	4.6183 cu. in.

Line B - Initial Combustion Chamber Volume

3927187	64.00 cc	3.9655 cu. in.
3927186	63.31 cc	3.8634 cu. in.
3965742	64.00 cc	3.9655 cu. in.
3991492	62.07 cc	3.7819 cu. in.

Listed here are the surface areas exposed to the combustion chamber and the volume added to the combustion chamber for AC spark plugs.

Plug Type	Area (Sq.In.)	Volume (cc.)
R45	1.362	.391
R44	1.354	.382
R43	1.268	.382
R43XL	.865	.066
CR43	.942	.290
CR42N	.801	.162
R43T	1.0125	.338
R44T	1.299	.479
R46T	1.420	.498
R44TS	1.571	.245
R45TS	1.592	.306
R46TS	1.618	.320
R43TS	.971	.235
R42T (1st production)	.792	.227
(Interim in '71)	.881	.160
R43T (Interim in '71)	.917	.208
R44XL	1.202	.126

One line on the chart is for heads measuring roughly 63 cc's per chamber; the other is for 75 cc's per chamber heads. Determine which you have before attempting to use the chart as a guide for milling cuts on your heads. Do not rely on the chart for any heads other than small-block Chevrolets and do not count on the chart for perfection in determining how much volume is being removed by a particular depth cut. Each chamber must be individually cc'd to determine its true volume.

Dropping a valve to bring the CCs up to snuff should be considered a last resort tactic. If the engine is to be run in a particular class of competition which will not allow metal to be removed from the combustion chamber, then the valve dropping will have to be used, but for any other form of running, the correct CCs should be obtained by removing metal from the combustion chamber. If valve dropping is part of the plan, then begin by removing metal from the valve and not the valve seat. This is nit-picking, however, because the vast majority of all competition and certainly all street engines can benefit by removing metal from the combustion chamber to bring all of the chamber volumes in line.

On the small-block heads chamber volumes will be very close — the end chambers are qualified in the plant which means the bulk of the variance will be between the two center chambers. The primary reason for CCing and making certain that all of the chambers are of equal volume is to control the spark. One CC difference in combustion chambers alters compression ratio quite a bit and if you are on the ragged edge of a knock anyway, one combustion chamber which is smaller than the others will produce a "spark knock" or detonation which can't be heard but can certainly be damaging to the engine in addition to creating a power loss. When this happens you can be down on power for a reason you don't understand and the normal guy can't detect.

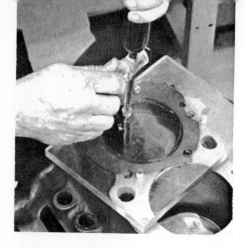

FIGURING COMPRESSION RATIO

These photos, drawing, descriptions and formulas take the mystery out of computing compression ratios.

Don't measure cylinder volume—compute it from the bore and stroke and mark it V_1.

Cylinder volume =
$$0.7854 \times bore^2 \times stroke$$

Deck-clearance volume V_2 is the volume between the piston top and the top of the block at TDC . . . if you are using flat-topped pistons. A micrometer, caliper or feeler gage can be used to measure the deck clearance and this measurement is figured as

Deck-clearance volume =
$$0.7854 \times bore^2 \times deck\ clearance$$

Gasket volume V_3 can be estimated by assuming that the gasket opening is round and computing the volume:

Gasket volume =
$$0.7854 \times bore^2 \times gasket\ thickness$$

But, the dome on most small-block pistons complicates figuring the c.r. And, for some classes, dome volume cannot exceed a specified amount or the engine will be ruled illegal. Therefore, you may need to know how to measure dome volume. The maximum number of cc's in the dome and minimum number in the chamber will give the most compression, of course. But, it is best to stay under the maximum compression by 1 to 2 cc's to allow carbon build-up without getting the combination into the area of illegality. If the pistons which you are using have too much dome volume, all can be reduced by milling off the dome. Be sure to get the valve notches correct before measuring dome clearance because such notching can remove a lot of cc's from the domes.

If a plastic or metal ring of known volume is sealed to the block over a cylinder, which has its piston at TDC, the ring can be filled from a burette. Subtracting fluid used from the ring volume gives exact dome volume *if the deck clearance is zero or above the deck.* If the deck clearance is below deck, the volume of the dome given by this method will be less than actual dome volume. The figure will be "off" by the volume between the flat surface of the piston and the deck at TDC. However, this method makes the compression ratio calculation faster and perhaps more accurate because you do not have to guess at deck-clearance volume V_2.

If a machined ring is not available, accurately locate the piston one inch down the bore. Use a plastic piece to seal the opening and measure the amount of fluid required to fill the cavity. The measurement is subtracted from the volume of a one-inch tall section of the bore. As with the ring method, this gives the exact piston-dome volume *if the deck clearance is zero,* but is off by the amount of the deck clearance if the deck clearance is below the deck. If your piston stands out of the bore or above the deck, the exact volume will be obtained if you move the piston farther down the bore by the amount that the piston protrudes from the block.

If your piston is below the deck, the exact volume of the dome can be obtained if you move the piston down the bore one inch *minus the deck clearance.*

Chamber volume V_4 is measured as described elsewhere in this chapter. If you are using domed pistons, the piston dome volume must be subtracted from the measured chamber volume to get V_4 for figuring compression ratio.

NOTE: Cubic inches from your cylinder volume are converted to cubic centimeters by the formula

Cubic centimeters =
$$cubic\ inches \times 16.4.$$

Just crank these figures into the following formula:

Compression ratio =
$$\frac{V_1 + V_2 + V_3 + V_4}{V_2 + V_3 + V_4}$$

Remember that cylinder displacement or volume V_1 affects compression ratio. Anything you do to increase V_1 (bigger bore and/or longer stroke)—or to reduce V_2 or V_3 or V_4—automatically increases the compression ratio. If you plan to rework your cylinder heads now for use on an engine which will be bored and stroked later, use the displacement of the final engine configuration to determine the head volume that you'll need eventually so that you can do the head work just once.

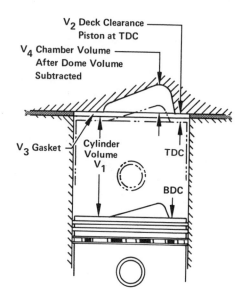

V_2 Deck Clearance
Piston at TDC

V_4 Chamber Volume
After Dome Volume
Subtracted

V_3 Gasket

Cylinder Volume V_1

TDC

BDC

This shows one method of checking piston-dome volume. The piston is installed with rings at TDC. A machined ring of known volume is placed over the cylinder and all fluid measured as it is dribbled in. Subtracting fluid used from ring displacement gives the dome volume if the deck clearance is zero. Eye dropper is filled from burette and used to add critical last few drops.

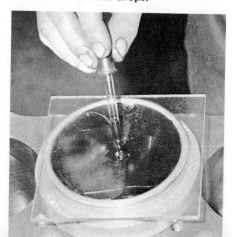

SCREW-IN ROCKER ARM STUDS

Beginning in 1970, Z-28, LT-1 and slant-plug (service package) heads have screw-in replaceable rocker-arm studs and hardened-steel push-rod-guide plates. Before that, rocker-arm studs were pressed into the heads. Guys used to pin the studs in the heads with small dowel pins. Then they would worry a lot because there was rarely a satisfactory fit to keep the stud from working in its hole in the casting when subjected to the rigors of high-performance use. Heads made prior to 1970 — and 1970-72 heads with press-in studs — can be updated and outfitted with Chevy screw-in studs and guide plates with minor machine work. Stud-mounting bosses must be milled to provide the under shoulder of the new studs with a flat surface and to allow room for the guide plates if these are used.

You'll have to pull the old studs out of the heads and then have the stud bosses milled 0.250 for Chevrolet production studs without guide plates; 0.320 for production studs and plates; or 0.410 inch for Mr. Gasket studs without guide plates.

Be sure to mill the stud bosses *before* tapping the existing holes to 7/16-14 NC for installation of the screw-in studs.

The threads of these studs must be coated with a liberal dose of sealant before they are screwed into the head casting. A number of accessory firms offer screw-in stud kits for this job. Some of the kits include the correct size drill, tap and cutter with which to face off the stud boss. These kits and the studs they supply are adequate for most high-performance street use. If you are in the process of building a competition engine and want screw-in studs in older heads, you'd best give serious thought to using stock Chevy studs.

You might be agreeable to all of the above until you get the old head up on the work bench and start trying to figure out how to pull the press-in studs from the head. Ain't no big deal. Just stack on some of the old rocker balls you were going to throw away anyway, top them off with a rocker nut and start tightening. If you have enough horsepower in the old bicep the stud will come up. Always check before you start this procedure to see if the studs have been previously pinned into place. If so, drill out the pin before pulling the stud.

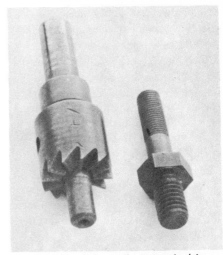

To install screw-in studs correctly (the stock version is shown) you'll need a spot facer to provide a clean register surface for the stud.

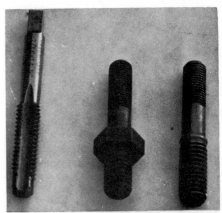

When converting press-in stud heads to the screw-in items you'll have your choice of stock stud or accessory item. The stock item was designed to clamp a guide plate to the head. Notice that the leading point of the tap has been ground away to aid straight starting in the hole.

Here's the trick for removing pressed-in studs. Stack up some old rocker balls, add a new SAE nut with some top-quality oil and turn on the impact wrench. Out comes the stud. You may have to take the nut off and add another rocker ball to get the stud all the way out. Use a new nut every four to eight studs. This can be done with a breaker bar and socket, but you'd better eat breakfast first.

CHEVY HARDWARE PRICES

Since we make constant reference to the fact that you should start with the very latest Chevy head hardware, it is only fair that we sketch what some of the hardware will cost. The slant-plug heads (bare) usually cost about $60 each. Valves (intake and exhaust) generally run about $3.75 each. Retainers are about .20¢ each. Guide plates — .40¢ each. Stock screw-in studs are .35¢ each and the Mr. Gasket set goes for about $11.00 and this doesn't include any of the cutters that are required to ready the heads for installation. Valve spring 3911068 will usually cost about .80¢ — but is a low-performance spring and should not be used with any of the late cams. Valve spring 3927142 costs about $1.30 each and is the Chevy spring to use on a performance engine.

N.H.R.A. HEADS

Getting your "stock" heads into an N.H.R.A.-legal state is worth about $125, regardless of who does it. There's cc'ing, surfacing of the heads and the detailed seat job which requires only three angles on the seat with the angle under the seat extending into the port a maximum of 1/4-inch below the seat i.d. The valve can have only one angle.

Paul Hogge, having fought his share of verbal battles with "drag-strip lawyers," insists that his customers get a sheet from the division N.H.R.A. technical director with the specifications to which the engine must comply. That way, the competitor has the information on an N.H.R.A. letterhead with a signature and a date to back up the specs to which he has built and checked his heads and other engine components.

Modified classes, on the other hand, can be run with multiple angles on the backside of the valve and multiple angles on the seat/port combination. Even the expensive-to-do radius seat job which blends a radius from the port right into the chamber can be used in modified classes.

STUDS

Many professional racing engine builders use studs in the cylinder block and then torque the head in place with nuts. When you make this kind of change you are beginning to spend dollars in a big way. Using studs does help cylinder-head clamping — but simply is not needed for less than a blown engine. You should also know that attempting to install and remove heads over all those studs gets to be a real pain after a while. If you encounter a problem with keeping head gaskets on an engine, make sure the mating surfaces of the heads and the block are true before spending time and money on studs. However, if studs are used, always tighten the nuts down on hardened steel washers to keep from galling the seating surface under the nut and also to distribute the loading of the nut. Studs, nuts and hardened washers in a kit cost about $65.

Aftermarket guide plates are available for the earlier heads which did not come factory-equipped with guide plates. These plates are held in place by head bolts and require some minor grinding in the area of the rocker-stud boss. Late stock guide plates can be installed on the early heads, but this requires a mill to face off the top of the rocker-stud boss. Stock Chevy guide plates clamp under screw-in rocker-arm studs.

STOCK PISTONS

Two basic types of stock pistons have been supplied in the little Chevy since the engine was built. Permanent-mold cast-aluminum flat-top pistons were supplied in all 265 CID engines. All 283 CID engines were supplied with cast pistons but some were flat-top and others had a 1/8-inch pop-up. Beginning in 1962 the 315 HP 283 CID Corvette pistons were notched for valve clearance due to a change in head design. Beginning in 1962, all 283 pistons were weighted differently than the older ones due to different crank counterweighting.

The first forged pistons showed up on the 1962 340 HP and they were used through 1968 in higher HP versions. All 327 pistons are designed for a 4-inch bore and a 3.250 stroke. Compression ratios varied slightly because of head variations.

All 302 pistons are forged and the original 302 offered in 1967 had the same dome design as the 327 piston. Since then the 302 has been supplied with larger domed pistons of the same design as used on the 350 CID. Does this mean that the 302 and 350 pistons interchange? NO! Here's why. The bore is the same but the stroke is different and some of the difference is in the pin location. Understanding that you must mate the piston with the correct crank and head is the key to all of this. While we're still on this, mull over this example given to us by Dino Fry. Fellow had a 327 which needed boring anyway which means the purchase of a new set of pistons. So the sharpie bores and hones the block for a set of stock Chevy 350 pistons. The 327 heads are retained, together with the 327 crank. The engine has no power. A compression check is taken. The maximum reading is 90 pounds — and that means no compression. What happened? The 350 piston pin is located higher in the piston than that of a 327. This lowers the piston in the bore — hence no compression. There are other combinations such as this which simply don't get the job done because the engine builder didn't think what was happening when the engine was going together. Had the builder checked deck height,

350 CID forged pistons. 1969-70 LT-1 10.5:1 is at left. This original piston was used with a floating pin and later with pressed-in pins. It has retainer grooves and pin oiling holes from ring groove. Piston in center is forged 10.5:1 unit with T-slot design, slot behind oil ring instead of drilled oil-return holes. It has no holes to oil the pin. Center piston would not be a good choice for a racing engine but would be o.k. for high-performance street machine if pin oiling added. T-slot design allows running closer clearances than solid skirt. Piston at right is 9:1 flat head with valve reliefs as used on 1971-72 Z-28 and LT-1 engines. It has retainer grooves and pin oiling from the oil ring.

Three 302 CID forged pistons. Note that only the 3946876 one at right has a pin with ground ends and pin locks. All are equipped with grooves for retainers. Difference is in weight related to crank journal diameter.

or compared a 327 piston with a 350, or measured chamber and dome volume (as described) the error would have been caught long before the engine was fired.

It is essential to measure all of the parts before starting to assemble the engine—or starting to do machine work on the individual parts. In the case of the 302, 327 and 350 CID engines which share a common block with 4.00-inch bore, the pistons look very similar. But, each one has a unique compression height. The 302

is 1.800, the 327 is 1.675 and the 350 is 1.560. Compression height is the dimension from the center of the pin bore to the flat or quench portion of the piston (not the dome top). It is easy to measure with vernier calipers by measuring from the top of the pin hole to the flat top of the piston, then adding 1/2 of the pin diameter to get the compression-height measurement. Do not be misled when you look at hotrod parts catalogs. Many of these specify compression heights

1969-70 base 350 CID cast-aluminum T-slot piston. Pads alongside of pin hole are used for balancing. Note indentations in top of piston for valve clearance.

(distances) which include the dome, but fail to note that fact in their explanations. Thus, it's often hard to tell what you are getting until you have the pistons in hand.

Back to the 350 CID with the dome — beginning in 1971 the dome was whacked off and the forged piston is now a flat top with far less compression than earlier engines. Thus a '71 350 can be updated by going back to the earlier 350 piston. Even in this case you check piston-to-valve clearance. Beginning in 1972 350 engines were produced with dished pistons for even less compression than the '71 engines. All of this is an effort aimed at reducing emissions.

All of the stock 307 pistons are cast and configured for a 3.876-inch bore and a 3-1/4-inch stroke.

At this writing all of the pistons produced for the 400 CID small block are cast and dished. A number of forged-aluminum aftermarket pistons have the correct pin location and feature a pop-up design quite close to the pre-'71 350 engines.

The stock piston dome shape is head and shoulders above any trick dome shape that you can buy on a special small-block piston. Domes on the TRW replacements are essentially the same shape as those on the stockers. Chevrolet spent thousands of hours in development programs to mate the combustion chamber and dome shapes for the best performance. And, an enormous amount of effort was invested to make these combinations give good performance *with low emissions*. Even though the lower-performance engines introduced in 1971-72 don't appear to be all-out winners in the horsepower race, don't overlook the fact that the search for low emissions is bringing us higher displacements to retain performance.

Most of the stock forged pistons (Chevy calls them impact-extruded) have solid skirts without slots. One of the ones for 350 CID, however, is a T-slot design, as shown in the illustration on the first page of this chapter.

Fits on factory-supplied forged pistons are typically a lot tighter than can be achieved with replacement pistons — with the exception of the TRW's. This is made possible by a barrel-skirt design which barrels the piston above the pin to a maximum of 0.0018-inch at deck height. This is done in combination with cam grinding and a tapered skirt which tapers outward 0.001-inch maximum at the bottom of the skirt. Chevrolet's forged-aluminum pistons are available in oversizes up to 0.030, as indicated in the Heavy Duty Parts List.

Piston-pins in most of Chevy's forged pistons are lubricated by oil scraped off of the cylinder wall by the oil ring. A hole at each side of the oil ring groove connects by another drilling into the top center of the wrist-pin boss on each side of the piston. Initially, all pistons were drilled from the bottom of the pin boss straight through the top of the pin boss and into the hole connected to the oil-ring groove. The practice of drilling through the bottom of the pin boss, at least on the high-HP engines, was abandoned because this proved to be a weakening factor.

Examination of the 302 and 350 pistons shows that only the top of the pin boss bore is drilled at an angle so that the bottom of the pin boss can be left solid. "Little things" like this show that Chevy's continuing development program benefits every enthusiast who'll just pay attention to what those factory cats are up to.

Pins are retained in the forged piston in one of two ways: (1) the pin is pressed into the rod eye and held there by an interference fit in all of the cast-aluminum-pistoned engines and in some of the forged pistons; and, (2) the pin is full-floating in some of the forged pistons and is retained by Truarc retainers in early models and Spirolox retainers in later models.

HOTROD PISTONS

The only time that you should consider using hotrod-type pistons made by the custom piston manufacturers is when stock Chevrolet or TRW replacement parts are not available in the bore size or stroke that you need. Hotrod-type pistons cost more money than the Chevy/TRW parts but we doubt that you'll find any more performance. Of course, if you are building a special-stroke engine, you will probably have to use pistons by Arias, Forged True, Jahns, J.E., Venolia, etc. A few extra inches will not usually provide enough extra HP to be worth the extra time and $$$ required for the hotrod pistons. Obviously, if you are building a giant "moose motor," special pistons will be required.

If you buy custom pistons, allow plenty of time for delivery because these typically take from several weeks to several months for the manufacturing process, especially if the size and compression height that you need is not scheduled into a production run of some type. Don't plan to build an engine on a double-quick overnight basis with special pistons. That's frustration-ville! Get the pistons in your hands before trying to establish a time schedule in which to complete your engine.

FORGED — OR CAST?

Some stock and replacement pistons can be used for racing, but not all racing pistons are suitable replacements for the stock items. Suitability of the various types depends on the intended use for the engine. Many replacements and racing pistons are available for the small block, including sand-cast, permanent-molded, die-cast and forged types. Of these, the forged piston is the ultimate for several reasons. Forged pistons are made by forcing aluminum slugs into a piston form under extremely high pressures to create a very dense grain structure in the finished part. Forged pistons are claimed to have up to 70% more strength and better heat-dissipation characteristics than conventional sand-cast pistons. Their strength at temperatures over 600°F is far superior to any other type of piston.

TRW, which makes more forged pistons than any other company in the world, has this to say about forged piston

Typical competition piston. Item on the left has a slightly higher dome for added compression ratio. Piston on the right has been fitted with Teflon buttons and is cut for Dykes rings — strictly racing stuff and not to be used on the street.

qualities and capabilities. "Forging starts with a billet of alloyed aluminum which is preheated to a working temperature-and then formed. A multi-stage forming process allows control of the internal grain flow in the head, skirt, pin boss and ring land areas. The resultant piston blank has exceptionally high density with virtually no porosity."

Sustained full-throttle, full-load operation substantially reduces the hardness and strength of the cast piston. The density and section shapes which are possible in the forged piston greatly reduce the temperatures in these critical areas, giving the forged piston a considerably higher operating strength range which makes it more resistant to head or ring-land distortion.

Several makes of pistons are available for the small block, and most of these come complete with pins, rings and cylinders — except the special pistons which are available from custom manufacturers.

Although forged pistons have a number of advantages over die cast and permanent-molded pistons, the initial investment required for the forging dies, and the use of more expensive production machinery, has kept most manufacturers from ever considering this method of manufacturing pistons specifically for the small block.

Almost any of the pistons — whether forged or cast — will work fine for road or street use. All

that you have to do is to make sure that the pistons are fitted with the correct clearances. Watch the mixture strength so that you don't run the engine too lean and don't try to crank in more than the recommended 38° to 42° BTDC maximum total advance.

MAXIMUM BORE SIZE

The small-block Chevy cylinder blocks are thin-wall castings which do not take kindly to massive overbores, unless you like to roll the dice.

265 CID blocks can *usually* be safely bored 1/8-inch to 3-7/8 inches for 283 CID. 1957 283's are limited to 0.060 inch, but '58 283's will *usually* accept a 1/8-inch overbore to 4 in. 1959-62's *usually* bore to 4 in. 327 blocks are limited to 0.030; *some* have made the 0.060 figure. 350 and 400 CID blocks are best limited to 0.030 over; *some* have been punched out to 0.060.

Whatever you do, don't take these recommendations as the troublefree gospel. There's always the chance for core shifts, pin holes in a bore, or cracks which are not detectable until after the cylinder has been bored — and it could be the last one to look at the boring bar, too. You still owe the man for the boring, even though the block is scrap. But, you knew that, didn't you?

Details on block identification and peculiarities are on page 14.

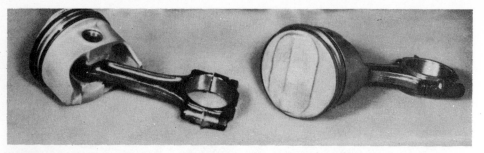

Z-28 piston and rod assemblies after prepping the rods and taking out all irregularities inside of the piston. Pistons can be glass-beaded inside and out if the ring grooves and pin bores are masked carefully. Rings just won't seal if you glass-bead the grooves because the beading destroys the sealing surface.

TRW piston modified for pin oiling, for 3/16-inch oil rings and 0.072-inch Spirolox. Piston is part of a very successful circle-track engine which was under construction by Dino Fry.

Two drills have been inserted in the pin-boss area of this forged Chevy piston. Note how oil from the back side of the oil ring connects to angled hole drilled into pin boss. Similar holes can be added to the TRW pistons for improved pin oiling.

NOTE: Photo at right shows preferred notching method for small-block pistons. A continuous notch allows better high-RPM breathing than two separate notches, even though a slight amount of compression is lost. Drag-racers can often get by with the separate notches, but it should be remembered that the sharp center divider (which is what reduces high-RPM breathing) also becomes a stress-raiser which can promote dome failure.

Top of TRW forged piston after notching for valve clearance as required by high-lift camshaft.

COMPRESSION RATIO

Dome size relates to compression ratio, of course, as does combustion-chamber and cylinder volume. When you bore the engine for larger pistons, the dome must be made smaller — or the combustion chamber increased in volume to keep the same compression ratio provided by the stock combination.

Keep in mind the fact that gasoline quality has been getting worse in most areas of the country. On the West Coast, the last good super-premium was taken off of the market in 1970. We understand that the problem is similar throughout the U.S. Of course, you can buy aviation gasoline for racing purposes, but your daily transportation needs the ability to run on what's available at any corner pump.

Use a compression ratio of 9.5 to 10:1. If you insist on using 12:1 because Chevy and TRW offer such pistons, you'll "go bananas" from your engine's continual rattling on low-octane gasoline. It's not smart to build an engine with a lot of compression for street use any more.

PISTON PREPPING

Before you do anything else to your new pistons, measure them for bore size and compression height. There's no sense investing a lot of preparation time on pistons that are wrong to start with. It's happened!

It is a very good idea to get your new pistons Zyglo-ed before you start deburring the domes. New pistons, even though they are forged, are not always perfect. Sometimes the metal does not flow into all of the places that it should have and any discontinuity could be the beginning point for an eventual crack.

When you get your pistons, go over the heads with sandpaper and files to get rid of all sharp edges.

PISTON FITTING

When you buy pistons for your engine, get them in your hands before you bore or hone the block to size. Measure each piston with a micrometer and check each bore with a snap gage and micrometer. Mate the pistons to the cylinders so that there is the least amount of honing to be done in each of the cylinders. You can also check the piston compression heights to see whether a certain combination of compression height, connecting-rod length and crankshaft rod throw will assist you in getting the best possible tolerance stack up for the right deck height at each cylinder. When boring to fit a class limit, stay three to five thousandths undersize to allow for wear or rehoning. Otherwise, it will be new-block time before you'd like to be there. Or, your engine could be declared to be oversize in a tech inspection teardown.

Pistons can be fit as closely as 0.0045-inch in the small block with little danger of scuffing—but the engine will not develop full HP until you've run it for about 30 to 50 hours under load. However, the long-term durability of the engine is improved because full HP is not being developed and the pistons do not rock as much in the bores. When pistons are fitted according to the factory hi-perf clearance recommendations (0.0055 to 0.0065-inch according to the table in this book) long-distance racers often find one or more pistons cracked at the end of a race. For this reason, any small block used in long-distance racing must always be torn down and fully inspected, including Zygloing the pistons, after each race event. The same is not true for circle-track and drag racers, because they do not spend extended periods of time at peak RPM's under full load. However, Zyglo-ing is recommended whenever the engine is torn down for rings, etc.

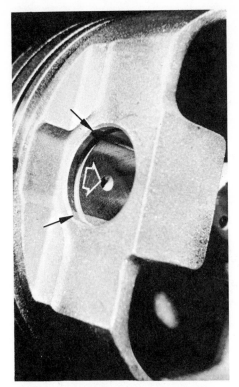

Drilled TRW piston shows new oil holes for the pin bosses (outline arrow) and grooves which TRW supplies for pin lubrication (black arrows). Interior has been glass-beaded and the exterior has been beaded around the wrist pin and on the head—but not on the thrust surfaces. Photo courtesy King Engine Service.

You may as well figure on getting all new pistons after every long-distance road race.

If your fire breather will live on the trailer and you're all set to change rings after about 30 hard passes through the quarter mile then you can get away with 0.0065-inch. Running 0.0065-inch piston-to-bore clearance on the street in any small-block Chevy is an engraved invitation for a noisy, oil-consuming, plug-fouling, short-lived engine. You'd hate it!

It's not uncommon to find four to six pistons cracked in the pin-web area when pistons are Zyglo checked after a long-distance event. Pistons and con rods must be considered as expendable replacements when racing the small block. Don't be cheap or hesitant when it is time to replace parts, especially if cracks or flaws are detected prior to assembly. And, it is much cheaper to find them then!

Here's what a double Tru-Arc setup will look like after being correctly installed. Rod is one of Fred Carillo's finest.

PISTON CLEARANCES

Type	Road Use	Street/Strip	Racing
Chevrolet cast-aluminum	0.0015-0.0025	0.0025-0.003	0.003-0.004
Chevrolet forged	0.004-0.005	0.005-0.006	0.0055-0.0065
Hotrod cast or forged	Follow maker's recommendations		

NOTE: Measurements of piston should be made perpendicular to pin, even with rod centerline.

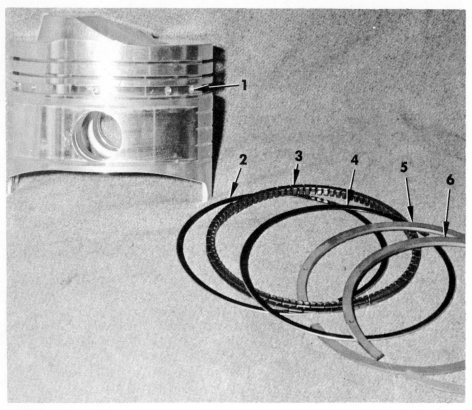

Holes 1 drilled in the oil ring groove allow oil to return to the sump. 2 is the lower rail for a three-piece oil ring. 3 is an oil-ring expander. 4 is the upper rail. 5 is the second ring. 6 is the first or compression ring. The dot on the top of the ring should always go up on the piston.

Bill Jenkins takes a close look at a piston ring with a lighted magnifying glass. How many rings have you ever examined by this method? Might learn something. Same illuminated magnifier is used to "read" spark-plug electrodes and porcelains.

PISTON RINGS

Piston rings are always a subject of interest among auto enthusiasts because they are almost always replaced during engine rebuilds and must, of course, be replaced if the bore size is changed. Few mechanics will hesitate to debate the merits of various brands of piston rings, but many do not understand the basic functioning of these vitally essential parts.

The sealing of combustion and compression pressures occurs as these same pressures enter the ring grooves, forcing the rings down against the bottom of the grooves and outward against the cylinders. Although outward stresses are built into the rings, these merely *assist* the gasses in sealing. Ring pressure against the wall does not accomplish much sealing. Tests made by Ricardo showed that rings operating *without* gas pressure behind them failed in a few minutes of operation.

Racing-engine builders frequently talk of "ring flutter." At high RPM the top ring may have sufficient inertia as the piston decelerates near TDC, so that it is held against the top of the ring groove. Gas behind the ring escapes to the crankcase and the top ring collapses *inward* under cylinder pressure, instead of being pushed outward as in normal operation. This results in vastly increased blow-by which pushes oil out of the crankcase, and drastically reduces power output. Ring collapse or "flutter" occurs only on the power stroke and always causes ring breakage if allowed to continue.

Designers of modern high-performance, high-RPM engines avoid ring flutter by reducing compression-ring width, thereby decreasing their weight and consequent inertia. Ricardo's famous book says, "Taking all of the arguments into account it would seem that the width of the ring should depend on the normal speed of the engine; the higher the speed, the narrower the ring." As proof of this comment we see high-speed two-cycle engines such as racing outboard and motorcycle engines using 1/32-inch-wide rings to prevent flutter at speeds which may exceed 10,000 RPM.

Any compression ring thicker than 5/64-inch or one-piece oil rings thicker than 1/8-inch are probably too thick to provide any oil control whatsoever in a high-RPM engine. Rail-type oil-ring setups which are combinations of very thin rings with wavy spacers can be wider, of course. If you have pistons with wider ring grooves, you might investigate Perfect Circle's spacers which allow using thin rings in wide grooves. Don't waste your time trying to build huge breather boxes to contain the oil from a bad blow-by condition. You will be way ahead horsepower-wise by eliminating the blow-by problem through the use of the correct rings.

A trend began to grow very fast in 1963-64: racing-engine builders turned to a 20-year-old idea to solve their ring-flutter problems on big-bore high-horsepower engines. They began installing an L-shaped ring invented by Dr. Paul de K. Dykes of Cambridge University. These rings are used almost exclusively in high-performance engines. Even so, because the rings use low tangential pressure against the cylinder wall, cylinder wear may be reduced during those strokes when the rings are not pressure-loaded. Dykes-type rings require a special stepped groove or a spacer can be inserted in a standard, non-stepped groove to allow using them in a piston which was not originally machined for Dykes rings.

Although there are many small-block Chevys and other engines equipped with the Dykes-type rings, they should only be considered for use on an all-out race engine.

RING TYPES

Moly rings - These are recommended because they seal instantly without any break-in time if the cylinder is round and smooth, even if the bore is used. Chevrolet claims that the moly rings give less friction than other types of rings, also. The instant seating is provided by a combination of features: (1) the cast-iron channel on each side of the moly inlay, and (2) the smooth surface grind on the ring face. When moly rings are made, they are lapped in a round cylinder until they are *light-tight*. Such processes are not used for ordinary cast-iron or chrome-plated rings.

Some makers enhance the sealing characteristics with a tapered face or a controlled torsional action to make sure that the ring will provide the initial hairline contact of cast iron against the cylinder wall. Moly rings are not pure molybdenum, but start out as cast-iron rings with a channel. This channel is filled with molybdenum-spray which molecularly bonds itself to the cast iron. About ten thousandths of cast iron is left at both the top and bottom of the ring.

With a melting point about 1000°F higher than chrome, moly is very resistant to scuffing. This scuff resistance is augmented by microscopic cavities in the moly coating. These fill with oil to give excellent pressure sealing and scuff resistance.

The moly rings are used only in the compression positions on the piston. The usual chrome-rail with wavy expander oil rings are typically used in moly ring sets. Chevrolet's moly ring sets have moly top compression rings. TRW, Perfect-Circle and Ramco sell "double-moly" sets with moly 1st and 2nd compression rings.

Regardless of who made the rings, examine the surfaces carefully for chipped or damaged surfaces. Reject any that are not right because there is no sense installing bad rings in your engine to start with.

Chrome-plated rings - Chrome-plated rings were the "hot tip" before the advent of moly-filled rings. And, in some instances, the extra abrasive-wear resistance of the chrome rings makes them the only ring to use. Chrome-plated rings gained widespread use because they are four times harder than uncoated cast-iron rings and therefore they cut abrasive-caused wear by as much as five times. Chrome-plated rings are therefore the best buy for any form of racing where the engine is not equipped with an air-cleaner system. Chrome rings will live approximately twice as long as moly rings in such applications.

You should only consider chrome rings if there is no way to run an air cleaner and if your round cylinders have the correct surface finish. Chrome rings cannot conform to an odd-shaped cylinder and may never seal in a worn cylinder. Hence, they are seldom used for re-ringing unless the cylinder has been honed round.

Chrome rings must be carefully inspected for chipped or damaged surfaces prior to their use or reuse. Such defects can cause serious cylinder-wall damage if the defective rings are used in an engine.

Head land rings — These rings are described on the next page after ring installation. A separate description is required because the piston-ring grooves are special. Take special note of the fact that these require cylinder bores which are *round.*

Enlarged view of stock Chevrolet moly-ring set shows top compression ring with cast-iron channel edges at each side of moly-sprayed center filling. 2nd compression ring is plain cast iron. Oil ring has chromed rails with wavy separator.

Checking groove depth or back clearance. When ring is bottomed, its depth should closely equal that of the groove in which it will operate.

121

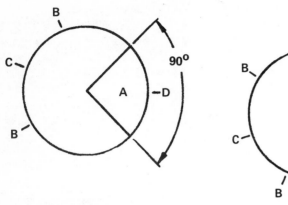

Cylinders
1 - 3 - 5 - 7

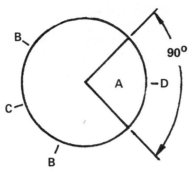

Cylinders
2 - 4 - 6 - 8

Here's how to install small-block piston rings on the pistons. A is the arc within which the oil-ring-spacer gaps should fall. Put the tang in the hole within this arc. B is the oil-ring-rail gap. C is 2nd compression-ring gap. D is top-compression-ring gap. This gap arrangement provides best oil control. This is the type of information that you will find in the Chevrolet Overhaul Manuals. You should have one to work on the engine with the assurance that you are doing things correctly.

OIL RINGS

Oil control is a separate subject. Dr. Dykes has also been responsible for research which proved that oil passes the rings in both directions and in large quantities. Although oil flows past the oil-control rings on the down-stroke, it is returned to the sump on the upstroke. There are at least two types of oil-control rings to consider: (1) the type using two chrome-plated rails above and below a wavy ring separator, which probably should not be used for re-ring jobs, and (2) the dove-tail design slotted cast-iron ring with an expander.

FITTING RINGS

In addition to the usual dimensioning of the rings to fit bore diameter and ring-groove width, three other measurements are quite important: ring end gap, groove clearance and "back" clearance.

End gap is measured by pushing the ring squarely into the cylinder about an inch with a piston. A feeler gage can be used to measure the end gap.

End gap on small block rings should be on the order of 0.015 to 0.018 inch.

End gaps which measure too small when the ring is installed in the cylinder can be opened up by holding the ring in a vise, protecting it with a cloth or cardboard, and carefully filing or stoning off the ends to get the desired gap. If your pistons arrive with the rings installed, don't be lazy —take them out and measure the ring gaps and the groove clearance as discussed herein and in the service manual.

Ring-groove clearance is also measured easily with feeler-gages. Stock-piston-groove clearance for compression rings should be from 0.0012 to 0.0032, measured between the ring and land. Oil-ring clearance, measured between ring and land, should be 0.002 and 0.0035. Replacement and racing pistons often specify 0.002 to 0.004 clearance for compression rings. Special groove clearances are needed for Dykes-type rings. Ring-groove clearances on the low side improve oil control and high-speed performance, but increase the risk of ring sticking in a short period of time, especially where engine is used only on the street. Too much groove (side) clearance increases oil consumption,

causes groove pounding, and finally ring breakage. Additional side clearance can be obtained when needed by sanding the side of the ring on a flat surface. Solvent-wetted Wet or Dry paper supported on a thick piece of glass works nicely.

"Back" clearance is the clearance between the groove "bottom" and the backside of the ring when the ring is at cylinder-bore diameter. The back clearance is o.k. if the ring width and groove depth are nearly identical—or perhaps the groove could be 0.010 to 0.030-inch deeper than the ring was wide. A common problem with oversize pistons was that the groove depths were left at the size which was correct for the stock bore, thereby providing an enormous amount of "back" clearance on oversize pistons. Ring-groove spacers have been made for years out of ring shim stock which was stacked into the groove after being formed into ring shapes. Enough ring shim stock was added to the top compression ring groove, and sometimes to the second compression ring groove so as to take up the unwanted clearance. However, this shimming procedure was time-consuming and not always satisfactory, especially if the shims stacked up unevenly to cause a bulge.

Bob Joehnck says that back clearance is no longer the problem that it once was because most oversize pistons are supplied with the correct ring groove depths and the oversize rings are made to provide minimal back clearance. If you are preparing a transportation machine, a quick check to see that the ring grooves are not excessively deep should be all that's required.

But, if you are building a drag-only engine, you may want to optimize the back clearance to get the highest possible compression pressures and perhaps longer ring life.

The current best way of shimming ring compression-ring grooves to reduce back clearance is to use a coiled spring which is placed behind the ring. The wire thickness which is used allows grinding the coil to a lesser thickness to make the back clearance exactly what the builder wants. One builder making such spacers is pro-stock-racer Ron Hutter of Chardon, Ohio. The spacers sell for $20 a set. He recommends using a back clearance of 0.015-inch per side, or 0.030 smaller groove OD than the ID of the ring when it is expanded against the cylinder wall. This

Head land piston at right is specially grooved to position compression ring just 1/16-inch below piston head. Compare this ring location with that on the conventional piston at left. Both forged pistons are made by TRW, but head land type is available from Sealed Power. Arrow indicates step in center of TRW pin which is discussed in paragraph describing various types of pins.

HEAD LAND RINGS

As the air-pollution problem grew in choking proportions several years ago, Sealed Power Corporation of Muskegon, Michigan began experimenting with ring locations on the piston. They thought they could reduce pollution by eliminating blowby. They did just that; but during the course of experimentation, a number of factors were discovered. Blowby was reduced, horsepower went up, operating temperatures went down and the concentrations of unburned hydrocarbons were reduced. Their piston went into production as the head land ring piston.

The ring is called head land because of the close proximity to the piston head. The area between the top of the piston head and the conventional top ring is known as the "head land."

Conventional rings, which operate under tension, can't be located as high up on the piston because they are more prone to fracture at the high temperatures prevailing near the combustion chamber. Keep in mind that with a conventional ring in a conventional

leaves the ring standing out of the piston somewhat when it is bottomed in the groove. By using this back clearance, which is much tighter than many builders use, Hutter claims that he can now get as many as 75 or 80 runs from a single set of double-moly rings.

RING GROOVES

Ring-groove condition is vital to the functioning of the rings. According to Richard MacCoon of Grant Industries, "Rings are just like valves and must have a good seat on which to seal. Groove finish is every bit as important as that of the cylinder or the ring itself. Piston makers machine piston-ring grooves with extreme care to ensure perfectly smooth surfaces. Yet you will often see 'mechanics' use a broken ring to clean out carbon from these finely machined grooves. They gouge and burr the groove and still expect the rings to work. Special tools for reconditioning grooves should always be used when fitting new rings to used pistons."

RING INSTALLATION

When you install the rings on the pistons, follow the instructions as to where you should put which rings. USE A PISTON RING INSTALLER to get the rings on the pistons without damaging the ring grooves or lands between the grooves . . . or the rings. If you don't own a piston-ring-installing tool, buy one! When the rings are on the piston, oil them and position the gaps in the relative positions indicated on the installation diagram.

A good ring spreader costs less than $10. They are simple to use and prevent ring breakage and "springing" of the rings, as well as piston scratching. To install piston rings correctly you'll need one of these neat tools.

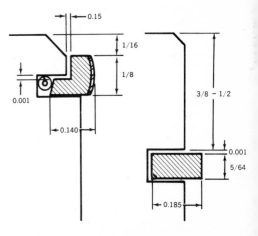

Head land ring (left) confines fuel vapors to the combustion chamber because it is only 1/16-inch down from the piston head. Conventional ring arrangement (right) has top ring 3/8 to 1/2-inch down, leaving a gap in which unburned hydrocarbons can collect. By keeping the mixture up near the flame, the new ring promotes more complete combustion, so there are fewer hydrocarbons left to get into the exhaust.

HEAD LAND RING DETAILS

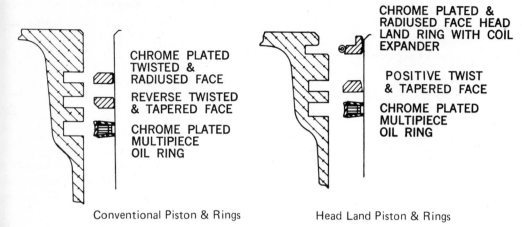

CHROME PLATED TWISTED & RADIUSED FACE

REVERSE TWISTED & TAPERED FACE

CHROME PLATED MULTIPIECE OIL RING

CHROME PLATED & RADIUSED FACE HEAD LAND RING WITH COIL EXPANDER

POSITIVE TWIST & TAPERED FACE

CHROME PLATED MULTIPIECE OIL RING

Conventional Piston & Rings   Head Land Piston & Rings

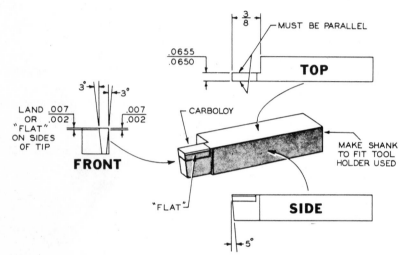

With a tool made like the one above, a competent machinist can turn many a piston for Sealed Power rings. Coolant such as kerosene or cutting fluid must be used to keep the tool and work cool and to prevent aluminum build-up on the tool. It also washes away chips to prevent scratching the groove sides. Dimensions below are for regrooving flat-top pistons or pistons with no valve reliefs near the outer edge of the head.

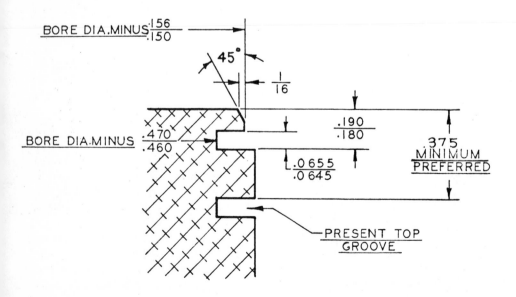

location, the gases must travel some distance down the side of the piston before exerting pressure behind the ring. This delays sealing, even when assisted by ring tension. In this period of time there is blowby. This space between the top of the piston and the top of the ring is also a storage place for unburned hydrocarbons which escape with the exhaust as atmospheric pollutants.

The head land ring has no appreciable tension itself — but mounts only 1/16 inch from the top of the piston and is gas-actuated. A stainless or carbon-steel coil-wire expander behind the ring keeps the ring in correct position during periods of high-vacuum, low-load operation. During combustion, expanding gases move in behind the ring's upper lip to begin immediate sealing. The net result is 50 percent less blowby compared to conventional rings and an increase in horsepower.

The location of the head land ring increases thermal efficiency of the engine because the combustion surface area is reduced. This means the engine will run cooler — and the piston-ring belt (area below the top ring) is also cooler because leakage of hot combustion gases is minimized by the head land ring's quick-sealing properties.

By the simple changing of stock pistons and rings to pistons grooved for the Sealed Power ring, a small-block Chevy can pick up 10 to 15 horsepower above 6000 RPM. Currently, Sealed Power can supply an engine builder with not only the rings, but also TRW-forged aluminum pistons designed specifically for the small block. The head land ring sets include moly-filled second compression rings and stainless-steel oil rings. The top ring is chromed.

"Down South" racer and crack Chevy-engine builder, Smokey Yunick, has had as much experience as anyone in the country with the head land ring assembly and reports that leakage past a conventional ring is five or six percent — compared to the Sealed Power's leakage rate of only two or three percent. Yunick is quick to point out that the head land ring is really quite sensitive to the shape hole it's used in. That is to say — it had better be round — and this means using that big steel plate clamped to the top of the block when boring and honing is done for a com-

Sealed Power piston has unusually high compression-ring location. Note bevel leading to the ring. This is a TRW forging.

petition engine. Yunick reports there is nothing special about the clearances to be used when running the Sealed Power ring set — if anything, the clearances can be just a shade tighter than normal because the piston stays straighter in the bore and the amount of scuffing falls. Gas pressure on the head land ring supports the piston and keeps it from rocking over during that part of the stroke where the piston would normally cock.

Just because the head land ring is L-shaped and relies primarily on combustion pressure for sealing, do not be quick to lump the head land ring with the Dykes ring. The head land ring might be thought of as a second-generation Dykes ring — or an expansion of the thought — because technically, the Sealed Power ring is a Dykes ring with an expander behind it. There is one very important difference in the two concepts. The Sealed Power ring is kept against the cylinder wall all of the time by the expander while the Dykes ring relies on combustion pressure alone to effect the seal — thus it doesn't seal on the intake stroke. This may or may not matter on a blown engine — but it is certainly important in the case of a normally aspirated (non-supercharged) engine.

Do not use a head land ring in cylinders having a wear ridge, or after removing one by ridge-reaming. When considering a piston for re-machining, several precautions must be observed. First of all, make certain there is sufficient top land width for the optimum groove, approximately 0.375-inch for adequate strength of the land below the groove. Care must be taken to ensure that valve pockets will not interfere with the optimum groove location.

Sealed-Power's instruction sheets provide details for machining pistons with valve reliefs near the outer edge of the piston, with valve reliefs cut into the top land, converting existing 5/64-inch grooves to the required 1/16, for "too-narrow" top lands and for special grooving for circle-track racing.

MIXING RINGS

From time to time we read of some engine builder who uses Company X top rings of a given dimension, a second ring by Company Y and an oil-ring combination made up of parts from one or two more manufacturers. In most cases this is really far out, teeny-bopper trick stuff which doesn't work any better than (or as well as) a good set of correctly installed rings that came out of one box. Rings packaged together were designed to work together — run them that way and stay out of trouble. There are exceptions to this rule, and the exception would be the guy with several engines he is keeping tabs on at the same time and using as test beds for some of his engine-building ideas. For the individual who builds one or two engines a year, the plan is to buy the ring *set* of your choice and install them correctly.

CYLINDER BORING

Many racing-engine builders use the CK-10 Sunnen Power Hone because the hone leaves the cylinder with the desired cross-hatch finish and the correct degree of smoothness to ensure that moly rings will seal correctly. Cost for boring a block varies from $55 to $80, depending on who is doing the work.

HONING

Chevy's own fine pistons are used to advantage when displacement is limited to stock size by class regulations, as in stock drag classes. And, these pistons should be at the top of your list if the available oversizes meet your displacement requirements. If you plan to use the engine for high speeds and drags, more clearance is needed. See the Piston Clearance Table for details.

Add clearance to the stock bore by honing the cylinders. You do not have to remove the pistons from the rods when you take the assemblies out carefully (after covering the rod bolts with plastic tubing) so that the cylinder walls are not damaged by the rods. But, like the old Indian scout—look for signs. Check the wear pattern on each piston to make sure that it is parallel with the piston-skirt centerline. If not, this is your "sign" that the piston is cocked and not travelling straight in the cylinder. Any piston showing uneven wear must be aligned with its connecting rod. Twisted or cocked piston/rod assemblies steal horsepower through unnecessary friction and create unwanted heat and wear. You'll also want to look at the cylinder bores for similar signs.

When honing the cylinder block it is essential to simulate cylinder distortion caused by installing the cylinder head. There's HP to be gained by this attention to detail — so don't neglect it. It is worth the extra time that is required. As pointed out in the chapter on block preparation, some racing mechanics bolt a plate to the top of the block — a plate with holes large enough to allow a hone to enter the bores — and which has the same bolt-hole pattern as a small-block cylinder head. We have seen some of these that are 4 inches thick. Chevrolet Engineering suggests that 7/16-inch NC capscrews with washers be installed in all of the head-bolt holes and torqued to 60 lbs. ft. The end result of this effort is that the bolts and/or plate simulates the stresses applied to the block by the cylinder head. The hone then makes a rounder hole . . . one which will be round when the engine is bolted together.

If you are getting a block honed to provide the correct clearance, expect to pay from $16 to $25 for the task. For high performance use, it is impossible to hone a cylinder too smooth.

Popular and much respected Powerforged piston manufactured by TRW. The .020 following TRW refers to the oversize (from stock bore) that the piston is machined to. L-2210A part number says this one is for a 4.020-inch-bore 302 engine.

Hot Rod City! More tricks here than a monkey in a mile of grape vine! A is a "fire slot" machined into the dome to "promote" flame travel. B indicates a Dykes ring located at the very top of the piston. C shows holes drilled in back of oil ring to promote drain-back. D are Teflon buttons to prevent aluminum piston from galling against bore. E indicates a tab which is supposed to keep the short-skirt piston from rocking in the bore. Groove F is supposed to hold oil in place to lubricate cylinder wall. G indicates how piston has been machined to accept button with which to retain the wrist pin. H is an area hogged out to reduce the weight of the piston. With all of this we've still got the sharp edge at I on the dome which is a sure horsepower loser. Strictly big-buck race-car stuff — of questionable value.

PISTON MACHINING

Numerous articles have appeared which illustrated engines being assembled with new pistons which were knurled to decrease clearance. Knurling, as often practiced in cheap engine rebuilding, deforms the piston skirt to decrease piston side clearance and thereby improve oil control and reduce noise from piston slap. Because of the deformation which occurs, new pistons should not be knurled on the skirts.

Some engine builders turn shallow grooves on the skirt of the piston to guarantee that the piston skirt will be lubricated by oil in these "reservoirs." Both the TRW and stock Chevy pistons have a wavy finish on the skirts for this reason.

PISTON BALANCING

Any replacement piston will probably weigh more than the stock item —especially if you are increasing the bore size. This is not a problem so long as all piston and pin assemblies weigh the same and the crankshaft, connecting rods, and flywheel and clutch are carefully balanced by a capable and experienced balancing ex-

pert. Avoidance of excessive piston weight improves engine life by reducing loads on the piston itself, pin, connecting rod, bearings, and the connecting-rod bolts. Material should not be removed from the slipper or load-bearing portion of the skirts or the pistons will be seriously weakened. Balancing pads are provided to permit equalizing the weight of all pistons in a set.

REPLACING PARTIAL SETS

Replacing a piston in an engine is not a quick and easy job, even if you buy genuine Chevrolet parts. It's even tougher if you buy non-genuine replacement parts. Piston weights may vary from part to part. If you replace the connecting rod, that's still another weight to consider. Compression heights also vary. When you add all of the possible ways that things can go wrong, replacing a piston and/or a connecting rod can be a lengthy undertaking which can require completely rebalancing the engine parts unless you have an accurate record of what went into the engine in the first place: connecting rod total weight, big-end weight and small-end weight, and piston type and weight (with pin).

Popular low-cost, readily available "rebuild" piston is the Triplex. This one delivers about 11.25:1 compression. The large eyebrows accommodate the newer (2.2-inch) intake valves. LH stamped on the crown stands for left side of the block as viewed from the flywheel end.

Stock forged 302 CID piston at left. The arrows indicate the oiling passage from the back of the oil-ring groove to the top of the pin boss. One arrow points to the ground end of the piston pin. Retainers are 0.042-inch-thick Spirolox.

An aftermarket piston, one of several which features a "fire slot" in the crown. Sometimes this is beneficial, sometimes not. Two oiling holes in the bottom of the wrist-pin boss are a no-no because they tend to weaken the loaded side of the boss.

An excellent example of the complications which arise when trick stuff is used. These specially made pistons work with a 5/8-inch stroker crank. Notice that the wrist pin has been moved all the way up into the lower oil-ring groove and that most all of the skirt has been cut away in order to clear the counterweights. These pistons went into a drag-race engine and the results were quite successful.

Forged piston for 327 was designed for use with pressed-in pin, has no grooves for pin retainers. Note slight dome and reliefs for valve clearance. Available for standard, +0.001 and +0.030 bores.

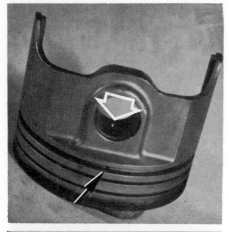

In TRW forged pistons, the oil hole which runs parallel to the wrist pin (arrow) is drilled through the oil-ring groove. It should be intersected by another 1/8-inch oil hole which is drilled on an angle through the top only of the wrist-pin boss (outline arrow).

TRW piston after drilling for oil to wrist pin. Keeper grooves have been widened for King Engine Service 0.072-inch-thick Spirolox. Taper-wall King pin is also shown here. Oil-ring groove has been opened to 3/16-inch and piston has been glass-bead blasted.

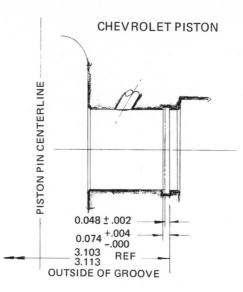

CHEVROLET PISTON

PISTON PIN CENTERLINE

0.048 ± .002
0.074 +.004 −.000
3.103 / 3.113 REF

OUTSIDE OF GROOVE

Detail for wide Spirolox:

1. Cut grooves as shown.
2. Install one 0.072″ Spirolox.
3. Use a groove micrometer to measure distance between grooves and grind equal amounts off each end of the pin to provide 0.000 end clearance between ends of pin and Spirolox on installation.
4. Or, grind 0.021″ from each end of the piston pin and install pin into piston. Grind one pair of Truarc locks to 0.072″ total thickness. Insert these and remove to check pin length. Keep shortening pin evenly on both ends (by grinding) until both Truarcs fit into the groove with zero end clearance for the pin.
5. Remove Truarc locks and pin.
6. Break pin end sharp corners with a stone.
7. Reassemble with second 0.072″ Spirolox at final assembly.
8. Do not reuse Spirolox retainers.

PISTON PIN RETENTION

There are a number of fancy ways to keep the wrist pin from sliding out of the piston and gouging the wall — buttons, clips, and rings. The best, most successful, sanitary, no-nonsense approach to the problem is using a 0.072-inch-thick Spirolox at each end of the pin. This requires machine work — but nothing that even a small machine shop can't handle. However, it is a job requiring a precise lathe and mandrels to hold the piston. The retainer grooves in the piston must be widened to contain the wider-than-stock unit. Stock width is 0.042-inch. King's Engine Service is one source of supply for the thicker-than-stock Spirolox. His part number 927020 covers a set of 20 for $12. In connection with this, King charges $20 to recut the pistons to accept the wider Spirolox, $20 to drill the TRW pistons for correct pin oiling and $18 to fit the pins.

Probably the second-best approach is to machine the grooves to 0.084-inch and use two of the stock-thickness Spirolox.

Double Tru-Arcs is another way to retain the pins. This requires that the grooves be opened up to 0.085 to 0.086-inch wide. Tru-Arcs — that's a brand name — are stamped out of sheet metal with one edge slightly rounded and the other edge 90 degrees to the plane of the ring for all practical purposes. These rings should be installed by placing the rounded edges of the two retainers together in the center of the groove.

Regardless of which of these methods of pin retention is used, there are several points which should be followed. On some pistons there will be enough room to make the groove wider toward the outside of the stock groove; on other pistons the widening cut will have to be taken from the inside of the stock groove. Some pistons will require that a slight amount of metal should be taken from both sides of the groove to obtain the correct width and still maintain a minimum of 0.080-inch of material left outboard of each groove in the direction of the cylinder wall.

Typical lathe setup used to turn wider pin-lock grooves in a piston to use the 0.072-inch Spirolox or Tru-Arc wrist-pin retainers.

KingPins are taper-wall pins designed specifically for small-block racing. Other makers offer similar pins, but avoid any which are chrome-plated because any irregularities in the chrome will cause the pin to break.

When shortening the wrist pin to fit this modified piston, shorten the pin an equal amount on each end; then before installing, break the sharp edge off the corners of the pin ends with a stone.

End play at initial building should be 0.0000-inch to prevent hammering and breakage — this goes for either Tru-Arc or Spirolox used in high-performance engines. Never reuse either type retainer — you're gambling pennies against hundreds of dollars in this situation.

Most any bearing supply house can supply the Tru-Arc snap rings, while the Chevy parts counter sells the thin Spirolox.

Last choice for pin retention is a single Spirolox or Tru-Arc at each end of the pin. This is adequate for street use, but any racing application needs one of the previously recommended methods.

OILING THE WRIST PIN

When using stock, TRW or Sealed Power pistons only a few but very important steps need be taken. First we must provide a film of oil to ride between the wrist pin and the piston. This is accomplished by drilling an oil hole of 1/8-inch diameter into the wrist-pin bore. Before grabbing piston and drill bit, you should know there is a right and a wrong way of doing this and because most of us have been doing it wrong for so long we'd best take some advice from Smokey Yunick. Smokey says this oil hole into the wrist pin bore is the most effective way of lubricating the wrist pin but that the hole should not be drilled into the bottom of the boss. Drill the hole into the top of the boss — in other words towards the top of the piston. Then intersect this hole with another hole of the same diameter drilled through the lower piston ring groove. Thus oil returning from the back side of the lower ring moves onto the wrist pin before returning to the sump. Yunick says that drilling the bottom of the boss disturbs the tensile strength in an area where you cannot afford to take chances. The bottom of the boss could be jerked out from a fracture started from that oil hole. Naturally, this procedure should be applied to both sides of the piston.

Those TRW replacement pistons with a 1/8-inch wide oil-ring groove should have the groove carefully opened up to accommodate the stock 3/16-inch-wide ring. This procedure helps oil control on high-performance engines.

TAPER WALL PINS

Pin durability can be a real problem on a high-RPM small block. Chevrolet's high-performance pins have squared ends, thick walls and are bored straight through the center. TRW's have a necked-down area in the center of the pin bore. This area is considered by some to be a stress-riser which could promote failure. Both of these pin types are certainly adequate for most street-driven machines. However, taper-wall pins are definitely recommended for the serious racer. The cost of the pins is cheap insurance as compared to the price of replacing an engine when a pin lets go.

You'll note that some of our photos show taper-wall pins. These weigh slightly more than stock pins, but they concentrate the major cross-sectional area of the pin where the load is greatest — in the rod "eye" (small end). The ones shown here are KingPins made by King Engine Service out of specially heat treated 9310 bar stock with squared ends to contact the retainers correctly. Some piston makers also offer taper-wall pins. The pins are usually available in a standard length for use with Spirolox or Tru-Arc retainers and longer pins are offered for those builders preferring to use end buttons.

PIN CONFIGURATIONS

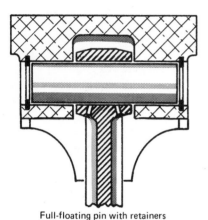

Pressed-in pin

Full-floating pin with retainers

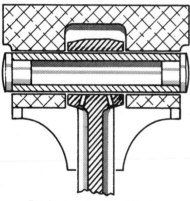

Full-floating pin with pin buttons

Pins can be installed in three separate ways in small-block pistons, as shown by these illustrations. The top two are stock methods and the bottom one is favored by some racing-engine builders. The two full-floating methods have pin clearance in the rod eye and two holes in the rod for pin lubrication. The illustrations do not show oiling the pin bosses from the backside of the oil ring, but this is essential.

PRESSED-IN vs. FULL-FLOATING PINS

Two types of piston pin installation are used in Chevrolet small-block engines. Most common is the pressed-in pin. In this situation, the pin oscillates in the piston pin bores, but is pressed immovably into the small end of the rod with an interference fit. The vast majority of all Chevrolets on the road today are so equipped. High-performance engines such as the 1969 Z-28 and LT-1 have full-floating pins. The pin is a floating fit in the piston-pin bores and in the small end of the rod. Spirolox spiral-wound steel retainers, 0.042-inch thick, hold the pin in the piston. All other small blocks, including those with forged pistons, have pressed-in pins. Except for some replacement Z-28 and LT-1 short blocks, the pistons do not have retainer grooves and there's no room to install them.

Full-floating pins are recommended for any engine that is to develop a lot of HP on a continuous basis. The reasons include longer life for the pin bores in the piston, for the pin itself, and for the rod—if the rod has adequate pin clearance and both rod and piston have suitable pin-oiling holes. The advantage of easy assembly and disassembly without danger of damaging the parts is especially useful for a racing engine which must be disassembled and reassembled often because it is being raced.

In a high-loading situation, a pressed-in pin tends to scuff in the pin bore because the pin is marginally lubricated and the same area always gets the load. Once the pin starts to scuff, the pin bore overheats and rapidly wears to an out-of-round configuration. Then the rod can cock and break in the middle. The same type of failure occurs if a full-floating pin is not lubricated in the piston or has inadequate clearance or lubrication in the rod. In this situation the pin galls or scuffs in the rod eye, seizes so that it no longer turns, then scuffs in the piston with a failure sequence identical to that of a pressed-in pin which scuffs in the piston pin bore/s. Such failures are nearly always blamed on the piston or on the connecting rod—instead of on the pin which was the real culprit.

Full-floating pins should have 0.0006 to 0.0008-inch clearance in the piston; 0.0008 to 0.001-inch in the rod. If the fit is made too tight, the broken-rod syndrome could occur in *your* engine.

As the rod moves back and forth on the crankshaft journal, there is a tendency for the pin to move back and forth with the rod. In a full-floating configuration this makes the pin act as a battering ram which tries to push the pin retainers out of their grooves. Keeping the pin-to-retainer clearance to a minimum (0.000 to 0.005-inch) - preferably to the zero clearance — and setting the rod side clearance at no more than Chevy's specs reduces or eliminates this battering-ram effect. If you machine or remachine grooves in a piston to use a thicker Spirolox, this must be done with great care to end up with the desired end clearance. It also requires grinding the pin ends to be square. This grinding process, in conjunction with machining the grooves to provide the desired clearance, is described in the section on Piston Pin Retention. If you are changing to a full-floating setup, pin bores should be opened up to provide the recommended clearance for the pin. Pin bores can be drilled to provide lubrication for the pin and the rods must be modified for use with full-floating pins as described in the Blueprinting chapter.

Retainers should be used *once!* After you have run the engine, use new retainers if you take them out of the piston for any reason. Truarc retainers supplied in many pistons are apparently adequate for street applications, but builders seeking maximum reliability use wider grooves with two Truarcs or the 0.072-inch Spirolox (preferred).

There's sharp disagreement among engine builders as to the relative merits of pressed-in versus floating pins. Engines are easiest to assemble when floating pins are used. But, some engineers insist that the engines will live longer and provide less trouble if the pressed-in pins are used. They point out that the pressed-in pin provides a "T-shaped" structure for the top of the rods so that the pistons are prevented from cocking on the rod axis, as occurs with the floating pins. This gives the pin only two bores to "wiggle" in, instead of three. There's no denying that correctly installed pressed-in pins are best for a street engine. The engine will stay quieter longer with the pressed-in pins than with the floating pins. However, pressed-in pins can be installed incorrectly and when this happens, disaster is certain to occur.

When fitting pressed-in pins, it is sometimes necessary to hone the rod "eyes" or small ends so that the interference fit for the pins will be reduced to an acceptable level. Too much interference galls or tears the rod eye or pin surface as the parts are pressed together, causing very rapid wear of the pin-bore in the piston. The interference fit should be in the range of 0.0008 to 0.0012. The tighter fit is preferable.

It is extremely important to ensure that the machinist uses the correct fixtures and measures the pistons, rods, and pins—and then corrects any misfits before proceeding with the installation. More pistons are ruined by faulty assembly to the pins and rods than by any other cause. After the correct fits have been established, use the right fixture to center the pin and rod in the piston. The fixture also guides the pin through the rod eye and into the other pin bore. The pin and rod eye must be lubricated prior to pressing the pin into the rod/piston assembly. And, the piston must be supported squarely and firmly. Some machinists heat the rod eye prior to installing the rod onto the pin and piston. Pin clearance in the piston should be 0.0005 to 0.0007-inch to ensure good oiling. Some replacement pistons from Chevy may have as much as 0.001-inch clearance (upper tolerance limit).

INSTALLATION CAUTIONS

Before shoving a piston in the hole with the backside of a ballpeen hammer assume that it is one of the most important, carefully designed and fragile parts of the entire assembly. Assume? Why? Because the proof is abundant in one of two areas. Performance is poor or destruction is imminent if the piston is not "right" and in the business of building high-performance engines, the term "right" is used to describe degrees and not an absolute. Consider: That the piston — with its ring assembly — creates more mechanical friction than any other component. That the piston and ring assembly has to operate over a very wide temperature range and because the heat capacity is quite small the piston may reach a very high temperature while the cylinder in which it is operating is relatively cool. At times like this you can count on the lubricant being chilled and relatively inefficient. That the piston must be as light as possi-

ble for the acceleration and deceleration constitute the bulk of mean loading on the rod journal of the crankshaft and the inertia of the moving piston constitutes the majority of cylinder wall loading. The inertia of the piston loading also constitutes the main disturbing force on dynamic balancing. That the piston has to receive millions of applications of the entire gas pressure exerted in the individual cylinder, transmit this from the piston head to the wrist pin and do this without any appreciable distortion to the head, skirt, rings or cylinder walls.

That the piston and ring assembly is charged with the duty of receiving and disposing of the major proportion of combustion heat. That the piston and ring assembly is charged with the duty of forming a gas-tight seal in one direction and a very effective oil seal in the other. That while the piston receives heat over the entire head surface, it may only get rid of heat to the cylinder walls through the circumference; thus the piston must be made of a material which will readily conduct heat to the walls. That the two conditions of light weight and high thermal conductivity are best met by using an aluminum alloy which introduces even more problems.

The thermal-expansion rate of most aluminum alloys is close to three times that of cast iron. As temperature of the alloy rises, the strength of the metal falls rapidly.

We mention all of these simply as a reminder that all is skittles and beer in the land of high-performance engines — no matter what the brand name on the valve cover. Unless you have more money and research facilities than General Motors, there is precious little you can do about the problems of a piston-and-ring assembly, but the few things you can do must be done without fail. Lubrication, temperature control and correct clearances head up this list.

WHAT DO YOU DO NOW THAT WE HAVE CONFUSED YOU?

If you are building a street/strip machine that is not being bored out or getting new pistons, you may now be in a dilemma. What to do? Make the pins full-floating — or live with the pressed-in pins? Change to forged pistons or live with the cast ones? Or,

Take it easy when you install those rings. Ring compressor must be flush with the block deck at all points before driving the piston down with a piece of wood.

perhaps you are wondering how you can lower the compression ratio now that the gasoline is so bad.

If the engine is only going to see an occasional trip to the quarter-mile strip and is more designed for transportation than racing — stick with the pistons and pressed-in pins that came in your engine, especially if you are not changing the cam and valve train to allow use at higher RPM's. They'll probably go right on working perfectly without a minute's trouble. If you have an engine that is equipped with a high compression ratio, consider changing to a lower-compression cast-aluminum piston so that life will become more livable.

But, if you are building an engine which is to spend its working hours on the racing scene, then by all means disassemble it completely for a full blueprinting. Make the necessary modifications to the rods and buy the pistons needed to allow the pins to float in both. If you are buying new pistons, then consider the forged ones in the HD Parts List — or TRW's. Most of the full-floating-pin pistons have deeper and perhaps even larger valve notches to accommodate large valves and high-lift camshafts. And, TRW's have 1/16-inch-thick rings which means that there will be even less tendency towards ring flutter at high RPM than the HD Chevy parts. However, for most uses, the TRW's should be modified for pin oiling, thicker retainers and 3/16-inch oil rings.

With changes happening fast because of emission requirements, it will pay to keep up to date on what Chevrolet is using.

COMPRESSION RATIO

In general, the average dual-purpose small-block — or even an engine used solely for transportation, should be equipped with a true compression ratio of 9:1 to 9.5:1 maximum. Premium gasoline is required with this compression.

Racing engines may be able to tolerate ratios up to 11.5:1, but anything this high will not run well on any gasoline that you can buy at the corner gasoline station. And, this problem is getting worse as gasoline quality continues to worsen in terms of actual octane rating. A racing engine can tolerate higher compression than a street-driven one because a camshaft with lots of overlap reduces the engine's low-speed-pumping capabilities. Higher compression ratios are used to offset the loss of low-speed torque caused by lots of overlap.

QUICK COMPRESSION RATIO CHECK

To measure the approximate compression ratio of any engine requires only a burette as described in the head CC'ing section. Bring a piston to TDC, seal the top piston ring to the cylinder wall with a smear of grease around the edge and install a head gasket of the same type to be used on the engine (a used one will be fine). Install the head and torque the bolts. Turn the engine so that the spark plug is vertical (easier to do if the engine is out of the car). Remove the spark plug and fill the cylinder head through the plug hole from the burette. Use the same fluid described for CC'ing heads. Note how many CC's this requires to fill to the bottom of the plug threads. Page 111 has a table of plug volumes. You can add this volume if you want to be accurate. Convert this chamber measurement to cubic inches by dividing the CC's by 16.386:

$$\frac{\text{chamber displacement} + \text{cyl. disp.}}{\text{chamber disp.}} = \text{C.R.}$$

Example: 4.001-in. bore x 3.48-in. stroke 350 has a cylinder displacement of 4.001 x 4.001 x 0.7854 x 3.48 = 43.752 cubic inches. Measured chamber capacity 76.3 cc's ÷ 16.386 = 4.618 cu. in.

$$\frac{43.752 + 4.618}{4.618} = 10.47:1 \text{ C.R.}$$

NOTE: The plug hole is seldom the highest point in the chamber, so there is nearly always some air left in the chamber that is not displaced by the measuring fluid. Therefore, calculations based on this method may give a slightly higher compression ratio than you actually have in the engine.

Want parts information?

Enthusiasts often complain about "tight-wad" manufacturers who won't answer requests for information or literature. Advertisements in the automotive magazines offer catalogs or instructions—typically for 50¢ to $1. Why should you pay a manufacturer for his catalog so that you can buy something from him? The answer has two parts: (1) you probably *won't* buy anything, and (2) his out-of-pocket costs for sending the catalog (printing, envelope, addressing and stamps) *are more than what he charges in every case.* He asks that you help to defray literature costs because he has no way of determining whether you are a literature collector, a discount-house shopper, or a bona fide cash customer.

How about letters with questions? Many questions which are asked obviously indicate that the writer has not done his "homework" by reading workshop manuals, magazine articles, or this book. Some intelligent questions would probably be answered if there was room for an answer on a neatly typed letter sent with a dollar for literature and a self-addressed, stamped envelope for an answer. Indicate on your letter that a handwritten scribble will be fine for an answer—and word one or two questions carefully so that they can be easily answered with a word or two. Some enthusiasts' letters contain such long and involved questions that $100 in time and research would be required to create an answering letter. Even if the manufacturer has the answer "in his head," a typed letter costs at least $4—not counting the man's time—whether you buy anything or not. Small wonder that so many letters are thrown out—or that manufacturers react with undisguised disinterest when called upon for information. Selling catalogs and literature is an absolute necessity in the automobile-accessory business. If you cannot grasp that fact, then don't be surprised when your requests go unanswered.

Although H.P. Books and the authors cannot answer requests for information on engine or chassis setups, your letter pointing out where this book could have been more helpful will always be appreciated and acknowledged. A suppliers list is on page 160. These firms can help you.

THE STOCK SYSTEM

Chevrolet's small-block V8 engine has one of the most troublefree and reliable lubrication systems and lower ends that's available in any medium-displacement engine you can buy today. And, this has been accomplished without any of the desperation measures that have had to be used to make other hi-perf engines live.

Chevy's design engineers spent an enormous amount of effort in making the bottom end right! Lower-end failures in these engines are very, very rare. This is only true if the factory's proved design is used *as is* — without the trick modifications which hundreds of experts have found to their expense to be completely unworkable. Incidentally, be sure to read the info on the types of bearings and crankshaft journals which are needed to make the engine live. If you missed that part of the chapter on building the hi-perf small block — one word tells it like it is and should be — *"stock!"*

The full-pressure lubrication system uses internal passages within the cylinder block, crankshaft and head. Oil supplied by the pump goes through a full-flow filter into a 1/2-inch main gallery atop the camshaft. Oil from this gallery proceeds through a hole to an annulus (groove) around the backside of the rear cam bearing. Lifter (tappet) and rear main oiling is provided from this groove. The four front cam bearings also have the grooves which connect to their respective main bearings.

Oil fed to the lifters gets to the rocker arms through hollow pushrods. A 1/2-inch-diameter pump inlet with a large suction screen produces minimum flow restrictions and eliminates pump cavitation.

Because everything that you do to increase power simultaneously increases heat production, don't overlook oil cooling as a heat-removal method. An external cooler helps, as does improving the heat-radiating characteristics of the engine surfaces. All of this is fully explained in this chapter.

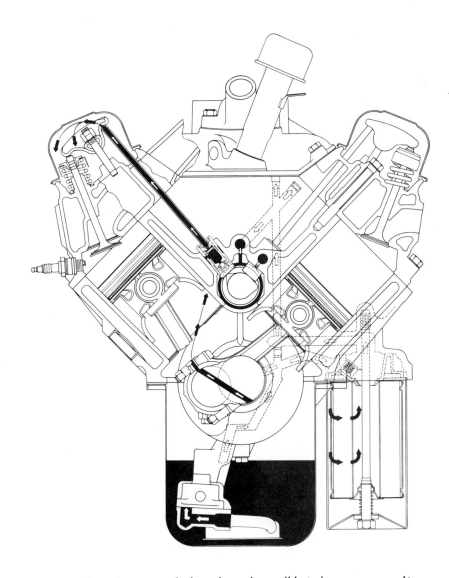

The stock Chevy oiling system is darned near impossible to improve upon. It can handle over 500 HP with complete reliability if you don't try to make trick changes. By leaving the system stock you can expect maximum reliability consistent with the thousands of hours Chevrolet spent in making it right in the first place. This is the early block with canister-type filter.

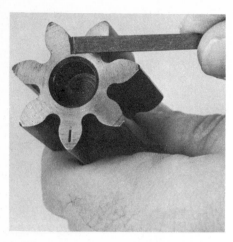

Lightly deburring gear-teeth edges with a fine file is highly recommended in preparing a pump for high-RPM running.

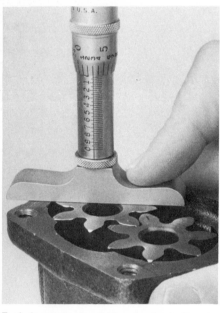

End clearance should be checked after the gears have been deburred at both ends. This oil-pump body — a Z-28 — had 0.003" clearance. It will be sanded lightly at the joint to reduce the end clearance to the recommended 0.0025 inch.

OIL PUMPS

You can foul up on the ignition, cam, pistons and intake system and the engine will be a "dog" . . . but it will still get you to the grocery store. Foul up on the oil system with some home-built, jury-rigged pump, pan and pickup arrangement and the whole ball of wax goes out the door. There is no need to do this of course, but some guys think they just have to "out-trick" the factory and that's when the trouble starts.

There are three pumps to use in the high-performance small-block Chevrolet: Z-28, big-block, or dry sump. For street, strip and a lot of circle-track applications the Z-28 pump will most likely suffice. If you need more of an oiling system than this you should probably go directly to a dry-sump system. The Z-28 pump, part number 3848907, bolts up to any of the small blocks. We called the local Chevy dealer, asked the price, and the parts man said $17.50. Buy one new — not rebuilt! Take it home, take it apart. Check the end clearance of the gears. There should be no more than 0.0025-inch between the ends of the gears and the cover plate surface when the gears are fully bottomed in the housing. If there is more clearance, the pump will be quick to lose prime and slow to regain it. This hurts. To bring excessive end play back in the ball park, sand the pump body cover-mating surface on a piece of solvent-wetted 220 Wet-or-Dry paper backed up by a machined plate or a piece of heavy glass. If the clearance is too small — less than 0.0015-inch — and this is really rare, the gears can be sanded down in the same manner.

Check the end clearance with a depth micrometer. Wash the pump out with clean solvent. Don't dry it off with a shop rag because that puts unwanted lint into the oiling system. Blow off the pump body and gears with compressed air or just let all of the solvent evaporate by allowing all of the components to rest on a clean surface. Some pictures in this section show how the gears should be deburred on the ends. This should be done if burrs exist. If they don't exist, don't try to create some in your mind. In other words, don't start looking for things to do

— and then get carried away with the project and do too much. Before putting the pump back together, douse the gears in a high quality motor oil.

Bill King has another suggestion: drill two 0.060-inch holes in the idler gear. These go on opposite sides of the gear, spaced about one-third in from each end. These serve to oil the center post on which the gear turns. Be sure to deburr the bore of the gear where the drill comes through.

A lot of guys are tempted to run the big-block oil pump on the small block. This provokes some differences of opinion. The big-block pump is an excellent unit — make no mistake about that. Contrary to popular belief, the big-block pump has no greater capacity than the Z-28 unit, but does have a pressure balance and 12-tooth gears instead of the 7-tooth gears used in small-block pumps. These gears — the argument goes — move more smoothly and thus keep the distributor from jerking around and producing spark scatter. The large-block pump does have a larger diameter pickup tube and a double bypass which helps to keep a more even oil pressure throughout the temperature range.

If the large-block oil pump is used in the small block, then you must measure the amount of pump shaft engagement with the distributor shaft. The tang on the end of the distributor gear must engage fully with the slot in the end of the pump shaft. If more engagement is needed, the drive gear shaft can be pressed out of the gear a fraction of an inch, or if the distributor will not seat in the block because of too much engagement, then the shaft can be pressed further into the gear. The only real bother to running the large-block pump is that a pickup must be fabricated to fit the small-block pan.

One of those who says that the Z-28 pump is the way to fly — Smokey Yunick — opines that the large-block oil pump takes quite a few more horsepower to drive than the Z-28 pump.

No matter what pump you use, don't get carried away with the old trick of shimming the spring for more pressure. This can gall and then stick the bypass and blow the filter can off the block. The only time that shimming may be needed is when a remote filter and/or cooler is used. In this case, it may be necessary to shim the oil pump spring 1/8-inch or install a stiffer spring to restore the desired 50 psi hot oil pressure which should be run in a high-performance Chevrolet engine. If the spring is shimmed, place the shims inside of the pressure bypass valve rather than at the other end of the spring.

Don't try to run too much pressure. When the oil is at operating temperature, pressure should never exceed 60-65 pounds. Anything over this just whips more air into the system. Another way of putting this is: more oil pressure doesn't help bearing life.

Don't go into any part of engine building blind. Do some thinking. This is especially true of the oiling system as it applies to the small-block Chevy. You'll note elsewhere in the book that the recommended clearances for the lower end of a little Chevy are 0.002-0.003-inch on the mains (with the minimum preferred) and 0.002-0.0025-inch on the rods. This doesn't sound like much and when the engine starts going together it looks mighty slim. So Herman J. Shankmaster thinks that the trick is to run 0.004 on the mains and 0.003-inch on the rods. He figures that he can "float" those journals in a heavier weight oil (like 50W) and get all the protection needed. There's no danger of the crank and bearing ever coming together because of the great film of oil in there, right? So the engine is fired up and at 1500 RPM, 8 pounds of oil pressure shows on the gage. So after tapping the gage for awhile, Herman chills the engine, sits in the front seat of his street car and thinks things over. What I need, he says to himself, is more oil pressure; and to get more oil pressure I need a bigger pump. And this is how poor Herman tries to solve one evil with another one. Herman spends a lot of time working on his car. Did you ever wonder why?

The pump attaches to the rear main bearing cap, so it is important to make sure that the hole in the pump aligns with the hole in the cap. Some chamfering may be needed to get the holes lined up with each other. A capscrew goes through the hole, so remember that the oil has to pass through this same area and exit on the opposite side of the capscrew.

Small-block oil pumps which are purchased from the dealer do not have a pickup installed. Remember to buy a pickup when you get the pump. The pickups are available with slightly different lengths — about 1-1/2 in. covers the span of difference to fit the various stock pans. If you are going to lengthen the pickup to fit a deeper pan, Dino Fry suggests buying the Chevy II pickup which has a tube reaching toward the front of the engine. This will give you some tubing to use as you place the pickup about 1/4 inch away from the bottom of the installed pan.

The pickup *must be brazed into the pump body.* If you have the Kent-Moore pickup installation tool No. J-8369, you can hold the pump body in a soft-jawed vise as you drive the pickup into the pump cover. Otherwise, you'll have to file or grind around the end of the tube until it slips into the pump cover. Before starting to braze the tube into the cover, take the pin, spring and relief piston out of the cover so that they will not be damaged by the heat.

The pickup and pan work together, so remember that whenever you start modifying a pan/pickup for any special purpose. Above all else, do whatever is necessary to keep the pickup submerged in the oil. No big deal, you say. Just shove the pickup down close to the bottom of the the pan, dump in a load of oil and "go racing." Unfortunately, it's not that simple.

Incidentally, when you are working on the pickup, don't be tempted to saw off the pickup to run a plain-ended tube. It won't work. And, the stamped-metal shield over the screen in the bottom of the pickup must also be left in place because it helps to prevent oil from leaving the inlet to the tube.

For the most part, small-block oil pans fit a particular chassis — thus there are many variations on a central theme of rear-sump design. From top to bottom: a '56-57; '58 to late '60's; the double-sump, larger-capacity pan is for most of the '62 and newer 327 blocks while the last pan is basically the same as the second example save for drain-plug location.

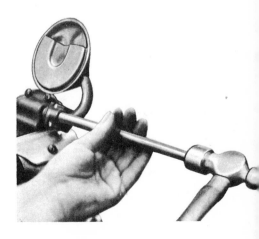

Kent-Moore Tool J 8369 can be used to install the pickup tube in the pump cover. You'll still have to braze the pickup tube in position — after taking out the relief spring and piston. Don't be tempted to skip this important step. It is an essential one for a high-performance engine. Photo is from Chevrolet Chassis Overhaul book.

The stock Chevy oil pickup — this one on a big-block pump — is hard to beat. Think long and hard before modifying it. You can bet that Chevy did more than just a little research on the subject before arriving at this design. Just be sure to keep it about 1/4 to 3/8 inch from the bottom of the oil pan that you use — which may require extending the pickup tube.

Drill indicates where a second hole has been added to oil the idler post. These holes (two are required, each one-third in from the gear end) in a "valley" of the gear can be from 0.040 to 0.060-inch. Be sure to deburr them where they break through into the gear bore so that the post will not be scratched when the pump is assembled.

The no-risk plan here is to safety-wire the capscrews used to hold the pump cover on the pump body. The pickup tube MUST be brazed to the body after removing the relief piston, spring and pin so that they will not be heat-damaged. Brazing a button over the hole in the screen is not a bad idea, but cutting away the shrouding as has been done here is a bummer! Leave the shrouding stock; cutting it away will allow the pickup to uncover quickly in turns or stops. Z-28 windage tray, pan and pump happen to be the lowest-cost most fool-proof hot tip for all street-driven small blocks and probably better than 75% of all the competition cars in the country. Baffle (arrow) prevents lube from sloshing forward during hard stops.

It is recommended that the pickup be repositioned for the particular use the engine will see. For oval-track racing, the pickup should be relocated on the right side of the pan. For drag racing, the pickup can be relocated to the extreme rear of the pan so that the force generated by the acceleration of the car will keep oil around the pickup. With such a setup, a vertical baffle must be placed ahead of the pickup to avoid oil starvation on deceleration.

Regardless of the position in the pan, the pickup should be spaced 1/4- to 3/8-inch above the pan bottom.

You have seen advertisements for swinging pickups which follow the body of oil during acceleration or hard braking. Swivelling-type oil pickups still need development to get full potential. At the present time they are largely used in funny-cars and in road-race machinery. When used in road-race machines, the pickups have strange quirks which you might not recognize or think about until too late. You don't need or want one for your street/strip machine.

The pickups work fine if there are sufficient "g" forces. If you declutch and shift, the pump will gulp air and drop oil pressure. If you "float" over a hill and are slowing down, the same thing occurs. Mechanics with whom we talked claimed swinging pickups can cause failures if the pickup happens to stick in the forward position just as you get back on the throttle to accelerate hard. Perhaps a pickup which swings 180 degrees from side-to-side only will be best because it will take care of cornering loads. Such a pickup could be used with baffles to take care of the acceleration and braking forces. Baffling the pan is a better solution for oil control. If you do choose to use a swinging pickup, for whatever reason, then the swinging joint should be pressurized (through a restriction) from the pump to prevent air entering with the oil and to keep the swinging joint well oiled.

The ultimate design will probably end up with ball bearings supporting the pickup, with a pressure-fed joint to eliminate sucking air. Such units are not manufactured as of this time.

Here's a pump trick worth remembering for road-course racers who don't want to go to
the expense of dry sumping. Z-28 pump has been fitted with a swinging pickup which
mates to a very large diameter inlet tube. The lower hose supplies lube under pressure
back to the pickup in order to eliminate aeration and to keep a film of oil between the
steel of the pickup and the cast-iron of the housing from which the pickup swings.
You'll have to make this one — there's nothing like it on the market. Right, Smokey?

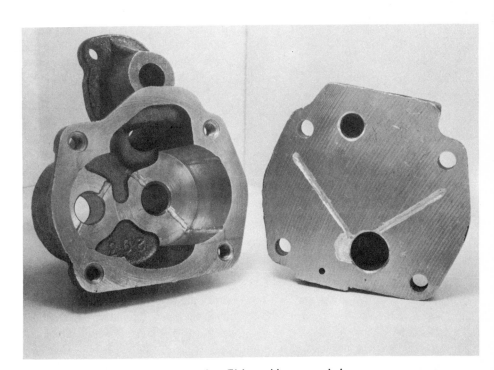

Z-28 pump modifications by co-author Fisher add pressure-balance grooves across
idler and drive-gear cavity ends to provide hydrostatic balancing of these gears. This
reduces spark-scatter which is caused by pump "chattering." Grooves are approximately 1/32-inch deep and 1/16-inch to 1/8-inch wide. Note the vertical groove
added toward the inlet side of the idler gear. A similar groove on the drive-gear inlet
side does not show clearly in this photo. These two grooves connect with the grooves
in the pump cover. Remove the idler post when doing the grooving. The cavity in
the cover has also been enlarged and smoothed somewhat so that it is similar to the
cavity in the pump body (at the inlet end). Pressure relief piston, spring and pin
have been removed in preparation for brazing the pickup tube assembly into the
pump cover.

OIL PAN & WINDAGE TRAY

To obtain "free horsepower" from the oiling system, keep the oil away from the "monkey motion" of the crank. To ensure the pickup an adequate pocket of oil, increase the capacity of the pan. Roughly three quarts of oil are "somewhere upstairs" in a small-block Chevy turning high RPM. Oil galleys are full; the lifters and pushrods are

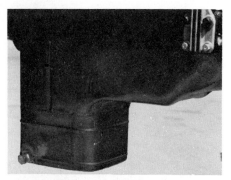

A number of manufacturers rework stock Chevy pans for added capacity — and at one time Chevrolet even got into the act with a fabricated pan that looked quite similar.

Low-cost modification performed by a home builder worked well on a drag-race car. Rear baffle prevented oil from climbing rear wall under acceleration. The front baffle prevents forward oil surging when braking or letting off the throttle.

full, the valve-train side of the heads are drenched, the timing chain is flooded and the pump passages are full — in addition to all of the lube on and draining from the cylinder walls. Figure one more quart gurgling through the filter can and you've got an engine with four quarts of oil not surrounding the pickup. In fact, the pump may have no oil available for the bearings and lifters, which can be bad news.

For serious competition on the drag strip, count on adding enough sump to bring the capacity of the pan up to eight quarts *without* raising the level of the oil in relationship to the crank. If you can extend the sump straight down without hitting the chassis, steering linkage or ground when the front end drops, this is the most effective and low cost way of modifying it. Make sure that the extended sump will not hit the ground even when the front suspension is completely bottomed out.

If the deep-sump method won't work, then you have to make the sump longer and/or wider. At this point, the chassis usually dictates what must be done. Longer or wider sumps increase the problems of keeping lube surrounding the pickup. Oil now has a lot more "floor space" to move around in. And more square inches of oil area are exposed to air forced down by the undersides of the pistons and churned by the crank.

If you could see into an oil pan while the engine was turning some "high numbers," the scene would be close to that achieved by firing a nozzled garden hose into a half bucket of water. Swinging gates and doors built into high-performance pans have a single purpose, which you shouldn't lose track of if you start building or modifying pans. Construct and place the gates so that horizontal oil movement within the pan feeds the immediate area of the pickup. Strips of piano hinge are readily available on which to swing the gates.

The semi-circular tray baffle 3927136 under the crankshaft drains the oil away from the crank and at the same time prevents the crank throws from hitting an accumulation of oil. This baffle should be installed on any small-block Chevrolet engine — regardless of the type of oiling system used. It's worth several HP at high RPM.

After installing a new trick baffled-and-gated pan and windage tray, keep track of oil pressure, ET slips and spark plugs. If oil pressure drops, that is a good indication the pickup is running out of oil to feed the pump. In short you'd best start over on pan and windage-tray design. If the car is going quicker or faster, that's a good indication you did some good. If the spark plugs come up looking oily or the breathers are dripping oil after one pass, the lube is most likely being restricted from adequate drainback.

For a street or road car, the wise move is probably to buy a Z-28 pan P/N 3974251, tray baffle P/N 3927136 and five main-bearing-cap studs P/N 3960312 required to mount the baffle. The Z-28 pan is internally baffled, has a rear sump and fits in most Chevy frames without reworking. The baffle keeps the oil away from the crank and in the higher RPM ranges, allows a few more horsepower to reach the flywheel. Remember that the Z-28 pan and tray are hard to beat — stick with it until you find a real need for something different. Use a magnetic drain plug.

Chevrolet makes a swinging gate pan P/N 3956670 for the small-block Corvettes but this should not be used in preference to the Z-28 pan, pump and windage tray.

For drag racing, you won't be far wrong with the Z-28 tray baffle along with the deepest sump pan you can stuff under the car without danger of it dragging the asphalt when the car settles.

You must always remember that the important thing is to keep the pickup immersed in the oil. Extend the pickup tube and the pickup itself in the oil when the pan is deepened. If necessary, add bracing between the pickup tube and the pump body to ensure rigid support. But, hanging the pump itself onto an extension is not recommended, according to Bob Joehnck, because the pump was not designed to be used with a long, unsupported intermediate shaft with no bearings.

A wide variety of performance-oriented pans is made by Aviaid, Ron Butler, John Mason, Milodon, and Tri-Metric Engineering. An array of baffles, swinging gates and sump sizes and shapes are available for a myriad of specific applications. Depending on the complexity, these pans cost from $50 to $200 or more.

Ed Pink built this pan for a circle-track car. A deeper sump could not be used in the car, so added capacity was gained laterally. Gates swing only in the direction of the arrows. You'd better have proof you need all of this.

There are a couple of ways of making a swinging gate in an oil pan. These shots show both sides of a gate. The ribbing in the bottom of the pan is for strength. It is especially helpful to stop fatigue from drumming. Lips (arrows) are used to mount a windage tray.

ENGINE BREATHING & VENTING

Nearly all mechanics start out with the idea that the stock breathing for the small block is inadequate. Nothing could be further from the truth. The stock covers are equipped with oil separators designed to prevent oil pull-over at air flow up to 10 cubic feet per minute — a lot of air flow. You can use these rocker cover vents to make a system adequate for any racing engine.

Just connect the two rocker covers by 3/4-inch ID or larger tubing which runs up and across the front of the engine with two or more breather-type oil caps in the piece of tubing which is at the highest point. If you braze elbows into the stock covers, be sure to leave the stock oil separators intact. When you install this type of system, you eliminate any need for expensive and ineffective hotrod breathers which usually blow oil all over your engine. The system which we have described was first used on the Dodge/Plymouth Trans Am entries in 1970 and was subsequently used on those monster engines that run in the NASCAR events. Success in both of these applications has proved that this is the system to consider.

There are cast-aluminum covers available for the small block — but most do not include any oil separators and special breathers must be constructed to bring back the crankcase pressure relief which was previously provided in the stock covers. This may be one instance where the cosmetic benefits of the special parts should be foregone in favor of the real benefits and built-in breathing of the stock parts.

If you're looking for cosmetics *and* the best rocker covers at the same time, the cast-aluminum cover currently offered by Chevy is the hot tip. Cast into the underside of the covers are small tips which "collect the oil" blowing around upstairs so it drips onto the rocker balls. Just visit the Chevy parts counter.

If an electric fuel pump is used, the stock fuel-pump mount can be used for venting hardware.

Why all this fuss about venting? The engine is nothing more than an air pump, which means that the same volume of air is moved around in the bottom of the engine as is inhaled into and exhaled out of the combustion chamber. Couple this with the air and oil mist whipped around by that massive rotating crankshaft and you quickly see that the bottom side of any large engine gets to be a violently active area when it comes to air velocity and direction. The engine simply needs a plenum chamber at the bottom end where all of the vented air from the downstrokes can be displaced through vents. High-RPM ring flutter is often directly traceable to pressure at the *lower* end — which correct venting helps to reduce.

The right venting also helps the engine to run cooler.

Upper rocker cover has been sawn through to show construction of the four-slat baffle which is built into every Chevy small-block cover. Although simple in construction, the baffle effectively stops oil pull-over with the escaping air from the engine's insides. Center cover is a die-cast aluminum cover from Z-28 or Corvette engine. Note the cast-in oil drippers which aid rocker-ball lubrication. Lower cover is a stock stamped-steel cover.

This is typical of the "hot-rod" breathers being sold. These top and bottom shots of a cast-aluminum accessory valve cover shows how the breather is mounted and vented. They're of very poor design and several of these won't equal the breathing ability of one stock breather.

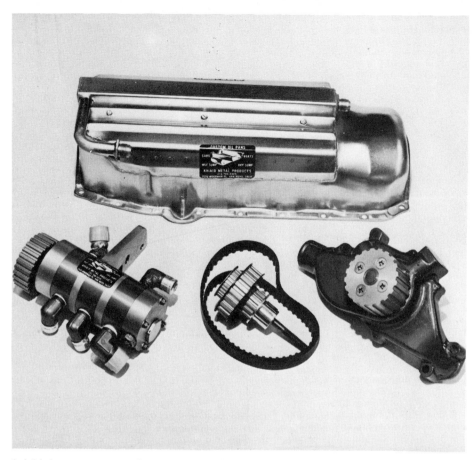

Aviaid dry-sump system for the small block is impressive and keeps boat engines and circle trackers out of lubrication problems. This is for all-out competition only. Pump is made by Weaver Brothers.

On a competition-oriented engine, the stock mechanical pump may be replaced with an electric unit. Several manufacturers offer cast fuel-pump-blockoff plates. This is also an excellent area for a crankcase vent.

Yunick breather arrangement for a road-race car. A ball bearing is captured in the section of tube indicated between the arrows. Slam on the brakes and the bearing rolls forward to seal off that outlet while the other section remains free to vent to a remotely-located puke can. This works!

Two breathers on tube connecting to the stock rocker covers will do the job.

Rear breather on this engine has been blocked off and breathers installed in the valve covers. This blocking off can also be accomplished with a 1-1/4-inch freeze plug driven into the block.

Oil-filter lineup: On left is canister-type filter with adapters to install the unit into small blocks. '56-67 blocks take adapter 5573979 (1), '68 and up police and truck engine adapter 3951626 can be used on any '68 and later engine (2). Canister is 5574535, cartridge is 5576054. Screw-on filters use adapter 3952301 on '68 and later blocks (3). Standard short filter 6438261 (PF-25) can be replaced with heavy-duty model 6438384 (PF-35). Canister filter has more filtering area and is cheaper to replace. Using the screw-on-type filter with the 1956-67 engines requires using adapter kits as made by Eelco or Mr. Gasket.

OIL FILTERS

In 1955 when the small block was introduced there was no filter on the engine and no provision for one, but beginning in 1956 Chevy has put the oil filter right on the block so there's no need to arrange for a remotely mounted filter at big expense. Some builders think that the screw-on filters introduced on 1968 engines and used on all blocks built since that time are necessarily better than the older canister-style filters. This is not the case, so don't rush to buy an adapter kit to put the late style screw-on filter on your pre-1968 engine. All that the later filters "buy you" is higher replacement cost. The canister-style filters are about $2.80 each, whereas the screw-on units are $4 or more. Don't complain when you are cleaning out the messy canister — think about the buck and a quarter or more that you are saving. And, you can take some pleasure in knowing that the larger canister-type filter has more filtering surface to clean your oil. In fact, some racing-engine builders won't use the screw-on filters. They convert the '68 and later blocks to use the early-style filter. These guys order a kit from Chevy, P/N 5574538, throw away the adapter that's in the kit—or swap it for adapter 3951626. This kit sells for about $11 list price.

Two canister sizes have been used on passenger cars: a long can on '56 and '57 engines; a short can was on '58 through '67. The two canister sizes are interchangeable, but naturally take different size filters. If you have a choice, and the clearance in the car permits, run the early (long) filter can to gain the extra filtering area. Incidentally, although 1968 was the changeover date from canister to spin-on filter, we are well aware that some '68 cars had canister filters — but they are the exception rather than the rule.

If you have an early block you can convert it to use a spin-on filter with the Fram adapter kit HPK-1 (there are others); and if you have a 1968 or later block you can convert it to the earlier (canister-type) filter using the parts described in the accompanying photo. By using Trans-Dapt fitting SP-328A any of the late (spin-on) blocks can be converted for dry sumping or for running a remote filter. By removing 0.030-inch from the seating surface of the Trans-Dapt casting, the same fitting can be used on the early block.

Thermo-Chem of Tulsa, Oklahoma has a casting which routes oil directly to a cooler from a spin-on filter. Their casting only fits spin-on style blocks.

On any of these adapters, check very carefully to see that the adapter seals against the block surface. Poor quality control or incorrect design will sometimes produce a "leaker." Traco's unit is highly recommended and used by most Trans Am and Formula A mechanics. Their part number 109 is priced at $22.50. The adapter is drilled and tapped to accept 1/2-inch pipe fittings.

For an engine going on the race track a pair of oil filters should be used instead of the stock setup. Some newer filters have a built-in check valve; if they're used in a remote location make sure they're hooked up correctly because they only flow one way.

So, as you can see there is more than one way to go with the oil filter on a small-block Chevy. The early blocks can be converted to spin-on style — which offers some convenience and added cost with less filtering surface. Late blocks can be converted back to the canister style. The canister-style filter will leak if the rubber gasket is not correctly installed — just make sure it's in the correct location when you start to tighten the big bolt. The spin-on filter almost never gives any trouble on the street (except for the idiots who don't bother to change them), but occasionally the spin-on filter will back off from vibration on a competition engine. Richard Catton of Reath pointed out that this is not uncommon on racing boats. If a spin-on filter is being used directly on the block of a competition car or boat, check it periodically to ensure that it is snug; if you're running two of them side by side in a remote location (Milodon kit), tape the two filters together with racer's tape (air conditioning duct tape) so they can't loosen.

Traco's adapter allows use with remotely-mounted oil filters, coolers and with dry-sump pumps. Because this adapter has no sealing problems — which some adapters have — it is used by the majority of Trans Am and Formula A engine builders. Notice drilled bolt head for safety wire and O-ring for sealing against cavity in block.

A heavy hauler ready for action from the stable of noted Chevy expert, Bob Joehnck of Santa Barbara, California. Filter can shown is called the "long can" but there is one available from a truck engine which is still longer.

Fram adapter for use with remote filter(s) and coolers on the '68 and newer blocks. Can be used on older blocks if underside of casting is reworked. The bolts supplied with the kit should be replaced by Grade 8 hardware.

When dry sumping, or running remote filters or cooler, follow the manufacturer's directions to the letter when it comes to routing oil. Some filter adapters for remote plumbing will install with the bypass in place, but you don't want a bypass because with the filter and cooler lines, all oil will tend to take the easy route and slip through the bypass — hence no cooling or filtering.

The first time that you fire up your engine, run it for 20 or 30 minutes at a fast idle. Drain the oil *while it is still warm* and promptly change both the oil and the filter cartridge. New engines are always full of lint and other trash — much of it from shop rags. This lint is the very worst culprit for plugging up filters. The price of the oil and filter that you throw away is cheap insurance against losing an engine. If you have plugged the filter relief, then the new filter ensures that you will have good oil pressure. If you have left the relief valve stock, dirty oil will bypass the filter whenever the oil is cold or the cartridge is plugged — and it will go directly to your engine's bearings and lifters.

The filter pressure-relief valve in the filter adapter is a disaster preventer for folks who refuse to change their filters and oil regularly. The valve should be plugged so that all oil is filtered before it can get to the engine. Watch that oil-pressure gage that you added. When the pressure starts to drop (assuming you are measuring the oil pressure *after* the filter), replace the filter cartridge because it's obviously become too clogged to work any more.

Of course, when the filter relief is plugged, you have to avoid jazzing the throttle when the engine is cold. You will have to let the engine warm up before running any high RPM's or the pump by-pass may not be able to cope with the pressure relief job — and your filter could be burst open by the high pressures which can occur with a cold engine.

So, what's so great about a full-flow filter and why should you continue to use the one that Chevy builds into their engines? Let's look at some facts and figures published by a competitor, the Ford Motor Company, in an SAE paper published in the 1950's. A full-flow filter reduced engine-component wear by the following amounts: 50% in crankshaft wear, 66% in wrist-pin wear, 19% in cylinder-wall wear and 52% in ring wear.

Much of the engine wear occurs from dirt or particles of metal which are seldom completely removed from the engine when it is first built or overhauled. Some of the engine wear comes from wear products—bearing particles, pieces off of the camshaft or lifters, minute bits of carbon which somehow manage to get past the rings, and tiny chunks of aluminum which are worn off of valve-spring retainers by the valve-springs. Of course, if you stick with steel retainers as supplied by Chevrolet, you'll eliminate one possible source of aluminum chips in your oil. Although the heads are iron, they should be equipped with steel shims at the bottom of the spring seats.

When these chips are recirculated through the engine with the oil, additional wear is caused, adding to the quantity of unwanted junk in the oil on a continually increasing basis so that the oil becomes a carrier of wear-producing material instead of a flow of life-sustaining lubricant.

WHAT KIND OF OIL?

Chevrolet has even provided an oil specification for the small block. They recommend 30 to 50 weight aircraft or other ashless high-performance oil such as Valvoline Racing Oil, Pure HP Racing Oil, or Sunoco 10/50 or 20/50 Multigrade. Most of the oils that you purchase at the discount store or corner service station are low-ash oils. The ash which remains, although small in amount, creates preignition-causing deposits. Many automotive oils were once ashless but have gone to the low-ash formulation as a result of incorporating anti-rusting agents and other agents required to make the oils—and engines—live with the attitudes prevalent today. However, you should realize that the oil companies cannot protect your engine when you start using oils without some of the long-life additives. You'll have to make sure that you change the oil and filter fre-

Engine used in Formula A competition exhibits effective but easy-to-fabricate crank-case venting system running from the valve covers to a single "puke can" which catches blowby oil, then returns it to the crankcase. Small radiator is for oil.

quently—something that most people have fallen out of the habit of doing in recent years.

DO NOT RUN HIGH VISCOSITY OILS. Stay on the lighter side of Chevrolet's recommendation. There is no need for the heavy stuff which merely complicates the oiling, perhaps creating bearing problems which you'll probably blame on something or someone else. Use the right grade of oil—usually 30 weight—of the recommended type and stick with it. High-viscosity oils do such terrible things as tearing up filter cans, not flowing to the bearings when the engine is cold, etc. Above all, stay off of the throttle until the engine is fully warmed up, no matter how cute the chick that wants to hear your engine go "rump-rump."

Stick with high performance ashless racing oil. For the street, 30 weight is about the ticket for most areas of the country. On the track, 30 weight is adequate unless temperature starts to get over 270°, in which case try 40 weight to see if that helps. If you have to go to 50 weight, chances are good you *really* need an oil cooler. Change oil and filters often. Drag racers will dump in a new load of oil in a clean engine, make three hard passes and discover that their oil is "dirty." Actually, the lube merely changes color — most of the multi-viscosity oils get dark very quickly when subjected to heat.

Bob Joehnck says, "Many engine failures are due to racing with too heavy an oil. Some drivers insist on 'jazzing' the oil. Some drivers insist on 'jazzing' the

throttle before the engine is thoroughly warmed up. Bearing failures inevitably result. We usually run 30 SAE oil in our engines—especially in the wintertime—making sure that this relatively 'thin' oil is thoroughly warmed up before ever revving the engine. Oil must be warm for these engines to function correctly. Some of the best-looking lower ends that we have seen have been in engines that have just finished a 200-mile race at Riverside where it is 110° in the shade. Naturally, we run coolers so that the oil temperature never exceeds 225°, but oil which is too cold cannot be recommended for these engines. When the oil is too cold, the pump can't move it regardless of the clearances that you have used. The Harrison NASCAR cooler is an absolute essential for the small-block which is being

143

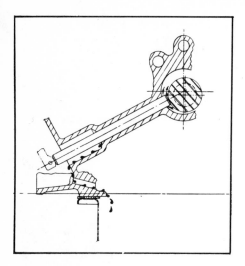

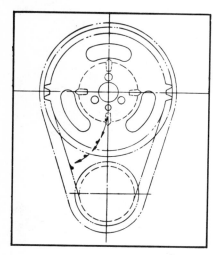

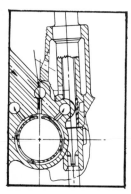

Before going off on a wild tangent to modify the oiling system, study these drawings of critical oiling areas to figure out why the factory did it that way to begin with. Clue: minimum trouble — maximum performance. Top drawing: fuel pump pushrod oiling; center: timing chain oiling; bottom: distributor shaft oiling.

road raced . . . so don't neglect to install one—or you'll wish that you had."

All of Chevrolet's tests are accomplished with 30-weight ashless oil. ALL such testing, including durability tests, is done with this type of oil. None heavier was ever required or used. Why, then, do so many drag racers insist on using 50-weight oil? Because this is the only weight that they can use which will give any oil pressure when the clearances are opened up unnecessarily. If you are getting excessive oil dilution, check why and fix the problem. When stock lower ends have the reputation of being hell-for-strong in stock configuration — and reliable as a locomotive — why not start off with a stock lower end and 30-weight oil? If the engine does not stand up to your kind of racing, maybe you didn't put the engine together right.

OIL ADDITIVES

Only one oil additive should ever be considered for use in the little 'ol Chevrolet and that is GM's Engine Oil Supplement (E.O.S.) which can be used on the cam and lifters — and on the rocker-arm balls — when the engine is assembled. But, don't use this additive in your engine on a continuing basis if you are racing it. Any additives which have calcium or barium in them will cause preignition — and E.O.S. falls into this category.

Additives ultimately cause pre-ignition in a racing engine because detonation in the end-gas area of the combustion chamber heats the barium and calcium deposits until they are glowing, thereby starting the preignition cycle which will completely destroy the engine if allowed to continue.

E.O.S. is available at GM dealers in 16 & 32 oz. cans. It is probably the best lubricant-additive that you can use in any new engine. With all of GM's research behind it —you can be sure you're getting your money's worth! Some cam grinders even include a can of it with every cam and lifter kit which they sell because the stuff really helps to avoid lifter scuffing and cam-lobe wear during those critical first few minutes of operation.

Avoid other oil additives because they may not be compatible with the additives which the oil manufacturer has used.

GAGES FOR PRESSURE & TEMPERATURE

If the engine is to be used in any kind of road racing, an oil-temperature gage and an oil-pressure gage should be hooked up. Read the oil pressure directly from the engine — not from a line to a cooler or remotely mounted filter. The same goes for the oil temperature. Go back to the oil plug near the distributor and take a reading there. The little Chevy just doesn't need a lot of oil pressure like some engines. If the engine is being worked hard and the pressure is less than 50 pounds, you're on the ragged edge of trouble. On the other hand, anything over 65 psi is too much.

Use a direct-reading oil-pressure gage with at least 3/16-inch ID line for rapid gage response. In this regard you should know that the majority of engine-bearing failures are a direct result of a severe drop in oil pressure when the oil pump picks up air while the car is in a high-speed turn. In a situation such as this, the driver is so busy that he does not notice the gage. A responsive gage mounted near the driver's line of vision is a must for a high-performance vehicle, but all of this is only as good as the driver's willingness to observe the gage.

One way to circumvent this problem is to install a Mallory "Sonalert" warning horn in a circuit with an idiot-light pressure sender. The vehicle battery can be used or a tiny Dura-Cell battery can be used. The 80-decibel blast—that's real loud—which this tiny (under 2 oz.) warning horn produces should wake your driver to the fact that he should get off the throttle until oil pressure returns.

Still another remedy is to install an engine shut off switch which turns off the ignition when oil pressure falls below a safe level. Ansen makes such a device.

If oil pressure does drop there are several areas to start exploring to locate the cause. Simply adding another quart of oil will sometimes cure the problem. Higher engine flow rates can also cause an oil void in the sump—thus a drop in pressure. This is often caused by excessive bearing clearances and higher than necessary oil pressure.

Incorrect oil-pan baffling (usually homegrown over-baffling) which prevents the engine oil from draining back into the oil pan while the car is in a turn or is accelerating can also cause problems.

Ideally, oil temperature shouldn't go over 270°F, but if you are leading a race and the temp gage starts to crowd 300° don't panic. In long races on a hot track readings in excess of 300° are not uncommon — but don't make a habit of it.

If your car only has the idiot light oil-pressure warning, consider that this is far too slow and unreliable for any high-performance activity. When your oil-pressure light goes on, this only tells you that the oil pressure is somewhere between 2 and 6 psi! Or, you could be down to zero pressure. By the time that the light comes on, damage has probably already occurred. For this reason an oil-pressure gage should be considered essential. However, you can keep the idiot-light circuit and sender intact and use it for a catastrophe warning by wiring it to a large clearance light on the dash or to a horn relay so that you'll either be blinded by the big light or awakened by the horn blowing in the event of oil-pressure loss.

OIL COOLERS

When installing your oil-cooler plumbing, keep all of the hoses at least 1/2-inch ID and avoid elbows or reducing fittings wherever possible. One 90° elbow is equivalent to 10 feet of pipe of the same diameter—so you can see how elbows can restrict the flow. Small hose also restricts flow through the cooler.

Keep the hoses short. Use hoses designed for hot-oil service. They must be specified for long life at temperatures to 350°F or so. Aero-Quip steel-braid-covered hose is possibly the best you can buy for remote oil cooler or dry-sump plumbing. This hose or non-sheathed hose for oil service can be found at firms specializing in truck or aircraft parts.

The oil-cooler hoses should be filled as they are installed. Or, if this is not possible, the pump must be turned with an electric drill until the entire system is filled. Failure to do this could cause bearing damage because the engine will have to turn over a lot of times before the bearings get pressure.

A big Harrison cooler, 3157804, is listed in the heavy-duty parts list. But it is not ready to use as it comes out of the box. You'll have to take it to a heliarc expert to get it cut apart and modified so that the oil flows into one end of the cooler and out the other.

Low-restriction coolers with the inlet/outlet on opposite ends are available readymade, so unless you get your heliarc work done dirt-cheap, you may want to start off with a non-GM part that needs no modification. A Boss Ford cooler made by Karmazin Products is one possibility, Ford P/N C90Z-6A642-A with mounting brackets C9ZZ-6B633-A and C9ZZ-6B634-A. The brackets are an absolute necessity, so don't overlook these rubber-shockmounted pieces when you place your order. The cooler is all-steel, so it weighs a bit more than the Harrison. It is 7" tall, 15.6 inches wide and about 2" thick. Ford high-performance engineer Jeff Quick told us that the cooler can be relied upon for about a 30°F temperature drop between the inlet and outlet, depending on inlet temperature, of course. He also cautioned us that the cooler should be mounted where it gets fresh air ducted to it with a free opening behind the fins. The cooler cannot be expected to work if it is mounted against a flat surface—or immediately ahead of the stock radiator. Either type of mounting will impede the flow of air through the cooler, which is what's essential in this instance. Mount the cooler so that it is out of the way of rocks and dirt which could clog the fins and reduce the unit's cooling capabilities.

Lest the over-$100 price of either the Harrison or Karmazin cooler tempt you to try to use an automotive heater radiator core for a cooler, let us assure you that such items are not designed to withstand oil-pump pressure. The pressures developed in cooling systems are far less than those in an oil system.

A common mistake when modifying an oiling system on a high-performance engine is over-cooling the oil. Oil should be kept at about 200°F to flow properly. Oil temperature should be measured where the oil comes back to the engine from the cooler. However, it is important to install the temperature sender so that it does not restrict oil flow in any way. A temperature range of 180 to 230°F is normal. Oil temperature should

Harrison cooler listed in HD Parts List is a good cooler if you modify it internally so that oil flows from one end to the other. The inlet must be at one end and the outlet at the other.

never exceed 230°F—but often will, regardless of how hard you try to keep it at a cooler temperature. Chevy suggests that the oil in the pan should never exceed 280°F.

If you've been building and racing small-block Chevys for years, don't be surprised if you're having problems keeping them cool — a problem you probably never faced in the old days. The reason for this is that the engines you're building now are probably larger than the older units you've put together. As displacement increases, the problems attendant to getting rid of excessive heat also rise. Thus temperature control on a 400-incher is much more critical than on a 283.

USE YOUR ENGINE AS AN OIL COOLER

The professional racers who paint their engine blocks, rocker covers and oil pans flat black are doing this for reasons with a sound basis in engineering fact. P. E. Irving, in his excellent book MOTORCYCLE ENGINEERING (available from Autobooks in Burbank, California) has this to say on page 183, "A polished surface emits less heat by radiation than a black one. Rate of heat emission from a polished surface is approximately one-tenth that from the same surface covered with a thin film of lampblack, and the emissivity of a cast-aluminum surface is increased about 10% by a thin coating of black paint." You only have to look as far as your stove to notice that tea pots are polished to keep heat in—so why do the same to an engine?

Thus, a black surface is *ten times as efficient* as a polished one. ALCOA's Engineering Handbook indicates that Irving's comment is quite conservative. ALCOA compares an as-cast surface with one which has been black-anodized to a depth of 1.7 thousandths. The black surface is *more than ten times better in heat-radiating ability than a plain cast surface.* Remember these facts when you are tempted to start polishing and chroming various engine parts which can contribute to cooling efficiency.

Another noted mechanical engineer, Mr. Julius Mackerle, in his book, AIR-COOLED MOTOR ENGINES (also available from Autobooks), states that it is an error to assume that using a greater quantity of oil will reduce oil temperature. Every ad for a big sump and almost every magazine article which discusses why racers install big sumps tells you that the use of larger quantities of oil reduces temperature. This common misunderstanding is completely untrue and utterly ridiculous! *Additional oil capacity does not lower oil temperature*—it merely increases the time required for the oil to attain a stable operating temperature: not usually of any real importance. Oil changes cost slightly more and the engine requires longer to cool off after it has been run. Additional oil capacity is helpful in a long race, providing the pickup is moved to the bottom of the bolt-on sump to make all of the oil available for use and so that the pump always gets the coolest oil. Additional capacity is insurance against losing an engine in the event that unexpected oil-consumption problems develop in a racing situation.

Mackerle further remarks that "A finned sump does not aid cooling to any great extent as the oil does not flow down the cooled sump walls. Cooling is more intense on the crankcase walls, over which the oil flows in a *thin*

film . . . Best oil cooling is obtained by a tube-type radiator . . ."

The reader should take note of the words "*thin film*" as these are the key to understanding the removal of heat from oil.

If you use the stock rocker covers, don't use the chrome-plated ones! Additional heat-removal capability can be added by welding or brazing sheet-metal fingers and/or baffles to extend into the hot oil to transmit the heat to the radiating surface. The orange-enamelled covers should be refinished with a *thin* coat of flat-black paint. The stock covers have a lot of surface area which you can use advantageously in helping your engine to rid itself of destructive heat.

If you have already purchased special aluminum rocker covers or chrome-plated ones, or if you have a chrome-plated pan, you can still use these parts to advantage. Either sell them to get your money back out of them so that you can buy new stock parts, or "de-polish" them by sand-blasting the polished surfaces. Black anodize the aluminum parts. Black anodizing is a plating process which many plating shops can provide for you at reasonable cost. Incidentally, the black obtained by anodizing may turn out somewhat spotty because castings do not usually anodize perfectly. This will not impair the heat-removal characteristics.

Parts which are not aluminum, or aluminum parts which are not being black anodized, can be painted with a thin coat of self-etching flat-black paint of the non-insulating variety. The entire block can also be painted on the outside with flat-black paint. This is one place where you don't want Sperex's fine insulating paint. You want to let the heat out—not keep it in. You can paint the headers or exhaust manifolds with Sperex paint so that these will not add as much exhaust heat to the engine compartment, thereby allowing the other parts to cool off more rapidly.

Although seemingly insignificant, these efforts will reward you with a cooler-running, longer-lasting engine.

You might think that some fins welded or brazed onto the bottom of the pan could assist the engine in getting rid of heat. Let's see what Phil Irving has to say about this on page 239 in the book already mentioned.

"While oil is good at collecting heat, it is very bad at getting rid of it again, because the layer directly in contact with a cool surface increases its viscosity and stays there, acting as an insulator and effectively preventing heat being dissipated from the hotter oil in the interior. Ribbing a sump which contains a quantity of oil is not very effective unless these are internal ribs also to transfer as much heat as possible from the body of the oil, but ribs placed on areas against which hot oil is violently thrown by centrifugal action can be made to radiate a lot of heat." From this we can see that ribs, if you add them to the pan, should really be added to the sides of the pan where the oil is flung against the walls by the crank.

Corvair rocker-cover retainers work like a charm to spread the bolt load on a stock tin cover to prevent leakage which sometimes occurs in long-distance, hard running.

Here's a low-buck trick. Longer-than-stock rocker-cover bolts are jammed with a nut. This is a lot easier to reach with a socket than a stock setup.

DRY SUMP SYSTEMS

Drag boats, ski boats, and a wide variety of road-racing vehicles can benefit from a dry-sump system instead of relying on the conventional single pressure pump.

The majority of internal combustion engines produced in the U.S.A. have "wet-sump" oiling systems. A wet-sump design carries the engine oil in a reservoir (sump or pan) directly below the engine crankshaft. An oil pump in the pan forces the oil to all engine bearings, rocker arms, etc. Gravity returns the oil to the pan for recirculation. The wet-sump system is impractical when racing with low chassis height and reduced ground clearance. These factors won't permit using a deep oil sump with an adequate supply of oil. A shallow sump produces oil foaming and excessive windage. At high RPM, the crankshaft can keep enough oil airborne by "windage" that 25 to 50 lbs. ft. of engine torque is lost.

Dry-sump systems have been used successfully in aircraft engines for many years. "Dry-sump" design uses a remote engine-oil reservoir, generally level or above the pump system so that gravity ensures priming. Oil is pumped from the reservoir to the engine bearings, falls by gravity to the "dry" sump and is returned to the remote oil reservoir by a separate pump system. In a dry-sump system, oil capacity is limited only by the size of the remote reservoir: two to three gallons is a common size. Auxiliary oil coolers and filters are readily accommodated.

The Weaver pumps have become the racers' standard for dry-sump-oiling systems. It allows holding oil-pan depth to a minimum—always less than flywheel depth. Two separate oil pick-ups should be used: one for the front of the oil pan and one for the rear. Due to pickup location, acceleration, braking, windage or turns do not

interfere with getting all the oil out of the sump so that it can be returned to the remote reservoir. The stock oil pump is eliminated and replaced by an externally mounted, gear-belt-driven pump consisting of at least three totally independent gear pumps. Two gear pumps are separately connected to the front and rear oil-pan pick-ups and pump oil back to the reservoir. The third gear pump delivers oil from the remote reservoir to the engine bearings through a filter and cooler. This pump is equipped with an externally adjustable pressure regulator. Aircraft-quality hoses, fittings and plumbing practice must be used throughout with oil filters and coolers as required.

If your racing machinery requires a dry-sump system, expect to spend over $500 for a simple dry-sump installation—more for a complex one with extra scavenge stages, injector drives, etc. Weaver Brothers also provide cog-belt drives for installations where only a water pump, or a water pump and an injector pump, are used.

For a steel pan with built-in screened pickups, you'll want to contact Ron Butler at Butler Racing in Culver City, California.

The following tips should assist you when installing a dry-sump system.
1. Eliminate the engine oil pump completely and plug the pump-to-filter-pad passage.
2. The scavenge pump/s should have three times the capacity of the pressure pump.
3. At least two scavenge stages should scavenge the oil pan and one stage should connect to the rear outside of the rocker cover on the predominant outboard side of the car. This depends on the course and whether it is run clockwise or counter-clockwise.

This is only for all-out competition engines. Weaver Brothers' three-stage pump is driven by cogged timing belt. This is same pump type (and brand) shown on the cover engine.

Hole indicated in the rear main cap must be plugged if a dry-sump system is used.

Fine example of a fabricated pan for a special application. This one is used in a boat where clearance required dry-sumping. Two outlets in pan connect to scavenge side of the Weaver oil pump.

Inside views of the dry-sump pan showing pickups in front and rear. Connecting the rear pickup to a fitting at the front of the pan eliminates outside lines and simplifies plumbing. This one was made by Mr. Yunick. Baffles had not been installed when photo was made.

147

Under 300-inch small block built by Bruce Crower was turbocharged, injected and produced about 700 HP on straight alcohol. Small photos show the accessory drive with hex drives for water, dry-sump, and fuel-injection pumps mounted on gear-drive cover. Gear drive and oil pump are produced by Crower Cams for all-out racers.

Another view of the Crower engine with part of the accessory gear drive in place. This is the prototype unit. This gear drive is now in production by Crower for the all-out racing engine. Hex drives turn water pump, dry-sump pump, distributor and fuel-injection pump — all of which mount on gear-drive cover.

Crower scavenge and pressure modules fit into a special gear-drive housing.

4. Do not run scavenged oil through the engine oil cooler but return it directly from scavenge pumps to supply tank through -12 or 3/4" line.

5. Use a -12 or 3/4" inlet line to the pressure pump from the supply tank. Install a coarse-screen aircraft filter in this line to keep contaminants out of the pressure pump and pressure-bypass valve.

6. Pass oil from pressure pump through engine oil cooler and remote oil filter and then into the block through the adapter. Make every effort to reduce restriction in the oil-cooler circuit. Do not connect oil coolers in series. If more than one oil cooler is used, connect them in parallel, i.e., tee the oil line and pass the oil into and out of both coolers simultaneously.

7. Do not over-cool the oil. Racing oil must be at about 200°F to flow properly. Measure oil temperature between the oil cooler and the engine. Keep it between 180° and 270°F when thoroughly warmed up.

8. Do not exceed 60-65 psi oil pressure (hot) because excessive pressure aggravates oil aeration and creates scavenging problems. Oil pressure over 65 psi is not necessary for good bearing life.

9. Run a full-length semi-circular tray baffle under the crankshaft with louvers to draw the oil away from the crank.

10. Design the oil supply tank as tall and as small in diameter as space permits. It should hold a minimum of 8 quarts of oil with enough air space above the oil to allow oil-air separation. The tank bottom must be level with or slightly higher than the pump inlet so that gravity will prime the pump.

11. Build the engine with the correct lifters, rocker arms, rear cam bearing and clearances to require a minimum of oil flow. Such attention to detail is the greatest asset to a correctly functioning dry-sump system.

12. Vent both the engine and the supply tank, or vent the engine to a correctly vented supply tank. Keep vent lines of adequate size (one -12 or two -10 lines) to keep from causing any pressure build-up in the crankcase. Making these vent lines too small is a common mistake. Existing breather holes in the engine rocker covers are an excellent place to vent from. Leave the production oil separators in the rocker covers under the vent holes. These are designed to handle 10 CFM without oil pullover—provided that the vent lines are of adequate size—out of the system. You'd be hard pressed to design something with this kind of oil-separation capability and GM gives it to you in the factory-direct low-cost parts.

CLEANING THE BLOCK

The first step in block preparation for a competition engine requires disassembling the engine down to the very last bolt — even if you are starting with a brand-new engine. So, whether the engine is new or used, remove all of the soft and screw-in plugs and cam bearings. New cam bearings can be reused if you take them out carefully with the correct driver — which is a MUST tool for any serious engine builder.

All of the oil-gallery plugs at the front and rear of the block must be removed. These plugs almost never cause any trouble — but for a competition engine we will not rely on "almost-never" situations. The primary reason for removing the pressed-in plugs is to allow free access to the oil galleries so they may be cleaned out. There can be grit, dirt, casting sand and metal shavings in the oil passages — and there's no way to get it out until the gallery plugs and cam bearings are removed. Tap the front holes with a 1/4 NPT pipe tap and round up some Allen-head (socket-head) pipe plugs to use here.

Main oil gallery feed holes to the cam bearings are smaller than the connecting passage from the cam bearing to the crankshaft bearings. This upper passage should be opened up to the same size as that which connects to the mains. The holes are of different size to simplify machining. Open up these passages on the rear four bearings only. The front one is o.k. as is. If the lifter feed passages are to be restricted for use with needle-bearing rockers, now is the time to do it. Limiting oil to the lifters is described at the end of the camshaft chapter.

If you are working with an engine that has been assembled with Teflon tape on plug or bolt threads, make sure that you remove all of this at the time the plugs and bolts are removed. Pick it out of the threads with a sharp-pointed tool such as a scribe. At this time the careful engine builder will run taps through all the threaded holes in the block. This loosens up any impacted dirt, putty, seal-er or whatever and allows it to float free when the block goes to the hot tank.

When you reassemble the engine, remember that Teflon tape can shred and flake off into the oil galleries if it extends beyond the first or second thread of the plug — and it can do the same thing when the plug is removed. When rebuilding an engine, extreme care must be used to re-cover all of these pieces so that they will not clog the oiling system. One sealant that you may want to consider is Loctite's Teflon Pipe Seal. It works well on the plugs and on cylinder-head studs or cap-screws to ensure against water leakage.

If the block has been used, have it "boiled out" or "hot-tanked." Most auto parts houses, automotive dealer-ships, or automotive machine shops can do this job — or at least tell you where it can be done. A block boil-out normally costs about five dollars. Sometimes you can get a set of scroungy heads in the tank at the same time at no extra cost.

A small bit of strategy can be used here, so work it into your plan of attack. Take the block to be boiled out on a Friday afternoon if the place of business involved is closed on Saturday. Check with the man in charge of the operation and request that your block be left in the cleaning solution over the weekend. Or, make arrangements for the block to "cook" for several days before it's pulled out.

If you don't build engines on a regular basis (at least two a year) another sly move can be effected by asking the man who boiled out the block if he'd mind taking a look at the block to see if he can find any cracks or problems which could plague you later on. This is done on the theory that two sets of eyes are better than one, coupled with the fact that a man who works at this all day can often spot items in an engine that a new-comer to the field wouldn't see or even understand. Look for fine hairline cracks in any of the main webbing, and double check all of the bolt holes for pulled or stripped threads. The chances of finding any cracks in the main-journal webbing are remote, but look now before you cart

All of the tapped holes should be cleaned up with the correct size taps to eliminate any burrs or dirt.

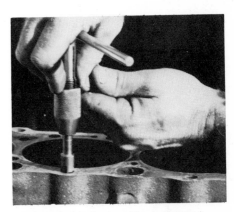

All threaded holes in a block should be topped off with a countersink before assembly. This prevents thread pulling.

NOTE - When you get an engine hot-tanked, try to find a place that uses a tank with agitation. This helps to ensure that the galleries will be cleaned. Otherwise, you can expect to have to use some kind of solvent and brushes to get the accumulated glop and guck out of the galleries, even though the block has been tanked. Use the brushes in any event to make sure that these areas are cleaned. A spray-nozzle-type cleaner will not clean the galleries, believe us!

Something went wrong somewhere — notice the deep scoring by the cam chain on the block plug. This is typical of the odd-ball things to look for when tearing down an engine to be rebuilt.

Oil-gallery plugs in the rear of a block can sometimes be a bear to remove. If they won't budge, you have to centerpunch, then drill them out.

NOTE - Tapping the front holes in the block for 1/4-NPT thread will give only one or two threads — and not full ones at that. This means that the pipe plugs will have to be epoxied in place when they are installed. If you are not going to display the block to all your friends to show your racing-engine-building expertise, you might want to put stock cup plugs in with Loctite and never mention it. We've never heard of any that gave trouble. Saves work!

the block home. Needless to say, if you find *any* cracks, pay the boil-out bill and point the block toward the nearest trash barrel.

MAGNAFLUX

Professional engine builders will always Magnaflux the block and caps to make sure that they are not overlooking cracks which could turn their expensive work into a pile of junk — perhaps in the heat of competition. If you get to Magnaflux equipment, this is cheap insurance against making a big investment in a block that should be broken up and melted down again.

ALIGN BORING

Align boring is a relatively simple machining operation done to ensure that all main-bearing saddles lie on a common axis. To accomplish the operation, a slight cut is taken from the mating surface of each main-bearing cap. The caps are then bolted to the block and torqued in place. A boring bar is then run the length of the block through all of the main-bearing bores. Because this operation must be done with a machine which does just this one thing, align boring simply cannot be accomplished in some small towns — or for that matter in many large communities. A local automotive machinist or garage should be able to tell you where the work can be accomplished.

Once you have located a shop which is equipped (physically) to do the job, things get more complicated. Despite the fact the operation is relatively simple, a lot of align boring is done wrong and blocks are ruined. Lempco, Quik-Way and Tobin Arp make quality align-boring machines — so you might keep an eye peeled for these labels on machines if you are talking the job over with a machinist — which brings up the next point. In a job shop (take on anything that comes in the door), a machinist must not only be good (reasonably good will suffice in most cases) but he must be *fast*. In a day he may align bore a block, mill a couple of heads, turn some brake drums, and do some free welding for a friend. He may have to yank a block out of the hot tank and it's for sure that he'll spend time on the phone and talk to a couple of customers in person. Be assured that whatever the job is, they want it "done yesterday."

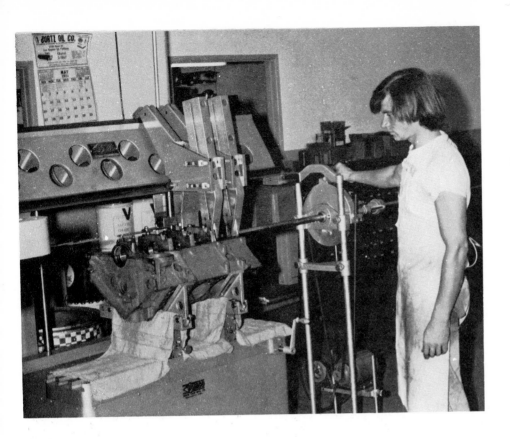

This is the way a quality align-boring machine looks. Notice the massive table and overhead arm which ensures that nothing shifts around during the operation. Photo made in Ed Pink's establishment.

Without wasting the machinist's time, tell him that the block is being used in competition — that you want it done right. You want as little as possible taken off the main-bearing caps and block-mating surfaces as possible. You also want the crank to be dead parallel with the cam. To get this job done right will require an align-boring machine which locates the block according to the crank centerline. The machines mentioned previously do that. The rub comes in the fact that, for the most part, the accuracy of the job is dependent on the operator and his willingness to double-check everything. The quick way to do the job is to mill 0.005-inch off the main caps and a like amount off the block, torque the caps in place and then bore. All of the holes may now be aligned but the cam is closer to the crank, thus the timing chain has some slop in it — which alters effective cam timing — which you don't want or need in a competition engine. So the machinist must remove the slightest amount of metal possible, especially from the block, to do the job correctly.

If you are line boring a block in which the main bearing insert has "spun," and get the block bored with a 0.005-inch cut in the block side, you can get a Cloyes True-Roller chain/sprocket set designed for the closer center distance. These sets must be special ordered. When you add up all of the costs which are involved, you may find that it is cheaper to junk the old block and start with a fresh new one.

If the engine is to be used for a steady diet of competition it should be align bored; if it is to be used occasionally for competition then you should pay a machinist to check the block with a mandrel or straight crank to determine if align boring is needed.

For a strong, but strictly street engine — you can get away with the following. Lay a straight crankshaft in the oiled bearing inserts and tighten the main caps. Do not install the rear seal. If the crank turns freely by hand, the assembly will most likely be trouble-free for the street. Details for checking the crank for straightness are provided elsewhere in this book.

Prices vary from shop to shop for align boring — but expect to pay $50 to $75 for the job. Don't shop price on this item — shop quality. One final word — don't ask the machinist for the job to be "done yesterday." Leave the impression you'd much rather wait and have the job done right than to pick it up in an hour and end up with something suitable only for use in a delivery truck . . . and maybe not that!

4-BOLT-MAIN CONVERSION KITS

Should you have a two-bolt-main block and be wondering what to do with it, the chances are good that you should run it as is for a street machine. If you are going to get into serious competition, then it is possible to use the block with a four-bolt-main conversion kit. These kits require align boring the block after the block has been drilled and tapped to mount the new caps. However, consider the total costs because a new high-performance block including new cam bearings for any standard displacement costs approximately $125. This could be far less than the cost for a conversion kit, line boring and a new set of cam bearings . . . plus a bore job if that's needed.

When you buy a fitted block, the deal gets even better. That arrangement gives you pistons, rings, pins and both main and cam bearings. Some of the factory-direct deals are so good that we wonder why anyone ever considers buying anything other than stock parts.

Two-bolt-main blocks can be updated and strengthened with Milodon bearing caps which utilize the stock stud locations with two angled bolts.

If you have a good two-bolt-main block, don't start throwing rocks at it. King Engines has built two 292 CID small blocks and Mauri Rose, Jr. also uses two-bolt-mains with aircraft steel studs and nuts with great success. So there are at least two quarter-mile circle track and one drag engine which are holding their own in weekly competition. Despite these successes, the four-bolt-main block is still the starting point for the average guy trying to build a performance small block.

Additional main-bearing bulkhead (web) durability can be achieved by using studs instead of bolts in the three intermediate main-bearing caps. The main-bearing caps should fit *tightly* into the case notches to prevent cap misalignment. Studs should fit snugly into the full length of the threads in the block. Use Loctite.

Bob Joehnck points out that the two-bolt blocks are often bored out for the larger crank journals when the four-bolt conversion caps are installed.

Another method of achieving lower end strength on two-bolt-main blocks is the use of steel blocks ground on four sides. Stock caps must also be machined and block should be align bored.

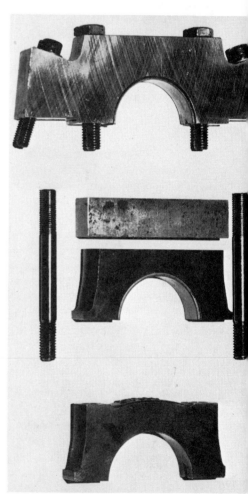

Top is four-bolt ductile-iron main cap manufactured by Milodon for converting two-bolt-main blocks. Center device remains a two-bolt cap, but is stronger than stock because load is distributed across the heavy bar. High-strength studs are used instead of the stock bolts. Stock cap has been milled off to accept the machined bar. Bottom is stock two-bolt-main cap.

DECKING

On all-out racing engines, block preparation and subsequent machining can be quite expensive because of the large amounts of time which are inescapably involved. Although this detailing is not necessarily required for a strong-running, street-only, small-block Chevy, the true racer would never think of overlooking it. That is the "decking" of the block. This operation gets the distance between the deck and the crank centerline equal at each end for each cylinder bank. It also makes the decks 90° to the cylinder bores and establishes them at a height above the crank which gives the desired deck clearance between the piston flat surface and the cylinder head.

Small blocks are usually out by as much as 0.004 to 0.012 inch from one end to the other and have been known to stray from parallelism with the crank by an average of 0.008 inch. Measurements can be made with a long depth mike from the deck to a mandrel installed in the main-bearing saddles, or with a large-throat mike from the deck to the bearing saddles at each end. Be sure to record the figure that you end up with on the corrected deck height so that you could build another block just like it if you had to make a replacement.

There are a couple of ways that you can go about the next sequence of events to get the deck height established and the decks parallel to the crankshaft centerline. If you are planning to reassemble the engine with the same parts, *check the deck heights before you take the engine apart!* Clean the carbon off of the flat portions of the piston tops. Use a dial indicator in a bridge-type holder or a depth mike with parallels (a couple of ground tool bits work just fine). Measure the deck height of each piston and record these dimensions so that you can refer back to them later on. Note whether the piston is above or below the block deck. If a piston is above the deck, put a + sign in front of that number. Mark the piston and rod assemblies before you take the engine apart, preferably stamping them with numbering stamps. That way you'll know "where you're at" if one of your buddies cleans the parts when your back is turned.

After the engine has been disassembled and the block hot-tanked as already discussed, check the main-bearing saddles for freedom from cracks and for true alignment as previously described. If align boring is required, do it now. If you are going to use the same pistons and rods, get the block decked to provide the desired relationship of the pistons' flat surfaces to the block deck.

But, you say, all of the pistons did not have the same deck height. Now you are getting down to the real nitty-gritty. You must use the lowest piston as your reference. Deck to *that* piston. The other pistons' flat surfaces will have to be machined to lower their decks to equal the lowest of the bunch. This can also mean that the piston domes will have to be machined off a bit, too, to keep the compression equal in all cylinders. Measuring piston-dome volume and calculation of compression ratio is handled in the cylinder-head chapter.

There are a lot of combinations of gaskets and pistons, but there are only two things that are really important in determining deck. You must maintain a minimum of 0.035-inch clearance between the piston and the cylinder head in any area they might contact. This 0.035-inch figure is established on the assumption that you are not running more than 0.008-inch piston-to-wall clearance. For every additional 0.001-inch piston-to-wall clearance, add another 0.003 to 0.004-inck deck. That's because of piston rock within the cylinder. A piston can be run 0.005-inch out of the hole (above the deck) with a 0.040-inch gasket or you can run the piston down in the hole and use a thinner gasket. Within reason, this is not important, but the amount of clearance between the piston and the head is important — and you'd better get it right!

The deck height mentioned above is for stock or other *steel* rods. If an engine is being built with aluminum rods, a deck of 0.045-inch minimum must be maintained.

Deck clearance is the difference between the top of the piston and the top of block. Measure it with a depth micrometer (shown here) or a dial indicator. Make certain that the piston is at TDC when making the measurement.

You can do a pretty fair "country-boy" job of checking the bottom of a block for being straight if you can lay a machinist's rule on the saddles and not be able to shove a piece of cigarette paper between the rule and the block. This block is in bad shape and a 0.001-inch feeler slides in easily.

Ron Armstrong checks out an air-inlet stack for a 327 engine being built for an "E" Racing Runabout owned by Wes Knudsen. The engine produced 572 HP at at 7500 RPM; set a new record in 1972 at over 104 MPH. Weiand hi-quad manifold has two List No. 1849 Holley carbs with vacuum-actuated secondaries.

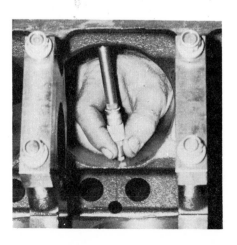

Don't measure bore like you were going to a fire. Take your time, make certain the inside mike or snap gage is 90 degrees to the bore and measure the bore near the top and near the bottom to determine the amount of taper.

Keep in mind the things which affect deck clearance. These include compression height (pin center to flat part of piston top), rod length (center of big end to center of small end), position of crank in the block (it will be raised slightly if the block is line bored), and crankshaft stroke at each rod journal.

Once the block is bored, assemble the engine loosely with the parts which are to be used and check the deck heights at each piston. Note the measurement on each piston top with a marking pen. If you merely had a preliminary cut made to parallel the decks to the crankshaft, a further cut may be required to get the deck correct for the piston which sits lowest in the block when it is at TDC. Once the deck is correct for the lowest piston, check the rod lengths and compression heights to see whether you can find a different combination which will reduce the amount of machining required on each piston. Because piston machining will nearly always be required in getting the deck height correctly established, you can see that any piston balance operations should be delayed until after deck height has been established. And, piston notching may also be required, as described in the camshaft chapter. You may want to make the piston-to-valve check for clearance at this time so that all machining operations on the pistons can be done at the same time.

Correcting the deck can be done in a block machine which grinds the deck surface, or you can use a large milling machine. Incidentally, a dead-smooth surface is neither wanted or needed. The surface, according to Bill King, should be rough enough to "catch your fingernail" in it. This helps to hold the gasket.

The cost for decking a block will vary, depending on whether the machinist is really "with it" or not. Top shops typically get $40 to $50 for the job, depending on the amount of time required by the specific job. This seems like a lot, but you want a nit-picking specialist who insists that the four corners of the block are at 90° to the cylinder bores, as well as equidistant to the crank centerline at each end. You might get by with a simple surface cut for $20, but doing it right may cost more.

BORING

Like all of the rest of automotive machine work, there is boring — and then there is boring. If the block is decked, the boring can be done with a first-class boring bar. If not, the work should be done with a machine which centers off of the main bearing saddles. Most importantly, a three- or four-inch-thick steel plate must be torqued down to the head surface of the block while the boring and honing is being done to that bank of cylinders. And, the main caps should be installed and torqued down during the boring and honing. This kind of machine work is hard to come by in many areas. Some shops wouldn't give it to you if you stood there and looked over their shoulders. Believe that!

Why go to all that trouble? Let's assume a normal boring bar is used to bore the holes. All four holes on one bank are bored and they are round. The honing is done and the holes remain round. The block is "sani-ed up" and the crank is bolted in. The main caps are torqued down and lower end of the block twists ever so slightly. The lower end of one bore is now slightly egg-shaped. Now the head is bolted on and the bolts torqued down evenly. Now the top of each bore is pulled toward the five bolts which provide the clamping. The result is the top of the bore becomes distorted and out-of-round.

If the boring is done while the main caps are torqued into place, the lower end of the block is stressed just as it will be once all of the components are installed. The same holds true for the top of the block when the large plate is clamped in place. As we've said this kind of boring and honing comes only in a machine shop which specializes in high-performance machine work.

If you are going to bore the block with a machine which references off of the deck surface, the deck must be trued parallel with the crank centerline prior to boring.

If the block deck is crooked—then the bores will be off. Although the factory uses automatic equipment which lines up on crank centerline, the bores are not always straight and true with the crank centerline. You can get the bores closest to straight by lining the boring machine up in the center of each cylinder, half way down the bore. This provides an average

Main-bearing saddles are clamped onto a mandrel in this boring setup. Note the three-inch-thick plate which is torqued onto block during boring and honing to simulate cylinder distortion caused by installation of the cylinder head. This is an essential thing to do when building a high-performance engine.

location which will be more nearly correct than if the boring machine is lined up with the top or bottom of the bore.

If the block is being bored with a machine which references from the crank centerline without regard to deck position, then you can skip this preliminary parallel-decking operation.

This is what you'll need to hone the cylinder walls smooth. This particular hone is an Amco which features removable stones. Keep in mind that the finer the grit, the higher the number in the catalog — and for competition you'll want the finest grit they've got.

An excellent example of cylinder-wall cross-hatching. Final passes should be made with a stone number close to 500.

If you are at all serious about deburring a block or reworking ports you'll need some high speed (15,000 to 22,000 RPM) hand grinders to spin a variety of grinding stones. This stuff doesn't come cheap and is a good example of the overhead involved in building a "right-on" high-performance engine of any kind.

DEBURR, CLEAN & PAINT

With a handful of grinding wheels and a 1/4- or 3/8-inch drill motor or high-speed grinder, go to work eliminating the rough spots all over the cylinder-block interior: the tappet chamber beneath the intake manifold, the crankcase and the timing-gear cavity. Most engine builders start grinding by using various shaped stones—then go back over all of their work with some of the fine-grit paper sanding sleeves. This gets rid of any small bits of sand or casting which might jar loose, work their way into the oil system and "do in" the engine. We don't want the oil to "stick" to the rough surface of the stock tappet chamber and crankcase either. Polishing and then painting (later) aids oil drainback to the sump. With this polishing and deburring the block is now ready to be fitted with the pistons. All pistons in a set will vary slightly in size and for this reason should be fitted individually into their respective bores per the piston clearance specifications in that chapter.

After all of the machining operations, move the block to an area which you don't mind being doused with soap and water. Mix up a dishpan or bucket full of solvent (from the local service station), dishwashing detergent (Tide, Cheer, etc.), and hot water. Start scrubbing that block with stiff bristle brushes and the solution. Give it the old "Dutch rub" inside and out. Industrial supply firms and some automotive and speed shops sell small bristle brushes attached to very long wire handles which will allow cleaning of the oil galleries over their full length. If you can't find such brushes, a local gun shop will fix you up because the gun-barrel-cleaning brushes work just fine in an engine.

After you have the engine (and yourself) thoroughly soaked, sudsed, and scrubbed, apply the nozzle and hose to get rid of all the suds and, hopefully, any small particles which might still be around. You may prefer to haul the block to your local do-it-yourself car wash to use the high-pressure spray equipment there. This approach works well. While the block is drying take another close look all over for hairline cracks, a bit of sludge hidden in an oil passage leading to a mainbearing—anything which needs to be taken care of now. Don't hesitate to use a magnifying glass—especially if you're over 30! Now that you've gone this far with the project, mix up a new batch of detergent—without the solvent—do the whole job a second time. Rinse away the suds and let the block stand in the sun or under a heat lamp or two to aid in drying. If an air hose is handy, use air pressure to aid the drying-out process. From here on in, you are working with a clean block and you must take every precaution possible to keep it that way. This includes speeding the drying process and getting the block under a large towel or plastic covering to keep it dust-free until you are ready to paint it.

Bob Joehnck points out that block painting certainly ensures that no loose sand will get into the engine, but he claims that it is almost impossible to paint blocks commercially—because it is too time-consuming. Here is another place where the occasional engine builder's "free labor" can ensure a good job.

Actually, if the costs of sonic cleaners were not so fantastic that only large industrial firms and aircraft or missile builders can afford them, the sonic cleaner would be the ideal way to clean the block. Then there would be no need for painting. Some cleaning tanks (not sonic ones) have jet nozzles that direct strong streams of cleaning solution against the various parts of the block. If such are used with lots and lots of elbow grease and subsequent cleaning in household detergent and hot water, Joehnck feels that this is adequate.

Painting the inside of a block serves two functions. The paint's smooth surface speeds oil return to the sump. And, the paint goes a long way toward holding any grit in place which might work loose from the casting even after your polishing and scrubbing operations. You'll need a small brush— one one-inch wide will be fine—and a pint of Rustoleum or Glyptal. Rustoleum can be purchased at most any hardware, paint store or lumber yard which sells paint. Glyptal may be more difficult to find but is well worth the effort. It is a material manufactured by General Electric for coating electric windings in generators and electric motors. Thus, your search for this should begin in the Yellow Pages for a firm specializing in rebuilding large electrical motors. Before dipping into either of these coatings, move the block into a dust-free area and rig a sun lamp or two over the block to aid the flow and to set up the coating harder than can be achieved by drying at room temperature. Paint the area in the front of the block which will covered by the timing chain cover. Paint the entire tappet chamber which is to be covered by the intake manifold. Flip the block over on the engine stand and cover areas between the cylinder bores. At the back of the block, paint the area which will be covered by the bellhousing. This painting is a rather slow

Don't start grinding away at the bottom of the bore (A). Leave the edge there as an oil wiper. Do deburr area B.

To build a "right on" small block, all of the areas indicated need to be touched with a high-speed grinder to eliminate burrs or casting slag. Yunick, Joehnck, Bartz and other top engine builders figure six to seven hours just deburring and generally cleaning up the block.

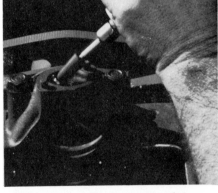

When going over the underside of the block, don't overlook the cavity in the rear main which matches up with the oil pump. Put a nice, smooth radius on the oil entry hole.

Sharp edges on the inside of the block should be rounded off and deburred — except those at the bottom of the bore as indicated in the photo above. A high polish is not needed.

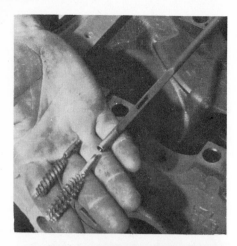

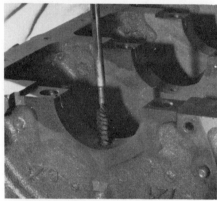

If you're gonna do it, do it right. A rifle-cleaning kit comes in handy for loosening up all kinds of grime and scale in those oil passages. After you've run the brush through all of the oil passages, you'll want to suds and rinse the block again to wash away anything which might have been dislodged.

There's no easy way to do this for the home builder — ask Dave Diamond — who demonstrates the fine art of applying hot soap and water to a small-block Chevy while he dreams of Saturday night at the digs. This is where you get wet. After the sudsing, fire up the trusty garden hose and apply the pressure to every hole, nook and cranny in the block. Put some water pressure down the cam bore and also the oil passages which supply lube to the lifters.

Another item you can't have too many of — small sanding rolls for removing casting irregularities on the inside of blocks and heads. There are a dozen or so shapes and sizes and they're available in industrial-supply firms and in some hardware stores.

Glyptal by General Electric is the trick for painting the inside of a block. Electrical motor rebuilders use it—so shop there.

process—or should be—because you should not brush any paint on the machined surfaces, such as the cylinder bores, head-mating surface or any of the machined surfaces adjacent to the main-bearing journals. Let the paint harden for at least 24 hours before getting back to the block. If at all possible, leave a couple of sun lamps pointed at the oil gallery and the crankcase to harden the paint.

If you are spray-painting your block with Rustoleum, use this procedure to get the best job: first, fog on a light coat and let this set for 24 hours; next, spray on a slightly heavier coat and let that set for 24 hours. Finally, spray on a heavy coat and let that set for 24 hours before removing your masking tape. Incidentally, corks or rubber stoppers are very helpful in keeping paint out of the lifter bores, distributor hole, etc. Don't hesitate to use them if they are available, as they speed things up as compared to masking tape.

BLOCK PREP SUMMARY

To recap this block-prepping procedure briefly — let's put it in the order the prepping should be done in — because it does make a difference.

Disassemble the engine, including removing all of the freeze plugs and oil-gallery plugs.

Run a tap of the correct size through all of the threaded holes.

Boil out the block, inspect and/or Magnaflux or Zyglo.

Align bore.

Straighten block deck to align with crank centerline.

Bore and hone with main caps torqued in place and a thick steel plate bolted to the head of the bank being bored and honed.

Scrub with soap and water.

Assemble the engine loosely for deck checking.

Disassemble.

Scrub the bare block for the second time with soap and water.

Paint the block interior.

Following the painting, the block may then be assembled.

Begin with the installation of the cam bearings.

BLOCK PLUGS

Some mechanics tap the block "freeze-plug" holes with a 1-3/4-inch pipe thread and install pipe plugs from an electrical supply house. These are installed with Loctite to eliminate any further worries about lost or leaky plugs. Others swear by the Neoprene expansion-type plugs which tighten in place with a nut. Still others use the stock cup-type plugs epoxied or Loctited in place. The size of the plug is 1-5/8-inch.

If the stock cup-type plugs are used they should be installed with the "cup" pointed out of the block. In other words, the concave side of the plug should face out of the block. The plugs of this type should always be forced into the opening with some type of mandrel or flat plate driven by a larger hammer to ensure that the plug does not cock in the bore. It is almost impossible to install this type of plug correctly with just a hammer.

If you have modified the lifter and main galleries at the front of the block so that these now have a couple of 1/4-NPT threads, clean the threads in the block and on the plugs with a non-oily solvent such as acetone, alcohol, methyl-ethyl-ketone or toluene. Coat the plugs with epoxy and install them with plenty of time for the epoxy to set up.

There's no particular trick to installing this plug in the end of the cam boss at the rear of the block, but if you blow one out after installing a "hot-rod cam" check the rear journal of the cam. There should be two holes in the end of the journal (parallel to the centerline of the cam) to prevent pressure from building up between the end of the cam and the plug.

Painted, O-ringed, align-bored, and "squared with the world," this small block from Ed Pink's shop is ready for assembly. Arrows indicate where dowel pins will be placed to ensure that the end manifold gaskets stay in place when the pressure builds up.

Just before the block is assembled, the exterior and interior casting surfaces should be this clean — all over.

Suppliers

Aero Design Products
891 West 16th St.
Newport Beach CA 92660
714/642-2478
C-D ignitions (Perma-Tune)

Ansen Automotive Engineering
13715 S. Western
Gardena, CA 90249
213/323-5263
    Catalog $1

ARE/Automotive Research Electronics
176 Gilman Avenue
Campbell, CA 95008
408/378-4005
    Catalog 50¢

Aviaid Metal Products
7570 Woodman Pl.
Van Nuys, CA 91405
213/786-4025

Bartz Racing Engines
15833 Stagg St.
Van Nuys, CA 91406
213/785-5754

George Bolthoff
Engine Systems Development
17722 Manchester Ave.
Santa Ana, CA 92702
714/540-4402

Racer Brown Cams
9270 Borden Ave.
Sun Valley, CA 91352
213/767-4062
    Catalog $1

Bud's Carburetor Shop
946 West 11-Mile Road
Madison Heights, MI 48071
313/399-9719 5 – 9 pm
Holley tuning/repairs

Butler Racing
11813 Major St.
Culver City, CA 90230
213/391-1785

The Carburetor Shop
1942 Harbor
Costa Mesa, CA 92627
714/642-8286

Champion Spark Plugs
Box 910
Toledo, OH 43601
419/536-3711

Chassis Engineering Co.
705 West 13th St.
National City, CA 92050
714/474-3861
    Catalog 25¢

ChevTec
140 South St.
Rochester, MI 48063
313/777-2584

Cloyes Gear & Products, Inc.
17214 Roseland Rd.
Cleveland, OH 44112
216/531-3264

Crankshaft Co.
1422 South Main
Los Angeles, CA 90015
213/749-6597

Crower Cams
3333 Main St.
Chula Vista, CA 92011
714/422-1191
    Catalog $2

Crown Manufacturing
858 Production Place
Newport Beach, CA 92660
714/642-7391
    Catalog $1

Diamond/Elkins Porting Service
Diamond Engine Service
3493 Ten Mile Rd.
Warren, MI 48091
313/756-4055

Diest Safety Equipment
9II S. Victory
Burbank, CA 91502
213/845-7866

Edelbrock Equipment Co.
411 Coral Circle
El Segundo, CA 90245
213/322-7310
    Catalog $1

Enderle Fuel Injection
1282 Los Angeles St.
Glendale, CA 91204
213/243-2175

Falconer/Dunn Racing Engines
5728 Bankfield
Culver City, CA 90230
213/390-3459

General Kinetics Co.
5137 Trumbull
Detroit, MI 48208
313/832-7360
    Catalog 50¢

Sam Gianino Racing Engines
4812 Leafdale
Royal Oak, MI 48073
313/576-0707

Go-Power
1800 Embarcadero Ave.
Palo Alto, CA 94303
415/328-7676

Grant Industries
3680 Beverly Blvd.
Los Angeles, CA 90004
213/382-1375

Grizzly Engineering & Machine
611 Sutter St.
Folsom, CA 95630
916/985-4074
    Catalog 50¢

Hank the Crank, Inc.
7253 Lankershim Blvd.
North Hollywood, CA 91605
213/765-3444

Charlie Hayes Racing Equipment
1560 E. Edinger Ave., Suite H
Santa Ana, CA 92705
714/547-5776
    Catalog $2

Hedman Headers
4630 Leahy St.
Culver City, CA 90230
213/838-1805

Helm, Inc.
Chevrolet Manual Distribution Dept.
Box 7706
Detroit, MI 48207

Hilborn Fuel Injection
25891 Crown Valley Parkway
South Laguna, CA 92677
714/831-1170

Holley Carburetors
11955 E. Nine Mile Rd.
Warren, MI 48090
313/JE6-1900
    Catalog $1

Hooker Headers
1032-A W. Brooks St.
Ontario, CA 91762
714/983-5871

Honest Charley Inc.
108 Honest St., Box 8535
Chattanooga, TN 37421
615/892-2114

J.E.B. Industries
4210 Vanowen St.
Burbank, CA 91504
213/984-1951

Joehnck Automotive
133 W. Figueroa
Santa Barbara, CA 93104
805/962-1773

K & D Accessories Co.
P.O. Box 276
Longview, WN 98632

Kent-Moore Tools
1501 S. Jackson St.
Jackson, MI 49203
517/784-8561

King Engine Service
1956 Hilton Rd.
Ferndale, MI 48220
313/398-2450

Kinsler Fuel Injection
3111 Middlebury
Birmingham, MI 48010
313/646-3223

Lakewood Industries
4800 Briar Rd.
Cleveland, OH 44135
216/267-5151
    Catalog $1

Manley Performance Engineering
13 Race St.
Bloomfield, NJ 07003
201/743-6577
    Catalog $1

Mason Engineering
15838 Arminta
Van Nuys, CA 91405
213/780-2642

Midwest Auto Specialties
5063 Turney Rd.
Cleveland, OH 44125
216/991-4900

Milodon Engineering Co.
7711 Ventura Canyon Ave.
Van Nuys, CA 91402
213/782-4373

Moldex Crankshaft Co.
25249 W. Warren Ave.
Dearborn Heights, MI 48127
313/561-7676

Doug Nash Racing
36360 Ecorse Road
Romulus, MI 48174
    Catalog $1

Nu-Metrics/Pentron
14055 Cedar Rd.
Cleveland, OH 44118
216/932-3100

Gail Parsons
1746 West Main
Newark, OH 43055
614/344-8010
Rochester FI repairs

Ed Pink Racing Engines
14612 Raymer
Van Nuys, CA 91405
213/873-3460
    Catalog $1

Racing Parts & Machine
1614 E. Joppa Rd.
Baltimore, MD 21200
301/823-2558

Rajay Industries, Inc.
2602 E. Wardlow Rd.
Long Beach, CA 90801
213/426-0346

Reath Automotive
32910 Cherry
Long Beach, CA 90807
213/426-6901

Simpson Safety Equipment
22638 S. Normandie Ave.
Torrance, CA 90502
213/320-7231

Kay Sissell Automotive
10829 Slack Ave.
South El Monte, CA 91733
213/444-8921

Sperry Fuel Controls
193 Pilgrim
Highland Park, MI 48203
313/398-2450

Stahl Associates/Drag Racer Parts
7 North Diamond
York, PA 17404
717/848-1711
    Catalog $1

Stahl Engineering/Headers
325 N. Queen St.
York, PA 17403
717/849-9129

Traco
11928 W. Jefferson Blvd.
Culver City, CA 90230
213/398-3722

Trick Stuff Engineering
12550 G.A.R. Highway
Chardon, OH 44024
216/285-2175

Tri-Metric Engineering
927 Industrial
Palo Alto, CA 94303
415/328-3707

Troy Promotions
918 W. 11 Mile Rd.
Madison Heights, MI 48071
313/399-7663
    Catalog 50¢

TRW Thompson Products
8001 E. Pleasant Valley Rd.
Cleveland, OH 44131

Warren Machine
33041 Calle Perfecto
San Juan Capistrano, CA 92675
714/493-1230

Warshawsky & Co.
1900 S. State St.
Chicago, IL 60616
312/939-4886

Weaver Brothers, Ltd.
14258 Aetna St.
Van Nuys, CA 91401
213/785-3622

Weiand
2737 San Fernando Rd.
Los Angeles CA 90065
213/225-1346
    Catalog $1.00

J. C. Whitney & Co.
1917 Archer Ave.
Chicago, IL 60616
312/939-3282

Now that we have discussed the ingredients for building various small-block Chevys, we'll get into how all the parts and pieces go together. Any of the following detail is meant to apply to any displacement small block unless otherwise noted.

PRODUCTION ENGINE — NOT A RACING ENGINE

Even if you buy a new fitted block, short-block — or even a complete engine assembly, don't assume that all of the machining operations have been performed correctly and that the block just needs to be cleaned and bolted together. The vast majority of Chevy employees have a lot of pride in the product they're turning out, but at the Chevrolet Engine Plant in Flint, Michigan alone, more than 300 small-block engines an hour roll off the assembly line. All of the engines are complete — down to a test firing on natural gas. At the rate of 300 complete engines an hour, you've just got to keep in mind that the little engine is strictly intended for production automobiles and not for racing. If racing is your goal, then approach the little engine with a lot of time, patience and understanding.

TIME IS ONE ESSENTIAL

Putting a little Chevy together in a winning combination is tedious. The job cannot be "flat-rated." If you are in a hurry — pass this book on to someone who can use it — because it will have been of little use to you. Despite an investment of hundreds of dollars poured into trick heads, special cam, double-pumper carb, and so forth, hurrying through the marriage of expensive and quality parts nearly always produces a "dog" because the marriage is not apt to be a successful one.

The unfortunate end to this story is that this same man is quickest to blame Chevrolet or the speed-equipment manufacturer for turning out such "lousy" merchandise. The old adage that haste makes waste can be no better applied than

to the tedious task of assembling a high-performance engine. It ain't easy!

One of the best, shortest and most meaningful comments on assembling parts to make a really good engine comes from Hal Klieves of Race/Chek in Pompano Beach, Florida.

"The best procedure for building any engine is patience, care and constant rechecking."

Engrave that statement on your headbone. Rechecking is the one outstanding trademark of the professional racing-engine builder. The average mechanic is quite content to bolt an engine together *once*, but his patience turns to anger if he ever has to take parts off or go back to do the job or some part of it over again.

Extra assembly —*even three or four times if that's what it takes* — measuring, disassembly, modifying, reassembly, rechecking and so on can be satisfying or frustrating, depending on your temperament. If you are easily frustrated and become angry when setbacks thwart your progress, forget about laying a wrench on the small-block or any other engine. Pay the cost and have the work done by an expert because engines jammed together hurriedly will never win races — or reliability contests, either.

This section is possibly misnamed because it also covers a great deal of information for preparing for the job at hand so that the frustrations will be reduced when you are doing the actual work. Additional details are provided on torque measurements and clearances so that you'll have these handy. Careful attention to details ahead of the time when you pull the engine can definitely shorten the time required to get the engine back together and into your automobile again. Such items are important whether the engine is used for competition — where it is important to get ready for the next race — or for transportation where the car must

For any serious engine work of any kind, an engine stand allowing rotation of the block is an absolute must.

not be kept out of service for long periods.

Many enthusiasts have difficulty getting all of the parts together at the right time so that the work can proceed without delays once it is started. You should make your shopping list carefully according to the engine which you are planning to build. Order all of the components which will take time for delivery. Note that high-performance, heavy-duty and off-road parts in the heavy-duty parts list may not be instantly available from the Chevy dealer's parts bins. Wait for the special parts to arrive and do whatever work is required on these parts — before even taking the engine out of the chassis. Pistons, rings, bearings, camshaft, crankshaft, valve springs and retainers — and many other parts — often take some time to arrive after you have ordered them.

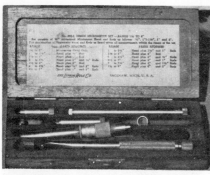

An inside micrometer set of the quality and size shown costs between $15 and $35 and is an essential part of precision engine building.

A magnetic-base dial indicator is another "must" tool for serious, precise engine building. The plunger should travel at least 1/2 inch. Cost of the indicator and base should be about $50.

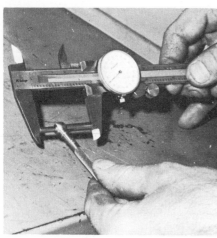

Sears, Montgomery Ward and any number of automotive-specialty firms supply moderately priced vernier gages. Accurate to within one-thousandth or better, this tool is indispensible for precise engine work.

WHAT IS BLUEPRINTING?

Despite all of the long-standing mystery and confusion associated with the term, blueprinting simply means rebuilding an engine to an exacting set of specifications. Some of these details are those originally set down by the factory; more often than not, however, the tolerances involved in rebuilding any high-performance engine vary slightly from factory-rebuilt specs. The thoroughness and care with which each component (and this goes for the last bolt you tighten) is measured and inspected pays off not only in added horsepower, but also in extended engine life.

Can an engine be blueprinted in a small garage or hobby shop? Yes, but! Unless you are well-equipped with tools and some special equipment, the job will be extremely difficult and very slow for the beginning engine builder. Because of special equipment needed for some steps, some operations may have to be by-passed, but for the most part an engine can be blueprinted in most any garage or workshop maintained by a performance enthusiast who is serious about his hobby.

If all of the measurements check out when the block, crank, etc. are returned from the machine shop, fine. If not, then the blueprint job is in deep water and there may be no way to save it short of buying new parts and starting over again.

Bear in mind that any steps left out, any variations in the clearances and specs means less horsepower and shorter life for the engine. Just before you decide to cut one little corner here or there, picture your engine with a rod sticking out the side of the block or a valve bent by a piston. Then consider what that will do to your bank account! The added time and care applied to an engine now can mean thousands of extra miles later on.

BLOCK PREPARATION

Block preparation is such an extensive procedure in itself that we have devoted an entire chapter to this subject. Preparing the block is an obvious requirement before proceding with the blueprinting and there are many blueprinting aspects in block preparation — as you will see when you study that chapter.

CRANKSHAFTS: Not so groovy!

Preparation of the crankshaft is another area where the guy building engines at home gets left out in the dark when it comes to an all-out racing engine. In this case, the crankshaft should be Magnafluxed. Some would try to tell you that the crankshaft should be "fully counterweighted" by adding extra weights at the center of the crankshaft, but the Chevy engineers did not think it was required or they'd have built the crank that way to start with. This is another area where you can examine Formula A and top drag-racing engines and discover that wise builders use the cranks as they come from Chevrolet.

Magnafluxing is a dye-penetrant electromagnetic process for detecting flaws or cracks in metal. Few machine shops offer the service — but if the service is offered in your area — take advantage of it. The cost involved, as opposed to the cost of replacing an entire high-performance engine, is a pittance. We mention this because we can think of little to save in a small-block Chevy once the crank "lets go."

All oil holes in main and rod bearing journals should be slightly chamfered and deburred with a high-speed hand grinder. First use a fine grinding stone, then switch to an emery-paper cone and finally polish it with a rubber-impregnated Cratex tool in the grinder. However, to observe Cratex's RPM limit, you may have to switch to a slower-RPM electric drill for the final polishing step. Lock that crank down tight and hold the grinder before you start this operation or you could badly score a journal. Don't be afraid to cover the rest of the journal with a couple of layers of masking tape—just to be safe.

Polish all journals with No. 400 sandpaper, using a shoeshining technique with paper strips.

Somewhere along the line before finally laying that crank to rest in the block, the bearings should be put into place, oiled, the crank laid in and the main caps torqued down. Remove them one at a time and set up a dial indicator over each main bearing in turn to determine how much the crank "runs out," if any. The factory allows up to 0.007 inch. A competition-engine crank shouldn't have any more than 0.001-inch run out. Don't let any lop-eared kid tell you that he straightened a small-block crank in a hydraulic press. This is a surefire method of cracking a crank - although it may be straight after it's cracked. Oddly, cranks are straightened with a hammer by the reputable crankshaft-specialty firms. This is a job for a professional hammer swinger . . . not a blacksmith or apprentice carpenter.

According to Bob Joehnck, the No. 2 main journal is the worst offender. If any journal runs out more than 0.001 in., the crank must be straightened. Jere Stahl says that you'll seldom find a Tufftrided crankshaft that is straight as it comes from Chevrolet. They must be straightened almost every time, so don't keep bugging the Chevy dealer to come up with a straight one because he's not likely to be able to.

So, what do you do to the factory high-performance crankshafts to make them right and good for racing use? According to Bob Gillian of Moldex, Chevy has made the process double-simple by providing a super high-quality part to start with. All that you have to do is to make sure that the crankshaft is straight — as we have already explained. If it is not, they can straighten it for you. Magnaflux the crank

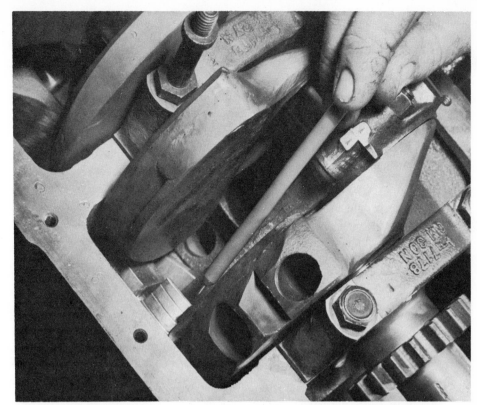

One of the continuing problems of a stroker is finding space on the underside of the block for the crank and pistons. Even the tab on this slipper skirt piston had to be notched to clear a crank throw. Build more than just one engine before you tackle this trick stuff.

Pen tip indicates radius which must be on all journals. Check bearing inserts to make sure that they do not touch this radius. Note chamfered and polished oil-hole edges. Tufftride cracks are not serious except at radius edges of throws. Magnaflux inspection may show small heat-treat cracks around oil holes which are not detrimental if they do not extend into the journal fillet radius.

Our big problem with a chain fall always seems to be one of where to hang it and how to support the rafter that always seems to be too weak and in the wrong location. Jere Stahl (Stahl Engineering) has solved the problem with an engine lift that will lift up to 1000 lbs. of engine or whatever out of the back of your pick up and then position it for installation into your boat or car. Taking out six bolts makes it a flat package for ease in carrying to the strip, Bonneville, or ?

to check for any hidden flaws — after the straightening routine. Polish the journals to eliminate any rough edges — after the oil holes have been chamfered to eliminate their rough edges. Moldex will check your high-performance crank for straightness, straighten if required, chamfer the holes, polish the journals and Magnaflux it for a mere $25. That's an all-time good deal, we'd say.

Gillian says that there is no reason whatsoever to shotpeen a Chevy high-performance crank that has been Tufftrided. The shot will merely bounce off of the crank's tough surface and does no good. You might notice a change in the surface color or appearance, but that is all that would happen. If the crank has to be ground undersize, re-Tufftriding will re-establish the tough surface at the journals. The price for this treatment at Moldex, not including any journal grinding, is about $40. Another bargain!

Back in the days when guys were finding more horsepower in flathead Fords and six-banger Chevys than the law allowed, they had a lot of problems with the lower ends. In fact, most nearly everything that got the hop-up treatment had lower-end problems of one kind or another. Bearings would score and scuff — cranks would gouge — and even seize. Oil pressure was either of the "tap the gage — I don't think it's working," or "oh my Gawd, I stretched the spring too far" variety. In this era the discovery was made that a groove turned in the main-bearing journal or a 360° groove in the main bearing gave better lubricant distribution to the rods so that they lasted a while longer. Unfortunately, this thinking is still with us and it is one of those holdover pieces of information that is on the ragged edge of being completely useless.

It is true that grooving a non-cross-drilled crankshaft provides a constant source of oil supply to the con-rod bearings, but cross drilling the main journals of the crankshaft eliminates the need for grooves because the connecting rods are then supplied from the oil in the upper bearing half groove, regardless of the position of the crankshaft.

When replacing a pan on a small block after inspection or rebuild always use new gaskets and apply a small amount of sealant in the area of the rear main cap to prevent leakage around the rear seal. Have a steady hand here and don't goop the sealer on the crank or the seal lip.

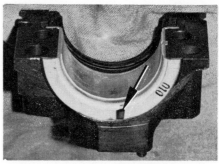

Front side of rear main bearing shows an oiling pocket (dark area) which supplies oil to the thrust surface. Note that this lower bearing is not grooved. Remember that no Chevrolet V-8 lower main bearings are grooved and no Chevrolet crankshafts are grooved, either.

Cranks, bearings, oil, oiling systems and so on have improved to the point where grooving the crank or both main bearing halves is not only not needed — it is not recommended nor used by Chevrolet! Any engine builder who insists on grooving a crankshaft these days is reducing the life of the engines which he builds. GM's best engineering efforts are incorporated in the stock parts, so put those old unsound ideas out of your head and take your gal out to dinner with the money you save by not grooving the crankshaft and not buying "special" bearing sets with 360° grooves.

A couple of points — or even three — need to be made. And, these are hardly ever thought of when this subject comes up in a bench-racing session. When the journal is grooved, you narrow it by the width of the groove — which may not be what you are really after. The groove weakens the crank because it reduces the diameter of all the journals which are thus machined. Third, and most important, even a very narrow groove in either the journal or the lower main-bearing insert reduces the bearing's load-carrying capabilities by at least 60%. That wasn't what you wanted, *was it?*

Fluid-dynamics sections of fluid-engineering handbooks tell us that the strength of an oil film across a bearing depends greatly on the width of the bearing. The pistons are constantly trying to push the crank out of the bottom of the block and the bearings and the oil film must also support the static weight of the crank and everything which is attached to it. Why would you want to reduce the strength of the all-important oil film with a grooved bearing or crank?

You really only need enough brainpower to heat your hair oil to see that such extra effort and expense to reduce the reliability of your engine borders on stupidity! If you forget these three reasons, fine. Remember this one.

There are great bunches of guys running small-block Chevys with non-grooved and non-extra-counterweighted Chevrolet cranks *without failures*. And a lot of them are using stock oil pumps, too.

If you are experiencing chronic crank or bearing failures, there are a number of areas in which to search before turning to crank grooving, which will not ever solve the most common problems which could occur. For instance — is the crank bent? Is the block straight? Were the rod and main clear-

Upper half of a main bearing which fits in the block is grooved and contains a hole for oiling. The lower half of the bearing which fits in the cap contains no groove and no hole. Get this wrong and you'll be buying more than a new set of bearings.

ances correct — or did you bother to check? Were the pistons aligned with the rods so that the bearings would not be subjected to abnormal load patterns? Did you blueprint the oil pump, checking that end clearance very carefully? Do you know what the oil pressure was? Did the engine run out of oil pressure consistently in the turns?

Do this. If bearing failure has you in a panic, check for the obvious wrong. If everything seems to be in order—keep looking—but don't even consider grooved lower bearing halves or a grooved crank. Face it. If a Formula A engine can run with a stock Chevy lower end done right, why can't yours?

Bearings used by Chevrolet are of the correct type, size and have the oil holes and grooves located and sized to lubricate the load-bearing surfaces and to distribute oil to the critical areas. Federal-Mogul's excellent booklet, "Bearing Down," points out that you should install bearings "as is" without enlarging or adding oil grooves which can disrupt the necessary oil film, cause a loss of oil pressure and reduce the fatigue strength of the bearing because of the reduction in total square inches of bearing area.

Now that you are convinced, don't become unconvinced by the parts that some auto parts counterman tries to sell you. Open the main-bearing set right there and examine it. If the lower main-bearing halves are grooved, give the set back. If the store does not have a correct set, go back to the Chevy dealer and have him order the right ones if he does not already have them in stock. Don't be confused. Several of the major bearing manufacturers offer 360^0 grooved main-bearing sets for the small block Chevy. Nearly all of these manufacturers, although they knew better, finally "gave in" and produced these sets to meet the demands of the buying mechanics who insisted that they had to have full-circle-grooved bearings. Some of these makers have tried to justify their position by saying that the bearings thus run cooler — and then they have the gall to advise you to run heavier oil, such as SAE 40 — and a heavy-duty high-volume pump. The pump costs you more money to buy and then steals HP to operate it — HP that you could use at the rear wheels. The higher viscosity oil doesn't help, either.

So, just because a large percentage of the buying public in-sists on buying the wrong parts because of a "fix" that worked 20 years ago does not give you any excuse to do the same thing. Now you know why Chevy does not sell grooved cranks or main-bearing sets with grooves in the lower halves, so don't be misled.

Rather than joining the ranks of the monkey-see, monkey-do mechanics, pay attention to what has been proved to work in the small block. When you see a whole pile of expensive drag-race engines stacked up at Bob Joehnck's or Bill King's Engine Service, check the bottom ends when you see them looking over an engine. Whether you are peering at Al Bartz's or Traco's Formula A engines, you'll see cranks without extra counterweights. Note that the main journals of the cranks are stock — with no grooves added. The main caps will hold stock non-grooved main-bearing inserts, too. When you see that some of the engines, especially those of the drag racers, are built with non-polished rods with only pin-oil holes added—you get the idea that their builders once travelled "the road to romance," but gave up on the trick stuff to settle down with stock-Chevrolet lower ends.

Main-bearing clearances are precision-checked with a dial-bore gage. Bill King sets all critical dimensions with bore gages, the most accurate method if precision gage rings are used to calibrate the indicator.

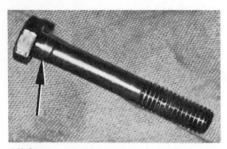

All factory main-bearing cap bolts feature an 11/16-inch head with a 7/16-inch shank carrying rolled threads. Keep this in mind when replacing with other than original bolts. All main-bearing bolts should carry the pilot area just under the head.

The rear main bearing on the Chevy absorbs the pressure-plate thrust. The slot in the cap between bearing shell and rear seal boss allows oil to drain back to the sump.

MORE ABOUT BEARINGS

There's still another old-mechanics' fable that persists in spite of all that the bearing companies have done to kill it. This is the one which says that bearings should be "lightly sanded or steel-wooled" before they are installed. This one makes the bearing engineers' hair stand on end. Multiple tens of thousands of dollars are spent in research programs to determine what coating should be put on bearings to resist the abuses of starting up a new engine. Then we "expert" backyard mechanics figure out every possible way to ruin their best efforts. Smart—we're not!

What do you do to install bearings? Clean them in solvent – CLEAN solvent. Dry them carefully with a lint-free rag. Make sure that the edges of the rod cap and rod have been chamfered slightly with a fine file. The block and main caps should also be chamfered slightly – right at the parting line. Install the DRY bearings in the DRY block, main caps, rod caps and rods. Oil should only be applied to the bearing insert on the load faces, definitely not on the backsides where the inserts seat against the block or rods.

We even found that some mechanics were using Loctite to install rod and main bearings. Bob Joehnck pointed out that Loctite is definitely going to reduce the flow of heat from the bearing into the rod or block because it is a heat barrier which destroys the intimate metal-to-metal contact which helps to allow these parts to live in the engine. Not only that, Loctite is a viscous material which sets up in a fairly thick layer which will reduce the clearance available at your rod or main bearings. Don't use anything on the backside of the bearings — including oil. And, don't chamfer the bearings with a knife, deburring tool or emery cloth. The bearing makers have put the required radius on the insert to match the radius ground into the crank. Save your effort for something that's needed!

BEARING CLEARANCES

Although the clearances recommended for these engines may seem to you to be conservative, they must be closely adhered to. Additional clearance might make for a "looser running" engine, but it won't give any more power. The Chevy small blocks must be set up "tight." They cannot be run loose, as is often done with other high-performance engines, or you will end up with lubrication problems. In checking with dozens of engine builders we could not find any who build engines with larger-than-stock clearances. Increased clearances at the mains and rods automatically increase the oil throw-off and increase the amount of oil which the pump must supply to keep up with what the bearings are throwing off. This can lead to a requirement for a larger pump and larger pumps take more HP to drive.

Additionally, you are creating more problems because the rings were not designed to cope with this additional oil throw-off. And, if you are working with a dry-sumped racing engine, you complicate the problem of getting the extra oil out of the sump and back into the supply tank — a problem which is bad enough without making it worse.

Although we've warned you about this in other places in the book, we'll say it again. *Don't try any trick clearances in these engines.* Build yours with the correct lifters, rocker arms, cam bearings and clearances to require a MINIMUM oil flow. This greatly aids the functioning of the rings and the oiling system. Ron Hutter of Trick Stuff Engineering comments on the lower end as follows, "The bottom end of the Chevrolet is *very durable* and the stock oiling system is completely adequate if the Z-28 pump and deep-sump pan are used. the only critical items are the rod and main-bearing clearances and the chamfer on the oil holes. The single most important thing to me seems to be the willingness of the individual to use good practice and common sense and be willing to take the time to pay attention to detail and cleanliness."

ROD SIDE CLEARANCES

Do not be tempted to open the con rod side clearances to more than the specified 0.020-inch per pair. That's measured between the two shoved-apart rods. More clearance merely increases the tendency to hammer out the pin retainer by allowing the pin more sidewise movement to act as a battering ram.

If you have to provide increased clearance, the usual way that this is done is to make a mandrel which is about 0.002-inch larger than the rod bearing ID. This mandrel is chucked in a lathe and the rod is clamped over it. The side of the rod which will be in the center of the rod pair should be turned off, taking care that you do not increase the clearance beyond the recommended maximum of 0.020-inch By taking the material from the surface which will rub against the other rod, you leave the clearance for the crank radius untouched. That way there is little chance that the rod chamfer at the cheek edge will ever touch the radius between the cheek and the journal. If the clearance has to be increased, take one half of the requirement off each rod. Example: A rod pair with 0.006-inch side clearance should be increased to the 0.010-inch (minimum) specification by taking 0.002 inch off of the center face of each rod.

Checking rod clearance

When you have installed the inserts and bolted the rod cap onto the rod and torqued the bolts, you can check the rod insert inside diameter. Then you can compare this against the diameter of the rod journal to see how much clearance that you have. Measurements of the rod insert ID can be made with a snap gage which is subsequently checked with an outside micrometer. Or, an inside micrometer can be used if it, too, is subsequently measured with an outside micrometer.

If you are going to build engines professionally, then plan to invest in the bore gages and ring standards that are required for the types of engines that you will be building. Although these tools are arm-and-a-leg expensive, they are definitely worth the extra cost and peace of mind that they'll give you in providing measurements that are undeniably accu-

A snap gage and a micrometer are used to determine rod side clearance accurately. Rods to be used together should be measured together and the clearance double-checked with a feeler gage after the rods are snugged up to the journal during a trial assembly of the engine. Note radiused edges of the oil holes in the rod journal and the radiused oil cavity in the rear main cap.

This is the only real way to check bearing-to-journal clearance — with a snap gage and and micrometer. Do not rely on Plasti-Gage for precision engine assembly.

NOTE: Measure the snap gage or inside micrometer with an outside micrometer which has been checked for accuracy.

rate and much faster than any other type of device.

Don't rely on Plasti-Gage measuring strips to tell you what kind of clearances that are in the engines that you build. This material does not always pro-

vide an accurate indication of the actual clearance. The only way to be sure is to measure ID and compare it against journal diameter. This is true for both rod and main bearings, of course.

Hole clear through main journal indicates cross-drilled crank. This one was done by Dino Fry. Note fine chamfering around the rod and main oil holes. All high-performance big-block cranks are cross-drilled. Any small-block cranks you'd buy from Moldex or Hank the Crank would also be cross-drilled unless you specified otherwise.

You can quickly distinguish between a forged-steel crank and a cast, nodular-iron crank by the parting line on the front journal arm. Crank at left with thin parting line is cast. One on right with wider, rib-like parting line is steel forging.

Standard undersize rod and main bearings are available from most all aftermarket bearing companies. You just have to be careful that you buy sets which do not have the 360° groove in the main bearings (the lower half must not be grooved). The usual span of undersizes is 0.002, 0.010, 0.020, 0.030 and 0.040 for rod bearings and 0.002, 0.010, 0.020 and 0.030 under for the main bearings. 0.030 may be the greatest undersize available for the 400-inch engine.

In addition to these sizes, your Chevrolet dealer can supply undersize bearings of 0.001, 0.002, 0.009, 0.010, and 0.020-inch for all small-block Chevy main journals and 1968 and later rod journals. All sizes except the 0.009 inch are available for the 1955-67 journals. The 0.001-inch undersize units can be very helpful in pulling in the clearances on a crank which is a trifle undersize to begin with. Rather than regrinding the crank, use these bearings to *reduce* clearance. And, as shown in the HD Parts List, there are 0.001-inch OVERSIZE bearings which can be used to *increase* clearance on the 1968 and later large-journal cranks (except the 400 CID cranks).

NOSE DRILLING CRANKS

Almost none of the crankshafts produced from '55 to '67 were drilled in the nose to retain the crank damper with a large bolt and washer. Beginning in '67 some were drilled, some were not drilled. After the larger diameter cranks were produced beginning in '68 most of the cranks (forged and cast) were drilled and tapped and outfitted with a bolt to retain the damper. Currently, most of the cranks get drilled and tapped, but occasionally one comes through where the crank damper is held on only by the force fit. This works fine on the street, but should never be relied on for even a small amount of drag racing. The dampers have a nasty habit of working off the end of the crank snout and into the fan and radiator at high RPM. Any automotive machine shop can drill and tap the end of any of the small-block cranks so that they may be outfitted with the stock Chevy retaining bolt and washer.

FORGED & CAST CRANKSHAFTS

If you are sorting through a garage-floor-full of small-block Chevy cranks someday and want to separate forged cranks from cast ones, look at the nose of the crank and the front side of the forward journal. You'll notice that all cranks have a parting line here. A forging parting line is much wider than that for a casting.

This can only be used for determining whether a crank is cast or forged and has nothing to do with the journal diameter or stroke.

CROSS-DRILLED CRANKS

We've already discussed cross-drilled cranks a few pages back, but we should mention that there are no factory-supplied cross-drilled small-block cranks, even though all high-performance big-block cranks are so machined. Racers who have gone to the trouble and expense of having a small-block crank cross-drilled admit that they could not find any benefits. Chevrolet engineers told us that the present RPM and bearing loadings don't require it for the small block.

CONNECTING RODS

Chevrolet builds four good-guy rods for the small block. All of these are specially cared for during production to ensure that the rods will withstand the stresses of heavy-duty use. In every instance, the latest rod is the one to use because it incorporates production modifications which have been made as a result of testing programs. These rods can best be described as high-quality parts with ground split surfaces between rod and cap, heat-treated for higher hardness than a normal production-car rod, shotpeened, run through a number of inspection procedures and 100% Magnafluxed for transverse flaws.

The best rod offered for small-journal cranks (through 1967) is the 3927145. Three deluxe rods are available for the large-journal cranks. 3923282 is a pressed-pin rod and 3946841 is a floating-pin rod with a coplated pin bore. The latest rod offered as we went to press was the 3973386 which was released for the Z-28/LT-1 engines. This pressed-pin rod is specially qualified for heavy-duty use as samples of it are endurance tested to 10-million cycles at 9400 lbs. in tension and 1450 lbs. in compression. Also, the bolt seats on the rod and cap are given an extra shotpeening. Price for these rods is about $24 each.

The same forging, finished with less-exacting specifications, is available as 3916396 for about $9. With a lot of hand work and a set of Develco bolts, these bottom-dollar rods can be modified into excellent racing rods as described in the following paragraphs. However, you'll be kidding yourself if you buy a set of these less expensive rods with the idea that you will be able to perform all of the special machine work and qualification tests, and so forth for less money than you'd spend by buying the completed rod from Chevrolet. Such would literally be self-deception of the highest order so we advise against it.

For an engine destined for heavy duty use, rods should be reworked to improve pin oiling by drilling two 3/32-inch holes from the bottom side of the rod "eye" or small end. Chamfer the holes from the underside and deburr the pin bore before honing to provide 0.0008 to 0.001-inch pin clearance for racing.

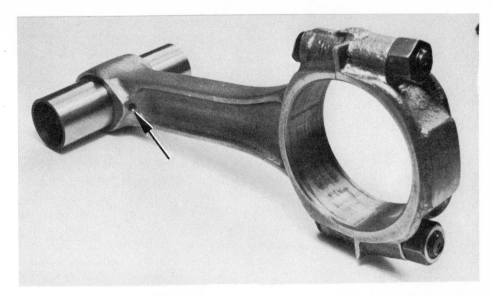

Bill King calls these his "Superized rods" — and no wonder. They're outfitted with his special taper-wall full-floating piston pins along with being trued six ways from sundown, Magnafluxed, shot-peened, and drilled for oiling the piston pin.

THIS IS THE WRONG WAY TO SUPPLY OIL TO THE WRIST PIN. But, it was once thought to be the correct way. Refer to the drawing in this chapter on the correct way to drill a rod for wrist-pin oiling.

NOTE: Connecting-rod bearing-tang slots are installed opposite the camshaft. Thus, the tangs will always be toward the outside of the engine on both the left and the right banks. Early rods had "spit holes" for cylinder-wall oiling. These were found to be unnecessary and were removed from later rods. Do not bother to install such "spit holes" when installing late rods in an early block.

169

Lightly polished stock rod is recommended for street use but not the aluminum racing piston. Grooves in the skirt are for oiling.

This is a rod vise. Build one or buy one, but use one when rod caps are torqued into place when out of the engine.

Pins should be individually fit into the rods. Non-floating rods can be reworked in this way to allow use with full-floating pins. Many builders add these holes and then follow through with all of the rod improvements described in the following paragraphs.

Connecting-rod life can be extended by rounding all sharp edges on the I-beam section of the rod and removing all excess flash at the forging parting line. You don't need to polish the rod, but getting the flashing off opens up any hiding places for cracks so that the Magnaflux will allow you to find them. All grinding must run lengthwise. Round all of the sharp edges around the rod-bolt head and nut seats and put that hand grinder to work smoothing out any nicks in the radius of the bolt and nut seats. If you have access to a hardness tester, check the rod bolts and nuts. They should fall in the neighborhood of 36-40 Rockwell "C." If not, pitch them in the trash. After you've gone through this with all eight rods, you'll probably wish you'd never seen a connecting rod.

Production high-performance rods are Magnafluxed after manufacturing, but the rods are then tumbled which tends to close up the die fold cracks. Removing the flash lays these longitudinal cracks bare, so the rods (and the bolts and nuts, too) should now be run back through Magnafluxing.

Now take the rods apart. Specify that the pin openings be masked off before peening. Tell the man that you want the rods and caps peened to 0.012 to 0.015-inch Allmen "A" arc height using No. 230 steel shot. *Do not shotpeen the rod bolts or nuts.* Have the rods resized after peening. Incidentally, it's low-cost insurance to use new, Magnafluxed rod bolts and nuts at each teardown.

In rebuilding a rod it is very important that the bolt-seat area be 90° to the bolt hole in the rod top. The same goes for the nut-seating surface on the cap. If this is not the case in both places, then the bolt head and the face of the nut will be cocked on the rod and cap. If the bolt is torqued down while cocked, it starts to bend and when this happens you've got the starting point for a crack in the bolt. Some engine builders figure that the rod bolt be-

ing cocked just slightly in the bolt hole of the rod and the cap is responsible for more rod bolt (and rod) failures than everything else put together. The seating surfaces for the bolt head and the rod nut need to be spotfaced so that the surfaces are dead parallel.

The accompanying drawings show what must be done to blueprint a stock small-block rod so that it will "live" to about 7,500 RPM. For continuous running above this figure, as in Trans Am racing, Carillo's rods are considered essential, regardless of their seemingly high price.

If all of this care and treatment of connecting rods seems a waste of time and money, keep in mind the fact that rods usually come apart when the engine is winding near its peak. When this occurs, the rod always wipes out other parts on its way out through the side of the block. The intake manifold and water pump are often the only salvageable parts from a small-block which loses a rod.

Here's how Bill King makes his "Superized" rods which have been used in drag racing, circle track and Formula A engines:
1. Sides of rods are ground for clearance so that sides are at 90° to the bore and parallel with each other.
2. Rod is taken apart for polishing and for drilling the two holes required to lubricate the pin. Nut and bolt seats are radius-ground around the edges so that there are no sharp corners from which a crack could start.
3. Rods are Magnafluxed. Any that don't pass are scrapped. Rods are then shot-peened.
4. Parting face of rod and cap is accurately ground.
5. New Develco bolts are center-drilled at each end to provide for location of the stretch-measuring tool.
6. Bolts are installed and tightened to provide correct stretch. This often requires more than specification torque.
7. Rod is sized at the big end and at the small end. All rods are identically sized for length.

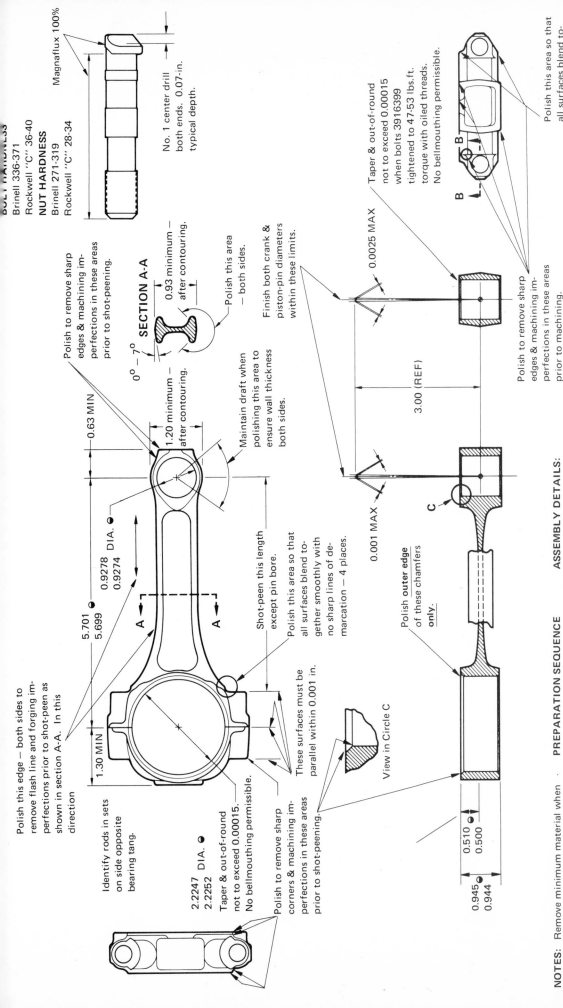

BOLT HARDNESS
Brinell 336-371
Rockwell "C" 36-40
NUT HARDNESS
Brinell 271-319
Rockwell "C" 28-34

Magnaflux 100%

No. 1 center drill both ends. 0.07-in. typical depth.

SECTION A-A

Polish to remove sharp edges & machining imperfections in these areas prior to shot-peening.

0.93 minimum — after contouring.

Polish this area both sides.

0° – 7°

1.20 minimum — after contouring.

Maintain draft when polishing this area to ensure wall thickness both sides.

Finish both crank & piston-pin diameters within these limits.

0.63 MIN

0.9278 DIA.
0.9274

5.701
5.699

Shot-peen this length except pin bore.

Polish this area so that all surfaces blend together smoothly with no sharp lines of demarcation — 4 places.

These surfaces must be parallel within 0.001 in.

1.30 MIN

2.2247 DIA.
2.2252

Taper & out-of-round not to exceed 0.00015. No bellmouthing permissible.

Polish to remove sharp corners & machining imperfections in these areas prior to shot-peening.

Polish this edge — both sides to remove flash line and forging imperfections prior to shot-peen as shown in section A-A. In this direction

Identify rods in sets on side opposite bearing tang.

View in Circle C

Polish **outer edge** of these chamfers **only.**

0.001 MAX

0.510
0.500

0.945
0.944

Taper & out-of-round not to exceed 0.00015 when bolts 3916399 tightened to 47-53 lbs.ft. torque with oiled threads. No bellmouthing permissible.

0.0025 MAX

3.00 (REF)

C

Polish this area so that all surfaces blend together smoothly with no sharp lines of demarcation — four places.

Polish to remove sharp edges & machining imperfections in these areas prior to machining.

B
B

SECTION B-B

PREPARATION SEQUENCE
1. Hand-select rods for minimum flash and die overlap. Equal but not excessive balance pads. Freedom from nicks & gouges.
2. Brinell hardness 269-321 3.7-3.4 mm dia. of impression Rockwell "C" 28-34
3. Magnaflux 100%.
4. Qualify dimensions marked.
5. Grind & polish indicated areas.
6. Shot-peen per note.

ASSEMBLY DETAILS:
1. Fit pins to 0.0007 to 0.0008 in. in rod.
2. Use new nuts & bolts for final assembly, oil threads & shank.
3. Stretch rod bolt to 0.006-in. with 50 to 60 lbs. ft. torque.

NOTES: Remove minimum material when contouring & polishing. Must be free from nicks & scratches. Coining not permitted. Shot-peen bolt head & nut seats after machining to Almen 0.012-0.015A arc height with No. 230 cast-steel shot. Protect holes to ensure quality.
Finish both crank and piston-pin diameters within these limits.

CONNECTING ROD PREPARATION FOR CHEVROLET P/N 3946841

Carillo rods are acknowledged to be the ultimate for racing engines. Eight will tear a $1000 bill in half.

King's rod-stretch measurer operates with center indents in bolts to indicate stretch. 1:1 adapter connects to torque wrench. Tool costs racers $84 with indicator and a bridge to use the indicator for deck-height measurements.

CHANGING ROD BOLTS

Changing rod bolts is not just a simple matter of hammering out the old and banging in new ones. If you follow this course of action, you'll probably distort the rod so that the bearing wipes unevenly—and wipes itself out on the rod journal. If you are replacing rod bolts, leave one bolt torqued up, with the rod assembled with a bearing on a crank journal. The crank then provides a mandrel as you tap out the old bolt, tap in the new one and torque the new one at least part way to full torque. Then you can do the same for the other bolt.

Save the full-torque installation until you are putting the engine together for the last time before running it. That way you can check the bolt for stretch with a micrometer prior to torquing it. Make sure that the rod does not stretch more than 0.0005 beyond the recommended maximum. A "stretchy" bolt is not wanted in any engine because one of those can stretch in use and cause a catastrophic failure which will demolish the engine and your bank account in one fell swoop. If you encounter a "stretchy" bolt, take it out immediately and destroy the threads with a hammer blow before pitching it in the trash. That way no one will "save it" for you.

Bill King sells a dial-gage tool which allows you to measure the rod-bolt stretch as you torque the nut in place. This makes the connecting-rod installation much easier than trying to tighten each nut a few degrees and then continually rechecking bolt stretch with a micrometer. Remember that stretch is the desired specification, even if you have to apply more than the recommended torque to obtain it.

If you have to clamp a connecting rod in a vise for any reason, be sure to protect the rod from the vise jaws by using pieces of wood or soft metal on each side of the rod. Any vise-jaw marks in the rod or cap forging should be considered stress-raisers which could lead to early rod failure.

ALUMINUM RODS

Aluminum rods are another of those "romance items" that are ever present in the speed-equipment business. It sounds so neat to say that an engine has aluminum rods that the buyers of these rods have usually overlooked the only reason for the existence of these parts. They are "shock absorbers" which help to soak up the hammer-like blows of occasional detonation which inevitably occurs in a nitromethane/methanol-burning drag engine. There is absolutely no reason to include aluminum rods in a gasoline-burning engine—and a lot of good reasons not to run them. They have a short life because aluminum work-hardens with use. The block has to be notched to provide clearance. And the super-large cross sections required to provide load-bearing strength equivalent to forged steel makes the aluminum rods weigh darned near as much as steel rods. This is another area where the money that you save by not buying the wrong parts can be used elsewhere. Maybe that money you were planning to spend on aluminum rods could be used to buy another set of rear end gears or a different set of wheels or slicks to get better 1/4-mile times.

Perhaps the explanation of why aluminum rods are so widely used is that they are a part of racing "romance." And, *they are cheap* — about $175 a set — as compared to $300 for a set of fully prepared Chevy rods or $500 for the ultimate H-Beam Carillo rods made by Warren Machine. If the aluminum rods are run for a limited time and then replaced, they could be the correct choice for some engines. Living with the wonder of when one will quit would cause us to recommend using the stock 3927145 (small diameter) or 3973386 (large diameter) rods modified for full-floating pins. At $150 per set (approximately), the price and quality are hard to beat and you know that they are plenty strong, even if you skip the clean-up and re-shotpeen processes.

Next time put the balancer on with the correct installation tool instead of driving it on. Hammering the balancer onto the crank is a sure way to destroy the rubber bonding between the balancer rim and hub. Even braided-steel lines won't withstand such shrapnel — nor did the bottom of this fiberglass boat! Although this photo is of a big-block, small-block balancers are identical in construction.

A novice gets into trouble very quickly when it comes to installing the crankshaft torsional damper — which is really a very simple operation if puller and the push tools which are readily available in most any auto parts houses are used. Putting the damper on or off with a hammer or pry bars is bound to lead to frustration and failure. Number shown is a Kent-Moore tool.

HARMONIC BALANCER

After seeing a harmonic balancer ring either explode or walk off the rubber mounting to its hub, we wondered whether there was any reason to become concerned about these items as a device requiring protection such as we give the flywheel with a scatter shield. According to Chevy's Bill Howell, who has run a flock of endurance tests on the engines, such behavior is not common. It may be your warning that the crankshaft is broken because the balancer soaks up torsional vibrations —which increase when a crank is cracked or badly out of balance, as in the case of a poorly done welded stroker. Such engines sometimes try to tell you about their problems ahead of time by shedding belts and/or pulleys and the harmonic-balancer damper ring. So, be sure to put that balancer in the box of things you were taking to be Magnafluxed.

Use the correct installation tool — Kent-Moore J-23523 — to install the balancer. This tool screws into the crank snout and the balancer is drawn into place with a nut which works against a thrust bearing. Do not, regardless of your hurry, ever try to install the balancer by driving it on with a hammer. The Shop Manual says, "CAUTION: The inertia-weight section of the torsional damper is assembled to the hub with a rubber-type material. The installation procedure (with correct tool) must be followed or movement of the inertia-weight section on the hub will destroy the tuning of the torsional damper."

And, don't follow the time-honored racers' scheme of heating the hub before sliding the balancer on the oiled crank. This leads to instant seal failure if the hub is hot enough. The installation of the balancer is another of the instances where the right way and the easy way turn out to be the same ones.

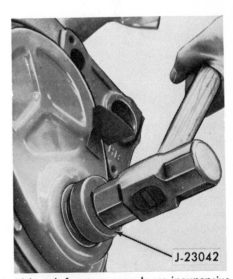

Although front-cover seals are inexpensive, they should still be installed correctly, which is to say — evenly, if they are to be effective. A mandrel or large, flat surface plate will work quite well.

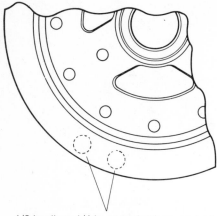

1/2-in. dia. x 1/4-in. max. depth as required to balance. On 3.62-in. radius. Optional on rear face.

To avoid harmonic balancer destruction, it is important to follow Chevrolet's specification for balancing holes. These must be centered on a 3.62-inch radius from the center of the hub on an 8-inch-diameter balancer. Holes in the front or rear of the rim must be 1/2-inch diameter on 3/4-inch centers, not more than 1/4-inch deep. Most important, the balancer rim should be tested to prove that its hardness is 187-241 Bhn. If it does not meet the hardness specification, get a new balancer.

You'll probably never need this, but a specialty crank shop can add a Chrysler crank snout to the end of a small-block crank to allow running blower-drive gear originally designed for the Chrysler.

BALANCING

Lots of engines are assembled and run with stock parts without being rebalanced. This is especially true where the assembled engine or short block came straight from Chevrolet.

Balancing is a must for ultimate horsepower and component life. For a street engine or trophy racer, though, balancing stock Chevy components should be considered on the luxury and unnecessary side of the ledger. However, if flycut pistons are used or the rod weight is changed, the engine should be rebalanced.

As part of finding more about balancing, we checked with Chevy Engineering to find out whether the old racers' tale of truing up and rebalancing the harmonic balancer/damper made any sense. We found that these are balanced as they come from the factory, even though they may be slightly out-of-round at the OD. If you "true them up" to be perfectly round, you destroy the factory balance job and you do have to rebalance the part. If you were wondering how the stock ones last without any special treatment, consider that a million hours of durability testing on engines with stock balancers showed no balancer failures. So, here's another place you can save by not trying to out-engineer what has already been done for you with cheap factory parts.

If you are having the engine balanced, get the harmonic balancer and clutch/flywheel assembly balanced at the same time — preferably with these units attached to the crankshaft as they will be run in the completed installation. This is essential with the 400, of course, unless the crank has been "internally balanced" by adding Mallory metal to the counterweights.

MACHINE WORK

The quality and cost of machine work varies more widely than you might think. This list is only a guide — and not the gospel on pricing. Far more important than pricing is the quality of work done — because in these days good work is a bargain at most any price. Without access to the machining processes shown on the list you are "dead in the water" when it comes to building a small-block Chevy correctly. At that point all of the trick hardware in the world won't bail you out.

MACHINE WORK — Typical Prices

ROD WORK

Complete rework 8 alum. rods . . .	$130.00
Complete rework 8 steel rods . . .	180.00
Bore, bush and pinfit, each . . .	6.00
Rebuild big end (steel rod), each . .	6.00
Rebuild big end (alum. rod), each . .	6.50
Pin fit only, each.	2.00
Steel rods hone & drill for floating pins, per set of 8	20.00
Side clearance, 8	18.00
Polish rods, each	8.00
Shot peen (disassemble & reassemble), set of 8	38.50
Shot peen (apart), each	5.00

PISTON WORK

Balance pistons to lightest piston . .	12.00
Machine fire lands to proper size (per piston)	4.00
Machine pin lock grooves for double locks (per piston) . . .	3.00
Shorten pins for double locks, each .	2.50
Pin bore pistons, each, in sets . . .	3.00
Pin fit pistons, each in sets	2.00
Drill pistons for pin lubrication, each in sets	2.20
Machine valve-to-piston clearance, per hour	12.00
Straighten or change ring grooves, per hour	12.00
Bead blast pistons	16.00

CRANKSHAFT WORK

Straighten, polish & chamfer crank .	25.00
X-ray crankshaft	30.00

Stroking customers' 283-302-327-350 crank includes Magnaflux, stroking using special short arc welding, reinforcing cheeks front and rear on 283 cranks, bead-blasting, grinding with radius throw, mains and micro finish. Prices shown for stroke increase in inches:

1/8 and 1/4 inch	$225.00
3/8 inch	245.00
1/2 inch	280.00
5/8 inch	300.00
3/4 inch	325.00

MANIFOLD MILLING

Often, when heads are milled there is a problem getting the intake manifold to fit properly against the heads. If the amount taken off the heads is slight, then the gasket can be compressed and the fit achieved — when this is not the case the intake manifold must be milled. The head-mating surfaces of the intake manifold should be milled 125% of the amount taken off the block-mating surface of the heads. The ends of the intake manifold — which mate directly to the block should be milled 175% of the amount taken off the block-mating surface of the head.

GLASS PEENING AND DRY LUBING

Glass peening (beading) is kissin' cousins to shotpeening — as you might suspect, tiny glass balls are fired by air pressure through a nozzle onto the hardware being peened. If you have access to this equipment, some benefits can be realized by having the pistons glass peened. The process puts millions of tiny irregularities on the surface of the metal which helps to hold a film of oil between the piston and the cylinder wall. The peening also relaxes the surface and strengthens it because the glass shot acts to stress-relieve the metal. The piston-pin bores and ring grooves MUST BE MASKED off for the process. Glass peening is also an excellent way to clean up a combustion chamber and can be of good use on the top of a head to dislodge small traces of casting metal before painting the area.

One note of caution on the use of glass peening — *anything.* Plan on at least three stages of cleaning after the part leaves the peening cabinet. We've had good luck with the first cleaner being clean solvent, then clean lacquer thinner and then alcohol — with the part allowed to dry between each bath. In the case of a part such as a piston with tiny holes, you should use an air hose several times after the peening to free the tiny glass balls from the oil holes or ring grooves. This cleaning procedure may sound overly elaborate, but unless you have access to one of the new sonic cleaners, we can assure you that the steps are necessary because the beads are so very small they literally get everywhere.

Dry-penetrant lubricants are making important contribu-

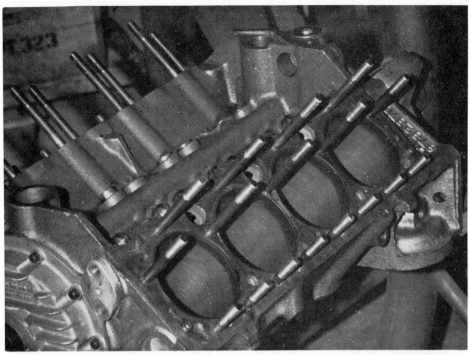

Studs (instead of bolts) are often used for head mounting on competition engines because more even clamping with less warpage is available. When installing, torque them to 60 foot pounds and use Loctite on the studs but not on the nuts. Studs also help threads to last longer when rebuilds are frequent.

tions to the aerospace industry but are somewhat harder to come by than glass peening. Basically the process consists of firing a dry-lubricant (powder) into the part being treated with a tremendous blast of air or gas from a nozzle. The treatment is especially helpful on gears, chains and such things as rocker arms and rocker balls. Some of the aftermarket rocker arms and balls are sold already dry-lubed to prevent the galling and scoring that is common when these parts are run hard. Because the material is so soft, crank and cam bearings should never be dry-lubed.

If you contemplate having a part dry-lubed, it should be the last process the part goes through. In other words, if part X is to be Magnafluxed, shotpeened, polished, etc., then take care of all of these steps before applying the dry-penetrant.

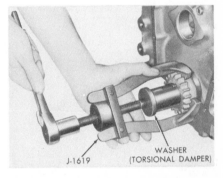

To remove a gear from the crank requires a gear puller. The quickest way to ruin a gear and a crank is to decide that you can do it without a puller. Pry bars and hammers are not the correct tools in this instance.

Here's what that piece of aluminum should look like after you've turned the drawing over to a machinist. It clamps the production pulley together and keeps it together at high rpm. The piece is most needed for a road-race engine.

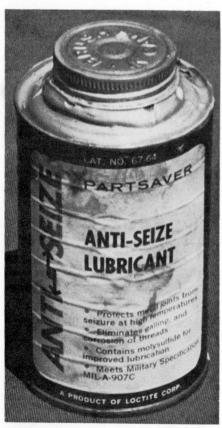

In time, most top engine builders come around to believing that if LocTite is not used on a bolt then that bolt should be lubricated. Any hardware store will have cans of anti-seize compound for sale — use just a touch on all threads not used with LocTite.

PULLEY REINFORCEMENT PLATE

With the help of the sectional drawing and the photo here of the pulley reinforcement plate you should be able to show a machinist what you need made of a good grade of aluminum — something on the order of 7075 machines nicely. This is another item which is not needed for the street, but should be a part of a racing small block. Seems that at sustained high RPM the stock pulley has a tendency to disassemble itself. The aluminum plate — if fashioned correctly — keeps everything together. Pay particular attention to the blending of the fillet radii on the back side of the plate (the side which mates against the pulley). If this does not match the pulley, then the plate itself can introduce a failure.

HEAD GASKETS

One of the problems you'll face with a high-winding, high-HP small-block is slight amounts of head warpage. There's no sure cure for the problem, but Chevy's own 0.016-inch-thick stainless-steel gasket, P/N 3916336, seems to help greatly. When this gasket is correctly installed and the bolts are torqued according to specs, the bolts need not be retorqued. However, some worry-wart types insist on checking the torque again *after the engine has cooled.* The standard Chevy gasket is a steel type (0.021-inch thick) which is not usually retorqued, either.

When adjustments are needed in deck height, you can turn to Fel-Pro, Fitzgerald and Victorcore gaskets which are available in thicknesses up to 0.048-inch. These composition gaskets usually compress to 0.035 to 0.040-inch — depending on initial thickness — when installed. It's important to use the same gasket type on an engine as was used when the deck was figured.

Make certain that all of the threads on all of the capscrews are clean. Use a non-hardening sealer on the threaded portion of these because they live in water. Permatex No. 2 works fine, or get a can of GM's sealer 1050805 in a spray can — or 1050026 with a brush. Use alcohol to clean up afterwards. In torquing down a head, follow the chart and take plenty of time to do the job. Go around each head 10 or 12 times to build up to the final reading in the specs.

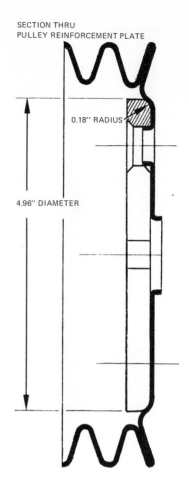

SECTION THRU
PULLEY REINFORCEMENT PLATE

0.18" RADIUS

4.96" DIAMETER

GUIDE PLATE PREPPING

If you are running guide plates of any kind, polish the grooves where the pushrods ride. Use a strip of crocus cloth to whip back and forth on both sides of the groove to eliminate any burrs or sharp edges which might dig into a pushrod when contact is made. Also, if the guide plates are used, be sure to use a production (or equivalent) pushrod because the non-hardened aftermarket chrome-moly pushrods and the guide plates don't mix. After about 10 minutes of hard running, the pushrods are ready for the trash because of deep scoring caused by contact with the guide plates.

If either the heads or the block are milled on an engine where guide plates are used, start eye-balling the guide plates in a hurry during preliminary assembly because you could get into a rocker-arm-geometry problem and bind the pushrod against the bottom of the guide-plate groove if the head was milled 0.060-inch and the head surfaces of the block got planed 0.020-inch to make it straight. Manley has a set of deep-slot guide plates designed to eliminate this very problem — or you can modify stock plates to accomplish the same result.

For the old timer, this is duck soup; but for the novice it's plenty shaky. Oil the rings and the inner surface of the ring compressor liberally before tapping the piston down in the bore. If it doesn't want to go, don't force it! Find out what the trouble is before proceeding.

To eliminate the hassle of belts coming off, turning upside down or breaking, Smokey Yunick built this engine (see cover) with a cog belt for water pump and alternator drive. Dry-sump pump (Weaver) at right side of the engine is not visible, but it is also driven by a cogged belt. Aluminum water pump is a National unit. Alternator bracket below left.

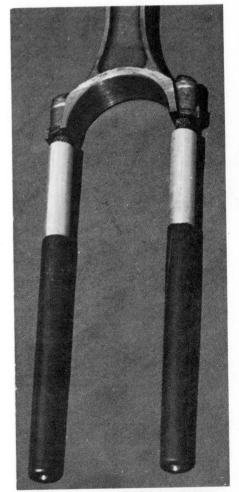

Ring end gap should be measured with the ring shoved squarely down in the bore. A flat-top piston can be used to seat the ring squarely in the bore 1/2 inch or so below the deck. This block has been grooved for use with O-rings.

Garbage-can liners are so inexpensive you can't afford not to buy a dozen or so to cover engines which are going together.

Some type of soft protective covering should be placed on the rod bolts while the rod and piston assembly is shoved toward the crank to prevent nicking a journal. Rubber, plastic or soft aluminum tubing will do.

RECOMMENDED CLEARANCES — To make your engine live

Piston-to-Bore
: 0.0055-0.0065 inch measured at *centerline* of wrist pin hole, perpendicular to pin. Finish bores with No. 500 grit stones or equivalent (smooth).

Piston-Ring Gap
: Minimum end clearances:

Top	0.022
2nd	0.016
Oil	0.016

Wrist Pin
: 0.0006-0.0008-in. in piston, 0.0008-0.001-in. in rod for racing with floating pin. End play 0-0.005-in.

Rod Bearing
: 0.002-0.025-inch, side clearance 0.010-0.020-inch, minimum preferred per pair of rods.

Main Bearing
: 0.002-0.003-inch, minimum preferred, 0.005-0.007-inch end play.

Piston to Top of Block (Deck Height)
: 0.012-0.015-inch average below deck. No part of piston except dome to be higher than deck of block. Deck height specified is for a 0.020-inch steel head gasket. If a thicker head gasket is used, a piston-to-cylinder-head clearance of 0.035-inch should be considered minimum.

Valve Lash (HOT)
: Camshaft:

3927140	0.022 In. - 0.024 Ex.
3849346	0.030 In. - 0.030 Ex.
3972178	0.024 In. - 0.030 Ex.
3965754	0.022 In. - 0.024 Ex.

Valve-to-Piston Clearance
: 0.020-inch exhaust, 0.010-inch intake at 0 valve lash during overlap. NOTE: These are absolute minimum clearances to allow for heat expansion only and will not accommodate valve float from overrevving.

NOTE
Additional specifications are in the Chassis Service Manual and in the Overhaul Manual.

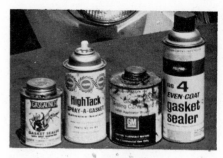

To each his own on the different compounds used to seal gaskets. All of those pictured are good and should be found on your workbench until you settle on a favorite brand.

SH-287S	
CONSISTS OF	**POSITION**
2 – SH 287	3 - 4
1 – SH 288	2
1 – SH 289	5
1 – SH 290	1

Printed in U.S.A.

Depending on the brand of bearings you buy — something like this will be packed with each set of cam bearings. The far left column shows the number of each bearing packed. The second number (such as SH 287) is the bearing number; the last row of numbers shows the position in the block that the bearings are intended for. Number one is at the extreme front of the block next to the water pump with the bearings being numbered consecutively after that.

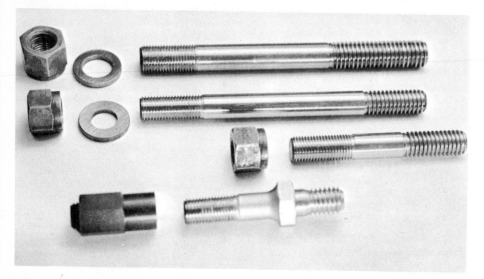

Dick Belleveau of J.E.B. (Air World) makes this beautiful hardware for professional small-block engine builders. Top is main stud, made in $50 sets. Center is cylinder-head stud. These kits are $65. $2 rocker stud (bottom) is squared across tip to allow correct wedging action with socket setscrew in positive-locking adjusting nut. You won't find better hardware than this.

Over the years Chevy has produced two different width rear cam bearings. Depending on application (truck, car or industrial) the 283's generally had the wide bearing while the 327's and larger had the narrow bearing. The width of the bearing is unimportant; nor does it matter if the hole is up or down in the block. However, IT IS IMPERATIVE THAT THE HOLE (EITHER HOLE IN THE WIDE BEARING) BE ALIGNED WITH THE GROOVE IN THE BLOCK. Either width bearing will fit any of the small blocks.

RECOMMENDED TORQUES — Keep it running stronger, longer

SIZE	USE		TORQUE (lb. ft., unless noted)	LUBRICANT[1] (oil, unless noted)
1/4-20	Oil Pump Cover		80 lb. in.	
	Oil Pan to Front Cover		80 lb. in.	
	Front Cover Bolt		75 lb. in.	
	Rocker Cover		25 lb. in.	Antiseize
5/16-18	Oil Pan Bolt		165 lb. in.	
	Camshaft Sprocket		20	
3/8-16	Intake Manifold		25	
	Water Outlet		20	
	Exhaust Manifold		25	Antiseize
	Clutch Pressure Plate		35	
	Distributor Clamp		20	
	Flywheel Housing		30	
	Flywheel		60	Loctite
	Water Pump		30	Sealant
3/8-24	Con-Rod Bolt		50[2] (0.006" stretch)	Loctite
7/16-14	Cylinder-Head Bolt		65	Sealant
	Rocker-Arm Stud		50	
	Oil Pump		65	
1/2-13	Main-Bearing Bolts,	Inner	70	Molykote
		Outer	65	Molykote
1/2-20	Harmonic Balancer		85	
	Oil Filter		25	
	Oil Drain Plug		20	
1/2-14	Temperature Sender		20	
14mm	Spark Plugs 13/16" Hex		25	
	Spark Plugs 5/8" Hex		15	

NOTES:

1. Many racing engine builders use Loctite instead of oil to eliminate possible problems caused by bolts or nuts loosening.

2. Although a rod-bolt torque "range" is recommended by Chevrolet, engine builders have found that the rod bolts often require 55 to 60 lbs. ft. torque to get the recommended 0.006-inch stretch. This stretch is essential to pre-load the bolt so that the nut will not come loose as the rod bolt head and nut "sink" into the rod body and cap during operation. Stretch is the preferred specification, even if torque exceeds values shown. It is a good idea to record the torque required to obtain the stretch for each bolt. Then if you have to check the lower end and get it back together in a hurry someday, you can torque each bolt to your pre-recorded specification without having to back the nuts off and retorque. All rod nuts should be Loctited so that the nuts will not loosen if the bolt stretches. Observe torque when taking an engine apart so you can spot trouble spots that might otherwise be overlooked.

3. Additional specifications are in the Chassis Service Manual and in the Overhaul Manual.

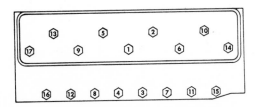

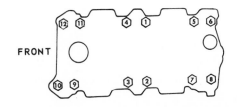

FRONT

SAVING TIME IN ASSEMBLY

Do not send your crankshaft, rods, pistons, flywheel and clutch out for balancing until *after you've made a trial assembly of the engine.* The rods can be assembled to the pistons and checked for alignment and end-for-end length — then marked so that all will be reassembled in the same groupings of rod, pin and piston. Mark the clutch and flywheel with paint daubs and bolt the two together without the disc. Cylinder-head reworking is another time eater and you may want to rework a set of new or used heads to reduce delays from this area. Buy or borrow another engine to use in the car while you are reworking your own. Then, if you have problems with your high-performance engine, you always have an everyday engine for getting you back and forth to work and to the pool hall.

It's a mistake to order a balanced assembly from a speed parts house if you are blueprinting your engine. If you should find that the rods have to be reworked or the pistons modified in any way for valve clearance or to get the deck clearance correct — then all of the parts would have to be rebalanced. You'll always be money ahead by making the trial assembly first, then getting the parts balanced.

SOMETHING IS MISSING —

A number of specifics have been left out of this blueprinting chapter because some portions of the engine are so important that they required detailed coverage in separate chapters. These included pistons, cylinder heads, camshaft and valve-train components, oiling system, ignition, exhaust, flywheel and clutch. Much of the special detail for assembling the small-block engine in high-performance form has been carefully detailed in these special sections of the book. When these recommendations are combined with an intelligent application of the information in this section and in the Service and Overhaul Manuals, you can expect to build a winning combination. Bolt torque and clearance specifications have also been included in this book for your guidance. These are the latest which were available from Chevrolet when this book went to press in January 1972.

We won't go into the science of flywheel and clutch selection — nor the modifications of transmissions and rear ends. All this is the subject of constant experimentation on the part of drag racers and the makers of clutches and flywheels. We can tell you what Chevrolet has done for you and has available in their parts bins.

Small-block Chevy engines produce a lot of torque, but due to Chevy's design work on clutches, the stock package can be made to last through all but the most grueling kinds of racing.

Slipping clutches are no real problem to the professional pro-stock racers because they have been known to set up their small-diameter clutches to give a small amount of slip on engagement so as to cushion the drive train from the shock which it would otherwise receive. However, such professional racers are hardly worried about the costs of rebuilding the clutch and carefully examining the transmission after every meet. You probably are concerned and would like to avoid rebuilding things any more than necessary. After all, it takes time to haul that big lump of an engine in and out of your chassis — and parts — even stock ones — aren't all that cheap. If you are building on a budget, then the best way is to put the right parts in to start, rather than just hoping that everything will work out o.k.

If you have a Turbo Hydra-Matic 400 or 350, you've been laughing as you read the previous paragraph because you have solved your clutch problems. And, if your converter has the correct stall speed, you are probably going as fast or faster in the quarter mile than you did with the clutch-and-four-speed arrangement . . . with no further worries about the clutch. You've wrapped your automatic in a protective shield blanket, of course. While the Turbo 350 is adequate for the street, and some drag strip work, the Turbo 400 should be considered for an all-out drag-race car. B&M Industries can supply modified valve bodies (harder shifts) and heavy duty clutch packages (longer life) for either of the units.

You can spend just over a hundred bucks to get the 10.5-inch L-88/ZL-1 single-disc clutch. This will hold onto all small-block engines fairly well and it has a reasonable pressure so that you can operate it without a continual case of leg cramps. The small-diameter light-weight flywheel has minimum inertia so that you can hang those quick shifts, too. The pressure plate, 3886066, must be used with a 12.75-inch-diameter flywheel, 3991406. This is a 15-pound flywheel, incidentally.

If an aluminum flywheel is desired, the Schiefer forged aluminum 30-22013 with the Schiefer Rev-Lok pressure-plate assembly 65-05600 (10.4-inch) unit is recommended. The flywheel saves 5.75 pounds and the pressure plate saves 3.75 pounds. These components are designed to be used with the Chevy 3886059 plate assembly.

In general, the Chevrolet clutches offer better quality at lower prices than the hotrod clutches. Here again, don't be misled by the decals on your hero's car. The clutch that he's running may be a far different animal than the one that you can buy as a standard part.

Should you decide to experiment with super-stiff non-Chevy single-disc clutches, you may end up having to buy a a hydraulic clutch-actuating mechanism to be able to drive the car comfortably. In this instance, look at the parts in the bins for the Chevrolet trucks.

In 1971-72, M22 transmissions with 26-spline input shafts and enlarged output shafts were introduced. Although the case is the same, the tail housing is slightly longer. Using one of these transmissions in a 1955-69 Chevy requires using a 26-spline clutch disc, a shorter driveshaft and a specially concocted U-joint. In general, the use of this tranny should be avoided in the earlier cars because adapting it is a bunch of work.

Installing a Turbo-Hydramatic in 1955-58 models is not recommended unless the block is changed to a later model. Holes for mounting the starter onto the engine block are not in the block and there really is not sufficient metal to install them correctly,

although such conversions have been made. Take a good look at such a project before starting and chances are good that you will decide to switch to a later block.

If a lighter or heavier flywheel is needed for any of the Chevrolet engines, a number of speed equipment firms can supply them. Some of the flywheel/clutch assemblies are streetable and some are not. Make sure you know what you're getting before you order. An overabundance of clutch pressure is not wanted for a street machine. Don't hesitate to include a scatter shield. The lightest weight ones are formed of steel sheet by Lakewood or Ansen.

When you add up all of the factors, the total real costs could cause you to rethink the problem. A Turbo Hydra-Matic could be your answer. Incidentally, if you go to the wrecking yards for a Turbo Hydra-Matic, you should be aware that asking for a Chevrolet "anything" automatically jacks the price into the stratospheric regions. The 400 transmission has the vacuum modulator on the right side towards the bell-housing end of the case. This says that the unit is a "400." A "350" has the vacuum modulator pointing backward at the U-joint end of the case. Any GM Turbo Hydra-Matic 350-400 will work — Buick, Oldsmobile or Pontiac — and most of the late ones have the multi-hole pattern that lets them fit any of the engines, including Chevrolet, of course. If you find one at the right price with a broken case, consider buying it and installing the guts in a new Chevy case.

NOTE: The 400 CID small-block has an unbalanced flywheel — or an unbalanced converter plate, as pictured on page 26. An unbalanced harmonic balancer is also a part of the package. Do not attempt to use a flywheel designed for any of the other small blocks unless the 400 CID crankshaft has been internally balanced or replaced with a crank and harmonic balancer from a 350 CID engine.

This is Lakewood's safety bellhousing designed to contain the most severe clutch or flywheel explosion. The unit bolts directly to the back of the block and allows the use of any of the popular clutch-flywheel combinations.

A safety blanket constructed of ballistics nylon will effectively accomplish the same thing as a safety bellhousing and can be used to go around a stock Chevy bellhousing or either of the Turbohydros. Use only the safety blanket that is designed for your particular hardware — in other words, don't try to fit the automatic safety blanket to the stick-shift bellhousing.

SAFETY BELLHOUSINGS & BLANKETS

Competition cars should always be outfitted with safety bellhousings or safety blankets designed to contain the clutch and flywheel assembly in the event it comes apart during the heat of battle on the race track. Lakewood and Ansen are two manufacturers that offer a safety bellhousing for the small-block Chevy which will bolt right up to the block and also mate correctly with the Chevy transmissions.

Diest, Simpson and some other manufacturers offer safety blankets constructed of ballistics nylon. These are designed to wrap around the stock bell-housing and protect the driver from disaster in the event of a clutch or flywheel mishap.

Don't think you've avoided the entire problem with an automatic transmission because they have a nasty habit of coming unglued from time to time when subjected to a steady drag-racing diet. Diest, Simpson and Lakewood offer safety blankets for all of the Turbohydros. When buying either a safety bellhousing or safety blanket, check with the National Hot Rod Association rule book ($1.00) to see if the product will pass their technical inspection. If it won't, you can be sure you don't want it on your car even if you never run an NHRA event.

If you are building a road-race car, check with the sanctioning body involved to see what is required and approved in the way of clutch and transmission safety devices.

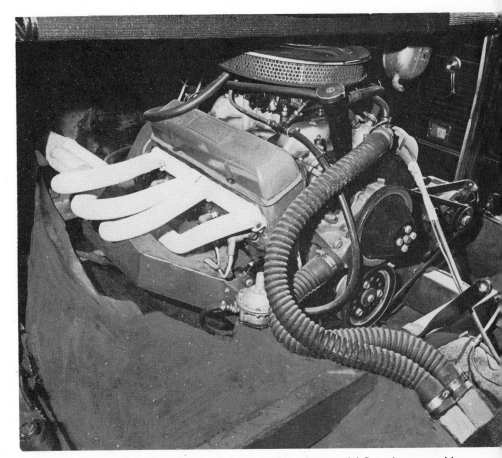

Got a yen to build something different? Interested in a late-model Corvair powered by a mid-engine small-block Chevy? Even with a stock engine the car corners like a Can Am car and accelerates like nothing you've ever driven on the street. Crown Manufacturing makes all of the necessary mounting hardware . . . which fits!

THE TUNEUP

Just because you build a 450-horsepower small-block Chevy is no insurance that you'll have within 100 horsepower of that reading one month after the engine goes to work in the car. Because of the enormous horsepower available from the small-block Chevy and the fact horsepower goes away gradually in normal driving, it is difficult to tell that your engine is not performing at its peak. After a sharp tuneup, you'll realize the engine had lost much of the potential response which was built into the engine.

Most modified engines never produce the horsepower of which they are capable because their builders fail to spend the extra effort required to make their creations run perfectly. You can make your investment pay maximum dividends through careful attention to details during assembly—and then tuning it to perfection after you have installed it—by using a chassis or an engine dyno. $10 to $30 worth of chassis or engine-dyno time will produce far more performance than you might imagine.

Items which deserve special attention include carburetor jetting, linkage, and synchronization (for dual carbs). Ignition timing—initial setting and centrifugal-advance rate and amount—is another area of importance. Transmission and rear-axle ratios must also be carefully selected to get the desired performance.

Multiple-carb installations do not stay synchronized, so buy a Uni-Syn or other synchronizing tool—and, use it frequently, or switch to a single four-barrel with the correct air-flow capacity for your engine. Prior to any tuning or competition efforts, check that the carb linkage works easily to open the carb/s fully and close them positively with no binding or sticking. This kind of action is well worth whatever time it takes to make it happen.

No gaskets should obstruct the carbs at their bases or the manifold castings where they join the heads.

Selection of the correct jets can be accomplished by observing the color of the porcelain insulators. However, new plugs may take time to "color"—so use an illuminated magnifier (Champion or A-C tool) to make this chore an easier one. These illuminate the base of the porcelain where it is buried in the plug shell. Because this is the first part of the plug to "color," the magnifier should be considered an essential tool for any racer's toolbox.

When you have installed the jets which give maximum performance (12:1 air:fuel ratio), you may have less economy than you'd like for daily driving. Should this be the case, use leaner jets for around-town driving and highway use—remembering that the engine is being fed a too-lean mixture for full-throttle operation. Re-jet the carbs when it's time to race. Part-throttle and cruise air/fuel ratios are usually set for 14 or 15:1—or even leaner on many cars which are set up for minimum emissions.

Air cleaners can affect mixture, so run your tests with the air cleaner/s installed. Dyno tests with and without the cleaners can quickly show whether the air cleaner/s are restrictive. The air cleaner base must always be left installed to provide correct air entry to the carburetor.

Set the ignition timing per factory specs, using added initial advance with caution as described in the chapter on ignition. Avoid setting the timing while the engine is being tested on a chassis or engine dyno—sometimes called "power timing" *unless you load the engine long enough for the temperatures to stabilize.* Flash readings made in conjunction with quick twisting of the distributor to get impressive readings are not the answer. Should you do this, and then run the engine with the same setting—especially at high speeds on the road or in competition—you can destroy the engine. Here's what happens—the spark setting which can be tolerated by the engine during a flash reading before spark-plug and cylinder-head temperatures have stabilized is more advanced than the engine can safely use after temperatures have reached the higher values in steady operation. As a result, the *dyno setting of ignition timing for the highest flash reading will always be too far advanced.* Using such settings for anything more than a quick blast through the quarter-mile will cause destructive detonation.

Tuning pays off in performance dividends. This is true with any engine, whether it is stock or highly modified. You may not have access to a dyno. Even so, you can do a lot of tuning on the road without traffic and with easy-to-see markers. Keep detailed records in a notebook—and *never change more than one thing at a time.* You'll be surprised at how accurately you can spot what is helping—or hindering—your car's performance. You can equalize air-density effects by testing during the coolest part of the day—and preferably on days with similar barometric pressures.

TOOLS REQUIRED

To perform a good tuneup you need a minimum of special tools—and a maximum of common sense. Let's start with the tools—you'll have to take care of the other. In order of importance we'd have to vote for a compression gage, a vacuum gage and a tachometer. Feeler gage, a spark-plug wrench, and various small wrenches and screw drivers should round out the list of items necessary to take care of a Saturday-morning tuneup.

HOW TO USE COMPRESSION GAGE

Let's begin with the compression gage—a quick and accurate way to discover if one cylinder is "laying down" on you. A compression gage can be used to discover broken valve springs, a blown head gasket, a crack in the cylinder wall, a broken ring or one that has lost its spring and bent or burned valves. In other words you either start by running a compression check on the engine—or spend a month of Sundays changing plugs, wires, carburetors, coils, points, beating on the fender and swearing Chevys are no good. A long parts bill later you'll discover that a broken valve spring accounts for the sour performance.

Use compressed air (a bicycle pump will do) to blow away any trash or debris that has collected around the base of the spark plugs. Disconnect the wires and remove all of the spark plugs. Pull the coil-wire out of the distributor and jam the carburetor linkage to full-open position. The way to go here is to remove the throttle return spring and then block open the linkage. Often this can be done by just wedging a screwdriver into some part of the linkage to prevent its movement. Number a piece of paper 1 through 8. Insert the compression-gage fitting into a spark-plug hole (#1). Have wife, buddy, or neighbor crank the engine over at least five revolutions. Record the gage reading. Release the pressure in the gage and repeat the procedure to read the same cylinder again. Record the reading beside the original reading. Move on to the next cylinder and repeat the double-reading procedure at each cylinder.

Watch the gage carefully as the engine is cranked. The needle should rise steadily as the piston rises in the cylinder. If the needle does not rise steadily on one or more cylinders suspect a stuck or sticking valve . . . either intake or exhaust. If the readings are about equal between cylinders but all are lower than the specifications call for the problem is most likely badly worn rings or leakage around the valve seats. To narrow this down, squirt a small amount of engine oil into the spark plug hole of one of the cylinders to help the rings seal. Then take another compression reading on this cylinder. If the reading shows a substantial rise over the previous readings then the compression leakage is past the piston rings. If the oil has no effect on the reading, then the leakage is past the valves. They could be bent, burned or a valve guide could be severely worn. If one cylinder reads much lower than the rest, check for a broken valve spring if the cylinder fails to respond to the oil squirt. If adjacent cylinders show a very low reading compared to readings obtained from the other six then you've probably got a blown head gasket on your hands. If compression readings are above those specified for the engine the combustion chambers are most likely covered with a thick coat of carbon from bad fuel, low-speed operation, general neglect or overly rich jetting. If you suspect a blown head gasket, put everything back in working order, fire the engine and pull the radiator cap. Often the ailing gasket will allow a stream of air bubbles to flow into the cooling system and these are readily seen when the engine is fired. Be quite careful in pulling a head off, if you do suspect a blown head gasket. Try to save the gasket—NOT FOR REUSE—but for examination. The trouble might not be a blown gasket, but a cracked cylinder wall or combustion chamber.

In a highly modified engine, compression-gauge readings taken at cranking speeds are not always a true indication of cylinder pressure. At lower crankshaft speeds, the camshaft is unable to create high cylinder pressure because of valve overlap.

HOW TO USE A VACUUM GAGE

A vacuum gage is an inexpensive tuneup tool that can be used to locate trouble while you are doing daily driving. It also doubles as a tuneup tool. If you've never used a vacuum gage on an engine before, hang on to the instructions that come with it because they'll usually include a chart and you'll be able to get much more from the gage if you'll commit some of the needle movements to memory. One profitable way to spend an afternoon is to connect a vacuum gage to an engine which you know to be in good tune and then make measured changes to the valve lash, or ignition timing or idle mixture to see what the gage does under each "bad" condition. Keep track of these changes on a piece of paper so that you can return the engine to its original state of tune—with or without the aid of the vacuum gage. Always allow the engine to reach normal operating temperature before using the vacuum gage.

Both good and bad news are foretold in this picture. A common practice to warm up the lubricant in the entire running gear is to jack the car up at the differential housing, open the hood and set the engine for 2000 RPM idle. This is fine . . . unless someone should lean against the car and either rear wheel touches the ground. Better place stands under two points at the rear instead of just one if you'd rather be safe than sorry.

Bob Joehnck produces this Compelator — a circular slide rule for the racer who wants to figure top speed, engine rpm, gear ratios and tire diameter for optimum performance. This low-buck item gives lots of answers in a hurry.

Notice that: A. There is no fan shroud. B. The radiator is "half-thickness." C. A Flexolite fan is used. D. That an outside mass Dayco fan belt is used. All of this is part of the drag-racing game.

One of the popular "outside mass" Dayco racing fan belts — in this case set up to eliminate the alternator. Spacer plates between block and water pump and between timing cover and block are for clearance required by a gear driven cam.

HOW TO USE YOUR TACHOMETER IN TUNEUPS

Let's say you're in a situation where the engine suddenly starts running rough or there is a noticeable loss of power. A compression gage is not handy, but you have a tachometer. Short each spark plug wire to ground one at a time and note how much RPM drops on the tach . . . or pull off the plug wires one at a time. A leak in a cylinder caused by rings, valve seats or cracks in the cylinder wall or combustion chamber will allow pressure to drop within the cylinder. That cylinder produces less power, affecting RPM.

A cylinder doing its share of work without serious leakage will drop 50 to 100 RPM when that plug wire is pulled off or grounded. If the tach shows a decrease in RPM of only 10 to 20 RPM, you've found a sick cylinder.

AIR LEAKS

Rough idle is usually blamed on bad plugs or plug cables. But, once in a while, the rough idle persists after the obvious things are corrected. In such cases, according to Champion engineers, you should always suspect air leakage into the intake manifold. The first step is to check the torque on the main manifold bolts and the carburetor base. But, don't overlook vacuum-hose connections such as heater/defroster controls, spark-advance connection to the distributor and other vacuum connections which are used for various control functions. Sometimes the hose itself will leak—and other leaks occur around stripped threads of manifold or carburetor fittings. A hose sometimes cracks on its underside where it's not immediately obvious.

STICKY LIFTERS

A sticking valve or lifter will often be the result of "getting into the throttle" on a Saturday night after several weeks of driving the car slowly on city streets. Fill a squirt can with carburetor cleaner and squirt small amounts of the liquid down the push rod toward the stuck lifter or around the valve stem while the engine is idling. Any number of carburetor cleaners which can be used while the engine is running at a fast idle can be effective remedies for unsticking a valve . . . but pouring such stuff in the carburetor won't do anything except create smog to annoy your neighbors.

ENGINE TEMPERATURE vs. PERFORMANCE

A cold engine sometimes feels stronger because the underhood temperatures are down and the carburetor is getting cooler air. If the engine is assembled correctly, it should run as well hot or cold, with less wear if it is warm. Chevrolet claims no difference in power between 145 and 195 degrees and they never run cold engines on the dyno.

THERMOSTATS

Don't let any would-be automotive expert talk you into taking out the thermostat. Thermostatically controlled cooling is an essential feature and only the stupid person who doesn't understand what is happening takes it out. If a part can be left out of an engine safely, you can be sure that the manufacturer won't put it on in the first place. Auto engineers always go by the slogan of the famous GM engineer, Boss Kettering, "Parts left out cost nothing and cause no service problems." If there was any way for Chevy's engineers to ensure that the engine got fast warm-ups to avoid sludge and acid formation—and therefore engine wear—other than by controlling the water temperature, you can be sure that they would do it in a minute. And, removing the thermostat can reduce the cooling which you get from the water circulation. It's also possible that taking out the thermostat will reduce performance because more HP is required to drive the water pump when the restriction is taken out.

Bear in mind that engine wear is increased when warm-up time is increased. A quickly warmed-up engine suffers less wear, especially when it is allowed to reach and maintain its normal operating temperature for a period of time prior to shutting it off. Short hops during which an engine never warms up increase oil dilution by gasoline, build up varnish and sludge accumulations, and greatly increase cylinder wear. High wear rate is caused by combustion products which condense on the cylinder walls to cause etching and rapid wear.

Cold cylinders also mean thick oil which increases the friction that pistons must overcome. The hotter the cylinder walls, the less friction loss.

You can check this oft-proved and well-documented series of facts in any internal-combustion-engine textbook.

Thermostats. If they stick closed (cold-engine position) the engine will run too hot. If they stick open (hot-engine position) the engine will run too cold in anything except hot weather. 1966-69 engines have 180° thermostats. 1970-72's usually have 195° units, unless the engine is a high-performance type such as a Z-28/LT-1, in which case 180° is used. Air-conditioned cars nearly always have the 195° thermostats.

COOLING SYSTEM

The cooling system should also be checked when you are going about your tune-up chores. Before starting the engine—while everything is still cold—check the coolant level. Models without a separate supply (header) tank should be maintained with the coolant level just below the top of the filler neck when cold. If a separate supply (header) tank is in the system—as on Corvettes—the level should be maintained at the half-full mark in the tank.

If you are filling the system for the first time, you may notice an overflow the first time that you get the engine up to operating temperature. This is perfectly normal and indicates that the system is leveling out due to expansion of the coolant. The level should remain where it belongs from then on . . . slightly below full in any case.

Engine overheating can occur even with a well-maintained cooling system if some other factors are overlooked. Radiator cleanliness is important. Bugs collected in the radiator core during the summer reduce the air flow enough to cause overheating. A high-pressure air hose directed at the back of the radiator will usually clean the little rascals out. It is a good idea to do this every fall.

Because the oil picks up and radiates a lot of engine heat, a low oil level can also cause a higher water temperature. A dirty engine and a thickly coated oil pan can hold a lot of heat and add to the cooling problem. And, an incorrectly adjusted ignition or Transmission Controlled Spark System can also cause overheating.

The structure around the radiator is extremely important to the radiator's overall cooling capabilities.

Shrouds at the back side of the radiator allow the fan to work more efficiently. Directional panels at the front of the radiator funnel the air through the radiator, using the forward motion of the car to assist in ramming air through the radiator. These must be intact and correctly installed with the appropriate seals.

IGNITION CHECKS

With these guidelines on how to locate hidden trouble you've got a sound foundation for a good tuneup. Follow through by cleaning, gapping and replacing the plugs, or replacing them with new ones. Always check the gap on new plugs before installing them. While you're shoving the protective boots over the plugs, check the rubber or Neoprene for cracks or insulation damage which could allow voltage to leak off. Do the same thing with all of the primary wiring. Then as a double check on wiring, run the engine at night with the hood open to locate any arcing from wire to wire, or wire to ground.

Install new points and condenser or inspect the points for pitting and adjust them for the correct gap. Take a close look at the distributor cap while it's off. Are the terminal posts corroded, burned or loose? These ailments and others related to the distributor cap can lead to some difficult-to-locate problems.

SPARK PLUG READING

Learning to read spark plugs is fundamental to keeping track of the performance of any engine. The guidelines on spark-plug reading in the ignition chapter should get you started. Spend plenty of time developing this skill of "reading" and if you believe it too difficult to bother with, keep in mind that this one skill separates the men from the boys at Indianapolis where alcohol and nitromethane fuel make plug reading a revered science!

RICH OR LEAN?

Air/fuel ratios are usually referred to as being rich or lean. A rich mixture is one that has a comparatively small volume of air; a lean mixture has a comparatively large volume of air in relation to the fuel volume. A lean mixture burns slowly and subjects the combustion chamber, plugs, cylinder walls and pistons to heat for a longer time. This can lead to

Never mind about all of the trick stuff like the fuel-injection pump and the spacer plate in back of the front cover — what you need is a degreed damper which can be read as easily as this one of Bob Joehnck's.

detonation, pre-ignition, burned valves and pistons.

Although some power is sacrificed, a slightly rich mixture is a safety measure in a racing application because the engine tends to run cooler and thus the problems normally associated with a too-lean mixture are avoided.

In an engine running excessively lean, combustion-chamber temperature will rise as an engine approaches lean-best power condition. This dangerous area must be jumped. In this case, jet the engine excessively rich, then work backwards toward the correct air/fuel ratio by progressively leaning the mixture. Keep an eye on those spark plugs.

Generally speaking, a colder plug is required to tolerate higher combustion temperatures.

A high-lift cam can also raise combustion chamber temperatures.

ALTITUDE AND POWER LOSS

An engine loses horsepower and efficiency as elevation increases. A three percent loss of shaft horsepower can be recorded at 1,000 feet compared to the reading at sea level. At 2,000 feet, the loss is more than double the drop at 1,000 feet. These losses stem from the fact that the cylinders can't take in as much air mass as air density decreases. Additionally, minor air/fuel ratio changes further reduce horsepower. The weight of fuel going into the engine stays the same, but the weight of air entering the chambers tapers off — it's the reduction in air density that causes the resulting loss of horsepower. With this in mind, if a race is held at an elevation considerably above sea level, the mixture should be leaned slightly to compensate for the altitude if the engine had been previously tuned and jetted for a lower altitude. At 4,200 feet, racers at the Bonneville Salt Flats have all sorts of tuning problems.

IGNITION PROBLEMS WITH RACING CAMS

Racing cams increase combustion efficiency and horsepower over a limited engine RPM band. Within this narrow range of operation, the cam will increase cylinder pressures and temperatures. If this efficient, narrow range of operation could be maintained for a considerable length of time, then the engine could require a colder than normal plug. However, because sustained full-throttle operation is rare, there is not a continuous increase in compression pressure; therefore a colder plug is unnecessary in most applications.

When the engine RPM range is consistently outside the working range of a particular cam, a colder plug may lead to extreme fouling. If sufficient room exists between piston and plug, projected-nose plugs of the proper heat range usually perform well with high-performance cams.

The ability of the projected nose plugs to run warmer under lower RPM, low cylinder pressure, low combustion-chamber temperature, and rich mixture minimizes plug fouling.

Because racing cams can alter effective cylinder pressures at a given engine speed, it becomes necessary to make corresponding changes in ignition timing. When to fire a plug is dependent upon when the intake valve actually closes in relation to the crank rotation. Altered intake-valve timing will require ignition-timing changes, and along with gearing, carburetion and effective cylinder pressures, becomes one of the several variables whose effects are best handled by a certain degree of experimentation. As a starting point, duration increases drop cylinder pressures in the lower RPM range and require more ignition lead.

COMPRESSION RATIO

There are a number of factors surrounding compression ratio (C.R.) which can get even an experienced engine builder in trouble from time to time. Without going into great detail on the subject, here are a few things to keep in mind about C.R.

Increasing the bore of an engine will raise the compression ratio of an engine just as surely as will using higher compression heads, pistons or a stroked crankshaft.

The level of heat produced within the combustion chamber depends greatly upon the extent and number of alterations (boring, stroking, etc.) which are performed.

COMPONENT LIFE

Don't expect small-block components to last forever. One reputable source surveyed Corvette owners and learned that a mildly driven small-block 'Vette would eat up a clutch on the average of 57,000 miles, but that a 'Vette driven hard would go through a clutch in only 38,000 miles. Spark plugs (any kind of driving) in a small block shouldn't be expected to do anything after 10,000 miles, and if you want the engine to stay in sharp tune (for the street) you'll change plugs after every 5,000 miles. Keep a record of when you change what — the best intentions of memory go astray after a few thousand miles.

TACHOMETERS

An accurate mechanically driven tachometer should be used on any small-block Chevrolet used for serious competition. The Jones Motrola tachometer is universally accepted as the best one. Several firms buy these tachs with special faces, including Charlie Hayes, Moon Equipment and Stahl Associates. These tachs cost about $60 to $75: the higher priced unit includes a "tell-tale" needle.

Electronic tachometers are fine for street use, but few professional racers will trust them for competition, with a possible exception which we've noted in the section on rev limiters.

REV LIMITERS

Recommendations from Chevrolet are clear and plain: if the valve train is matched with the cam and there is adequate clearance between valves and pistons, 7800 is the limit for drag racing, while track racing gets limited to 7200.

Balanced, blueprinted and tricked-up small-block Chevys have been taken to RPM's in excess of ten grand, but this is a short sure way to saw it in half. Even the handful of professionals who occasionally experiment at such wondrous "R's" are quick to admit that they occasionally lose an engine. For this reason, and because no one sells engine insurance, pay the "premium" required for a rev-limiter system.

There are two basic types of RPM limiters: electronic and mechanical. Mechanical types operate from a cable connected to the distributor tach drive. If a mechanical tachometer is also used, a dual-drive connector is required.

Stahl Associates is one firm offering Jones mechanical tachs and a mechanical rev limiter/ignition shut off. The rev limiter costs about $65. The coil primary wire is wired to the limiter switch. When the pre-set RPM is reached, the ignition is turned off until the engine slows to 100 RPM below the shut-off point. You should be aware that the mechanical type shut off shuts off the ignition completely until the RPM's get back to the desired level, which may not be what you really want . . . especially on a supercharged engine, because the manifold can get well loaded with fuel, as can the exhaust system, during the time that the ignition is completely turned off.

This can be perfectly o.k. on a drag-race machine with open headers, but an electronic type limiter will probably be better for a street/strip machine that uses mufflers. Why? Because the drop-dead mechanical shut off loads the mufflers with fuel and it is not unusual for the mufflers to be completely blown off of the exhaust system. How are you going to explain that to the passing gendarme?

In the area of electronic rev limiters, ARE, Inc. probably supplies more units than all of the others. Their Revgard RPM Limiter and a similar unit with a built-in "dwell stretcher," can be pre-set to any desired RPM. When the engine reaches that RPM, some of the ignition pulses are removed to hold the engine at the RPM limit. The limiter sells for $40 for point-triggered systems; a more expensive one is required for GM's magnetic-impulse system. Two wires connect the ARE Revgard unit into the ignition system.

An optional rev limiter is built in to the digital display or light-bar tachometer offered by Nu-Metrics. This is another "stutter" type system which deletes some of the ignition pulses to hold RPM to a pre-set "safe" level. Although the digital display in these tachometers is only changed every 0.6 second, the rev limiter is instantaneous. It will immediately begin to delete ignition pulses at any time the RPM starts to exceed the pre-set limit. These tachometers are available with light "bars" which glow green as long as the RPM is below the pre-set limit and then glow red when RPM is reached, at which time the built-in rev limiter automatically operates to prevent engine over speeding.

Although these units were initially introduced early in 1971, they will probably be widely used because the light-bar units provide an instant visual cue to the driver. This is much easier to see—and harder to ignore—than a tachometer with a swinging needle. A plug-in rev limiter and an optical sensor which photocell-triggers the tach from the flywheel or crank pulley are options.

OTHER ITEMS TO CHECK

Don't overlook the ordinary in a tuneup. Now is the time to inspect the fan and various accessory belts for wear and cracking. Starting at the fuel-pump fittings, visually move along the fuel line to the carburetor, checking the fittings for gas stains that would indicate leaks. If flex hose is used, check it very carefully for cracks or evidence of seepage where the flex line joins the steel fitting. Inspect the radiator hoses—especially the lower one because it is often overlooked until it's too late to change at your convenience.

Remove corrosion buildup from the battery, terminals and starter connections with a mixture of household baking soda and warm water.

If you're running a set of headers on the car, check each bolt to see that it is tight. On a new set of headers this should be done at least once a week for several weeks until the header flange takes a "set." Then the bolts will remain tight for longer periods of time. At this time, they can be removed one at a time, touched with a couple of drops of Loctite and tightened down.

Pull the valve covers, remove the breathers and clean both with solvent. They can soak while all of the head bolts are checked for the correct torque loading and the valve lash is adjusted. When installing new gaskets, apply your favorite gasket cement to one side (the side that goes against the valve cover) and stiff wheel bearing grease along the other side of the gasket. The valve cover and gasket may now be removed as a unit several times before the gasket need be replaced.

DZUS of West Islip, Long Island, New York now makes a special fastener for fast removal and positive installation of covers. One-quarter turn with a screwdriver releases each fastener. No machine work is required for installation.

Numetrics' digital tach updates at 0.6-sec. intervals, includes light bars for shift-up/shift-down RPM limits which can be pre-set, is available with RPM limiter option. Tach operates from distributor or can be had with photocell sensing for racing.

Jones Motrola tachometer is cable-driven. Tell-tale is optional.

K-D air density meter is an essential tool for the serious tuner.

YOUR OWN TIMING DEVICE

Numetrics Division of Pentron Industries, Inc. has introduced a Performance Speed Computer which allows you to test your equipment for drag starts and ET's, and to time corner speeds or lap times for setting up suspensions, gear ratios, etc., for oval racing. The device weighs only a pound and can be permanently mounted or temporarily taped in place in the cockpit for use when you need it. The computer transfers easily from car to car because the sensing indication is a series of reflective strips which are stuck on the inside of the front wheel rim with a light and photocell to provide a counting system. One connection to the 12-volt electrical system makes it ready for use.

The computer is pre-programmed by dialing in a few numbers related to tire diameter. Digital readouts can be quarter-mile times in seconds and MPH — or lap times in seconds. Seconds readouts are to hundredths accuracy; MPH is to tenths at over 100 MPH. If you want ET first, that's what it reads out. Then you can push a button to see what your terminal speed was, or vice-versa. With one of these devices, which sell for much less than a day's rent for a track facility, you can get your equipment into shape with a minimum of trouble. We'd recommend using the computer because it can practically eliminate the frustration of trying to get things right by making trip after trip to the strip where you can only run two or three times on each trip.

While it is especially tempting to tune by the "seat of your pants," stopwatches, dynamometers and the Numetrics Performance Speed Computer are more meaningful indicators of what progress you are making in your tuning efforts when you are trying to get your car ready to win trophies at the drags or autocrosses.

Strip Tips for a Small-Block CHEVY

by Bill Hielscher

Tuning a car — to me — means doing whatever is necessary, allowable or financially feasible to make a car perform to the fullest. It has almost nothing in common with the ordinary garage tune-up. It's just where that tune-up stops that a tune-up for the drag strip starts — and never ends. Changing the plugs, points and boiling out the carburetor are a necessary part of a basic tune-up. By the same token, jet changes are part of a strip tune-up. Changing jets might occur three or four times during a day of racing and jet changing is just one small part of tuning a performance car. So, where does the performance tune-up start and stop?

In an attempt to give you a baseline from which to start, let's suppose we have a '67-'69 Camaro set up for drag racing. We'll aim our remarks at the 302, 327 and 350 engines, all with a single four-barrel carb, a close-ratio 2.20, 2.43 or 2.54 low-gear, four-speed transmission. To keep things equal — we'll count on making the car weigh 10 pounds per cubic inch. In other words, if the car has the 302 engine, we'll pull the weight down to 3020 pounds and if we're running the 350 CID engine, we'll make certain that the vehicle weighs 3500 pounds on the starting line.

This may be going a long way around to make a point: the same car with engine size changes up or down the cubic-inch ladder and accompanying weight changes will run within 2/10 second with almost no change to the car itself! So race or run what you've got and try to make your particular combination work with little, inexpensive, but important changes.

For serious performance work you'll want a camshaft on the order of 320 degrees with roughly 0.500-inch lift. This is not recommended for the street and is not recommended for the track unless a change is made in gearing. For street and strip use I couldn't possibly recommend using a cam with more than 280 degrees in any small-block Chevy. For the strip, plan to make the car work

between 4000 and 7200 RPM. About here, a lot of you are probably mumbling about twisting the little engine to 8000 or 9000. Sure it can be done — and is every day — but usable horsepower and torque take a giant sag around 7300 or so, so the car doesn't run any faster (sometimes slower) no matter how much tighter it's turned.

The numbers game as applied to the gear ratio is fascinating and can be played endlessly as horsepower is gained, tires get better or strips are changed but the fascination is quickly dulled by the cost of gears and the work of installing them. A 4.56 is a baseline gear for a performance-oriented street car which sees the strip on weekends. If the gear is selected only for drag-strip use, we can be more selective. The 302 incher is slightly down on torque as compared to the larger displacement engines, so we'll need a little more gear. About 5.57 will move the car out quickly. A 10-pound-per-cubic-inch-car using a 327 will be competitive most of the time with a 5.38 gear. A 9 lb/CID 350-engined car will also run this gear while the 10 lb/CID 350 engine can use the 5.57 cogs to move the weight from a standing start. Don't look on these gear ratios as the gospel, but these combinations will provide a base from which to start without buying and changing gears every weekend. To be on top of the situation you've got better things to do with your race track time than changing gears, such as driving.

Driving loses — and wins — more races than all of the broken and "sick" cars put together. Driving a stock-bodied, carbureted, stick-shift car into the 10-second bracket and keeping it there week after week is a difficult and exacting job. If you are new to this, don't get discouraged quickly and don't be ashamed of the "butterflies" because the best drivers in the sport still fight the problem every round.

I'm frequently asked by the beginner, "How do you leave the line?" This is a very important question and the answer can only be, "Quickly," because the majority of races are won or lost in the first 300 feet and that comes very quickly indeed. The days of 4000 RPM starts are over. A competitive car, such as what we've described, should leave the line at no less than 7200 RPM with a 9-inch wide tire. Because of increased wheel spin, the same car with a 7-inch wide tire should come off the line at about 6200, depending on track conditions and horsepower.

Current tire compound technology demands that the tires be hot as they leave the starting line. The heat softens the rubber and tends to make the tire grip instead of spin. Clean and heat the tires at the same time by making a series of short burn-outs just before staging. If you use a traction compound, whether liquid or powder, do some experimenting. Chances are you'll wind up using some form whenever it's allowed. As a rule of thumb, a 7-inch wide tire should be mounted on a 5 or 6-inch rim. Most 9-inch wide tires work best on 6-inch rims only. Keep in mind that most stock wheels are 6 inches wide. A 10-inch-wide tire should move up to a 7-inch rim and a tire 11 inches or more in width will need an 8-inch rim width. Start with 12 or 14 pounds pressure and work down from there. You'll probably find that 8 pounds pressure (hot) is just about right.

To get into the ball game you'll probably want to start with a flywheel and clutch package of 30 to 40 pounds. A wheel too heavy for the job will "flywheel" the tires, making them spin excessively and delaying the car "hooking up" to the track. There are situations in which a much lighter flywheel can be used effectively, but keep in mind that a missed shift with a light wheel often means disaster. Everyone misses a gear now and then — the question is when and how many! Always use a scattershield or competition bellhousing and keep in mind that none of the flywheel/clutch combinations offered by Chevrolet were designed for 7000 RPM starts or shifts. This is one area where money can be saved and injury averted by using products specifically designed to do the job.

Adjust the clutch and clutch linkage so that the clutch is fully engaged about two inches off the floor. Don't make a big project of this. If the clutch works perfectly well at four inches off the floor, simply place a 2-inch-

Cowboy boots, a smile a mile wide and small-block Chevys — they're all trademarks of Bill Hielscher from Irving, Texas whose fleet of drag-race Camaros and Corvettes win their share in the AHRA pro circuit.

thick wood block under the clutch pedal to limit downward travel of the 2-3 and 3-4 shifts.

Just because hundreds of 7000 RPM standing starts are made by scores of cars at dozens of strips each week doesn't mean you should ever try it. On the contrary, starts should be tried at 4500, 5000, 5500 and so on until an appreciation is gained for what can happen at this RPM. Get a feel of the car before moving up to more critical and expensive starts.

In case you're wondering, the guys that win on the strip will come out of the hole at seven grand, side step the clutch and leave the accelerator on the floor as they work through the gears. This takes some practice and don't be ashamed if it takes you a while to get there. At this point I would recommend that a guy put his left hand at about "11 o'clock" on the steering wheel and be ready to "do some steering." Just because a drag race is held in a straight line doesn't always mean the car wants to go straight. More than one stock-bodied car has swapped ends on the strip and more than one has chewed off a piece of guard rail. A car wants to jump sideways from the torque and as the tire begins to grow as speed picks up, the rear end wants to skate around.

As I've already pointed out, driving is what ultimately wins the race and in drag-racing the start is everything. Because I consider staging as part of the start, we'd suggest that you start there. Watch the pros at the strip you plan to run. Do they wait for the last yellow — or can they leave even sooner? This takes a lot of practice, so plan on getting in some running. Don't run, though, without trying to learn something. Concentrate hard on just one thing at a time and get it down pretty good before moving on to something else.

All of what I've been talking about I consider important if a guy wants to have any kind of success at the drags, but more important than all of this is "living with the car." By this I mean that you pretty well know if you have a good run going or not by the time you're in second gear. You stay with the car, and drive it so often that you develop a feel for hooking the car up to a particular strip. You can tell when the rings start going and you can also tell when you've found ten more horsepower. A good man that lives with a drag-race car can spot trouble before it starts. And, in a season of racing, this is the guy who will win a lot more than he loses — which is what it's all about.

PART NO.	DESCRIPTION		QTY.	SPECIFICATIONS OR NOTES

400 CID Engine Parts — 3.75-inch stroke. Engine is externally balanced with special flywheel and harmonic damper, uses short connecting rods.

PART NO.	DESCRIPTION		QTY.	SPECIFICATIONS OR NOTES
3977677	Block Assembly partial-1970, 265 HP		1	Short block, hydraulic cam
3977676	Block Assembly fitted cylinders		1	Block & pistons only
3951510	Block		1	Bare block 4-1/8 bore

350 CID Engine Parts — 3.48-inch stroke.

PART NO.	DESCRIPTION		QTY.	SPECIFICATIONS OR NOTES
3965748	Engine Assembly, 370 HP Z-28/LT-1		1	11:1 comp. ratio, forged crank and pistons, mechanical cam, 4-bolt mains, distributor w/o tach drive
3966921	Block Assembly partial 1969, 370 HP		1	Short block, mechanical cam, 4-bolt mains
3970653	Block Assembly partial 1969-70		1	Short block, hydraulic cam, 4-bolt mains
3966920	Block Assembly fitted cylinder 1970, 370 HP		1	Block & pistons only
3970016	Block, all		1	Bare block, 4-bolt mains
3997748	Crankshaft semi-finished		1	Rough turned on main journals only
3941184	Crankshaft		1	Balanced for use with following pistons
3942541	Piston, Forged Std.		8	Use with 3941184 crankshaft, with pressed-in pin
3942542	Piston, Forged .001 OS		8	As above
3942543	Piston, Forged .030 OS		8	As above

The following four P/N's are earlier pistons which may still be available:

PART NO.	DESCRIPTION		QTY.	SPECIFICATIONS OR NOTES
3959448	Piston Std.		8	Forged, with floating pin
3959450	Piston .001 OS		8	Forged, with floating pin
3959452	Piston .020 OS		8	Forged, with floating pin
3959454	Piston .030 OS		8	Forged, with floating pin
3946848	Retainer		16	Spirolox, for floating pin, .042-inch thick

327 CID Engine Parts — 3.25-inch stroke.

PART NO.	DESCRIPTION		QTY.	SPECIFICATIONS OR NOTES
3970166	Block Assembly partial		1	Mechanical camshaft
3970158	Block Assembly partial		1	HP hydraulic cam
3933044	Block Assembly partial		1	HP hydraulic cam, 1968 crank
3914681	Crankshaft 1968		1	Large journal, tufftrided
3838495	Crankshaft 1967		1	Small journal, tufftrided
3871208	Piston Std.		8	Forged, with pin
3871210	Piston .001 OS		8	Forged, with pin
3850139	Piston .030 OS		8	Forged, with pin
3931636	Block Assembly fitted cyl.		1	For 1968 crank
3970016	Block, 1968 and later		1	Bare block, 4-bolt mains
3933181	Block, 1967 and earlier		1	Bare block, 2-bolt mains

302 CID Engine Parts — 3.0-inch stroke.

PART NO.	DESCRIPTION		QTY.	SPECIFICATIONS OR NOTES
3970657	Block Assembly partial 1968-70		1	Short block with 4-bolt mains
3970162	Block Assembly partial 1967		1	Short block with smaller crank
3970647	Block Assembly fitted 1968-70		1	Block & pistons only
3970140	Block Assembly fitted 1967		1	Block & pistons only
3970016	Block		1	Bare block only, 4-bolt main
3917265	Crankshaft, 1967		1	Small journal diameters, tufftrided
3965727	Crankshaft semi-finished forging		1	Rough turned on main journals only
3923278	Crankshaft 1968		1	Large journals, tufftrided
3941176	Crankshaft 1968		1	Large journals, tufftrided, improved radii throughout
3946841	Connecting Rod 1969		8	Floating-pin
3927145	Connecting Rod Asm., 1967		8	Pressed-in pin, for small-journal crank
3946876	Piston & Pin Assembly, Std. 1969		8	Forged, floating-pin
3946878	Piston & Pin Assembly, .001 OS 1969		8	Forged, floating-pin
3946880	Piston & Pin Assembly, .020 OS 1969		8	Forged, floating-pin
3946882	Piston & Pin Assembly, .030 OS 1969		8	Forged, floating-pin
3946848	Retainer, Piston Pin		16	Spirolox for floating pins, 0.042-inch thick
3927177	Piston Assembly Std. 1968		8	Forged, pressed-pin
3927178	Piston Assembly .001 OS 1968		8	Forged, pressed-pin
3927179	Piston Assembly .020 OS 1968		8	Forged, pressed-pin
3927180	Piston Assembly .030 OS 1968		8	Forged, pressed-pin

PART NO.	DESCRIPTION	QTY.	SPECIFICATIONS OR NOTES

Parts for all small-block Chevrolet engines (except as noted).

PART NO.	DESCRIPTION	QTY.	SPECIFICATIONS OR NOTES
3916336	Gasket, Cyl. Head, 0.018-inch thick	2	Stainless-steel
3987376	Head, Cyl. 1970 bare, thick intake port	2	Large ports and valves
3965742	Head, Cyl. 1970	2	Same as 3987376, except slant-plug
3899696	Washer, Cyl. Head Bolt	34	Hardened, use requires spot facing intermediate-length-bolt bosses (2 at ends under rocker cover) so there will be a seal. Do not use with stock cyl. head capscrews or there will not be adequate thread engagement in block. Use with Mr. Gasket or other longer head bolts.
3849814	Valve, Intake	8	2.20 diameter
3849818	Valve, Exhaust	8	1.60 diameter
3973416	Stud, Rocker-Arm, 1970	16	Screw-in for 1970 and later cylinder heads with 2.02 intake
3973418	Guide, Pushrod, 1970	8	Hardened steel, for use with 3973416
3927142	Spring, Valve, Intake & Exhaust t	16	For use with cam 3927140, not for 3965754
3817173	Damper, Harmonic, 67-68, 302 CID	1	8.0-inch diameter, use with small or large journal crank
3947708	Damper, Harmonic, 69, 302 CID	1	8.0-inch diameter, for 4-bolt-main engine with large-journal crank
3947712	Damper, Harmonic, 70-72, Z-28/LT-1	1	8.0-inch diameter, for 350 CID with 4-bolt mains, large-journal crank
3974251	Oil Pan Assembly	1	Z-28 Camaro
3927136	Tray Baffle	1	Semi-circular for pan 3974251
3960312	Stud, Main Bearing Cap	5	For mounting tray baffle
3848907	Oil Pump	1	High pressure, Z-28/LT-1, does not include pickup screen asm.
3157804	Oil Cooler	1	Aluminum reverse-flow design
3881803	Bracket, Oil Cooler	1	
3879938	Hose Asm., Oil Cooler	1	
3879940	Tee, Oil Cooler Outlet	1	
444215	Elbow, Oil-Cooler-Inlet Hose (45°)	1	
444058	Elbow, Oil-Cooler-Outlet Hose (45°)	1	
444044	Elbow, Engine-Oil-Cooler Hose (90°)	2	
9417840	Nipple, Oil-Cooler-Inlet Hose (1/2 x 3)	1	
144042	Bushing, Oil-Cooler-Inlet Hose Reducer	1	(3/4 x 1/2)
3825416	Clip, Oil-Cooler Hose	1	
3995664	Piston Ring Unit, Std. (one cyl.)	1	Low-tension design, 4.0-inch bore
3995665	Piston Ring Unit, .005 OS (one cyl.)	1	Low-tension design, 4.0-inch bore
3995666	Piston Ring Unit, .020 OS (one cyl.)	1	Low-tension design, 4.0-inch bore
3995667	Piston Ring Unit, .030 OS (one cyl.)	1	Low-tension design, 4.0-inch bore
3849346	Camshaft Asm., 1964-69 Street Mechanical	1	0.455/0.455-inch intake/exhaust lift, 313°/313° duration
3972178	Camshaft Asm., 1970-71 Street Mechanical	1	0.438/0.455-inch intake/exhaust lift, 320°/312° duration. Used in 350 CID Z-28/LT-1.
3927140	Camshaft Asm., Service Package Mechanical	1	0.463/0.482-inch intake/exhaust lift, 322°/326° duration. For off-road use.
3965754	Camshaft Asm., Service Package Mechanical	1	0.495/0.510-inch intake/exhaust lift, 325°/331° duration. For off-road use. Requires aftermarket springs, see text.
5231585	Valve Lifter, Mechanical	16	Use with all mechanical cams
3927145	Connecting Rod Asm., 1967	8	Pressed-in pin, for small-journal crank
3923282	Connecting Rod Asm., 1968	8	Pressed-in pin, for large-journal crank
3946841	Connecting Rod Asm., 1969	8	Floating pin, pin bore coplated, for large-journal crank
3973386	Connecting Rod Asm., 1971	8	Pressed-in pin, special shotpeening of bolt/nut seats, for large-journal crank
3916399	Bolt, Connecting Rod	16	3/8-24 bolt
3866766	Nut, Connecting Rod Bolt	16	3/8-24 nut
3965718	Main Bearing 1-4 position	4	.001 oversize
3965719	Main Bearing rear	1	.001 oversize
3965720	Rod Bearing	8	.001 oversize

PART NO.	DESCRIPTION	QTY.	SPECIFICATIONS OR NOTES
3972144	Intake Manifold, Production Z-28/LT-1	1	High-riser single 4-barrel
3972121	Carburetor, Production Z-28/LT-1	1	780 CFM Holley, vacuum secondary
3965736	Carburetor	1	830 CFM double-pump mech. sec. 1-11/16 throttle bores
3940077	2x4 Carburetor Conversion Unit	1	Consists of the following
3941126	Manifold, Inlet	1	Lower half of manifold
3941128	Manifold, Inlet	1	Upper half of manifold
3941132	Gasket, Inlet Manifold Cover	1	
120229	Bolt, Inlet Manifold Cover	16	
3794836	Washer - Inlet Manifold Cover Bolt	16	
444588	Plug, Heater-Hose Hole	1	
444588	Plug, Temperature-Switch Hole	1	
179840	Bolt, Inlet Manifold	12	
3864910	Stud, Carburetor	8	
3957859	Carburetor Assembly	2	Holley 600 CFM double-pumper
120368	Nut, Carburetor	8	
3881847	Gasket, Carburetor	2	
3942593	Pipe Asm., Fuel Pump	1	Fuel pump to fuel manifold
3942594	Manifold, Carburetor Fuel	1	
3942595	Pipe Asm., Carburetor Fuel	2	
3942596	Pipe Asm., Carburetor Fuel	1	To left carburetor
3942597	Pipe Asm., Carburetor Fuel	1	To right carburetor
3941160	Rod Asm., Front to Rear Carburetor	1	Connects carburetors
3928326	Rod Asm., Accelerator Pedal	1	Converts to cable accelerator pedal
3941168	Cable Asm., Accelerator Control	1	
393292	Retainer, Cable to Accelerator Pedal Lever	1	
3942592	Bracket Asm., Accelerator Control Cable	1	
3921617	Clamp, Accelerator Control Cable	1	
120706	Bolt, Accelerator Control Cable Clamp	1	
9419727	Screw, Accelerator Control Cable	1	To dash
3942584	Screw, Special 10-32 x .92 Socket Head	2	
3942587	Spacer, Special	2	
9416980	Nut, Carburetor Rod to Lever Screw	2	
3946801	Bracket, Accelerator Pull Back Spring	1	
3939748	Spring, Accelerator Pull Back	1	
3836247	Gasket, Ignition Distributor	1	
3953866	Carburetor Installation Instruction	1	Last part with conversion unit
6415325	Fuel Pump, High Capacity	1	Corvette 1964
3963832	Hood, Ducted-Air, Fiberglass	1	For 67-69 Camaro
3963824	Plate, Air-Cleaner Base, 2 x 4	1	Use with 3963832 hood
3963823	Seal, Air-Cleaner-to-Hood, 2 x 4	1	
3963825	Element, Air Cleaner, 2 x 4	1	
3941146	Cover, Air Cleaner, 2 x 4	1	
6484655	Cleaner Asm. for Firewall Duct	1	1 x 4 bbl. carb
3916621	Duct, Cleaner to Firewall	1	1 x 4 bbl. carb
6422544	Element for Air Cleaner Asm.	1	1 x 4 bbl. carb, use with 6484665
6485788	Cleaner Asm. to Fiberglass Hood	1	1 x 4 bbl. carb, 1968-69
6421746	Element, Air Cleaner	1	1 x 4 bbl. carb, 1968-69, use with 6485788
3963822	Seal, Air Cleaner to Hood	1	1 x 4 bbl. carb, 1968-69, use with above 3 part numbers
3949708	Hood, Ducted-Air, Steel	1	Part of ZL-2 '69 Camaro option, use with insulator 3949716, 3909199 retainers (20) and misc. air-cleaner, seal, air-valve and other parts detailed in parts book.

WHAT YOU SEE IS WHAT YOU GET

There are several ways to buy a small-block Chevy from a dealer and you should be aware of what hardware is included in each basic package.

Fitted block — block with pistons, pins, rings, main and cam bearings, and rear oil seal.

Short block — assembled parts consisting of block with pistons, pins, rings, rods, crank, cam (no lifters), bearings, rear oil seal, timing sprockets and timing chain (but no timing cover) and a can of E.O.S. (engine oil supplement).

Complete engine — assembled engine with intake manifold (no carb), distributor (no wires or coil), water pump (no pulley), oil pan, rocker arm covers and harmonic balancer. Flywheel or converter flex plate and a bell housing are also included. No alternator, starter or oil pump is included.

Take a look at what you are buying and don't hesitate to ask for the parts man's advice as to what else you'll need to complete the engine which you are putting together.